*How the States
Got Their Shapes Too*

HOW THE STATES GOT THEIR SHAPES
··· TOO ···

The
PEOPLE
Behind the
BORDER-
LINES

MARK STEIN

Smithsonian Books

WASHINGTON, DC

Published by Smithsonian Books
Executive Editor: *Carolyn Gleason*
Production Editor: *Christina Wiginton*
Editor: *Duke Johns*
Designer: *Mary Parsons*
Maps: *XNR Productions, Inc.*
Photo Researcher: *Amy Pastan*
Indexer: *Clive Pyne*

ISBN-13: 978-1-58834-314-7

Manufactured in the United States of America

Book Club Edition

Contents

Preface

No child has ever been known to say, "When I grow up, I want to establish a state line." But somebody had to do it. Who were those people? How did they end up in that endeavor?

As it turns out, the people involved in America's states being shaped the way they are have come from all walks of life. Some are famous, such as Thomas Jefferson and John Quincy Adams, though how they participated in shaping our states is not widely known. Others are famous, but *why* they're famous is not widely known. Daniel Webster, for example: is he famous because of his extraordinary debate in *The Devil and Daniel Webster*? Stephen Vincent Benét's tale may well be why Webster remains famous. But Daniel Webster never debated with Satan—at least not in public. He did, however, create one state's lines.

Most of those who participated in the location of our state lines are not famous. Moreover, they are not exclusively white men. Women, African Americans, Native Americans, and Hispanics have also been involved in shaping the states.

For none of these people was the establishment of their state line their primary objective in life. Their participation in the creation of a boundary resulted from some personal quest. Those quests differed, yet each quest emanated from the issues of the time. Today those historical issues, and the personal quests they spawned, are imprinted on the map in the form of state lines.

The borders of the United States, however, do not fully enclose those quests. Many others sought, unsuccessfully, to create additional states in Canada, Mexico, Cuba, and—still an issue—Puerto Rico. Their stories further enhance our perspective of the United States.

The American map is so familiar that even its straight lines begin to seem a part of nature. But looking at it through the individuals involved in its creation, that map becomes a mural. Its lines reflect an ongoing progression of Americans. Who, when, and where they were explains much of why we are who we are today.

Lyman
Cutler

James K. Polk

Richard Rush

Sidney
Edgerton
and
James
Ashley

Stephen A.
Douglas

T

h

John Meares

Standing
Bear

o

m

John
Sutter

a

Stephen
Dougla

s

J

Brigham
Young

Robert W. Steele

e

Clarina Nich

Brigham
Young

Stephen
Dougla

"Alfalfa Bill" Mur
Edward McCa
Chief Green McCurta

Francisco Perea
and John S. Watts

Stephen A.
Douglas

James Gadsden

Jo
Quin
Adar

William
Seward

James
Gadsden

Sam Houston

Queen Lili'uokalani
and Sanford Dole

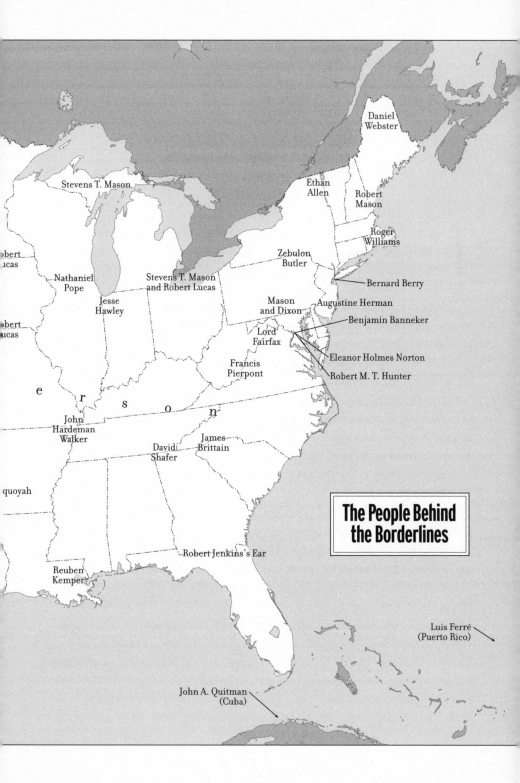

Daniel
Webster

Stevens T. Mason

Ethan
Allen

Robert
Mason

Roger
Williams

obert
ucas

Nathaniel
Pope

Stevens T. Mason
and Robert Lucas

Zebulon
Butler

Bernard Berry

Jesse
Hawley

Mason
and Dixon

Augustine Herman

Benjamin Banneker

obert
ucas

Lord
Fairfax

Francis
Pierpont

Eleanor Holmes Norton

Robert M. T. Hunter

e   r   s   o   n

John
Hardeman
Walker

David
Shafer

James
Brittain

quoyah

Robert Jenkins's Ear

**The People Behind
the Borderlines**

Reuben
Kemper

Luis Ferré
(Puerto Rico)

John A. Quitman
(Cuba)

Acknowledgments

I was fortunate, after the publication of *How the States Got Their Shapes*, to be urged by my late and much missed editor, Caroline Newman, to offer a follow-up book. But having been a writer in theater and film, as opposed to nonfiction, I had difficulty framing an idea that fit the bill. So I called my longtime friend Mark Olshaker, author of several best-selling books, and asked if we could get together for lunch to see whether we could generate an idea. He said (and this is truly what he said), "Sure. Next week is good. Or how about this? A book on the people, like that guy you mentioned in the first book with Missouri."

That is this book.

First and foremost, then, and with awe, I thank Mark Olshaker for an idea that, as it further developed, captured my imagination as much as my passion for maps drove me to write the first book. "As it further developed" refers in no small measure to the insights of Elisabeth Dyssegaard, who took over as my editor. Elisabeth did not have to fill Caroline's shoes, because her own editor shoes fit beautifully. Too beautifully, since Elisabeth soon advanced to become editor-in-chief at another publisher. But her parting gift to me was an introduction to Kenneth Wright, who became my agent and navigated my now orphaned project in more ways than I can enumerate here, though I cannot leave unsaid the importance of the encouragement and clear thinking he provided. Ken succeeded in placing the book where I most hoped it would end up, at Smithsonian Books, copublisher of *How the States Got Their Shapes*, where I knew I would be in good hands with its director, and now my editor, Carolyn Gleason. I knew Carolyn was ideally suited because of an offhand remark she had made when we first met, shortly after *How the States Got Their Shapes* replaced my original title, *Why Is Iowa?* "I liked your first title," she said, "but it didn't work." I knew then we had the same sensibility, except she knew what worked.

Both my copy editor, Duke Johns, and the schoolteacher who taught him grammar and syntax deserve gold medals. Duke's mind is a lens of clarity. He is also an intimidatingly thorough fact-checker, for which I am extremely grateful. The treaties and legislation that created our state shapes are complicated and often overlap. To my astonishment, Duke dug them up, checking and adjusting my efforts to explain them. If any errors have slipped past him, it only shows that no goalie can block every shot. (He even nipped and tucked this paragraph.)

For the images in this book I was privileged to have Amy Pastan searching out photos and portraits with such enthusiasm that she discovered, and connected me with, a descendant of Jesse Hawley, the subject of one of the book's chapters. Trudy Hawley's family records provided information not otherwise available. I was also delighted to be reunited with cartographer Rob McCaleb of XNR Productions, who had created the maps for my previous book. Once again he has turned words into maps that reduced me to one word: "exactly." His geodetic eye also spotted an element in the battles fought by James Brittain that had gone unnoted by historians of North Carolina and Georgia's violent boundary dispute, leading to its being noted for the first time in this book.

I also want to express my gratitude to the Bender Library at American University for the privileges it extended to me. And a special thanks to Professor William W. E. Slights—a profound influence on my life when I was his student at the University of Wisconsin, and a dear friend ever since—who generously shared his knowledge of colonial era English abbreviations. I also received valuable assistance from Robert S. Davis Jr., Frank Drohan, and Paul Schmidt, in addition to Lauren Leeman of the State Historical Society of Missouri, Kari Schleher of the University of New Mexico Library, and Arlene Balkansky of the Serial and Government Publications Division of the Library of Congress. Ms. Balkansky, in addition to all her help with the resources of the Library of Congress, devoted time to reading each chapter as it was first drafted, spotting textual errors and even problems in the flow and arc of the draft. All of this not only exceeded the duties in her job description but also those in our wedding vows from over thirty years ago.

ROGER WILLIAMS
The Boundary of Religion

It has fallen out sometimes that both Papists and Protestants, Jews and Turks, may be embarked in one ship.... All the liberty of conscience that ever I pleaded for turns upon these two hinges: that none of these Papists, Protestants, Jews or Turks be forced to come to the ship's private prayers or worship, nor compelled from their own particular prayers or worship, if they practice any.

—ROGER WILLIAMS, 1654[1]

R oger Williams believed in the separation of Church and State ... for *religious* reasons. A devout Puritan minister, he fervently believed that Christians violated the word of God when they mandated religious acts.[2] Williams's views were too pure for the Puritans. They kicked him out of Massachusetts. In the wilderness lands of the Narragansett Indians, Williams arranged to create a haven for people of all faiths (and of no faith), which came to be called Rhode Island.

The story of Rhode Island's founding for purposes of religious freedom typically omits Williams's religious motive. Teaching his reasoning in a public school risks, ironically, crossing the boundary between church and state. Aside from that, his religious motive has often been omitted because it makes his achievement less purely secular, less "American."[3] The American quest for a purely secular govern-

Roger Williams (ca. 1603–1683)

ment reveals the odd couple who became the nation's cultural parents: the Enlightenment and the Puritans.[4] Consequently, the church/state conflicts Williams confronted in creating Rhode Island continue to this day.

One of the first issues Williams faced began as soon as he arrived in Massachusetts in 1631: who owns the earth? Did the king of England, ruling by divine right, have the authority to claim possession of land upon which non-Christians lived? Williams maintained that the answer was no. Here again, his reasons were religious: a state that, on the basis of Christianity, asserts authority over a land where non-Christians live violates the Christian (meaning Puritan, as interpreted by Williams) necessity of separating church and state.

Williams's view was not likely to sit well with British authorities, upon whom the Massachusetts colonists depended for protection. Williams also believed that the Puritan Church, to remain pure of the corruption in the Church of England, should officially separate from the national church— also a view that Massachusetts officials wished he would keep to himself. In 1633 Governor John Winthrop noted in his journal (referring to himself in the third person):

> Mr. Williams also wrote to the governor ... very submissively professing his intent ... [and] offering his book, or any part of it, to be burnt.

In 1634 the governor noted:

> Mr. Williams of Salem [has] broken his promise to us, in teaching publicly against the king's patent, and our great sin in claiming right thereby to this country.

And the year after that:

> The governor ... sent for Mr. Williams. The occasion was, for that he had taught publicly that a magistrate ought not to tender an oath to an unregenerate man, for that we thereby have communion with a wicked man in the worship of God, and cause him to take the name of God in vain.

Williams was driving the governor crazy. He was also genuinely angering fellow ministers and others in the colony's power structure. This time around, he was put on trial for advocating against the Church of England, against the colony's religious laws, against the use of oaths in the name of God prior to giving testimony, and against England's right to the land. In his defense, Williams stated, "I acknowledge the particulars were rightly summed up, and I also hope that ... through the Lord's assistance, I shall be ready ... not only to be bound and banished, but to die also, in New England, as for most holy Truths of God in Christ Jesus."[5]

He was convicted.

The court ordered Williams to leave the Massachusetts Bay Colony within six weeks. Technically, he was banished for religious reasons. In reality, he was banished for secular reasons. His views undermined British authority. Here again, the events have frequently been told in a way that flips their religious/secular basis. In this instance, however, the story was given its secular spin not by post–Revolutionary War Americans but by the Puritan colonists as justification for his banishment.[6] Ironically, among those same colonists were some who privately sympathized with Williams—including none other than Governor Winthrop himself. "When I was unkindly and unchristianly, as I believe, driven from my house and land," William revealed some thirty-five years later, "Governor Mr. Winthrop privately wrote to me to steer my course toward Narragansett Bay."[7]

Williams arranged with the local Indians to build a homestead on a plot of land on Narragansett Bay's northeastern edge. But, as he soon learned from another private friend, this location had a boundary problem. Massachusetts, at that time, comprised the Massachusetts Bay Colony and the Plymouth Colony, and the governor of the Plymouth Colony informed him that he would have to leave there, too. That governor also turned out to be a secret sympathizer. "I received a letter from my ancient friend, Mr. Winslow, then governor of Plymouth," Williams later recollected, "advising me, since I was fallen into the edge of their bounds, and they were loath to displease the Bay, to remove but to the other side of the water and there, he said, I had the country free before me."

Williams consequently relocated to the bay's western edge, where, to accommodate the arrival of his followers, he arranged with the Narragansetts for a larger area upon which to settle. Because the land he was accorded resulted from acts of kindness by native peoples and colonial governors—all ostensibly enemies—Williams accorded it a special name: Providence.

During the time that Williams was arranging to relocate outside the boundaries of the Plymouth Colony, another group of exiles arrived from

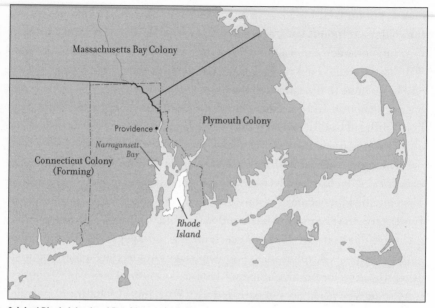

Original Rhode Island and Providence plantations

Massachusetts. Anne Hutchinson had been banished after Williams, in her case for religious beliefs that undermined the power of ministers (as opposed to Williams's beliefs, which undermined the power of magistrates). Williams welcomed Hutchinson and her followers. As he set about establishing Providence, she and her followers paid the Narragansetts for the use of land on a nearby island in the bay, known to the Indians as Aquidneck and to the British as Rhode Island. To this day, the official name of Rhode Island is "the State of Rhode Island and Providence Plantations." And to this day, its constitution asserts religious freedom for religious reasons. "We, the people of the State of Rhode Island and Providence Plantations," it begins, "grateful to Almighty God for the civil and religious liberty which He hath permitted us to enjoy, and looking to Him for a blessing upon our endeavors to secure and to transmit the same, unimpaired, to succeeding generations, do ordain and establish this Constitution of government."

This intertwined religious/secular duality that remains in Rhode Island's constitution also characterized Williams's efforts to establish the colony and form its government. The Narragansetts' permission to use the land carried as much weight with England as did Williams's opinions about England not having the right to claim Indian land. For Williams, however, this was a solvable problem. He would simply follow the words of Christ (Matthew 22:21) and render unto Caesar that which is Caesar's. The problem had to do with identifying Caesar. The king was Charles I, but royal authority in England was under attack in a civil war being led by Oliver Cromwell, a Puritan.

In 1641 Williams opted to render unto Cromwell after Parliament enacted laws restricting the authority of the king—notably, the king's power to dissolve the Parliament and his authority over the colonies. Still, Williams had to proceed carefully. Cromwell, like the Massachusetts Puritans, believed that Christian governments were required to protect the word of God. When Williams arrived in London in 1643, he stayed at the home of Henry Vane, a longtime friend and highly influential Puritan in Parliament. Vane disagreed with Cromwell about many things, including separation of church and state, and in time he would find himself imprisoned by Cromwell after the king had been beheaded and Cromwell had become lord protector of Great Britain. But at this early point in the struggle against the monarchy, the two had joined forces. Through Vane's offices, Williams got what he wanted:

> By the authority of the aforesaid Ordinance ... the Lords and Commons, give, grant and confirm to the aforesaid inhabitants of the towns of Providence, Portsmouth, and Newport, a free and absolute Charter of Incorporation, to be known by the name of the incorporation of Providence Plantations, in the Narragansett-Bay in New-England, together with full power and authority to rule themselves, and such others as shall hereafter inhabit within any part of the said tract of land, by such a form of civil government as by voluntary consent of all, or the greater part of them, they shall find most suitable to their estate and condition.

Cromwell died in 1658, and two years later the monarchy was restored under Charles II. Williams was now unsure of the validity of the parliamentary patent granting his colony its land—land that Williams theologically doubted England even had the right to grant. But once again he deemed it best to render unto Caesar—even a Caesar claiming a Christian divine right to rule. Fortunately, Charles II, uncertainly perched on the throne, was not looking for fights. Newly chartered Connecticut, however, was—since its borders included present-day Rhode Island. But Connecticut, being a Puritan colony, limited its protests when, in 1663, Charles II issued a royal charter to Rhode Island. What particularly irked Connecticut was that the boundaries of Rhode Island and the Providence Plantations were enlarged by Charles to include other outcast communities that, over the years, had settled near the communities founded by Roger Williams and Anne Hutchinson. The new boundaries were, with some later adjustments, the shape Rhode Island has today.

In his later years, Williams faced a fundamental church/state challenge in his relations with the colony's Quakers. He had participated in a public debate of theological issues with the Quakers at their settlement in Newport. Many of the Quakers in attendance, adhering to the Inner Light that was central to their beliefs, began to pray aloud when he spoke, thereby preventing him from expressing his beliefs. Williams subsequently urged Rhode Island's government to suppress those who would suppress others. The younger generation now running the colony opted instead to take their chances, even with religious expressions others considered rude or potentially dangerous.

From the founding of Rhode Island to the present, Americans have wrestled with the question, in what instances does divine authority negate civil authority? The fact that, under the Constitution, Americans agree on the validity of the question has not resulted in agreeing on the answer. From prayer in school to the teaching of evolution, to polygamy, same-sex marriage, medical decisions, and even the performance of autopsies, nearly every aspect of life in the United States has confronted questions of divine versus civil authority.

Did Roger Williams know the answers? If he did, it resides in his one work that seemingly has nothing to do with church or state. In 1643 he published *A Key into the Language of America: Or, An Help to the Language of the Natives in that Part of America Called New England*. The title suggests that the book is simply a guide to the language of the region's Indians. Each chapter presents a group of indigenous words and phrases, explaining their meaning within the context of the tribe's culture, noting their differences from European culture, and concluding with a scriptural reference placing that aspect of the natives' culture within the context of Christian precepts. Williams's "dictionary" was in fact a profound effort to increase understanding between the colonists and their Narragansett neighbors. As such, the most significant statement in *A Key into the Language of America* is its opening words: "I present you with a key.... A little key may open a box, where lies a bunch of keys." In the life of Roger Williams, there is a key.

AUGUSTINE HERMAN
Why We Have Delaware

By way of a little discourse on the supposed claim or pretence of my
Lord Baltimore's patent unto our aforesaid South River or Delaware ...
we utterly deny, disown, and reject any power and authority ... that may
or can legally come to reduce or subdue the said river and subjects.

—AUGUSTINE HERMAN, 1659[1]

D elaware is a little rectangle with a scoop on top that occupies what would
otherwise be the eastern end of Maryland. Since Maryland wouldn't
be that big even if it included Delaware, why do we have Delaware?

We have Delaware for the same reason the world had Bohemia—the
birthplace of Augustine Herman, who grew up to become the man responsible for the existence of Delaware as a separate colony. Bohemia's core
was the western half of today's Czech Republic, though at times it included
various adjacent regions. Its popu-
lation was a mix of Germanic people
(among whom many, in the wake of
Martin Luther, had left the Catholic Church to become Protestants),
Slavic people (who adhered to the
teachings of the Orthodox Church),
and a sizable number of Jews. For
Bohemia, creating a sense of itself
as an entity was further complicated
by the fact that it was periodically
ruled by far more powerful enti-
ties that were sometimes Catholic,
sometimes Protestant.

Delaware too began as a mix of

Augustine Herman (ca. 1621–1686)

people—Dutch, Swedes, Finns, and British Marylanders—living in a region that was periodically claimed by far more powerful colonies, both Catholic and Protestant. The Dutch laid claim to Delaware in 1624. They considered it the southern end of the New Netherlands, Holland's vast North American colony that extended up from the Delaware Bay, crossed the Hudson River, and continued northeastward to the Connecticut River. England too laid claim to Delaware in its 1607 charter for Virginia, which included all the land from the top of New Jersey to the bottom of North Carolina, from the Atlantic to the Pacific. England's King Charles I, figuring Virginia could spare 12,000 or so square miles, created Maryland as a colony for Catholics in 1632. The boundaries stipulated in its royal charter included what is now Delaware.

Dutch New Netherlands

Even though Delaware was claimed by both Holland and England, no Europeans lived there, with the brief exception of a failed Dutch settlement in 1631. Not until 1638 did Europeans settle permanently in Delaware, and they were Swedes. In time the Swedes branched out, and Dutch settlements were established. As in Bohemia, the two primary groups were gradually joined by minority populations of other groups.

For twenty years Delaware's settlements prospered and grew, their conflicts confined to fighting local Indians and each other. But in 1659 all the settlements were threatened by the larger colony of Maryland. In August of that year, Maryland sent word to the Dutch along Delaware Bay that they must depart from the colony. The danger resulted in a response from Peter Stuyvesant, governor of the entire New Netherlands. Stuyvesant dispatched two emissaries from Manhattan: a native-born Dutchman named Resolved Waldron and a Bohemian-born immigrant, Augustine Herman. In selecting Herman,

Stuyvesant made an astute choice. Herman's efforts—commencing here but enduring for the remainder of his life, and then continued by his son—displayed insights and instincts that were likely connected to the similarities Delaware shared with Bohemia.

Herman had been born in Prague in 1621, a critical time in Bohemian history. One year earlier, German Catholics had regained ruling power in the region. In the wake of this event, 36,000 Bohemian Protestants emigrated, many of them to Holland. Herman's family was among those emigrants.

Herman's parents oversaw an education that endowed their son with skills that would be of value both regardless and because of borders. He became a businessman in the import-export trade and a highly skilled cartographer and surveyor. As an adult he relocated to Manhattan, where his skills led to his becoming a member of the Board of Nine, assisting Governor Stuyvesant in his decisions and actions.

Herman's relations with Stuyvesant were bumpy. Herman had, at one time, written to Stuyvesant's superiors in Holland complaining of the governor's high-handedness, vengefulness, and morals: "The basket maker's daughter, whom he seduced in Holland on a promise of marriage, coming and finding that he was already married, hath exposed his conduct even in public court."[2]

While the two apparently patched things up sufficiently for Stuyvesant to appoint Herman as an emissary to Maryland, here too the younger man's approach differed markedly (or more aptly perhaps, "Bohemianly") from the governor's instructions. Stuyvesant had told Herman and Waldron to assert that Lord Baltimore's demands were "contrary to the 2nd, 3rd, and 16th articles of the confederation of peace made between the Republic of England and the Netherlands in 1654." They were then to demand that Maryland, by virtue of that treaty, pay reparations and damages caused by its "frivolous demands and bloody threatenings."

Herman's report of his and Waldron's meetings with Maryland governor Josiah Fendall and the colony's proprietor, Phillip Calvert (the Maryland-based younger brother of Lord Baltimore), reveals that such demands and counterthreats were virtually absent from their discussions.[3] The two emissaries did reference the 1654 treaty, but Herman's efforts were far more focused on documents issued by England itself, which supported the view that England had long recognized the right of the Dutch to their settlements along the Delaware Bay. Most effectively, Herman cited the English charter that had created Maryland, which stated that it was to be a British colony "in a country hitherto uncultivated in the parts of America, and partly occupied by savages having no knowledge of the Divine Being." Herman argued that the land *had* been hitherto cultivated by people with knowledge of the Divine Being—namely, the Dutch who had attempted a settlement in 1631. Admittedly, they had been entirely wiped out by Indians within a few months, but their settlement predated Maryland's 1632 charter.

Fendall and Calvert did not buy this argument. Twenty-three years later, however, Charles II bought it, invoking it to refute a later effort by Maryland to claim Delaware. Herman thus pointed the way for future generations to defend Delaware's independence from Maryland.

Though Calvert did not cotton to the claim, he did cotton to the man who made it. His good feelings toward Herman were sufficient to defuse the preparations Maryland had been making for an invasion of Delaware. In this respect, Herman and Waldron's mission succeeded, which in itself was a considerable accomplishment.

In addition, Calvert's good feelings gave the canny Herman an opportunity to further ingratiate himself with the government of Maryland. He offered his services as a cartographer to make a detailed map of the colony and the adjoining regions for Lord Baltimore in return for a grant of land in Maryland on which he and his family could live (and thereby put some distance between himself and his frequent nemesis, Peter Stuyvesant).

Herman's offer was accepted, and the grant of land was made shortly thereafter. But not just any land. Lord Baltimore, himself quite canny, saw an opportunity presented by Herman's offer to acquire more than just a map. He issued Herman a grant for land in which the eastern portion lay in the disputed area but the western portion was indisputably within Maryland. Lord Baltimore was thus undermining Herman's loyalty to the Dutch. Herman, for his part, named the tract of land Little Bohemia—which is exactly what it was.

It took ten years for Herman to complete the map he had promised—but they were a particularly eventful ten years, not conducive to concentration. During that period he relocated his family to the land he had been granted. England and Holland went to war, resulting in the ouster of all Dutch authorities in the New Netherlands. Charles II deeded most of Holland's former claims to his brother, the Duke of York—but, aiming to avoid conflict with his Maryland colony, the king did not include Delaware in the land deeded to his brother. Delaware was not, however, subsumed under the government of Maryland, since Catholic and Anglican tensions were so hair-trigger tense in England at that time. Consequently, the Duke of York became the de facto proprietor of Delaware, extending the "Duke of York's Laws" to the region and overseeing the appointment of its British officials. With this ascendancy of British rule, Herman opted to become a citizen of Maryland.

The map Herman ultimately delivered in 1670 was a masterpiece of its era. So appreciative was Lord Baltimore that he granted additional land to Herman, who now possessed some 30,000 acres.

Meanwhile, rapid political change continued. In 1672 England and Holland went to war again. This time the Dutch initially ousted the British from Delaware and other settlements. But in 1674 control once again reverted to England. A year later, Lord Baltimore died and his title passed to his son Charles Calvert, who repressed the rights of the colony's Protestants, among whom was Herman.

It was in this era that aging Augustine Herman passed the "Bohemian" baton to his eldest son, Ephraim. One year after Calvert became proprietor of Maryland and commenced repressing the rights of Protestants, Ephraim Herman became a court official in Delaware. Five years later, he was at the helm, navigating Delaware's status in the wake of the region's next major political shift—the 1681 British charter creating Pennsylvania.

Pennsylvania's charter caused immediate conflict with Maryland regarding the location of their mutual border. This conflict raised William Penn's concerns regarding Pennsylvania's access to the sea. His colony's only waterway to the ocean was the Delaware River (Pennsylvania's eastern boundary) down into the Delaware Bay (dividing Delaware and New Jersey), then out to the Atlantic. If Maryland should prevail in its continued claim that Delaware was within its borders, it could block Pennsylvania's access to the sea.

Penn, whose Quaker beliefs prohibited warfare and the forms of aggression that led to war, did not seek to possess Delaware. The semicircular top that Delaware has today originated in Pennsylvania's charter, when Penn urged that it include a southeastern border with a twelve-mile radius away from the Dutch town of New Castle, so as not to create conflict. He did, however, seek proprietorship over Delaware, to assure that Pennsylvania had free navigation to the sea. By seeking proprietorship, Penn left Maryland no choice but to contest the issue again. For Delaware's mostly Protestant residents, the choice of incorporation into Maryland under the anti-Protestant Charles Calvert or proprietorship under the pacifist William Penn was a no-brainer.

England, not wanting colonial conflicts it could avoid, ruled in favor of Penn. In granting him proprietorship over Delaware, England implicitly recognized Delaware as an entity unto itself. The Board of Trades and Plantations, which arbitrated the case for the king, cited the reasoning first posited by Augustine Herman regarding Maryland's charter excluding land previously cultivated by Europeans.

Following this act, Penn journeyed to Delaware, where he was officially greeted at New Castle by John Moll and Ephraim Herman, who presented Penn with the key to the town's fort. Augustine Herman, now an elderly man quietly living out his final years on his vast manor, had succeeded in achieving what Bohemia did not.

ROBERT JENKINS'S EAR
Fifteen Minutes of Fame

Official persons ... endeavored to deny, to insinuate in their vile newspapers, that Jenkins lost his ear nearer home, and not for nothing.... Sheer calumnies we now find. Jenkins' account was doubtless abundantly emphatic; there is no ground to question the substantial truth of him and it.

—Thomas Carlyle[1]

In today's society, people often refer to "fifteen minutes of fame," pop artist Andy Warhol's notion that mass media have become so prevalent that everyone will be in the spotlight at some point in their lives. Warhol actually said that in the *future* everyone will have fifteen minutes of fame, but in fact there is nothing new in this phenomenon. Mass media have created fleeting fame for as long as mass media have existed—which is to say, since the printing press or even the politically charged graffiti of ancient Rome.

Such was the case with one Robert Jenkins, the captain of a British merchant ship in the eighteenth century. At a key moment, the newspapers of the day put the spotlight on Jenkins—technically, on his ear, or more technically, on the absence of his ear—and in so doing provoked a war between England and Spain. Though the war had nothing to do with Florida and Georgia, it resulted in the boundary between those two states that exists to this day.

In April 1731 Jenkins was at the helm of the *Rebecca*, carrying a cargo of sugar from the British colony of Jamaica to London. While off the coast of Cuba, Jenkins's ship was overtaken by the Spanish coast guard, which boarded and searched for contraband goods from Spanish ports. Finding none, Captain Juan de León Fandino brandished his cutlass and ordered Jenkins to reveal where he'd hidden the contraband. When Jenkins continued to insist he had none, Fandino sliced his sword across Jenkins's ear. Still, Jenkins maintained he could not confess to what was not there. Fandino then had his men tie Jenkins to the yardarm using a neck halter. But even as the Spanish captain ordered the halter incrementally raised, thereby approaching the point of a lynching, Jenkins maintained there was nothing to tell. Frustrated and furious, Fandino took hold of Jenkins's wounded ear and tore it off, handing it to Jenkins and saying (depending on which version one reads), "Carry that to your king, and tell him of it!" Clearly an act of war.

But not in 1731. George II, the last British monarch born outside Great Britain, was uncertain as to his clout and allowed leadership to be exerted by Robert Walpole, who is thus recognized as England's first prime minister. Walpole's success was due in large part to his policy that England's economy was best maintained and strengthened by avoiding war. Consequently, he had negotiated the Treaty of Seville in 1729, which led to the episode involving Captain Jenkins two year later. Under the treaty, England agreed not to trade with Spain's North American colonies and, to enable verification, allowed British ships to be inspected by Spain for cargo from those ports.

The treaty was highly controversial in England. While peace was good for the economy, such severe limitations on its overseas trade were not. Nor did it sit well with the nation's pride. Many merchants and the sea captains and crews they financed did not abide by the treaty's prohibitions.

These violations explain, in part, Captain Fandino's frustration and violence. From Prime Minister Walpole's perspective, Fandino's rage reflected Spain's reduced circumstances. Spain was increasingly desperate to preserve its monopolies in the New World—the totality of which it had originally possessed following the voyages of Christopher Columbus. But that had been over two hundred years earlier. Spain's efforts to control the New World's supply of sugar and gold created a lucrative black market. Pirates engaged in hijacking, initially on their own and later with secret financing in some instances by other nations. By the time Robert Jenkins was at sea, otherwise legitimate shipping companies engaged in periodic smuggling as well.

When Jenkins returned to England in June 1731, a full account of his misfortune appeared in the press, but fame did not ensue. Such occurrences were not particularly unusual. The article in London's *Universal Spectator* also included:

The *Bacchus*, Captain Stephens, which is arrived at Bristol from Jamaica, was taken the 27th of April by a Spanish pirate sloop or *guarde costa*.... They treated her captain and crew very barbarously, putting their fingers between gunlock screws till they flattened them, and some had lighted matches between, in order to extort a confession where their money [Spanish doubloons from smuggling] lay, of which they had none on board.

Still, as these depredations continued, Walpole's efforts to avoid war met with increasing opposition. The tipping point came in 1737 with the death of Queen Caroline, through whose friendship Walpole had maintained the approval—or mitigated the occasional disapproval—of George II and the Prince of Wales (the future George III).

The future king's opposition to his father now emerged more boldly, and with it Walpole's political opponents commenced a drumbeat for war. Parliament held hearings regarding instances of mistreatment of British seamen by Spain. And just as the U.S. Congress has demonstrated its flair for the dramatic through the stage-managed appearances of star witnesses, Parliament's star for 1738 was Robert Jenkins. His presentation was electrifying: he related his breathtaking experience and climaxed his testimony by unfolding a square of cotton and producing his severed ear.

Or so later accounts state. The parliamentary records of his testimony do not record the ear being displayed. Nor is it mentioned in any of the newspaper accounts that immediately followed his testimony. Nevertheless, those news accounts, augmented by politicians expressing newfound outrage, generated a public uproar. Walpole had no choice but to accede to war.

In Georgia these distant events created considerable concern, since the colony was adjacent to the Spanish colony of Florida. Fearing an attack, James Oglethorpe, Georgia's founder, raised troops and improved defenses along his colony's coast and nearby islands. In July 1742 the Spanish attacked, with a vastly larger force than that of Oglethorpe, and quickly overtook one of the two forts on St. Simon's Island.

Oglethorpe still occupied the island's second fort, which was protected by a surrounding marsh with only two roads of access. The greater number of Spaniards was countered by the Georgians' greater knowledge of the pathways and marshes, and by Oglethorpe's skill in creating the impression that he had more forces than he actually did. The Spanish, believing Oglethorpe's numbers far larger, cautiously approached and were confused by the pathways. These factors enabled the Georgians to engage them successfully in what became known as the Battle of Bloody Marsh. The victory resulted in a new boundary with Spain, establishing the St. Marys River as the eastern segment of the Florida-Georgia border.

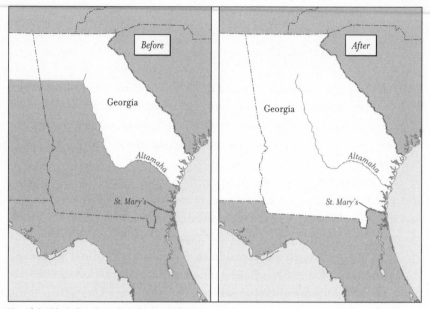

War of Jenkins's Ear: Georgia before and after

The larger war, however, was not as successful. England suffered a massive defeat in its campaign against the Colombian port of Cartagena. The war ended soon after, as did the career of Robert Walpole. All in all, little had changed as a result of the war—except for the Georgia border.

As for Robert Jenkins, he returned to work and obscurity. For a time he administered affairs for the British East India Company on the small island of St. Helena, midway between Africa and South America, then resumed his career at sea.

ROBERT TUFTON MASON
Winning New Hampshire

Prudence Gatch, aged sixteen years, servant to Robert Mason, Esq, maketh oath that Thomas Wiggins ... did give her master ill language; that her master bid Thomas Wiggins several times to be gone out of the house ... but he would not; that she, seeing Thomas Wiggins laying hold of her master by the cravat and hair, did run forth to call the neighbors, crying out that her master would be murthered.

—DEPOSITION OF PRUDENCE GATCH, 1686[1]

The colonial relationship between New Hampshire and Massachusetts has a long and tangled history, hardly evident in the relatively simple line that separates the two states today. That history was, in effect, a political chess tournament, with contestants that included not only England, Massachusetts, and New Hampshire, but also individual players with particular interests. One such individual was Robert Tufton Mason. His match, as much or more than any, determined the tournament's final outcome.

What is today Massachusetts began as an effort by the British Crown to maintain control in England amid religious turmoil. Vying for influence were Anglicans and Catholics, with Puritans and Quakers later joining the fray. To mitigate the conflicts, the Crown created a colony in America for Catholics (Maryland) and another for Quakers (Pennsylvania). Massachusetts (first settled by the separatist Pilgrims) became the colony for Puritans.

When Robert Tufton Mason was born in England in 1629, New Hampshire already existed. It had been created in 1622 when the Plymouth Colony's parent company granted land to his grandfather, John Mason, and Ferdinando Gorges for purposes of economic development. The two later divided the land—Gorges's portion becoming Maine, and Mason's becoming New Hampshire. Mason's plans for the land never got off the ground. The advance staff he sent found it not as expected, and John Mason died before

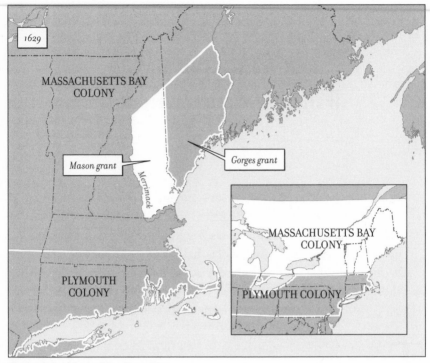

Mason grant: embryo of New Hampshire

ever setting foot on it. The land eventually was inherited by his grandson, Robert Tufton. Robert, however, was only a child. Consequently, the land was administered by an executor in England and the staff that had remained in America. They sold it off. During this same interval, Massachusetts came to administer jurisdictional functions in the region.

Thus, for his twenty-first birthday, Robert Tufton got nothing except a new last name, Mason, which he acquired to comply with his grandfather's will. He also acquired legal standing, enabling him to bring suit over the sale of his land, if he so chose. He chose not to, just yet. The year was 1650, and Robert Tufton Mason didn't like his odds given the political climate in England and the colonies.

One year earlier, the religious conflicts in England had climaxed with the beheading of Charles I. The government was now led by Oliver Cromwell. Cromwell was a Puritan, and so were the colonists in Massachusetts, where Mason's land was located. Both secular and church leaders wrote to the newly empowered Cromwell to express their Puritan joy: "We acknowledge ourselves in all duty bound, not only to take due notice of that tender care

and undeserved respect your excellence hath, upon all occasions, vouch-
safed unto the poor despised colony of Massachusetts," the General Court
declared.[2] "Intimate our sufferings under the tyranny of the Episcopacy
which forced us into exile, to our great hazard and loss, for no other offence
but professing that truth which, through mercy, is now acknowledged," wrote
a leading group of ministers.[3]

Not only was Robert Tufton Mason not a Puritan; his relatives had actively opposed the overthrow of the king. One cousin had been Charles I's master of bequests. Another cousin had been a member of the Parliament that
Cromwell dissolved. That cousin fled to Virginia.

Puritan rule turned out not to be the Garden of Eden its backers had
hoped. In England the Puritans closed theaters, prohibited dancing, and
even banned celebration on Christmas. Less amusing than the suppression
of amusement was the Puritan government's confiscation of property from
Catholics, accompanied by horrific ethnic cleansing in Ireland. After little
more than a decade, England had had enough. Puritan rule ended when
Charles II, son of the beheaded king, was restored to power in 1660.

Shortly after Charles II took his seat on the throne, Mason took a seat
in his London attorney's office. The time was right to petition the king.
His plea hearkened to the king's dethroned and beheaded father, who had
"become a Sacrifice" of Puritan rule—the same Puritans who, it stated,
"did surreptitiously … get a Confirmation of the [New Hampshire] Grant
… [and] aspired to Extend their Bounds and spread into a Larger Territory
than they had yet usurped."[4]

Massachusetts indeed had some explaining to do. Extending its jurisdiction into New Hampshire was but one of a list of dubious actions it had taken
during England's years of Puritan rule. With the monarchy now restored,
Governor John Endicott quickly wrote the new king:

> Most Gracious and Dread Sovereign,
> May it please your Majesty in the Day wherein you happily say you
> now know that you are King over your British Israel, to cast an Eye
> upon your poor Mephibosheth … we mean upon New England
> Kneeling, with the rest of your Subjects, before your Majesty as her
> restored King.… Touching complaints put in against us, our humble
> Request only is that … your Majesty would permit nothing to make
> an Impression upon your Royal Heart against us until we have both
> opportunity and leave to answer for ourselves.[5]

Charles II wasn't looking to resume the conflicts from his father's reign. He was looking for ways to reassemble the shattered authority of the throne. He embraced Massachusetts, while slipping Mason's petition to his attorney general. Massachusetts heaved a sigh of relief. Mason held his breath in hope. And Charles II had some time to be everybody's friend. Then his attorney general weighed in. "I am of the opinion," he reported to the king, "that the Petitioner Robert Mason, who is Grandson & Heir to the said John Mason, hath a good & legal Right & Title to the Lands Conveyed by the name of New Hampshire."[6]

Good news for Mason, followed by bad news for Mason. The king currently had more pressing concerns in America, where Holland and France, like Massachusetts, had feathered their jurisdictional nests during the turmoil in England. To regain his standing, Charles II needed the assistance of New England's most populous and influential colony, Massachusetts.

The attorney general's opinion was therefore filed away while the king, in 1665, sought New England's help in ousting the Dutch authorities from what is today New York. Massachusetts grudgingly scraped together 200 men, who ended up not serving in what turned out to be a less than successful venture. The following year, the king urged his New England colonies to join forces and oust the French from the present-day province of Quebec. Massachusetts humbly said no. In 1673 England again sought to oust the Dutch, once more without the help of Massachusetts, which flatly rejected the request for assistance of a British commander who landed in Boston en route to war.[7] This time England prevailed over the Dutch, taking control of their settlements in 1674.

With this final victory, Charles II decided the time had come to send Massachusetts a message. The case of Robert Tufton Mason was ideal for composing cutting remarks. *Literally* cutting: "We have been for a long time solicited by the Complaints of Our Trusty and Well-beloved Subject, Robert Mason," the king wrote to the governor of Massachusetts, "to interpose Our Royal authority for ... relief in the matter of [his] Claims and Right ... to the province of New Hampshire.... We have therefore directed that ... [Massachusetts] show cause why We should not afford the Petitioner that Relief."[8]

Faced with the loss of New Hampshire, Massachusetts commenced legal maneuvers that were countered by Mason. The case was finally adjudicated in 1677. During the maneuverings, Mason sought to improve his chances by relinquishing to the Crown any claim to governing the land. Before the judges, Massachusetts cited an impressive list of documents and precedents.

But the issue was no longer about law; it was about power. To a king seeking to solidify his control, particularly a king who had experienced recurrent difficulties in controlling Massachusetts, Mason's pretrial move was checkmate. Mason, however, did not win. The judges concluded that because "the said lands are in the possession of several other persons not before us"—living, as they did, across an ocean—"if there be any course of justice upon the place having jurisdiction, we esteem it most proper to direct the parties to have recourse thither for the decision."[9]

The place having jurisdiction? Couldn't Their Honours have been a bit more specific? In point of fact, their lack of specificity was the significant element in this decision. No one, based on the evidence presented, had demonstrated clear jurisdiction over the disputed land. Mason may not have won his case, but he had not lost it, either. The loser was Massachusetts.

Mason's next move was another avowal. In this instance, he promised not to demand back payments from the residents, and to sell their land to them "according to the just and true ... value of all houses built by them, and of all lands ... improved by them."[10]

Following this avowal, Charles II was ready to continue cutting Massachusetts down to size. In 1680 he decreed to the people of New Hampshire that they were now under his direct governance. Two years later the king sealed the deal with Mason. "We have received the Opinion of Our Attorney & Solicitor General that ye said Robert Mason ... has good and legal Title to ye Lands conveyed to him," the king informed Massachusetts, nailing down his proclamation by adding, "We do strictly charge & command you to secure him, his servants & agents from any arrests & molestations whatsoever during his or their abode within ye limits of your Jurisdiction."[11] Translation: Mason had won his match.

With the king having secured the way, Mason arrived in America for the first time. What he found, however, was that selling the land in New Hampshire to its occupants was a whole other game—one at which he was less adept. In 1685 settlers Thomas Wiggins and Anthony Nutter came to the home of New Hampshire's governor, where Mason was staying, to protest having to pay for what they viewed as their own property. Wiggins stated his views on real estate law in language so colorful that Mason decided to throw him out. Or tried to; Mason ended up being the one who got tossed. Wiggins hurled him into the fireplace, where Mason's clothing ignited, and one leg was badly burned. The governor quickly intervened and just as quickly lost a tooth and received two broken ribs. One of Mason's male servants, hearing the scuffle, dashed in brandishing his master's sword. It ended up in Nutter's possession as the two obstreperous settlers left, delighting over their prize.[12]

Mason returned to England later that year, having faced so much animosity he feared for his life. Now fifty-six years old, he died soon after. The conflict over New Hampshire's sovereignty, however, continued to drag on through the following decades.

In the same year that Mason returned to England, Charles II died and James II ascended to the throne. The extent to which Charles had reassembled royal authority encouraged James to seek *absolute* authority. To consolidate his grip on New England, James decreed that Massachusetts, New York, New Jersey, Connecticut, Rhode Island, New Hampshire, and Maine would

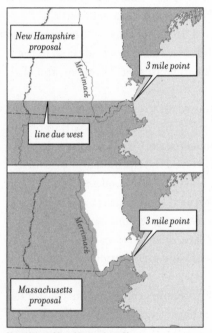

be combined and called the Dominion of New England. New England was now one big angry colony. Old England, for similar reasons, also became one big angry country. In 1688 James II abdicated the throne.

New Hampshire once again became its own province under the jurisdiction of the Crown. But not for long. It now had its own internal conflicts, one of which was the Mason grant. Robert Tufton Mason's heirs had opted out of this conflict by selling the grant to a London merchant named Samuel Allen.[13] This made no difference to those living on the land. They despised Allen as much as Mason. But as farmers on difficult soil, they were poor and virtually powerless. To augment their power, they sought to

New Hampshire–Massachusetts border proposals

have New Hampshire given back to Massachusetts, that colony being happy to help their cause. Those *with* power in New Hampshire opposed the move.

In addition, a new conflict had arisen regarding Massachusetts. The original 1622 grant to John Mason, reflecting the charter of the Massachusetts Bay Company, separated New Hampshire along a line three miles north of the Merrimack River. Europeans had assumed that the Merrimack flowed along a relatively straight line. In time the colonists discovered that the river made a major turn to the north, and they wondered if the border, at that turn, instead became a line three miles east, as opposed to north, of the river. Colonists west of the Merrimack, being beyond the Mason/Allen land, preferred New Hampshire over Massachusetts since taxes were lower. They maintained that north was not east and that a new line was needed. In 1695 New Hampshire's legislature proposed one. Massachusetts, for its part, ignored it.

New Hampshire's boundary proposal had been shelved when Queen Anne ascended to the throne in 1702. She sought to mitigate the conflict by appointing the same man to be governor of both New Hampshire and Massachusetts. Her policy was continued by subsequent monarchs for nearly fifty years.

On paper Anne's solution was brilliant; on earth it made little difference. The various parties continued to maneuver and countermaneuver. In the final round of this now century-old jurisdictional tournament, the ghost of Robert Tufton Mason returned to the game. Those in New Hampshire seeking a clearly defined separation from

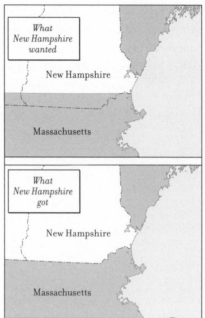

Final border decree, 1741

Massachusetts began making "Robert Mason moves"—moves based on the awareness that laws were not the rules of this game; power was. While Massachusetts cited royal charters and other documents in making its case to the British government, New Hampshire's representative sought to brush aside such legal details, closing his arguments with that era's version of a simple country lawyer:

> Your Petitioner doth most humbly appeal to your Majesty ... that in case any defect in Form should be found in the Appeal from New Hampshire, your Majesty may be graciously pleased to Consider in how surprising a manner your Loyal Little Province of New

Hampshire has been treated by the Governor who was pleased, though very Improperly, to call himself a Common Father to both the Provinces.... [Massachusetts] hath acted to usurp your Majesty's undoubted property.[4]

New Hampshire's history of loyalty appealed to the Crown. Massachusetts's history of disloyalty did not. In 1741 George II completely severed New Hampshire from Massachusetts by appointing separate governors and decreeing that surveyors mark off a new boundary. It is the boundary that exists today. Its location embeds in the American map the fact that power can supersede law—not simply because Massachusetts got less than it sought, but rather because New Hampshire got *more* than it sought.

LORD FAIRFAX
What You Know or Who You Know?

Surveyed five hundred acres of land on ye South Fork of ye branch.
On our way shot two wild turkeys.... This morning we began our
intended business of laying off lots. We began at ye Boundary Line
of ye Northern [Branch] ... & run off two lots.
—Seventeen-year-old surveyor George Washington[1]

Here's *what* we know. Maryland came into existence under a 1632 charter that stipulates its southern border as being "the first Fountain of the River of Pattowmack ... and following the same on the West and South, unto a certain Place, called Cinquack, situate near the mouth of the said River." We also know that the Potomac, as with every river, results from the confluence of numerous waterways. And we know—or surveyors do—that, from among these numerous waterways, the one most distant from the mouth of the river is considered the source (or in the charter's more lyrical language, "first fountain") of a river. We know that the South Branch of the Potomac, originating farthest from the mouth, would therefore be the southern border of Maryland. But we know that instead the North Branch is the southern border of Maryland.

Lord Fairfax (1693–1781)

Since half a million acres is at stake, and since Maryland diligently and repeatedly protested this obvious error, how did Virginia succeed in pulling it off?

The answer is Thomas Fairfax,

the 6th Lord Fairfax. In terms of "who you know," he of course knew his father, the 5th Lord Fairfax. The 5th Lord Fairfax had known and married the only legitimate child of Lord Culpeper, who knew and had remained loyal to Charles II during his French exile in the 1640s. Charles, essentially penniless while in exile, rewarded his supporters with land grants in the New World—a shrewd move since, in order to obtain their rewards, his supporters needed to return Charles to the throne.

Lord Culpeper's IOU was proprietorship over all the land in the Virginia colony between the Rappahannock and Potomac Rivers. That was a nice hunk of real estate but, being south of the Potomac, it had nothing to do with Maryland. It was, however, the seed of Maryland's boundary conflict with Virginia.

Following the restoration of Charles II to the throne, Virginia's colonial government was less than thrilled to see the taxes from this region going to Lord Culpeper and, upon his death, the 5th Lord Fairfax and, upon his death, the 6th Lord Fairfax, the gentleman who caused the boundary conflict with Maryland to surface.

Thomas Fairfax was the first of the proprietors of this region to see the family's American domain. Like his predecessors, he initially arranged for a relative to live in Virginia and manage his land. After a young woman whose name has not survived broke off their engagement, Fairfax left England to live on his American estates. He built a home for himself in the Shenandoah Valley, distant even from Virginia society, then centered around the ports of Williamsburg and Alexandria.

Lord Fairfax was not, however, in the wilderness. Virginia's growing population had by then pushed westward to the point that disputes were arising regarding the boundary between the two rivers cited in what was now known as the Fairfax Grant. Consequently, he and Virginia's governor commissioned a survey to settle their dispute by locating the western boundary of the Fairfax Grant—a line from the source of the Potomac to the source of the Rappahannock. Among those who participated in marking the Potomac portion was a young surveyor hired because he knew Lord Fairfax's cousin. This "who you know" factor would also affect Maryland's boundary dispute, since the young surveyor was George Washington.

In October 1746 Lord Fairfax's and Virginia's team placed a marker, known as the Fairfax Stone, at what they agreed was the source of the Potomac. That agreement located the source at the headwaters of the North Branch of the river, since that branch behooved both parties.

Whom it did not behoove was Lord Baltimore. Had the Virginia surveyors determined that the South Branch of the Potomac was the true source of the river, the land between the two branches would belong to his colony, Maryland. But Lord Baltimore did not then know (nor did anyone else) which branch of the Potomac extended farthest into the heavily forested western mountains. Over the next several years, however, his suspicions were aroused, and he had his colony's governor dispatch a surveyor to determine the respective locations of the source of both branches. The surveyor reported that the South Branch extended sixty to eighty miles farther from the mouth of the Potomac than did the North Branch. Learning this, Lord Baltimore sent instructions to his governor, stating:

> Lord Viscount Fairfax has a Grant of a large Tract of Land lying and running along the Banks of Patowmack River on the Virginia Side and ... I am informed The Powers of Government in Virginia have taken the Liberty to ascertain the Bounds and Limits of his said Lordships Grant.... I am informed that Commissioners have proceeded therein and instead of their stopping at the South Branch,

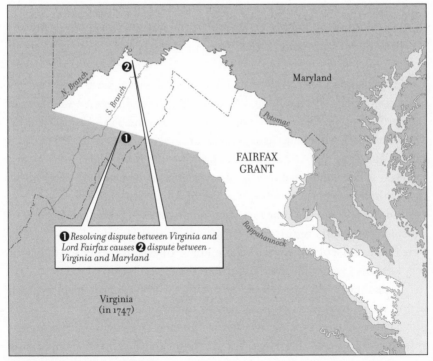

The Fairfax Grant: three-way dispute

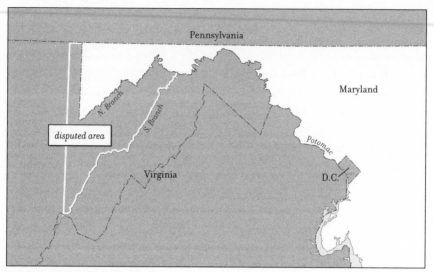

Maryland and Virginia: disputed border

which runs from the first Fountain of Patowmack River, one of the Boundries of Maryland, have cros't to a Branch runing North.... Communicate to Lord Fairfax that I am very desirous of Settling Proper Limits Conclusive between him and me in regard to my Province of Maryland and his Grant in Virginia.[2]

Lord Fairfax politely declined. Lord Baltimore then sought to have a survey commissioned by Maryland. But the colony's House of Burgesses was engaged in a battle over taxes with Lord Baltimore and postponed funding the survey. The issue was further delayed by the dangers and expenses of the French and Indian War (1754–63). Once recovered from the war, Maryland commissioned a survey. When completed in 1774, it revealed what by now both sides knew: the South Branch of the Potomac was the more extensive branch.

But this was not the time for colonies to fight each other, particularly in a dispute that would require the king to adjudicate. Maryland and Virginia were in the midst of uniting with their fellow American colonies to fight that very king over issues far more important than this chunk of land.

The boundary dispute resurfaced during the first years of the new nation within the context of a new issue. Under the Articles of Confederation, no provisions existed regarding interstate commerce. One state could tax another for use of its roads and rivers. For Maryland and Virginia, a compact was necessary to protect Virginia's use of the Potomac, which was entirely within

Maryland's jurisdiction, and Maryland's use of the lower Chesapeake Bay, which was entirely within Virginia's jurisdiction. In 1785 negotiations were mediated by, of all people, George Washington. At this time, Washington was retired from the army but was not yet the president, as no such position existed under the Articles.

Maryland navigated these negotiations carefully, since contesting the North Branch as the proper border would have been awkward enough when one of the line's original surveyors was mediating the negotiations. Given that the mediator was also the nation's foremost military hero, Maryland opted to cooperate. But it kept an ace up its sleeve. The legislation that appointed its negotiators stipulated that only when the two states agreed to their respective borders would the compact be submitted to the Maryland legislature for approval. Virginia agreed to such a discussion, but only regarding the border's western terminus—the Fairfax Stone having been lost in the intervening years. (Decades later it was rediscovered under forest foliage.) Virginia would not discuss which branch was the border.[3]

Maryland knew it could take the dispute before the Supreme Court. But here again, doing so would be asking the court to invalidate a boundary that the father of the country had helped establish. Fearing the impact of "who" over "what," Maryland's legislature debated less confrontational options. Its deliberations, however, were interrupted by—yet again—the need for unity in wartime, this time the War of 1812.

Virginia, meanwhile, had been continuing to deed land in the disputed region. These deeds further diminished Maryland's chances of prevailing before the Supreme Court. Maryland sensed (correctly, as it turned out) that the court would tend to rule in favor of states that had deeded land, despite an incorrectly surveyed border. The court's privileging of deeded lands protected citizens who would be adversely affected by suddenly having their property in another state.

Maryland made a last-ditch effort in 1818. The state proposed to Virginia that it would accept the North Branch as the boundary if Virginia agreed to a survey to relocate its source—since it is from that point that Maryland's western boundary is located. (The state that presently shares this boundary with Maryland, West Virginia, was still part of Virginia at the time.) Virginia, sensing advantage, agreed only to a survey that would reestablish the location of the Fairfax Stone, regardless of whether or not that location was truly the source of the North Branch.

In other words, Virginia won.

MASON AND DIXON
America's Most Famous (and Misunderstood) Line

The white man's right to freedom's wide as universal nature;
But beyond the Mason-Dixon line the black's ain't worth a 'tater.
In fact I rayther calkilate that *this* side of it either,
If white man's justice had its way, 'tain't worth a 'tater neither.

—ANONYMOUS[1]

T he Confederate anthem "Dixie" may contain a reference to Jeremiah Dixon, cosurveyor of the Mason-Dixon Line, but Jeremiah Dixon was not a Southerner, and Charles Mason was not a Northerner. They weren't even Americans; they were British. And the line they surveyed had nothing to do with slavery or the Civil War. In fact, it's not even a line—it's *three* lines.

In 1763 Mason and Dixon were hired to locate the boundary between Maryland, Pennsylvania, and Delaware. Why import two Englishmen when

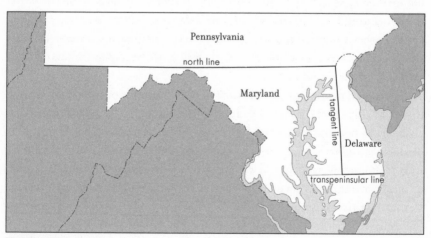

The Mason-Dixon line(s)

surveyors were falling all over each other in America? Why not hire George
Washington or Peter Jefferson or his son, Thomas, all of whom were surveyors? The reason was that this boundary's stipulations had political and
mathematical conflicts. Mitigating those conflicts required surveyors who
were not only mathematically brilliant but also politically impartial.

These conflicts began when Charles II granted a charter for the creation
of Pennsylvania in 1681 that included a semicircle at the colony's southeast
corner to provide a twelve-mile buffer around a preexisting Dutch settlement at New Castle. On the other hand, to protect Pennsylvania's navigation to the sea, it was given hegemony over Delaware and therefore would
negotiate on behalf of Delaware if a boundary dispute should arise. One did,
since the region that comprises Del-
aware had been included fifty years
earlier in Maryland's charter. But
Maryland had never governed the
region, because Holland had controlled it since 1631. The British had
recently ousted the Dutch regime,
but Delaware's Dutch settlers, who
were Protestant, opposed control
by Catholic Maryland. All these
complications, however, eventually
became even more complicated.

First, England sought to solve
the problem by creating Delaware
as a separate entity and leasing it to
Pennsylvania. Delaware was defined
as including all the land below its
semicircular northern border

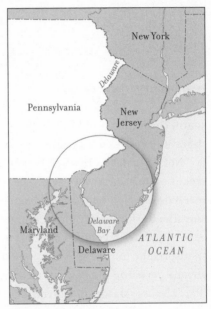

Pennsylvania's access to the sea

extending to the latitude of Cape
Henlopen. Then it was discovered that the borders in Pennsylvania's charter didn't connect. To make matters worse, Pennsylvania's southern border
at 40° N latitude turned out to be above Philadelphia, whose downtown is
39°57′ N latitude.

Again both sides presented arguments to the Crown. An alternative
solution was devised. Another map was then discovered to be wrong. Arguments resumed, and seventy-eight years later an agreement was finally
reached. It set the Maryland-Pennsylvania border fifteen miles below the

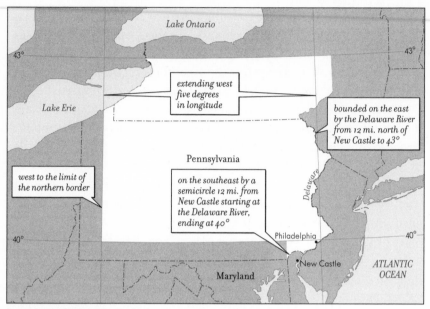

Lake Ontario

43°

43°

Lake Erie

extending west
five degrees
in longitude

bounded on the east
by the Delaware River
from 12 mi. north of
New Castle to 43°

Pennsylvania

west to the limit of
the northern border

on the southeast by a
semicircle 12 mi. from
New Castle starting at
the Delaware River,
ending at 40°

Delaware

Philadelphia

40°

40°

New Castle

ATLANTIC
OCEAN

Maryland

Pennsylvania: 1681 charter borders

southern boundary of Philadelphia, and the southern border of Delaware at the latitude of Fenwick Island.

Not wanting any further disputes, Maryland and Pennsylvania agreed to seek the finest surveyors available. Pennsylvanian Benjamin Franklin—so revered as a scientist that he'd been inducted into England's foremost academy, the Royal Society of London for the Improvement of Natural Knowledge—may have recommended Mason and Dixon. Their recent work had been sponsored by the Royal Society, and Franklin certainly knew of it, as would anyone perusing the news in 1762. *London Magazine*, for example, reported that "Messrs. Mason and Dixon, sent out by the Royal Society to observe the late transit of Venus over the sun, are returned from the Cape of Good Hope and have brought with them a most ... excellent and satisfactory observation, for which they have received the thanks of that learned body." The transit of Venus is a rare event in which the planet passes between the earth and the sun. It can be used to calculate the size of the solar system. How this is done was explained in the Royal Society's report, published immediately after Mason and Dixon's return, presenting their data and formulas computing parallaxes of latitude and longitude.

Asking Mason and Dixon to survey a boundary in America was thus akin to asking Mozart to play at a prom. Charles Mason was born in 1728, the son of a miller and baker. He demonstrated such brilliance at a young age that a mathematician in his home town of Gloucestershire helped finance his education. He joined the staff at the Greenwich Observatory, cobbling together an income from his nominal salary, a grant from a cartographic organization, and any fees he could earn for performing scientific tasks. With this he had to support a wife, who died young, and their two sons.

Jeremiah Dixon, five years younger than Mason, never married. The son of a coal mine owner, he was born in Bishop Auckland, County Durham, over 200 miles north of London. His family could well afford his schooling and introduced him to many eminent scientists with whom he established lasting relationships. Dixon was not, however, the stereotypical science nerd. He opted not to pursue an advanced education. He once told a job interviewer that his "seat of learning" for astronomy was "a pit cabin on Cockfield Fell"—the site of his father's coal mine. Indeed, he may have learned astronomy in order to map mine shafts.[2] A brief but revealing entry regarding young Dixon, whose family was Quaker, appears in the records of his local meeting: "Jery Dixon, son of George and Mary Dixon of Cockfield, disowned for drinking to excess."[3] At that time Dixon had already established himself as a surveyor who could, despite any love of liquor, walk off a line (or an arc or squiggle) on the ground exactly where it should be. His surveying skills were so highly regarded that the twenty-seven-year-old was chosen in 1760 to accompany the renowned scientist Charles Mason to the Cape of Good Hope to obtain data on the transit of Venus.

To survey the Pennsylvania-Maryland-Delaware boundary, Mason and Dixon began by establishing that Philadelphia's southern boundary was the street wall at 30 South Street. From here they went thirty-one miles due west, where arrangements had been made at a farm for an observatory that would be their headquarters for the next four years.

But how did they know they had traveled due west? Apparently, following a compass isn't sufficiently precise, as Mason and Dixon's field notes reveal. "Computed the right ascension of the mid-heaven," they noted, "when the *s [selected stars] passed the azimuth that would intersect the parallel of the post marked West, at 10′ to the westward of the said parallel."[4] Observing stars and crunching numbers, Mason and Dixon proceeded to locate a point fifteen miles due south of the southernmost latitude of Philadelphia—the negotiated latitude of the Maryland-Pennsylvania border.

They next surveyed the Maryland-Pennsylvania border eastward to the Delaware River. But the Maryland-Pennsylvania border doesn't extend to the

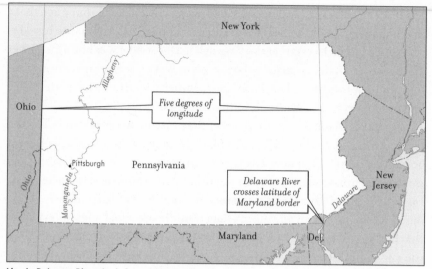

Line to Delaware River: basis for western border

Delaware River; it ends at Delaware's circular border. Why, then, did Mason and Dixon go tromping through Delaware? They did so to locate Pennsylvania's *western* border.

Pennsylvania's charter had fixed its western border at five degrees from its eastern border. But its eastern border was now entirely composed of the Delaware River, based on an agreement with New York. Since the Delaware River is not a straight line, what point would be used to measure five degrees westward? Based on an agreement with Virginia (whose borders at the time included West Virginia and parts of Ohio), the starting point was where the latitude used for the Pennsylvania-Maryland border met the Delaware River. (Confusing? It gets worse, which is why the states sought out Mason and Dixon.)

It was no picnic for these two eminent surveyors, plodding back and forth over a boundary spanning more than 300 miles, in good weather and bad, often far from shelter—but never far from observing American Indians. Precautions had been arranged, however, as noted in Mason and Dixon's journal: "July 16, 1767—We were joined by fourteen Indians deputed by the Chiefs of the Six Nations to go with us on the line. With them came Mr. Hugh Crawford, interpreter."

Coping with Indians was only one of the additional challenges. They also had to cope with boundary stipulations regarding Delaware's circular northern border, which unavoidably resulted in a wedge of uncertain jurisdiction. (In 1921 the wedge was awarded to Delaware.) To the west, they fretted

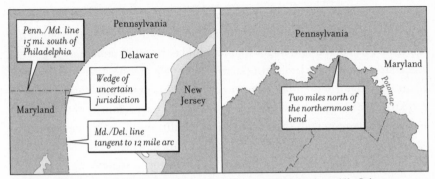

No man's land (left): the Delaware Wedge; Close call (right): Pennsylvania border and the Potomac

about colliding with the Potomac River, Maryland's southern border, since it was not included in the boundary agreement with Pennsylvania regarding Maryland's northern border. In this instance, they got lucky; their journal noted, "Capt. Shelby again went with us to the summit of the mountain, and showed us the northernmost bend of the river Potomac ... from which we judge the line will pass about two miles to the north of the said river." With the Indians, however, their luck ran out:

> Oct. 9, 1767—The Chief of the Indians which joined us the 16th of July informed us that the ... war path [east of the Monongahela River] was the extent of his commission from the Chiefs of the Six Nations ... and that he would not proceed one step further.
> Oct. 26, 1767—Continued the line to the river Monongahela.
> Nov. 5, 1767—Mr. Hugh Crawford with the Indians ... left us.
> Nov. 21, 1767—Seven of our hands left us.
> Nov. 29, 1767—Discharged most of our hands.

Their work was not quite done, but they had done all they could without risking warfare with hostile tribes across the Monongahela. Mason and Dixon returned to England in 1768. They next became involved in studies of gravity—but not as Mason and Dixon. Mason was hired to perform experiments in Ireland; Dixon's work took him to Norway.

Dixon returned to his hometown at the conclusion of this research. His family's wealth enabled him to live comfortably, engaging, when he chose to do so, in local surveying projects. He passed away in 1779 at the age of forty-five.

Mason, on the other hand, remained active in scientific endeavors and in seeking sufficient income. Two years after his return to England, Mason's

financial needs multiplied when he remarried, as he and his second wife produced six children. Following the American Revolution, Mason brought his
family to Philadelphia in hopes that he could earn more money, owing to his
and Dixon's boundary line being so widely known among American leaders.
Upon arriving in September 1786, he contacted his now eighty-year-old associate from years gone by, Benjamin Franklin. "I have a family of wife, seven
sons, and a daughter, all in a very helpless condition, as I have been confined
to my bed with sickness ever since I came to town, which is twelve days," he
wrote. "Had I been able I would have laid before you something curious in
astronomy. The expense of putting it in execution would be very trifling. I do
hereby send you a plan of the design."[5] What that celestial oddity was remains
unknown. Mason died shortly after sending Franklin his letter.

His name, however, along with that of his surveying partner, lived on,
engraved in the American psyche as the border between North and South.
Its earliest recorded use for this purpose may well have been when Virginia
Congressman John Randolph ominously declared in 1824 that "we who
belong to that unfortunate portion of this confederacy which is south of
Mason and Dixon's line, and east of the Allegheny Mountains, have to make
up our mind to perish ... or we must resort to the measures which we first
opposed to British aggressions and usurpations."

Why was this said in 1824, as opposed to, say, 1800? Very likely because
the 1820 Missouri Compromise established a line above and below which
slavery was prohibited or permitted in the Louisiana Purchase. That line
was the latitude 36°30′ (with the compromise exception of Missouri). No
such boundary existed in the eastern states. Indeed, when Randolph made
his reference to the Mason-Dixon Line, slavery was still allowed in Delaware,
New Jersey, New York, Connecticut, and New Hampshire. But—and herein the
reason for Randolph's reference—three of those states had already enacted
laws for the gradual abolition of slavery. New Hampshire did not enact a law
to end slavery until 1857, and Delaware remained a slave state through the
Civil War, though of course it was not a Confederate state.

But the Mason-Dixon Line to which Randolph referred didn't include
its transpeninsular and tangent lines defining Delaware. He meant only
the line dividing Pennsylvania, the nation's southernmost free state, from
Maryland, the nation's northernmost slave state. As for the exceptions—
Delaware extending slightly north of Maryland, and New Hampshire with
(as per the 1800 census) a total of eight slaves—neither was enough to stand
in the way of a catchy phrase.

ZEBULON BUTLER
Connecticut's Lost Cause

> Whereas the petition of Zebulon Butler and others, claiming private right of soil under the State of Connecticut, and within the Commonwealth of Pennsylvania ... the claims of Zebulon Butler and others be, and hereby are, repealed.
> —*Journals of the Continental Congress*, September 21, 1785

Zebulon Butler was Connecticut's foremost military leader in its boundary war with Pennsylvania over Wyoming. Connecticut and Pennsylvania fighting over *Wyoming*? Didn't these people have maps? Didn't they notice that New York and the northern end of New Jersey are in between Connecticut and Pennsylvania, and that Wyoming hadn't even been invented?

They did have maps—pretty good ones, by then—and the Wyoming they were fighting over was the *original* Wyoming, which was the name of a valley along the Susquehanna River. The conflict resulted from the fact that Connecticut's colonial charter gave it reason to lay claim to Pennsylvania's northern tier. The dispute led to warfare—forts, cannons, deaths—three times over thirty years. Though Connecticut ultimately lost, those battles that it won were led by Zebulon Butler.

Butler grew up in Lyme, Connecticut. The hilly and rocky nature of the area likely contributed to his purchasing, at the age of twenty-nine, newly available land being sold by Connecticut's Susquehanna Company in the fertile Wyoming Valley. Like his fellow pioneers, Butler knew that Pennsylvania disputed the legality of their purchases. Pennsylvania's reasons were quite simple. The land being sold and deeded in Connecticut was well within the borders stipulated in Pennsylvania's 1681 charter.

The boundaries in Connecticut's 1662 charter, however, overlapped those of Pennsylvania. It had granted Connecticut a northern border along its (yet-to-be) agreed-upon boundary with Massachusetts, a southern bor-

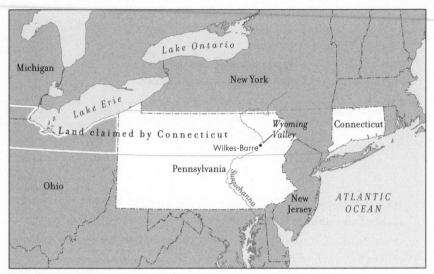

Connecticut land claims

der at Long Island Sound, and a western border at the Pacific Ocean. Massachusetts and Connecticut ultimately agreed upon a line located just above the 42nd parallel. Its southern coast at Long Island Sound extends as far south as the 41st parallel. Hence, colonial Connecticut could make a claim to a swath of land that crossed the colonies of New York, New Jersey, Pennsylvania, and onward to what is today the northernmost tier of California and a thin slice of Oregon.

Connecticut gave little thought to this vast western wilderness during its first hundred years. There was land enough for cultivation and expansion surrounding its settlements in the bays and rivers leading to Long Island Sound. But its population grew exponentially as the initial hardships and dangers in the New World dissipated.[1] By the mid-1700s, Connecticut needed more land.

Connecticut first asserted its western claims in 1754, when Governor Roger Wolcott allowed the Susquehanna Company to purchase land from the Iroquois along the Susquehanna River. The fact that Connecticut made no effort to assert its claim to the intervening lands in New York and New Jersey would later become legally significant. Politically and militarily, however, Connecticut knew it could not achieve a claim to land already populated by New York and New Jersey. The land in Pennsylvania, however, was still populated primarily by Iroquois tribes. If Connecticut thought that Pennsylvania's pacifist Quakers would enable it to settle the disputed land without a fight, that notion was soon corrected. When the first forty pioneers arrived in January 1769, three were promptly arrested and the others ordered to leave. Leave they did, but en route they encountered 200 other Connecticut settlers heading for the valley. Joining their ranks, they returned and were joined by even more in the months that followed—one of whom was Zebulon Butler.

When Butler arrived in July 1769, he was simply another settler, though he had distinguished himself in the recently concluded French and Indian War. The group's leader was Major John Durkee, who named the first settlement after two members of England's Parliament who supported the growing protests of the nation's American colonists: Isaac Barre and John Wilkes. To this day Connecticut's imprint, and an imprint of the approaching Revolutionary War, remains in the name Wilkes-Barre, Pennsylvania.

In early November Pennsylvania Governor John Penn sent troops to attack the Connecticut settlements. (This Governor Penn, whose father had returned to the Anglican Church, did not hesitate to use force.) The Pennsylvanians captured Durkee, and within two weeks the Connecticut settlers surrendered and again agreed to leave.

In the wake of this defeat, Zebulon Butler's leadership began to surface. No sooner had the settlers returned to Connecticut than they began to plan their return, with Butler among those mapping out their strategy. He served as a key aide to the newly released Durkee when the Connecticut settlers departed yet again for the Wyoming Valley in March 1770. To clear the way for their return, Connecticut settlers availed themselves of the services of a group of Pennsylvania vigilantes known as the Paxton Boys, for which they would later pay a heavy price. In the series of skirmishes, cannonades, and sieges that ensued, both Butler and Durkee were captured. This time Pennsylvania kept Durkee imprisoned. But Butler was released after four months and emerged as the new leader of Connecticut's forces.

Butler displayed a keen sense of when to attack, when to wait, and when to lay siege to an enemy settlement. In mid-August 1771, the Pennsylvanians, trapped and without provisions, surrendered to Captain Butler, thus ending the first eruption of what became known as the Pennamite War.

A stalemate prevailed over the next four years as both colonies awaited a ruling from King George III regarding their conflicting claims. The king, however, was in no hurry to issue such a ruling. Since relations with his American colonies were deteriorating, conflict *between* colonies served his purposes by obstructing efforts by many of the colonists to unite.

Meanwhile, Connecticut's settlements in the Wyoming Valley prospered under Butler's leadership. Connecticut officially named the area Westmoreland and declared it to be part of Litchfield County. Governor Penn, aware that silence could be interpreted as concession, responded with a proclamation in March 1774. Published in the *Pennsylvania Gazette*, it pointedly included:

> AND WHEREAS I have received information that a certain Zebulon Butler, under pretence of authority from the government of Connecticut, hath lately presumed to issue and disperse, through the counties of Northampton and Northumberland, in this province, a summons, or advertisement, setting forth, that the General Assembly of the Colony of Connecticut had appointed him a Justice of the Peace for the County of Litchfield, and in a town lately made and set off by the Assembly of the said colony, called by the Name of Westmoreland ... I do hereby strictly prohibit and forbid the inhabitants of the said Counties of Northampton and Northumberland, and all other the inhabitants of this province, to yield any obedience or to pay the least regard whatsoever to the aforesaid summons, or advertisement, or to any orders which may be hereafter issued or given by the said Zebulon Butler.

Prosperity in Connecticut's settlements led to growth and, in August 1775, a new settlement was founded along Warrior Run, a tributary to the Susquehanna and, most significantly, the first Connecticut settlement located on the river's western side. This westward push raised Pennsylvania's concerns beyond the battle of words. Should Connecticuters come to occupy regions west of the Susquehanna (the extent of its initial purchase from the Iroquois), they stood a greater chance of ultimately prevailing in their larger claim to possess the entirety of what they had come to call their Western Reserve. One month after the Connecticut settlers broke ground at Warrior Run, they were attacked by 500 soldiers from the Pennsylvania militia.

In response, Zebulon Butler led 400 Connecticut soldiers along the river's western side, where, on suitable terrain, he erected formidable defenses. Never before had so many men faced off in the conflict. Butler, however, knew his forces need not attack. They simply had to maintain a presence west of the Susquehanna. He also knew that Pennsylvania, to support its claim to the area, could not allow their presence to go unchallenged and would have to attack. On Christmas Day 1775, the Pennsylvanians did just that. But Butler's shrewdly located fortifications served their purpose, enabling Connecticut's militia to repel the Pennsylvanians. That in itself constituted victory in this second eruption of the Pennamite War.

Almost immediately, both militias turned to fight side by side in the American Revolution. Even then, however, the conflict continued to haunt them. In late June 1778 approximately 400 British soldiers and 600 American Indians approached the Wyoming Valley. On June 30 they attacked, driving back Butler's outnumbered forces. Butler retreated to a nearby fort, where he received word that reinforcements were en route. He and his officers decided to remain in the fort until the additional troops arrived. But many among the rank and file believed that, while waiting, they could be surrounded and destroyed.

Leading the opposition were Connecticut's earlier "shock troops," the Paxton Boys, who had good reason to fear for their lives. Their name derived from their hometown of Paxtang, Pennsylvania, where, under the leadership of Lazarus Stewart, they had formed a notorious anti-Indian rangers group. Twice they had raided peaceful Conestoga villages, massacring men, women, and children. Their fellow Pennsylvanians were outraged—most notably Governor Penn, who ordered them captured, and Benjamin Franklin, who published a pamphlet attacking their actions.[2] It was then that the Paxton Boys thought it best to ally themselves with the newcomers from Connecticut.

Now, in 1778, finding themselves at risk of being surrounded by 600 Indian warriors who had joined forces with the British, Stewart and his fellow Paxton Boys impressed upon the Connecticut soldiers the extreme jeopardy they were in. Butler, facing disapproval and terror among his men, and not entirely certain they were wrong, reversed his order and agreed to a counterattack. Their position was weak, however, and they were promptly outflanked. Butler ordered his men to retreat but, in the confusion of the rout, many never received the order.

Then came payback time. The Indians tortured and murdered the captured men, including Stewart. Despite efforts by the British to restrain them, the warriors spread into the neighboring communities, plundering and burning homes and barns.

The poison of prior conflicts did not end there. Connecticut blamed Pennsylvania for not sending nearby troops to protect the civilian population. Pennsylvania, in turn, blamed Butler for undertaking a foolhardy counterattack before the arrival of reinforcements. In similar fashion, the venomous relations between the Americans and the British explain what came next. Despite the fact that no civilians were killed during the rampage, and despite the fact that the British commander immediately offered sanctuary to those left homeless and restitution for their property, the American press blamed England for the disaster.[3] To this day, accounts of the Wyoming Massacre, as it has come to be known, often perpetuate this wartime propaganda.

The Continental Congress did not blame Butler, who was soon promoted to colonel. He continued to serve in the Wyoming Valley and elsewhere along what was then America's western frontier.

Congress also created a commission to rule on the Connecticut and Pennsylvania boundary dispute. It ultimately decided in favor of Pennsylvania. The decision was based on the fact that Connecticut had made no prior effort to assert its claim for nearly a hundred years, that it had previously (during a boundary dispute with New York) recognized that it was bounded on the west by New York, and that it had never asserted claims to areas of New York and New Jersey that it could have asserted for the same reasons it used in Pennsylvania.[4]

Zebulon Butler accepted the ruling. After the Revolution, he worked to validate the settlers' land titles in Pennsylvania. His efforts led to his being arrested four times, though he was never indicted. Violence erupted again in March 1784 following a flood that wiped out fences, houses, and barns in the valley. When the residents commenced rebuilding, they were driven away and ordered to evacuate by Pennsylvania troops still on active duty. Numerous men, rather than evacuate, hid in nearby caves and engaged in insurgent attacks. Butler was not among them. His fighting days were over.

When Pennsylvania's troops in the Wyoming Valley were finally discharged, Butler and his fellow settlers returned, and issues involving land titles were eventually resolved. Butler lived out his days in what became Luzerne County, Pennsylvania.

ETHAN ALLEN
Vermont: The Fourteenth Colony

Lately purchased by Allens and Baker, in company, a large tract of land situate[d] ... on Lake Champlain containing about forty five thousand acres.... The land will be sold at a moderate price. Whoever inclines to be a purchaser may, for further particulars, apply to Ethan, Zimry and Ira Allen or Remember Baker on the premises, or Heman and Levi Allen of Salisbury, per Ethan Allen & Company.

—ADVERTISEMENT IN THE *CONNECTICUT COURANT*, 1773 [1]

E than Allen was not a furniture maker. He did, however, burn a good deal of it as the leader of a self-proclaimed military force known as the Green Mountain Boys. Their mission was to defend homesteads whose land titles had been issued in New Hampshire but were being claimed by New York.

The dispute, based on conflicting colonial charters, had actually already been resolved. In 1764 King George III ruled that the region above Massachusetts, between the Connecticut River and the Hudson River, was part of New York. Prior to his ruling, however, New Hampshire had begun selling land in the region and issuing titles. In an effort to strengthen its claim, New Hampshire's land sales suddenly increased between 1761 and 1763.[2] The landowners themselves, for the most part, didn't have particularly

Ethan Allen (ca. 1738–1789)

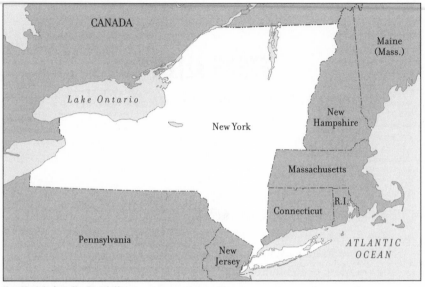

New York before the Revolution

strong feelings whether they were part of New York or New Hampshire—until New York declared their deeds invalid.

In order to validate a deed, New York required that a fee be paid for registering it in New York. The fee was based on the current value of the land, which, following occupation and settlement, was far higher than when it had been purchased as uncleared property. Consequently, registration fees were often as much as the original purchase price. This did not set well with the settlers. To make matters worse, New York frequently sold land titled in New Hampshire but not in New York. When surveyors appeared to stake out these lands, they began to face increasingly large groups of hostile New Hampshire-based settlers. Among those settlers was Ethan Allen.

Allen was the eldest of eight children, born and raised in Connecticut. His plans for a college education were derailed by the death of his father, which obliged Ethan to become a farmer while continuing his education informally. In time he added lead mining and iron manufacturing to his endeavors. With his profits he began purchasing land, often in partnership with his brothers, in what would eventually become Vermont. By the time New York declared the "New Hampshire Grants" invalid, Allen had extensive holdings throughout the region, including the 45,000 acres advertised in the *Connecticut Courant*.

When, in 1770, the owners of land titled by New Hampshire were named in lawsuits being brought by New York claimants to their lands, the defendants turned to Ethan Allen to take the lead in coordinating their defense. Allen collected official documentation of New Hampshire's deeds and, for the trial, secured the services of Jared Ingersoll, a prominent attorney who later served in the Continental Congress and participated in the writing of the Constitution. The trial was presided over by Judge Robert R. Livingston, who himself owned 35,000 acres of Vermont land deeded, in his case, by New York. Livingston refused to admit into evidence the documents Allen had gathered, and the subsequent verdict in favor of the New York plaintiffs surprised no one.

Before returning to his home in Bennington, Allen was visited by the attorney general of New York, John Taber Kempe, and James Duane, attorney for the New York plaintiffs in the case. They told Allen that if he and other leaders in Vermont could understand New York's view, and convey the justice of that view to the people in Vermont, Kempe and Duane could arrange for Allen and the other Vermont leaders to acquire considerable amounts of land in the region on highly favorable terms. Allen did not say no. He said, "The gods of the valleys are not the gods of the hills." When Kempe asked what that meant, Allen suggested he accompany him to Bennington, where he'd find out.

The following summer, New York's deputy surveyor general, William Cockburn, arrived in Rutland to divide it into lots. As his crew commenced work, he was approached by two property owners with New Hampshire deeds. In a letter to the land's New York proprietor (none other than attorney James Duane), Cockburn related that, "Your acquaintance Nathan [sic] Allen was in the woods with another party [of men], blackened and dressed like Indians.... By all accounts, we should not have been very kindly treated."[3]

The incident was the first of many that would ensue between New York surveyors or property claimants and Allen's Green Mountain Boys. It took place against a backdrop of increasingly violent confrontations. What had begun as spontaneous gatherings of angered residents were now evolving into organized groups of as many as a hundred men, dressed in a lurid mixture of American Indian headwear, women's caps, and powdered wigs. They had taken to brandishing clubs, swords, and rifles, issuing threats, knocking down fences, destroying crops, and burning haystacks. Often these frightening mobs were led by a man named Seth Warner. But New York's worst Vermont nightmare was about to take place: Seth Warner and Ethan Allen joined forces.

Allen's furniture-burning days were first recorded that fall in an October 1771 deposition regarding a dispossessed New York claimant. "One, surnamed Allen," a witness recounting what the victim had told him, vowed that "they had resolved to offer a burnt sacrifice to the gods of the world in burning the logs of that house. That they then kindled four fires on the logs of that house.... Allen and Baker, holding two clubs over the deponent's head, commanded him to leave that land."[4] Allen and others named in the proceedings soon found their efforts widely publicized in notices offering a reward of £25 for their arrest.

Allen's response revealed his continuing outrage at the corruption he had encountered in the New York legal system now seeking his arrest. He posted notices saying:

TWENTY FIVE POUNDS REWARD

Whereas James Duane and John Kempe of New York have by their menaces and threats greatly disturbed the public peace and repose of the honest peasants of Bennington and the settlements to the northward ... any person that will apprehend these common disturbers, *viz.* James Duane and John Kempe, and bring them to Landlord Fay's at Bennington, shall have fifteen pounds for James Duane and ten pounds for John Kempe, paid by,

ETHAN ALLEN
REMEMBER BAKER
ROBERT COCHRAN

With confrontations escalating on both sides, New York Governor William Tryon sought the assistance of British troops. But the last thing England wanted, with its American colonies already a political tinderbox, was to have its army firing upon its subjects. Likewise, the residents living on land obtained through the New Hampshire Grants turned to New Hampshire for assistance from its militia. New Hampshire, with its own concerns about potentially igniting the tinderbox politics in the colonies, abstained. Vermont was, as it would remain, on its own.

By August 1773 Ethan Allen and Seth Warner were burning entire settlements that had recently been established under grants from New York. Governor Tryon increased the reward for Allen's arrest to £100. The New York legislature upped the ante, declaring that if Allen, Warner, and six other named cohorts did not turn themselves in within seventy days, they would be deemed guilty of felonies for which they would be (if caught) put to death.

As before, New York's declaration was answered by a declaration, this time issued in the name of the Green Mountain Boys, though widely believed to be the voice of Ethan Allen. It met New York's bet ... and raised it:

> And furthermore that we will kill or destroy any person or persons whomsoever that shall presume to be accessory, aiding or assisting in taking any of us as aforesaid; for by these presents we give any such disposed person or persons to understand that, though they have license by the law aforesaid to kill us, and "indemnification" for such murder from the same authority, they have no indemnification for doing so from the Green Mountain Boys.[5]

Going all in with their chips, Allen and the other leaders of the Green Mountain Boys set up their own government. New York claimants now found themselves being put on trial in courts created by the Green Mountain Boys. Floggings and other sentences were administered as homesteads continued to be burned.

A major confrontation with New York was on the verge of exploding. Then suddenly it ended—silenced by a gun fired 137 miles away. On April 19, 1775, British troops marching to Concord, Massachusetts, to destroy a cache of weapons, encountered an armed group of colonists in the village of Lexington. In moving to disarm them, a shot was fired, triggering a battle that triggered the American Revolution.

Allen recognized a major opportunity here, but it required a critical choice. His writings attacking the tyranny of New York's royal governor had always made a point of expressing nothing but devotion to the king. Moreover, Vermont, positioned like a dagger from Canada wedging through New England before piercing the upper reaches of the Hudson River, could be of inestimable value to the Crown. Should Vermont make good on Allen's professions of fealty, it would undoubtedly gain control over the conflicting deeds to its land—if the British won the war. On the other hand, by denying the British this weapon and instead joining forces with the colonists, Vermont stood to gain independence as a state in an independent nation—provided the colonists won.

Being, if nothing else, an independent man—tumultuous, riotous, licentious, in the words of New York's legislature[6]—Allen opted for the colonists. At first the Continental Army wasn't sure what to do with this audacious man

and his Green Mountain Boys when they ran into each other, both heading
for the stronghold guarding the main highway to Canada: Fort Ticonderoga.
Confusion over protocol, however, was quickly resolved, and their combined
forces ousted the British on May 10, 1775—less than a month after the battle at
Lexington and Concord. By surprising the British through such quick action,
the Americans gained control of a vital artery.

Allen quickly seized the political opportunity afforded by this victory.
He wrote to the Continental Congress, asking that the Green Mountain Boys
be incorporated as a regiment in the Continental Army. The members of the
Continental Congress were well aware of the group's vigilante reputation,
but under the circumstances, how could they say no? In June they passed a
resolution stating "that it be recommended to the Convention of New York,
that they, consulting with General Schuyler, employ in the army to be raised
for the defense of America, those called Green Mountain Boys, under such
officers as the said Green Mountains Boys shall choose." Representatives
from Vermont's towns soon met to elect the commander of their now respectable and official regiment. The choice of either Allen or Seth Warren was a
foregone conclusion. By a vote of 41–5 they elected Warner. Evidently, Allen's
independent nature, while ideal for rebellion, was not ideal for friendship.

To his credit, Allen continued to serve, accepting an offer from General
Schuyler to perform assignments as needed. Schuyler availed himself of
Allen's persuasive skills by sending him to seek support from the French
Canadians of Quebec. Allen wrote to Schuyler that he was returning with
both recruits and information he'd been given regarding local pathways
and routes. While returning, however, Allen's independent nature surfaced
again. He and a fellow officer, Major John Brown, concluded that the British
in nearby Montreal, being focused on Schuyler's advance, could be ousted
by a surprise attack in which Allen and Brown divided their small force and
slipped into opposite ends of the city under cover of night. Not wanting to
lose precious time by awaiting approval, they went ahead with their plan.
Allen's men made it across the St. Lawrence River; Brown's did not. In short
order, Allen and his men were surrounded.

Allen's defeat was no small thing. The Continental Congress had been
sending letters and emissaries to the French Canadians, hoping that the
province of Quebec would become the fourteenth colony to join the rebellion.
Allen's debacle, Warner wrote, "put the French [Canadian] people into great
consternation.... The Canadians were before nine-tenths for the Bostonians;
they are now returned to their duty."[7]

For Allen, the consequence was that he spent the bulk of the American Revolution as a prisoner of war. From a public relations point of view, it was the best thing that could have happened to him. After being released in a prisoner exchange in 1778, he was widely hailed—in no small part because of his book, published within a year of his release, *A Narrative of Colonel Ethan Allen's Captivity.* As before, his skill with words served him well: the book quickly sold out several printings and went on to be reissued in 1807, 1814, 1838, 1846, 1849, 1930, 1961, 1992, and 2000.

Allen returned to Vermont, which, during his absence, had declared itself an independent republic. Arriving to a hero's welcome, his compatriots immediately sent him back to Philadelphia—three times, in fact—to lobby the Continental Congress for statehood. By the time of his third effort, in 1780, he was secretly contacted by an agent for the British who suggested that a negotiation regarding Vermont joining England's efforts to win the war might yield mutually beneficial results.

Ever the high-risk negotiator, Allen commenced negotiations with the British and also secretly informed the Continental Congress that he was negotiating with its enemy. "Vermont had an indubitable right to agree on terms of cessation of hostility with Great Britain, provided the United States persisted in rejecting her application for a union with them," he wrote, arguing that Vermont "would be the most miserable were she obliged to defend the independence of the United States, and they at the same time claiming full liberty to overturn and ruin the independence of Vermont."[8]

Congress yielded. But another eleven years would pass before the details regarding land deeds and restitution could be ironed out, enabling Vermont to enter the union in 1791. While Allen had led Vermont to the threshold of statehood, he did not live to cross it with them. He died in 1789 at the age of fifty-one.

THOMAS JEFFERSON
Lines on the Map in Invisible Ink

With respect to the new States, were the question to stand simply in this form: *How may the ultramontane territory* [the land west of the Appalachians] *be disposed of so as to produce the greatest and most immediate benefit to the inhabitants of the maritime States of the Union?—* the plan would be ... laying it off into two or more states only.... Good faith ... requires us to state the question in its just form: *How may the territories of the Union be disposed of so as to produce the greatest degree of happiness to their inhabitants?*

—THOMAS JEFFERSON[1]

Whether or not the Founding Fathers truly shared a common vision, there is no question that Thomas Jefferson possessed and expressed a vision that gazed far into the nation's future. And while many of his views are difficult to pin down, his views regarding the American map were crystal clear.[2] Yet, looking at what that map has become, the United States appears to have closed its eyes to his vision. Or is it that his influence can be difficult to detect?

One example of Jefferson's mercurial legacy is the eastern border of Iowa. He was responsible for establishing what is today the eastern border of Iowa, yet not responsible for the same border of its neighboring state, Illinois. The border separating

Thomas Jefferson (1743–1826)

Louisiana Purchase: boundary uncertainties

Iowa and Illinois is the Mississippi River. It was the eastern boundary of the Louisiana Purchase, which was completed by Jefferson as president in 1803. Subsequently the river became the eastern border of present-day Iowa, Missouri, Arkansas, and segments of Minnesota and Louisiana. Since the Mississippi had been the western boundary of the United States prior to the Louisiana Purchase, it was already in place as the western border of present-day Illinois, Kentucky, Tennessee, and segments of Wisconsin and Mississippi.

Other than those states with eastern borders on the Mississippi River, no other state has a boundary reflecting Jefferson's historic purchase. The Louisiana Purchase is now all but invisible on the map because of the language in Jefferson's treaty with France conveying the land to the United States. It declared that, after Spain officially ceded the land back to France, France would sell to the United States "the Colony or Province of Louisiana with the same extent that it now has in the hand of Spain, and that it had when France possessed it." Compared to today's government documents, the treaty, running less than 1,500 words, was extraordinarily brief and clear. On the other hand, it lacked certain details—such as the precise boundaries of the land it conveyed. This was because Jefferson knew that Spain (and England) disagreed with France as to the extent of the province of Louisiana. But Jefferson also knew that Napoleon's offer wouldn't last long, so he accepted it without quibbling over that detail.

Though the Louisiana Purchase is Jefferson's most famous geographic contribution to the United States, back in his days as Virginia's representative to the Continental Congress, he made other important contributions that, by contrast, provided highly specific details of his vision for the future of the United States. Today, however, only the ghosts of that vision inhabit the lines on the American map. Their geodetic life ended when Congress began tinkering with Jefferson's vision.

While in the Continental Congress, Jefferson chaired a committee that had been created to prepare a plan for the temporary government of the western territory of the United States. At the time, the nation's western territory consisted of the land acquired in 1763 by England and the American colonists in the French and Indian War (the Northwest Territory) and all the

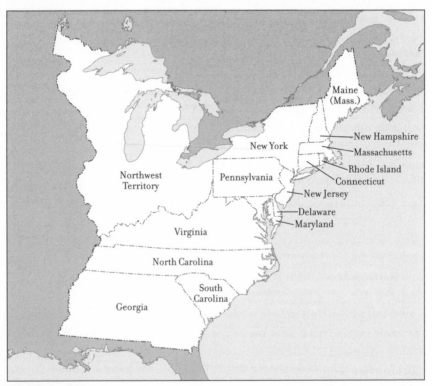

United States, 1784

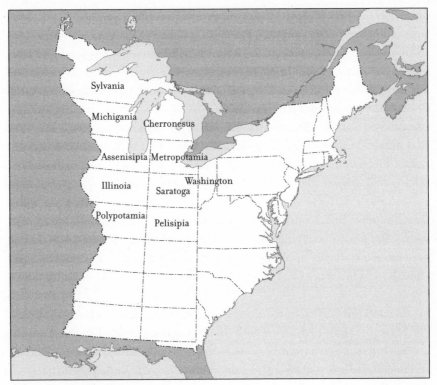

Jefferson's 1784 proposal for new states

other land west of the Appalachian Mountains. Prior to the Revolution, this second area of land had belonged to a number of the colonies. After the onset of the Revolution, these colonies—now states—eventually, if not happily, ceded their western regions to the federal government to create additional, more equally sized states.

Jefferson's committee reported back to Congress in March 1784. It proposed boundaries for the future states to be created in the western lands, the process by which they would become states, how these areas would be governed prior to becoming states, and even names for most of the proposed states. While the report was issued by a committee, considerable evidence suggests that the states it proposed reflected the vision of Jefferson.[3]

The boundaries of these states and even their names tell us a good deal about this particular Founding Father. The names he assigned included Sylvania, Michigania, Cherronesus, Assenisipia, Metropotamia, Illinoia, Polypotamia, and Pelisipia—all neoclassical constructions hearkening back to the ancient democracies of Greece and Rome. The two remaining names,

Saratoga and Washington, memorialized the American Revolution. In addition, while the monarchs of England often named American colonies after individuals, Jefferson named only one of his proposed states after an individual—an ethos that continued long after Jefferson. In the years ahead, Congress would reject Tennessee's originally proposed name (Franklin) and Colorado's first proposed name (Jefferson). Most senators and representatives viewed only one American as worthy of having a state named after him, that person being George Washington. Other than Washington, however, none of Jefferson's proposed names was ever used, although Illinoia and Michigania, once declassicized, did become state names.

Similarly, Jefferson's proposed boundaries were also scrapped between then and now. But the principle underlying his boundaries is all over the map. Jefferson's underlying tenet was that all states should be created equal, or—characteristically applying pragmatism to his ideals—as equal as possible. Jefferson's report stated:

> The territory ceded or to be ceded by individual states to the United States ... shall be formed into distinct states bounded in the following manner, as nearly as such cessions will admit, that is to say: northwardly & southwardly by parallels of latitude so that each state shall comprehend from south to north two degrees of latitude.

Still, as can be seen from the map of his proposed states, Jefferson did not consider size to be the sole factor in determining equality; he also considered geographic and agricultural factors. Consequently, the widths he proposed varied slightly:

> Eastwardly and westwardly they shall be bounded, those on the Mississippi by that river on one side and the meridian of the lowest point of the rapids of Ohio on the other; and those adjoining on the east by the same meridian on their western side and on their eastern by the meridian of the western cape of the mouth of the Great Kanhaway [the present-day Kanawha River].

In effect, Jefferson proposed two tiers of states with slightly different dimensions to mitigate differences in resources. While his lines do not appear on the American map, their prototypical dimensions do. Indeed, two tiers of states ultimately did emerge, side by side, further west: Kansas, Nebraska,

South Dakota, and North Dakota all have three degrees of height. Neighboring them, the mountainous states of Colorado, Wyoming, and Montana all have four degrees of height. Wyoming, Colorado, North Dakota, and South Dakota all have seven degrees of width, as do (allowing for coastal wiggles) Oregon and Washington.

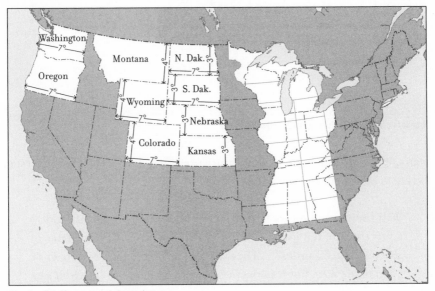

Ghosts of Jefferson: prototype shapes

When did Congress begin fiddling with this Founding Father's vision? Answer: eighteen days after his report. The report was delivered to Congress on March 1, 1784, and on March 19 Congress began altering it. Three days later, Jefferson presented additional revisions, to which additional amendments were made the following month. But the largest change came in 1787, when Congress enacted the Northwest Ordinance. Jefferson's proposed state names were now gone and, with the Northwest Ordinance, his proposed boundaries were also swept under the carpet. Moreover, the new proposed state borders were now confined solely to the Northwest Territory.

By then Jefferson himself was no longer in Congress; in fact, he was no longer in the country. He was in Paris, serving as the American ambassador to France. But he was not happy with what Congress was doing to his plan. The Northwest Ordinance stipulated that the region would be divided into "not less than three nor more than five States." It then described where those divisions were located. These new boundaries were largely the work of Jeffer-

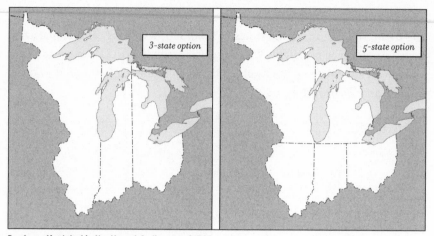

3-state option

5-state option

Borders stipulated in Northwest Ordinance of 1787

son's fellow Virginian (and fellow future president) James Monroe. Jefferson wrote to Monroe, his friend and protégé:

> Will their inhabitants be happiest divided into states of 30,000 square miles, not quite as large as Pennsylvania, or into states of 160,000 square miles?... They will not only be happier in states of a moderate size, but it is the only way in which they can exist as a regular society. Considering the American character in general ... a state of such extent as 160,000 square miles would soon crumble into little ones ... and if they decide to divide themselves, we are not able to restrain them. They will end up by separating from our confederacy and becoming its enemies.[4]

Indeed, 160,000 square miles is the approximate size of the westernmost state proposed in the Northwest Ordinance, composed of present-day Illinois, Wisconsin, and regions of Minnesota and Michigan. Had such a state ultimately been created, it would be roughly the size of California.

As can be seen on today's map, Congress eventually divided the Northwest Territory into five states. It also relocated numerous borders stipulated in the Northwest Ordinance. Nevertheless, each of the states that finally emerged exceeds 30,000 square miles.

Knowing when Congress tinkered with Jefferson's vision begs the more important question: why? The congressional resolution that ultimately altered Jefferson's boundaries stated that increased knowledge of the regions involved revealed that some of the proposed states would be deprived of navigation and others would consist almost entirely of barren mountain land. Indeed, this was true, but it wasn't the whole truth. The rest of the story wasn't openly revealed in Congress until 1845, during the debate over Iowa's statehood. Arguing for a return to more Jeffersonian boundaries, Ohio Congressman Samuel F. Vinton explained how the result of Jefferson's proposed borders

> would have been ultimately to give the country beyond the mountains a majority of the States.... Shortly after the conclusion of the war with England [the Revolution], very serious difficulties arose between Spain and the United States respecting navigation of the Mississippi. Our settlers in Kentucky and Tennessee ... looked to the Mississippi and its outlet through the Gulf of Mexico as their early road to market.... An opinion seems to have sprung up in the Atlantic States that the interests of the transmontane country would always be adverse to theirs.

That earlier Congress did indeed have cause for concern. The residents of North Carolina's land west of the Appalachians (present-day Tennessee) had grown impatient at the delays preventing it from becoming a separate state, and in 1784 they declared themselves the state of Franklin. Many of its residents further agitated for the state of Franklin to declare itself an independent republic and commence negotiations with Spain.[5] This risk not only spurred Congress to begin at once creating states in the land west of the Appalachians, but also to create larger and therefore fewer states than Jefferson had recommended. Fewer states in the region, Vinton went on to point out, would translate into fewer votes in the Senate. And treaties could be ratified only by the Senate.

One other of Jefferson's proposals, however, did survive the crucible of democracy. At the same time that he was proposing the division of the nation's western lands into future states, Jefferson offered a separate proposal stipulating the method by which the boundaries of and within these western lands would be located. "It shall be divided into Hundreds of ten geographical miles square ... by lines to be run and marked due North and South, and others crossing these at right angles," he urged. "These Hundreds shall be subdivided into lots of one mile square each ... marked by lines running in like manner due North and South, and other crossing these at right

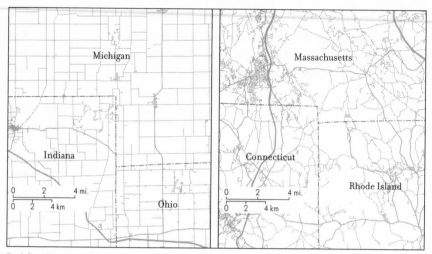

East Coast roads and Midwest roads

angles."[6] Jefferson, whose many accomplishments including surveying, did not invent this approach. It was already known as the rectangular survey system, one of several methods used by surveyors at that time.

Today airline passengers flying over the eastern states and the Midwest can look down and see a clear change in the pattern of the roads. East of the Appalachians, the roads generally conform to geographic features. In the Midwest, where the Northwest Ordinance was implemented using the method proposed by Jefferson, they conform primarily to a right-angled grid, positioned north–south by east–west. While Jefferson's influence on the American map can be difficult to detect, in that grid of roadways we can see his literal imprint on the United States.

JOHN MEARES
The U.S. Line from Spanish Canada

The Spaniards have seized three British vessels in the fur trade at … Nootka Sound, on the western coast of North America.… Their crews are sent to Mexico in irons.… [The incident] has been transmitted and presented to the government by a Mr. Meares, who came home a passenger.

—*London Chronicle*, May 1, 1790

A multistate boundary line separating the southern ends of Oregon and Idaho from the northern ends of California, Nevada, and much of Utah owes its existence to both Spanish Canada and China. Canada is not typically thought of as Spanish, nor are American state lines usually connected to Chinese influence. But a glance at a map of Canada's Vancouver Island reveals remnants of Spanish Canada in names such as the Juan de Fuca Strait, Flores Island, Cortes Island, and Estevan Point.

Spain, as the first European nation to plant its flag in the New World, proclaimed that it owned it all. And from 1492 into the early 1600s, it did. But then other nations began infiltrating uninhabited coves and bays along the New World's Atlantic coast and Caribbean islands. By the late 1700s, foreign infiltration also began on the western coast, as China became more open to European trade. One of the most valuable exports to China was the lustrous fur of the sea otter.

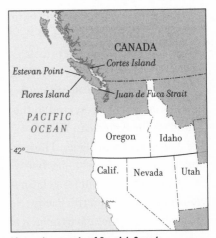

Line and remnants of Spanish Canada

John Meares (ca. 1756–1809)

Enter the adventurous English sea merchant, John Meares.

From obscure origins, Meares struggled his way up the ropes of British seafaring to its top knots. Born in the mid-1750s in or near the town of Bath, he joined the Royal Navy at fifteen as a cabin boy. By the end of the American Revolution, he had shown enough intelligence and skill to rise to the rank of lieutenant. With the war's end, however, his service was no longer needed. Meares needed to find a new avenue to wealth and fame. Quite possibly he found it by reading the newspapers. "The importance of Botany Bay will appear by all who examine Capt. Cook's chart of his discoveries," London's *Evening Post* wrote in 1786. "Its situation is well adapted for carrying on a trade between Nootka Sound and Cook's River on the American coast, and the islands of Japan and the Chinese Empire, in sea otter skins." Botany Bay (present-day Sydney, Australia) was but one of British naval captain James Cook's discoveries in the Pacific Ocean. In 1778 he discovered a way station for ships crossing that vast ocean en route to North America. The way station was a chain of tiny islands now known as Hawaii. It too would figure into Meares's plans.

England was not the only nation reaping the riches of lands newly discovered by Europeans. All of Europe, joined now by the fledgling United States, elbowed for opportunities. But Spain remained the best positioned, having been the first to establish settlements and naval forces in these regions. Evidence of Spain's power even permeated the previously cited news item, when it referred to the importance of Cook's River and Nootka Sound on the American West Coast but made no mention of San Francisco, Los Angeles, or San Diego. Those better-known locations were controlled by Spain. (Seattle was yet to be discovered by Europeans.)

Though Spain had lain claim to all the Americas, and its explorers had ventured throughout the Pacific Northwest, identifying their claims by the Spanish names they gave them, it had not sought to settle the northernmost regions. History might have been different indeed had Spain learned there was gold in the Yukon and Alaska. As it was, Spain saw little profit to be reaped from the region and great expense in protecting it, since it was some 600 miles from its nearest available naval harbor at San Francisco.

On the other hand, Spain was well aware of profits to be had from trade with China. Early on it had established a Pacific base for such commerce by colonizing the Philippines. Spain was also well aware when China became an open market for sea otter furs, and it acted immediately to stop other nations from establishing trading posts along the coast of the sea otter's habitat in the Pacific Northwest.

Into these waters John Meares set sail from Calcutta in 1786 on the first of his two voyages to the Northwest. His plan was to establish a permanent trading post for sea otter furs, which he would trade in China for goods to be sold in England. Meares was a raw newcomer, never having headed a commercial enterprise, nor commanded a ship. His apparent self-confidence, coupled with an independent streak, is revealed by the fact that neither of his two voyages was licensed by the East India Company—a risky move on his part. Just as Spain had sought to monopolize its discovery of the New World, so too did the British East India Company seek to monopolize its markets by prohibiting other Englishmen from engaging in trade with its markets.

For his first voyage, Meares arranged financial backing to secure two ships, which he named the *Nootka* and the *Sea Otter*. With himself in command of the *Nootka*, and a fellow navy lieutenant, William Tipping, commanding the *Sea Otter*, the two ships left India in March, 1786. Tipping's *Sea Otter*, carrying opium, sold its cargo in Southeast Asia before setting a course for the Northwest. There the two ships were to rendezvous, if they had not met up already.[1]

Meares arrived at Cook's River, in present-day Alaska, in August. He began trading with the natives for furs and learned that Tipping's *Sea Otter* was just ahead of him. Meares followed in its direction, continuing to trade along the way. As winter weather approached, Meares had yet to acquire a full cargo. He had three choices. He could depart for China (as the *Sea Otter* apparently had done) but with fewer furs than he wanted. He could harbor for the winter in Alaska and resume trading when warmer weather returned. Or he could winter at the way station discovered and described by Captain Cook: Hawaii.

Meares feared that his crew would never leave the tropical paradise described by Cook, and he also feared the financial consequences of returning with inadequate cargo. What he didn't fear was the Alaskan winter ...

because he had no clue of what it was. Few if any Europeans did. Just how bad did an Alaskan winter turn out to be? Newsworthy bad. "The *Nootka* ... arrived at Oonalaska the beginning of August and arrived in Prince William's Sound the end of September," the *London World* reported in October 1787. "By the severity of the winter they lost their 3rd and 4th Mates, Surgeon, Boatswain, Carpenter, and Cooper and twelve of the foremast men; and the remainder were so enfeebled as to be under the necessity of applying to the Commanders of the *King George* and *Queen Charlotte*, who just at this time arrived."

The rescue of Meares and his crew by the *King George* and *Queen Charlotte* was not particularly cordial. Both ships were licensed by the East India Company. From their point of view, Meares and his men were poaching. Their captains demanded that Meares pledge a £1,000 bond against his promise not to engage in any trade en route back to India, and that he turn over the metal and beads he was using to trade with the natives. In return, they provided Meares and his men with the bare necessities.

The news of Meares's rescue was followed a week later by news of his venture's sister ship. A brief item in the *London World* reported, "The *Sea Otter*, Capt. Tipping, sailed from Calcutta a few days after the *Nootka* ... and arrived in Prince William's Sound in September.... She left the Sound the day after, supposed for Cook's River ... but having never since been seen or heard of, there can be little doubt of her being lost."

Once rescued, Meares and his crew set sail for Hawaii, where they replenished themselves and then went on to Macau, a Portuguese colony on the coast of China. Meares sold what cargo he had and his badly damaged ship, then immediately started in again. In less than two months, he had arranged financing for two other ships. To protect himself from the East India Company, he contracted to sail from Guangzhou (Canton), China, for a Portuguese merchant, enabling his ships to fly Portugal's flag. Meares also protected his men against winter on this second voyage—and commenced his larger plan—by having his crew construct a permanent trading post in Nootka Sound. The one thing Meares was *not* protected against was Spain, whose ships soon entered Nootka Sound, where they too were arriving to establish a fur trade with China.

Meares himself had already departed with his newly acquired cargo, leaving behind a staff of Chinese craftsmen and seamen who, in addition to having constructed the trading post, had also constructed a ship, the *North West America*, as the next step in the expansion of Meares's enterprise. It was to sail under the command of one of the few Englishmen left to oversee operations at Nootka. Because of the presence of these Englishmen, the arriving Spaniards needed neither hounds nor accountants to sniff out British control of these Chinese settlers working for a Portuguese merchant. What happened next, Meares later reported to Parliament, was that "on the 9th of June, [the *North West America*] was boarded and seized by boats manned and equipped for war, commanded by Don [Esteban José] Martinez, that he did ... take possession of her in the name of his Catholic Majesty.... that the commander of the *N.W. America*, his officers and men, were accordingly made prisoners ... and some of her men were ... afterwards put in irons."[2]

Public response in England to Meares's carefully worded report was one of outrage. "The Court of Spain cannot be so devoid of understanding as to make a serious quarrel with this country upon so idle and ill-founded a pretence as her hitherto unheard of claim to the sovereignty of the seas to the northwestward of America," London's *Woodfall's Register* exclaimed in 1790. "The Court of Madrid might, with as much reason, lay claim to the clouds, the stars, and the hemisphere."

Not unlike today, the clamor was quickly exploited. Within a month, London's Covent Garden Theatre had presented a topical play entitled *Nootka Sound, or England Prepared*. British militants accused Spain of creating a crisis to divert its people's attention from democratic movements in other nations. In response, British peace advocates reminded their fellow citizens about the profitless war with Spain that had resulted from Robert Jenkins's dubious account of a Spaniard lopping off his ear.[3] (See "Robert Jenkins's Ear" earlier in this book.)

Ultimately, England and Spain did not go to war. Instead, they signed an accord known as the Nootka Convention, which would later affect the locations of California, Nevada, and Utah's borders with Oregon and Idaho. Under the Nootka Convention, Spain accepted the principle that a nation could not claim possession of land simply by having discovered it; rather, a nation must have established a permanent settlement on the land.

Nearly thirty years later, Secretary of State John Quincy Adams invoked the Nootka Convention in negotiations with Spain regarding the western boundaries of the Louisiana Purchase. By that time, an American settlement had been established at the mouth of the Columbia River in present-day Oregon. Adams cited that settlement as the basis for a border with Spain's California settlements.[4] Spain did not challenge Adams's logic, though its representative quibbled with the boundary he proposed. Adams noted in his diary, "I showed him ... the line offered in my note, upon which he only

42°: the watershed line

remarked that we might have taken the Columbia River from its source to its mouth, instead of the forty-first parallel of latitude." In the 1819 Adams-Onis treaty that resulted, the boundary was fixed at the 42nd parallel. North of this parallel, virtually all the waterways flow to the Columbia River; south of it, virtually all flow to what was then Spain's settlement at San Francisco.

But England also invoked the Nootka Convention, claiming its right to possess Oregon, based on British settlements along the Columbia River and the waterways leading to it. Having just concluded the War of 1812, neither the United States nor England wanted to renew hostilities, so the two nations agreed jointly to hold Oregon, which at the time extended to Alaska. This joint occupancy lasted some twenty-five years, at which point an American rallying cry for the region—"Fifty-Four Forty or Fight!"—once again brought the United States and England to the brink of war during the presidency of James Polk.

As for John Meares, he went on to undertake what many in his situation would do today: he wrote a book.[5] His adventures on the frozen seas with enemies from Spain and bullies from the British East India Company, combined with the tropical splendors of natives in Hawaii and the mysteries of Canton, made the book a longtime favorite of many readers. One dissatisfied reader, however, was George Dixon, who had captained one of the East India Company ships that had rescued Meares. Dixon took offense at being depicted as an extortionist. So he wrote a book, too:

> This Day is published, price 3s.6d
> *Further Remarks on the Voyages of John Meares, Esq.*
> in which several important facts, misrepresented in the voyages, relative to geography and commerce, are fully substantiated. Likewise is inserted a letter from Captain DUNCAN containing a decisive refutation of several unfounded assertions of Mr. MEARES, and finally a reply to his answer.
> By Captain GEORGE DIXON[6]

Meares, meanwhile, returned to active duty in the navy, where he was promoted to commander and with it received a substantial salary. George III proclaimed him a baronet, enabling him to be Sir John Meares. With his military rank, a hereditary title, and his book still being issued and advertised, Meares returned to his hometown of Bath in 1796 and got married. He had achieved all he sought.

With his success, Meares disappeared from the public stage. His death in 1809 went unremarked by any known obituary. Still, his name remains engraved on the map in Meares Island, British Columbia, and Cape Meares, Oregon.

BENJAMIN BANNEKER
To Be Brilliant and Black
in the New Nation

Benjamin Banneker, the sooty astronomer ... is to be associated
with our Genevese money-changer [Swiss-born Treasury Secretary
Albert Gallatin] for the purpose of "correcting" some part of this
foreigner's "procedure." ... The African scholar, if he could correct
nothing else, might very easily correct Mr. Gallatin's English; nay,
if Banneker had just arrived from the Gold Coast or the kingdom of
Whidau, he would be superior to our imported financier.
                                   —*THE PORT-FOLIO*, AUGUST 22, 1801

The largest historic site in Washington, DC, seen by more people (albeit
unaware) than any other, commemorates the eighteenth-century
work of a free African American named Benjamin Banneker. The
site is the city's northern and southeastern boundary line, separating the
District of Columbia from Maryland, which was surveyed by Banneker and
Andrew Ellicott. Signs at the site, however, currently say only "Welcome to
Washington—Cell Phones Illegal While Driving," without explaining how, in
1791, an African American got hired for such a prestigious assignment.

Banneker was not only a surveyor, which entailed a mastery of mathematics and astronomy. He was also a clockmaker, the author of the most
widely published almanac of his day, and even a bit of a poet.[1] Mostly, however, he was a tobacco farmer. For the first sixty years of his life, he cultivated
his crop in a sparsely populated area west of Baltimore, located between what
later became Catonsville and Ellicott City.

Banneker was thirty-one years old when the Ellicott family arrived in
the area and met the African American on the adjacent farm. Twelve-year-
old George Ellicott was fascinated by the functioning clock Banneker had
carved out of wood, based on his observations of a pocket watch. Banneker

was likewise fascinated by young Ellicott's newly learned mathematical insights, and delighted in the books the boy began to lend him. The Ellicotts had moved to Maryland from Pennsylvania, where they were part of a highly respected Quaker family, among whose members were a clockmaker, several surveyors, and an author of an almanac. Given the family's influence, perhaps it is not surprising that Banneker too became a surveyor and the author of an almanac.

Since slavery was integral to Maryland's economy, how did Banneker come to be a free man and the owner of a farm? His father, Robert, had been a slave until offered his freedom as an incentive for hard work. He toiled with a vigor that remained even after his liberation and marriage to Mary Bannka. Robert took his wife's last name because her father, too, had been a slave, whose African name was Bannka. When Bannka had been brought to America, he was purchased by Molly Walsh, who turned out to know a thing or two about involuntary servitude. Molly had been convicted of

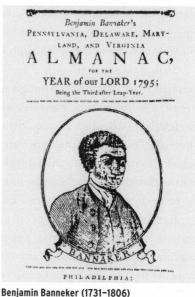

Benjamin Banneker (1731–1806)

stealing milk when she was a teenager in England and sentenced to seven years as an indentured servant in the colonies. After serving her period of bondage in Maryland, she farmed a small plot of wilderness land that she was able to rent. In time Molly earned enough to purchase two slaves. She did not, however, impose English names on them, and after two or three years she granted both their freedom. Then she married Bannka.[2]

After Molly and Bannka's daughter married Robert, the young couple took on the farm work, while Molly took on the task of educating her grandson, Benjamin, and his younger sisters. For a brief period, Benjamin attended a nearby Quaker school (the Quakers being not only abolitionists but continually in the forefront of equal rights). As with most rural children in that era, Benjamin stopped attending school once he was old enough to assist his parents on the farm. In time Robert and Mary purchased additional acreage, the records reflecting their name often being listed as Banneker.

As his parents aged and his sisters married, Benjamin took over the farm.

Despite his relationship with his Quaker neighbors, Banneker's journal reveals that he was as vulnerable as other African Americans at that time and for centuries to come. On December 18, 1790, he recorded, "XXXXXX informed me that XXXXXX stole my horse and great coat, and that the said XXXXXX intended to murder me when opportunity presented and further gave me caution to let no person in my house after dark."[3] If Banneker had been white, he could have taken this information to the sheriff. Rather than report it, he later carefully crossed out all the names in this entry, fearing what might happen should his journal fall into the wrong hands.

Still, in other segments of society, being black could be an asset, albeit sometimes as an oddity. Though no publisher accepted Banneker's first almanac in 1791, some considered it at length, thinking there might be interest in mathematical calculations performed by an African American. Through George Ellicott, now thirty-eight years old, Banneker's unpublished almanac came to the attention of the Pennsylvania Society for Promoting the Abolition of Slavery, one of whose members was George's cousin, the prominent surveyor Andrew Ellicott.

Banneker commenced preparing an almanac for the following year. Andrew Ellicott, meanwhile, started work on his recently received commission to survey the boundary of the newly created District of Columbia. To assist him in this task, he offered a position to his fellow surveyor and cousin, George. George, however, was unable to accept the offer and suggested Benjamin Banneker.

Politics in the eighteenth century being no different than politics now, Andrew Ellicott aimed to protect his posterior before making such a righteous choice. He sought the approval of President Washington's secretary of state, Thomas Jefferson—a shrewd move, since Jefferson's views on race were conflicted but his political ambitions were not. Jefferson approved the choice.

The wisdom of Ellicott's marshaling support soon became evident. During the course of the project, Ellicott lodged at various inns; Banneker slept at the base camp, since few if any local inns would provide accommodations to African Americans. Even in camp, Banneker ate his meals separately from the other members of the engineering corps. Without Jefferson's approval, Banneker's very presence on the project may well have been rejected.

Ellicott himself, however, regarded Banneker as a colleague. He placed him in charge of the astronomical instruments and asked him to perform the mathematical calculations. Ellicott supervised the field measurements. The city whose boundaries they were to locate was a square with ten-mile sides, occupying land on both sides of the Potomac River and encompassing the ports of Georgetown on the north bank and Alexandria on the south bank. Today, that part of the original city south of the Potomac is no longer part of Washington, DC, having been returned to Virginia in 1846. (See "Robert M. T. Hunter" in this book.)

Banneker's work on the survey made him an instant celebrity, since his achievement was of value to people in influential positions. First and foremost were the abolitionists, whose arguments against slavery were greatly strengthened by examples of the intellectual equality of African Americans. Even while the survey was under way, a meeting of the Maryland chapter of the Society for Promoting the Abolition of Slavery heard a report regarding "an almanac for the year 1792, the astronomical calculations thereof performed by Benjamin Banneker, a black man, a descendant of African parents. The calculations appear to be attested by a number of respectable characters as very accurate."[4] With the publicity generated by the society, printers were now more confident that an almanac created by an African American would sell well. They were wrong; it sold *very* well.

Banneker, his golden opportunity at hand, then did an extraordinary thing. He sent a copy of his almanac to Thomas Jefferson, but his cover letter said not a single word about his almanac. It spoke instead about slavery. After noting how, under the rule of the king, Americans had experienced a kind of enslavement, Banneker went on to say:

Your abhorrence thereof was so excited that you publicly held forth this true and invaluable doctrine, which is worthy to be recorded and remembered in all succeeding ages, "We hold these truths to be self-evident, that all men are created equal; that they are endowed by their Creator with certain unalienable rights, and that among these are, life, liberty, and the pursuit of happiness." ... But, Sir, how pitiable is it to reflect, that although you were so fully convinced of the benevolence of the Father of Mankind, and of His equal and impartial distribution of these rights and privileges, which He hath conferred upon them, that you should at the same time counteract His mercies, in detaining by fraud and violence so numerous a part of my brethren.[5]

The fact that Banneker wrote to Jefferson suggests that he was as keen an observer of politics as he was of planets and stars. Having witnessed Andrew

Ellicott seeking Jefferson's support for his appointment, Banneker knew that the present political constellation made Jefferson an ideal ally. Less than two weeks later, Banneker received the following letter:

Sir,
I thank you sincerely for your letter of the 19th instant and for the almanac it contained. Nobody wishes more than I do to see such proofs as you exhibit, that nature has given to our black brethren, talents equal to those of the other colors of men, and that the appearance of a want of them is owing merely to the degraded condition of their existence, both in Africa & America. I can add with truth, that nobody wishes more ardently to see a good system commenced for raising the condition both of their body & mind to what it ought to be, as fast as the imbecility of their present existence, and other circumstances which cannot be neglected, will admit. I have taken the liberty of sending your almanac to Monsieur de Condorcet, Secretary of the Academy of Sciences at Paris, and member of the Philanthropic society, because I considered it as a document to which your whole color had a right for their justification against the doubts which have been entertained of them. I am with great esteem, Sir
Your most obed't humble serv't.,
Thomas Jefferson[6]

Banneker and the abolitionist societies recognized the immense value of Jefferson's letter—as no doubt Jefferson did in writing it. The two letters immediately appeared in pamphlets and newspapers throughout the country. The publicity led to Banneker's 1793 almanac outselling all its competitors, and the 1794 edition outselling that of 1793.

But fame did not eliminate the racial abuses that Banneker faced. Too old to continue working his land, he rented it out to small farmers in the area. Often they refused to pay the rent and on occasion threatened him over the matter. He noted that on August 27, 1797, "Standing by my door, I heard the discharge of a gun, and in 4 or 5 seconds of time after the discharge, the small shot came rattling about me, one or two of which struck the house, which plainly demonstrates that the velocity of sound as much greater than that of a cannon-bullet."[7] Possibly the incident was an accident, not an act of intimidation. That the entry is ambiguous may itself be a clue to the experience of being black at that time and place. Does Banneker's observation about the velocity of sound reflect his fascination with science even when his life was in danger? Or does it reflect how, for the sake of safety, he disguised his recording of a racist event in scientific garb?

Likewise, what others wrote about Banneker reveals how one's true feelings about race could be just as difficult to know then as they often are today. The same year that the bullet was fired into Banneker's home, *The Time Piece & Literary Companion* published a satiric article, purporting to be the last will and testament of one Peter Porcupine. It included the curious-to-decipher bequest, "Should the said Thomas Jefferson survive Banneker, the almanac maker, I request he will get the brains of the said philomath carefully dissected, to satisfy the world in what respects they differ from a white man."

Benjamin Banneker could not satisfy the world. But he could cope with it. And prevail.

JESSE HAWLEY
The Erie Canal and the Gush of Redrawn Lines

> The common purpose of government is protection. But can it not be made to do more?... To the cultivation of the arts of peace, we have to ask our government to adopt another principle: that of a nation's wealth ... is best promoted by applying the surplus revenue of the state to internal improvements, roads, canals, &c.
>
> —JESSE HAWLEY[1]

Jesse Hawley contributed to the location of more state lines than any other individual except Stephen A. Douglas. But Hawley did it from jail. In 1807 he published a book-length series of fourteen newspaper essays while cooling his financially overextended heels in debtors' prison in Canandaigua, New York. The essays detailed the means by which the Great Lakes could be connected to the Hudson River and, via the Hudson, to the Atlantic. Doing so would have an incredible result, according to Hawley, who predicted with astonishing accuracy that "the trade of almost all the lakes in North America ... would center at New York.... In a century its island would be covered with the buildings and population of its city."[2]

Hawley was not the first to speculate on a waterway connecting the hinterland to the Hudson. As early as 1724, surveyor Cadwallader Colden wrote of the potential for waterways connecting New York's Mohawk River, which flows into the Hudson, to the Great Lakes:

> Many of the branches of the river Mississippi come so near to the branches of several of the rivers which empty themselves into the Great Lakes, that in several places there is but a short land-carriage from one to the other.... If one considers the [Mohawk] river and its numerous branches, he must say that, by means of this river and the

lakes, there is opened to view such a scene of inland navigation as cannot be paralleled in any other part of the world.[3]

In addition to the extraordinary commercial advantages of connecting the Hudson to the Great Lakes, Colden also emphasized its national security value—from the point of view of England before the Revolutionary War. He argued that the French, who had come to control the vast swath surrounding the Mississippi River, the Great Lakes, and the St. Lawrence River, "plainly showed their intention of enclosing the British settlements."

National security remained an important element when Hawley published his 1807 essays, but from a substantially changed perspective. The St. Lawrence still belonged to another nation, but now that nation was England, which had conquered French Canada in 1763. And while the Mississippi River was now entirely within the United States, owing to the Louisiana Purchase, that same purchase triggered a growing fear that someday the lower half of the Mississippi might also be part of another nation composed of the American slave states.

Between Colden's report to the colonial governor of New York and Hawley's newspaper series, numerous others had discussed aspects of what was to become the Erie Canal. Hawley's essays revealed that his passion for the topic had recently been augmented when Thomas Jefferson, in his second inaugural address, urged "an amendment to the Constitution [enabling surplus funds to] be applied in time of peace to rivers, canals, roads, arts, manufactures, education, and other great objects within each state." Amendment to the Constitution? Indeed, the Con-

stitution limits Congress to funding internal improvements only if they are roadways that convey mail or provide access to forts; it specifically prohibits Congress from acts that favor commerce in one state over any other. Apparently, Jefferson's vision differed from that of the other Founding Fathers.

Jefferson's views on the role of the federal government inspired not only Hawley but also others who contemplated a canal connecting the Great Lakes to the Hudson.[4] New

Jesse Hawley (1773–1842)

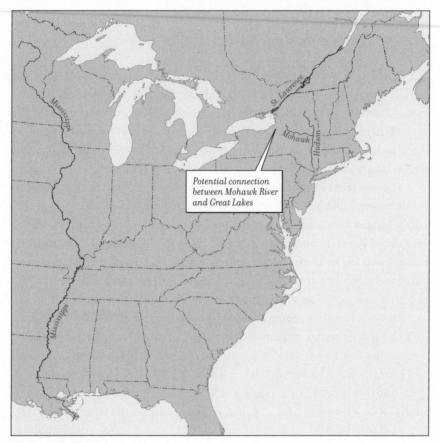

Erie Canal: significant rivers

York State Assemblyman Joshua Forman met with President Jefferson in 1809, seeking federal funds for the New York canal. But even Jefferson's jaw dropped. "You talk of making a canal of 350 miles through the wilderness!" he told Forman. "It is little short of madness to think of it at this day."[5]

Jefferson's insights into madness proved to be limited. Hawley's essays provided so much detail regarding the project's geography, hydrology, and cost that they became the introductory textbook for those joining with Forman to undertake the building of the Erie Canal. Hawley himself was not an engineer. Nor was he a surveyor, wealthy patrician, military man, or even a college graduate. He was just a middle-class flour merchant. His passion regarding the canal was so intense because the absence of such a waterway had landed him in debtors' prison.

Jesse Hawley had been born and raised in Connecticut, a sixth-generation American whose father was a carpenter. As an adult he migrated westward for the economic opportunities that beckoned to those in New England's coastal regions, where the growing population limited one's options. In western New York, Hawley became a flour merchant, milling wheat and shipping it east via waterways being made navigable by the Western Inland Company. Though the shipping costs devoured his profits, the Western Inland Company had declared its commitment to further improvements along the rivers that would reduce the cost of shipping. But the company changed its policy on waterways, causing Hawley's business to sink. Unable to pay his debts, Hawley was arrested in 1806. A friend posted bail. Hawley then jumped bail and went where he felt he would never be found: Pittsburgh.

While on the lam, Hawley published his initial essay using a pseudonym. To his credit, guilt over having jumped bail brought him back to New York, where he was sentenced to twenty months in debtors' prison. There, expanding his initial writing, Hawley continued to publish under his pseudonym, now fearing that readers would dismiss his ideas if they knew the author was in debtors' prison.[6] The projected canal was, after all, so grand that many Americans dismissed the idea even when proposed by worthies such as State Assemblyman Forman, former U.S. senator (and Constitution coauthor) Gouverneur Morris, and future New York governor DeWitt Clinton. Clinton relied heavily on Hawley's essays when, as governor, he got the state legislature to appropriate $7 million to create what opponents called "Clinton's Ditch." The governor committed his subsequent career to the Erie Canal and, after its completion and enormous success, continued to credit Hawley as the foremost progenitor of the project.

While commercial benefit was the primary reason for building the Erie Canal, there were two related factors that were also of great importance. One involved national security; the other, internal security.

Prominent New Yorker William Cooper (founder of Cooperstown and father of James Fenimore Cooper) connected the canal's economic benefits to national security when he wrote of the Great Lakes region: "The trade of this vast country must be divided between Montreal and New York, and the half of it lost to the United States unless an inland communication can be formed from Lake Erie to the Hudson."[7] Trade would be lost to the United States because it had to rely on the St. Lawrence River in Canada. The Treaty of Paris, which ended the American Revolution, guaranteed England free navigation of the Mississippi River but made no mention of American rights to navigate the St. Lawrence. Indeed, Americans did not enjoy smooth sailing on that river. Prior to Hawley's essays, the Senate considered legislation authorizing the president to acquire "by negotiation, or otherwise, as he may deem most expedient," free navigation along the St. Lawrence.

But the British were not the only impediment to navigation on the St. Lawrence. Boulders, rapids, and, in the winter, ice also hindered that waterway connecting Lake Ontario to the Atlantic. Canadians, equally aware of the vast market to be tapped by connecting the Great Lakes to the sea began to create their own series of canals.[8]

The Erie Canal also represented a means of further uniting the states. Despite the failure of the Articles of Confederation, which loosely linked the states, many Americans continued to cling to that document's distrust of a national government. An 1822 article in the influential *North American Review* said of the idea of an Erie Canal:

> It connects the east with the west by a reciprocal and advantageous commerce ... and thus a strong but mutual interest will ultimately unite them with a chain which neither the fervors of party nor the mutual jealousy of state will ever be able to destroy.... The union of the states is our only safety.... Remove it, give an absolute independence to every state, and the promise of our youth is blasted, and with it the world's best hope laid low.

The Great Lakes, if given access to the sea, would become more than lakes; they would become major avenues of commerce. Illustrating this fact on the American map, five states today have boundaries that were adjusted to provide access to the Great Lakes.

The boundary adjustment that most clearly reveals a state reaching for the Great Lakes was the tab at the western end of Pennsylvania's northern border. But this adjustment cannot be ascribed to Jesse Hawley's influence, since it occurred in a 1785 agreement between Pennsylvania and New York, more than twenty years before Hawley's essays appeared. It was, however, after Cadwallader Colden's report regarding connecting Lake Erie to the Hudson, and the numerous editions of his report published in the mid-eighteenth century indicate the high level of interest in the prospect of such a waterway.

That interest also contributed to Ohio's boundary adjustment in 1805, though in this case Ohio's primary goal was to possess the entirety of its western river, the Maumee. That goal could only have been augmented by the

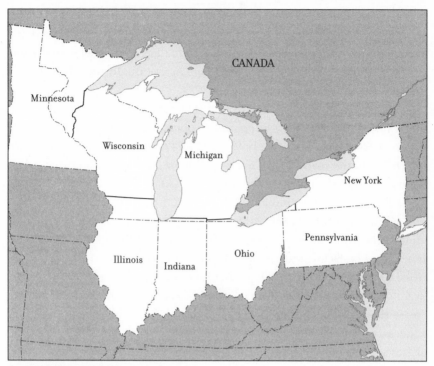

Border adjustments for Great Lakes access

fact that the segment of the Maumee originally located in Michigan was its outlet on Lake Erie at Toledo. Congress allowed Ohio to adjust its border with Michigan to include this port. If this irked Michigan, the territory was too sparsely populated for its irk to be heard. But after the Erie Canal was built, its irk grew into fury. The land that had been transferred to Ohio was now so valuable it sparked the Toledo War (see "Stevens T. Mason" in this book).

After the publication of Hawley's essays, Indiana's boundary with Michigan was moved north to give it access to the Great Lakes at Gary. Illinois's boundary with Wisconsin was moved north to give it access at Chicago. And Minnesota's boundary with Wisconsin was moved east from the Mississippi to the St. Croix River to give Minnesota access to the Great Lakes at Duluth.

While the impact of Hawley's writing was thus surfacing on the map, Hawley himself went back to being the businessman he used to be. "Notice is hereby given that ... the subscribers have been duly appointed as assignees of Jesse Hawley, an insolvent debtor," a legal notice in a Canandaigua, New York, newspaper stated in 1812. "Creditors of the said insolvent [are] to appear at Freeman Atwater's inn ... on Tuesday the 19th of May at ten o'clock A.M....

to receive a dividend (if there be any) of the said insolvent's estate." Hawley managed this bankruptcy in a way that avoided debtors' prison, though his financial difficulties may have contributed to disputes he had with his sisters, his in-laws, and his wife, from whom he eventually was divorced—an unusual recourse in that era.

But he kept bouncing back. In 1817 DeWitt Clinton's election as governor resulted in Hawley being appointed collector of revenue for the port of Genesee, New York. Three years later, he was elected to the New York State Assembly on the coattails of Governor Clinton. Two years after that, when Clinton was not renominated, neither was Hawley.

Though Hawley's prominence had been confined primarily to New York—and, within New York, to those involved in the legislation enabling the creation of the canal—he did have one brief moment in the national spotlight. It occurred on October 26, 1825: "The columns of the New York papers are filled to overflowing with the particulars of the grand celebration of the event of finishing the Erie Canal," the *New Hampshire Statesman* reported. "Jesse Hawley, of Rochester, in behalf of the visitors, made a congratulatory address, which was replied to by Judge [Joshua] Forman, in behalf of the citizens of Buffalo. On a discharge of cannon, the boat started in fine style, drawn by four horses."

Jesse Hawley died in January 1842. In his one-time hometown of Rochester, New York, his obituary consisted of three sentences. In Albany, the terminus of the Erie Canal, four sentences were devoted to his passing. But in Milwaukee, of all places, two full-page columns were devoted to his memory.[9] The length and location of these obits reflect Hawley's impact on the nation. Rochester, a port on Lake Ontario, and Albany, a port on the Hudson River, were prosperous before the canal was created. But Milwaukee, a port on Lake Michigan, would likely not have existed without the Erie Canal. Not until several months after ground was broken for the canal did the American Fur Company form a settlement in what is now Milwaukee.

The Erie Canal remains in use to this day despite the subsequent development of railroads and interstate highways. While it transports far less cargo than during its heyday, it has remained a shipping channel even after the United States and Canada created the St. Lawrence Seaway in 1959. Jointly operated by both nations, the seaway annually transports more than 200 million tons of cargo between the Great Lakes and the Atlantic.

JAMES BRITTAIN
The Man History Tried to Erase

Raise as many Militia of your Battalion as you shall think necessary
and pursue [the Georgians] from place to place ... until you have taken
their Leaders, if possible, and show them that we have law sufficient
to suppress unruly Citizens.
—LT. COL. WILLIAM WHITSON, NORTH CAROLINA STATE MILITIA,
TO MAJ. JAMES BRITTAIN, DECEMBER 17, 1810[1]

Had it not been for the actions of James Brittain, the boundary
between North Carolina and Georgia might well be twelve miles
north of where it is today. Until recently, however, one would be
hard-pressed to find any history book that mentioned Brittain. The reason
his name has now resurfaced is the flip side of the reason it was suppressed:
convenience/inconvenience.[2] Brittain's story is an important part of North
Carolina and Georgia history, but it has become more important for what it
reveals about history itself.

James Brittain was born in the mid-1700s, served in the American Revolution, and afterward settled in Mills River, North Carolina, with his wife
and children. The various surviving documents in which his name appears
suggest he was a leading citizen in the region, though never its preeminent
leader. He represented Buncombe County in the North Carolina Senate for
six (nonconsecutive) terms.

He was not always an illustrious leader, as a 1792 resolution suggests:

The commissioners appointed to fix the center and agree where the
public buildings in the County of Buncombe should be erected have
failed to comply with the above recited Act, and the inhabitants of
said county much injured thereby.... For remedy ... Joshua Inglish,
Archibald Neill, James Wilson, Augustin Shotes, George Baker and

John Dillard ... [shall] be appointed commissioners in the room and stead of Philip Hoodenpile, William Britain, William Whitson, James Brittain and Lemuel Clayton.[3]

Ten years later, Brittain's name crops up in another snafu over public buildings, as revealed in an 1802 directive issued by the Buncombe County Grand Jury:

> The Court house and Jail, the former of which being 35 feet long, stands partly on the Town street, and partly on the lot of Samuel Chunn and Zebulon Baird, and the latter on the lots of James Brittain and Andrew Erwin, so that the County, after expending a very considerable sum of money in executing said Buildings, have not the slightest title to the ground on which they stand ...
> (Signed) William Whitson, Foreman[4]

Brittain subsequently appears to have opted to donate the land inadvertently used to build the county jail, unlike others on the list.

Brittain's personal finances were considerably more involved in his state's boundary dispute with Georgia. In 1802 he purchased 100 acres of land, and in 1806 an additional 200 acres, elsewhere in Buncombe County, North Carolina—or, from Georgia's point of view, in Walton County, Georgia.

Technically, this land had originally belonged to South Carolina. But South Carolina had ceded the region to the United States in 1787. At the time, it was within the domain of the Cherokee nation. In 1798 the government "negotiated" a treaty with the Cherokees that required them to relocate to a reservation west of the Mississippi River—a forced migration now known as the Trail of Tears. In the absence of the Cherokees, the land South Carolina had ceded to the United States remained outside *any* state's jurisdiction. It came to be called the Orphan Strip.

The difficult access in the mountainous Orphan Strip provided ideal terrain for people who didn't want to be found. So many such people repaired to the region that, in 1800, a congressional committee proposed that it be given to South Carolina.

South Carolina, however, passed on the offer. It had no interest in extending its jurisdiction into this labyrinth of mountains, where many residents had repaired to escape jurisdiction.[5] North Carolina and Georgia weren't interested either. But in 1802 the federal government found a new solution. Georgia (which then still included present-day Alabama and Mis-

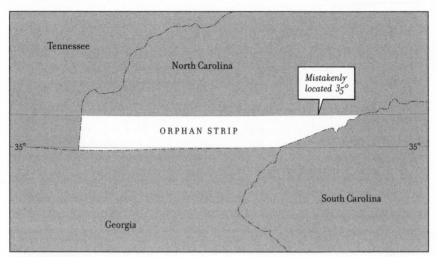

The Orphan Strip

sissippi) had gotten in hot water regarding land fraud in its western region. The federal government offered Georgia a deal. In return for relinquishing the land that would become Alabama and Mississippi, the United States would let Georgia off the hook for land fraud if it also agreed to accept jurisdiction over the Orphan Strip.

North Carolina did not protest this offer, though some North Carolinians suspected that the state's border with Georgia had been inaccurately surveyed. The border was stipulated as being a line along the 35th parallel. As it turned out, the 35th parallel is twelve miles south of where the border had been located.

Still, the United States had rid itself of a pesky problem, and Georgia dutifully organized the land as Walton County (not to be confused with present-day Walton County, Georgia). Georgia went on to appoint officials to govern its new county. What had been a notorious no-man's-land was looking better and better ... to North Carolina. That state now declared that the land was part of its Buncombe County. North Carolina likewise appointed officials to enforce state laws and register land titles.

Among those buying land and having the title recorded in North Carolina was James Brittain. Such purchases by absentee investors were precisely what most fueled Georgia's ire. Often the investors sought to charge rent to those living on their land titled in Buncombe County, North Carolina. This did not sit well with those living on the land who held title to it in Walton County, Georgia. In some instances the North Carolina owners turned to the region's North

Carolina authorities to evict those who refused to pay their rent. Those Georgians living on such land who held title to it in Georgia turned to the region's Georgia authorities for protection. Confrontations, often violent, ensued.

In December 1804 one such confrontation involved Buncombe County constable John Havner and several Walton County residents. It ended when Havner was struck in the face with the butt of a rifle, an injury that proved fatal.[6] In response, North Carolina sent a unit from its state militia, under the command of Brittain. Walton County residents quickly massed to defend themselves. In Georgia the *Augusta Chronicle* reported the following in February 1805:

> On the 19th of December, a party of horsemen consisting of 70 or 80 men, and headed by a Major James Brittain, marched into [Walton] County from Buncombe, North Carolina.... They took and made prisoners of Richard Williamson, James Lafoy, J. Cloud, G. Williamson, esquires, and several others.... Five they discharged and ten were kept and marched off like prisoners of war to Morganton, North Carolina.

Brittain's foray resulted in the battle of McGaha Branch, where his forces quickly overtook the Georgians. Those who escaped regrouped atop Selica Hill. But once again Brittain's men prevailed. Both "battles" might be more accurately described as skirmishes. The number of casualties is uncertain but known to have been low. Some accounts say one to fourteen people died, others say no deaths resulted.[7] What is certain today is that, unbeknownst to those involved, both clashes took place *north* of the Ophan Strip. Neither side knew, at the time, just where the boundaries were.

North Carolina-Georgia engagements

Those arrested and taken to the Morganton jail included the leading officials of Walton County. All escaped. How they managed to do so was not recorded. Notably, however, they did not continue to attempt to enforce Georgia's jurisdictional claims in the region. Though Georgia and North Carolina continued to dispute the region—periodically agreeing to surveys, then disagreeing on the results—only North Carolina's officials exerted jurisdiction. The people in the region also continued to conflict, often resulting in assaults and vandalism. These acts, along with Brittain's foray, constitute what has come to be called the Walton War.

In 1810, with North Carolina solidifying its control, Georgia hired Andrew Ellicott, one of the nation's foremost surveyors, to locate the 35th parallel. Milledgeville's *Georgia Journal* reported in 1812 what his findings were rumored to be (and, in fact, were): "No official communication has yet been made by Mr. Ellicott to our Executive; but we learn that no part of Walton County belongs to this state." Georgia took no official action in response to Ellicott's survey. In fact, it came to act in ways that sought to render the dispute invisible.

During that time, James Brittain too began to disappear from the public mind. When he died (likely in the years near Ellicott's survey), he was buried in what would become the family gravesite in Mills River, North Carolina. Today his grave is invisible, covered by tract homes.[8]

More pressing needs also erased his memory. In 1860 Georgia scrapped the constitution it had been using, which included a description of its boundaries, and replaced it with the constitution of the Confederate State of Georgia. It contained no boundary descriptions, since the last thing the Confederate states needed was conflict among themselves. Georgia's Confederate constitution was replaced during Reconstruction with a constitution that also included no assertion of boundaries. In this instance, those writing this constitution were imposing an end to a national conflict; they too had no wish to stir up local trouble.

For the same reasons, regional historians minimized or totally avoided any reference to the Walton War, seeking to suppress the fact that the North Carolina militia was once led into battle against fellow countrymen from Georgia. One multivolume history of Georgia informed its readers, "For several years a bone of contention between Georgia and North Carolina was the matter of locating the 35th parallel of north latitude, recognized as the boundary line between the two states. In 1806, surveyors representing both states ..." Even though 1806 was only two years after Brittain's foray, this highly detailed history of the state simply skipped it.[9] On the North Carolina side, even historians focused solely on the state's western end ignored the event. One such historian acknowledged the Walton War but wrote of it:

> Georgia, about December, 1803, created a county within this territory and called it Walton County. Georgia naturally attempted to

exercise jurisdiction over what it really believed was its own territory, and North Carolina as naturally resisted such attempts. Consequently, there were great dissentions, the said dissentions having
produced many riots, affrays, assaults, batteries, woundings and
imprisonments. On January 13, 1806 ...[10]

In both instances, the transition to 1806 leaves Brittain's 1804 foray in the
narrative's dust.

In 1971 Georgia suddenly renewed its boundary dispute with North Carolina, though modifying its claim. It also took up a similar dispute with Tennessee. The North Carolina dispute was triggered to maintain consistency in
Georgia's boundary claim with Tennessee. That dispute had been triggered
by Georgia's need for access to the Tennessee River to help supply water to
rapidly growing Atlanta, rising in the wake of the civil rights movement
as the preeminent city of the New South. Reflecting that change, Atlanta's
leading African American newspaper followed the boundary challenge with
equal concern. "Georgia Rep. Larry Thomason ... chairman of the Georgia
Boundary Commission, contends the state's present northern boundary is
about a mile south of where it should be," Atlanta's *Daily World* reported in
September. Noting that the U.S. Geodetic Survey had announced a meeting
to be held with representatives of the three states, the article continued,
"Georgia has accepted the invitation and is waiting for responses from North
Carolina and Tennessee."

Apparently, Georgia is still waiting. No boundary adjustments have
ensued. What has ensued, however, is an awakened awareness of the basis
for the conflict, and with it the name of James Brittain has begun to reappear
in historical accounts.

REUBEN KEMPER
From Zero to Hero?

The outrages of the Kempers a few years ago are not yet forgotten. That family has on the recent occasion displayed its accustomed contempt for the laws of society, and was very active in ... erecting Florida into a government independent alike of Spain and the United States.
—PHILADELPHIA *WEEKLY AURORA*, MARCH 3, 1811

W
hy is the Museum of the Republic of West Florida located two states away in Louisiana? The answer has a lot to do with Reuben Kemper, an American immigrant to Spain's province of West Florida.

After the Revolution, what had been a trickle of Americans migrating to West Florida turned into a flood. Reuben, Nathan, and Samuel Kemper moved there from Virginia around 1800. Like many Americans, they were attracted by the fact that Spain made it easier for the average person to acquire land than did the United States. In the United States, to obtain title to land one had to have the money to purchase it. In Spanish West Florida, one could apply for title to land, and ultimately obtain that title, simply by living on the land and cultivating it—and by professing loyalty to Spain.[1] The policy aimed to discourage absentee land speculators and reward individual productivity. To the extent that it was enforced, Spain's policy resulted in an industrious—and loyal—population.

The Kempers, however, were not happy campers. In 1804 the *Natchez Herald* reported that Reuben and his brothers,

with a party of about 30 men, with colors flying and horns sounding, marched from the neighborhood of the line of demarcation between this territory [Mississippi] and West Florida ... against the fort of Baton Rouge.... They arrived on the following morning about day-

Spanish Florida, 1783–1810

light near the fort. The Spanish commandant ... had posted a piquet of 18 or 20 men, who hailed the party as they approached. They immediately answered by a volley from their rifles, which dispersed the Spaniards, two of whom were observed to fall.

The newspaper account reported that the Kemper party then returned to its headquarters at St. Francisville, without explanation of why they retreated. Instead, the account quoted, in its entirety, a broadside that the Kempers had posted at points along the way.

The posting spoke of "the despotism under which we have long groaned," and their resolve "to throw off the galling yoke of tyranny, and become free men, by declaring ourselves a free and independent people." The message closely resembled the Declaration of Independence, though at no point did it say they sought to join the United States. Nevertheless, their declaration raised Spanish eyebrows. Earlier that year, President Thomas Jefferson had signed the Mobile Act, stating that the 1803 Louisiana Purchase included West Florida. But Jefferson also stated that, because of the ambiguity of the document defining the Louisiana Purchase, along with the ambiguity of land transfers between Spain and France, he would not assert American claims militarily.

Although Kemper and his brothers were not in cahoots with the U.S. government, weren't they freedom fighters nevertheless? Probably not, despite their rousing posters. One month after their attack at Baton Rouge, New York's *Republican Watch Tower* revealed that "Mr. [Reuben] Kemper, the leader of the association, was for some time in the service of Mr. Smith, of

Tennessee, to whom he became indebted to a considerable amount. Being prosecuted, he fled to Florida, where, at the head of thirty men, he raised the standard of revolt."

The details were actually somewhat different. Mr. Smith was John Smith, a resident of Ohio—in fact, a U.S. senator from Ohio. He owned land in West Florida, which he paid the Kemper brothers to manage. Smith's absentee ownership was in violation of Spanish policy, but Spanish policy was laxly enforced (especially for a U.S. senator).[2] The debt mentioned in the news account resulted from Smith's providing the Kempers with dry goods that they were to sell to local residents. When the business failed, Reuben Kemper was deeply in debt to Smith, but he did not flee to West Florida, since that is where he lived and where the litigation took place. The judgment in favor of Smith resulted in efforts by West Florida authorities to evict the Kempers from Smith's land. These efforts became increasingly violent confrontations that, not unlike a barroom brawl, began to involve additional people.

Spain's governor of West Florida viewed the Kempers as ne'er-do-wells who attracted bandits and a few otherwise innocent bystanders. He thus sought to isolate them from their followers by pardoning all those who had been arrested during the eviction confrontations, with the exception of the Kempers. The policy succeeded, as evidenced by the fact that the Kempers' response—the 1804 attack on Baton Rouge—attracted only some thirty men.

What, meanwhile, did the U.S. government think, since it claimed this region? William Claiborne, governor of the neighboring Louisiana Territory, reported to Secretary of State James Madison that the Kemper incident was "nothing more than a riot, in which a few uninformed, ignorant men had taken part."[3] Madison, in turn, repudiated the Kempers' actions and vowed to arrest them if they entered American territory.

But what the federal government actually thought turned out to be less clear. When the Kemper brothers, seeking to evade capture by the West Florida militia (composed primarily of American immigrants), fled into American territory, they were not arrested as promised. So Spain arrested them. But to do so, the West Florida militia had to step over the line into Pinckneyville, Mississippi. Because they had crossed the boundary, the United States justified its forces' freeing the Kempers as they were being transported down the Mississippi River to Baton Rouge.

For the next six years, the brothers tended to their own affairs. When Reuben surfaced again in December 1810, the situation had clearly changed. Baltimore's *Federal Republican* reported:

> Col. [Reuben] Kemper, in service of the [Republic of West Florida] convention, was on the Alabama River with 340 men, where he will probably remain until he receives a reinforcement.... We learn from St. Francisville that the Legislature assembled there last week under the new constitution ... that in consequence of dispatches from Col. Kemper, a detachment of 1500 men (with a suitable train of artillery) under the command of Col. Kirkland, marched from St. Francisville for Pensacola.

How had Reuben Kemper gone from being a debtor corralling a gang of bandits to a leadership position in a rebellion against Spain? Two underlying elements contributed to his success: deteriorating relations with Spain and political uncertainty in the United States. One deteriorating relationship involved the United States' need for unrestricted access to the sea via the Gulf of Mexico. After the Louisiana Purchase, Spain and the United States quarreled over the tariffs charged to American vessels at Baton Rouge and at Mobile (the mouth of the Alabama and Tombigbee Rivers). These tensions heightened three years after the Kemper incident, when President Jefferson signed the 1807 Embargo Act, prohibiting trade between the United States and any other nation. This extraordinary ban resulted from frustration with France and England's refusal to recognize American neutrality. Both nations, then at war, had repeatedly seized U.S. ships engaged in trade with their respective enemy. The act, which sought to curtail all trade until the war ended, aimed to hasten that end by withholding American supplies. To prevent smuggling, the Embargo Act also called for a blockade of Spain's West Florida ports. Spain was not pleased.

Spain had other problems that also contributed to the change in West Florida. Its Latin American colonies, following in the footsteps of the United States, had begun to seek independence, most notably under the leadership of Simón Bolívar. With its position in the world so uncertain, Spain closed immigration from the United States to West Florida. Even American relatives of West Florida citizens were prohibited from entering the province. The immigration restrictions created widespread animosity among the citizens of West Florida toward the nation to which they had previously been loyal.

Uncertainty on the American side also contributed to Reuben Kemper's reversal of fortune. This uncertainty emanated from a man whose involvement with West Florida is all but forgotten, but whose duel that killed Alexander Hamilton is not: Aaron Burr.

Burr, who had been vice president during Jefferson's first administration, never stood trial for the duel, but his reputation was in tatters. He subsequently traveled a great deal, often in Louisiana, in Mexico (where he had leased 40,000 acres that were being cultivated by armed "farmers"), and in West Florida. Burr's travels raised American suspicions, particularly in light of meetings he had held with the U.S. military commander in Louisiana, James Wilkinson. Though a highly talented general in the Revolution, Wilkinson later negotiated with Spain as a private citizen, seeking privileged navigation for Kentucky along the Mississippi River. Many in the Jefferson administration now wondered whether, in the event of war with Spain, the two men were conspiring to coordinate Wilkinson's forces and Burr's "farmers" to separate the Louisiana Purchase, Burr's Mexican lands, and all or some of West Florida into their own country. Wilkinson ultimately revealed this plot, though questions regarding his credibility only added to American uncertainty.

People don't like uncertainty, and many cope with it by finding a way to fill in the blanks. Reuben Kemper, who was also entangled in the alleged Burr conspiracy, was able to rehabilitate his reputation by providing the public with a way to fill in the blanks. The opportunity to do so presented itself, ironically, following his arrest by the federal government, which was reported nationwide. In January 1811 North Carolina's *The Star*, reprinting a story from the *Rhode Island Republican*, reported:

Since the [Republic of West Florida] Conventional Party have declared themselves free and independent of Old Spain ... a number of the inhabitants of this part of the [Mississippi] Territory wishing well to the cause have taken an active part in the business and about a fortnight since several men, to the number of sixty-five, went below the line of demarcation.... All who have returned above the line have had writs served upon them for the purpose of a prosecution, on account of having engaged in an expedition not authorized by the government of the United States—among whom are Col. Kennedy and Col. Kemper.

Because Kemper had lain low for six years, his dubious past escaped the notice of most newspapers. But his arrest risked revealing his days at the head of what the U.S. government had declared to be a gang. Shrewdly, he seized this moment to publish his own account in newspapers throughout the country. He related how he had been contacted by a man named Lewis Kerr, who knew of his past attack at Baton Rouge and invited him to an important meeting, at which he would have to take an oath of secrecy: "Before taking this oath, I told Mr. Kerr that was there anything in opposition to the government of the United States, that it must not be made known to me on any terms whatever! He assured me there was not." Kemper then employed some classic name-dropping, citing Kerr's assurance that the secret project "was set on foot by men higher in office than any others in the United States—I believe meaning the president." Kemper's article related that the venture being planned—technically not by the United States—was to take possession of West Florida. He was asked how many men he could raise and allowed as he could "fill the place."

The crux of Kemper's article followed this account of his recruitment. It sought to separate his participation from Aaron Burr's alleged conspiracy to create a new country:

> I asked him if he had ever learned or could conjecture what Mr. Burr's plans were, in coming to this country the year before.... His route was a strange one. Mr. Morgan said so it was, but he knew nothing of Mr. Burr's plans; that he was not in the habit of telling him, but said there was a man in this place some time prior to this had told him that he expected Burr was on some revolutionary plan or other toward Mexico.... I observed that, in my opinion, Burr was an intriguing character, who would stop at nothing in his situation. Mr. Morgan said very true, he was all that, but he was a man of too much sense for that.

Kemper concluded by relating an extraordinary effort he undertook to eliminate any uncertainty about the military action in which he was becoming involved:

> I at length determined in going to see Mr. Jefferson, and in June I left the Mississippi Territory for Washington city. On my route, I had planned a thousand ways of introducing the inquiry, knowing the unfavorable impression that had been made on the mind of the president through my particular "friends," Mr. Claiborne, Governor of Louisiana, Mr. John Smith, Senator from the State of Ohio, and some others.

But the climax of the article—Kemper's meeting with President Jefferson—engaged in the very thing the article hoped to eliminate: uncertainty. "I rather bungled the business," Kemper wrote, "obtained no information, and I suppose gave but little. The president thought he had received a novel visit, and I thought he treated his guest in a novel manner." Meaning what? Who knows. What we do know is how Kemper rehabilitated his reputation by skillfully exploiting uncertainty.

Uncertainty continued to accompany the Kempers as they passed into history. The 1874 *American Cyclopaedia* described Reuben Kemper as one of the "leaders in the movement to rid West Florida of its Spanish rule." Extolling Kemper, it says, "The Spanish authorities caused the Kempers to be kidnapped, but they were rescued.... After these occurrences, Reuben Kemper devoted himself to the task of driving the Spaniards from the American continent." Other histories have viewed Kemper more along the lines of William Horace Brown, who in 1906 described him as "a man whose lawlessness has found respectable apologists—who has even been lauded, like many others of his brutal breed, as a gallant knight of the frontier."

As for the portion of Spanish West Florida that was "liberated" in September 1810, it constituted itself as an independent republic. But before the year was out, the United States dissolved the Republic of West Florida, taking possession of the western half of the region and annexing it to Louisiana. This action created the segment of southern Louisiana east of the Mississippi River.

RICHARD RUSH
The 49th Parallel:
A New Line of Americans

As regarded the ... boundary line, I remarked [to Lord Castlereagh]
that the ground of the objection was that the only line that could be
run in the direction proposed under the Treaty of 1783 would not,
as had been ascertained since ... strike the Mississippi; and to run
it lower down would bring it through territory within the limits of
the United States.

—AMBASSADOR RICHARD RUSH[1]

The longest boundary line in the United States is the 49th parallel,
separating the United States and Canada from Minnesota to the West
Coast. The American most largely responsible for this line is Richard
Rush, who, as ambassador to England, negotiated the first use of this latitude
as a border. The simplicity of this boundary line is deceptive. Its location on
the map preserves several elements reflecting the development of the United
States in its infancy among the family of nations.

Rush himself was one of those developing elements. Born in 1780 amid
the American Revolution, he was the son of a Founding Father, Benjamin
Rush, one of the signers of the Declaration of Independence. As the son of
a political celebrity, Rush—like his friend, John Quincy Adams—carried
an extra burden in establishing an identity. Rush developed an identity
complementary to that of his father, a revolutionary whose revolution had
succeeded, by becoming a diplomat, thereby devoting his career to forming
bonds rather than breaking them. Characteristically, he prefaced his memoir
of being ambassador to England by stating, "Enough has been written and
said on both sides to irritate. My desire is, and such my effort, to soothe."

Though his father's contacts opened doors, Richard Rush strove mightily
to achieve his own laurels, graduating from Princeton University at the age

of fourteen, far and away the youngest member in his class. At Princeton he honed his oratorical skills, an effort that served him well in establishing his reputation as a lawyer. He was appointed attorney general of Pennsylvania in 1811, and later that year he was chosen to be comptroller of the U.S. Treasury by President James Madison.

The commencement of the War of 1812 made that year particularly pivotal for Rush and, separately, the 49th parallel. Because of his oratorical talent, Rush was selected to give a Fourth of July address before both houses of Congress, the president, and his cabinet. In effect, Rush was addressing the nation's founders on behalf of the next generation, and his words reveal the passing of the torch. "Thirty years, fellow citizens, is a long time to have been exempt from the calamities of war," he said to these veteran leaders of the Revolutionary War. "It is a fact that affords, in itself, the most honorable and incontestable proof that those who have guided [this nation] … have ardently cherished peace … [despite] abundant provocation.… Let the blood of Concord and of Lexington answer again!"[2]

The speech was reported by newspapers throughout the nation. It led to Rush's becoming an unofficial spokesman for the administration on behalf of the War of 1812, the causes of which were understood by the American public then about as well as they are today. Using the pen name of John Dickinson, Rush published an extensive series of articles justifying the war.[3]

On the same July 4 that Rush spoke before Congress and the president, an item appeared in the *Charleston City Gazette* speculating that America's opening thrust in the War of 1812 would be an invasion of Upper Canada. The report explained that Upper Canada was bounded "by Hudson's Bay [Company] in the 49th parallel of north latitude, extending due west indefinitely." As early as 1812, then, the 49th parallel had surfaced as the Canadian-American border. In the American press, that is; not in the act of Parliament that had defined Canada. The 1774 Quebec Act had stipulated the southern border of Canada's western region as being "the southern boundary of

Richard Rush (1780–1859)

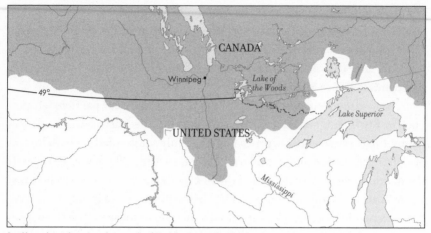

Southern boundary (western end) of Hudson Bay watershed

the territory granted to the Merchants Adventurers of England, trading to Hudson's Bay." The boundaries of the Hudson's Bay Company had previously been stipulated in 1670 as being all the land within the drainage basin of Hudson Bay. That drainage basin, however, dips *below* the 49th parallel, while further west it ends *north* of the parallel. Just as important, mapmakers in 1774 did not know how far these tributaries extended. When the news article about Upper Canada appeared in 1812, more was known, but much remained uncertain.

These uncertainties intersected with Rush's career when, after the War of 1812, President Monroe appointed him to be the ambassador to England, replacing John Quincy Adams, who was returning to become secretary of state. While awaiting the return of Adams from London, Rush served as acting secretary of state and negotiated the 1817 Rush-Bagot Convention, demilitarizing a key frontier between the United States and British North America (present-day Canada) by limiting the number of warships England and the United States could have on the Great Lakes.

The Rush-Bagot Convention boded well for Rush's upcoming boundary negotiations. But upon Rush's arrival in London, his endeavor to resolve differences with England did not get off to an easy start. Charles Bagot, the British ambassador to the United States with whom he had just negotiated, wrote disparagingly of one bridge-building effort by Rush:

> It is not true that the New England states preserve the manners of
> old England at the time of their settlement to the degree that Rush

thinks.... The real truth is there is very little similarity between the two people, and that little is becoming daily less.... All the young generation, nearly without exception, are of the Democratic Party, the creed of which being hatred of England, leads them to reject as much as they can what they conceive to be an England usage. And, let Rush say what he pleases ... in the Southern States ... the climate itself would soon induce a great change in English manners, customs, and feelings.[4]

Rush let such comments pass and focused on his goals, listing them in a paper he gave the British side. His list of eleven items provides insight into what is now the long straight line across most of the top of the United States. Item three was the "Northwestern boundary line," and item four was the "Columbia River question."[5] Imperceptible on the map today, the long boundary along the 49th parallel resulted from two separate issues.

In undertaking his new responsibilities, Rush sought advice from a key Founding Father, former president John Adams. Adams had been a member of the delegation that negotiated and signed the Treaty of Paris ending the American Revolution in 1783. That treaty stipulated boundaries, fishing rights, and commerce—all of which were now back on the table for two reasons. Some of the issues came to be contested in what had eventually exploded into the War of 1812 and were still unresolved. Other issues stipulated in the 1783 treaty now required renegotiation owing to the expansion of the United States via the 1803 Louisiana Purchase.

The advice Adams gave Rush reveals both the passing of the torch and the evolution of the new nation. Adams described an aspect of that evolution when he replied to Rush, "Not that we were British subjects at the Treaty of 1783, but as having been British subjects ... our right was clear and indubitable to fish in all the places in the sea where British subjects had fished or ever had a right to fish." Passing the torch, Adams went on to advise this rising leader: "Former treaties, not formally repeated in a new treaty, are presumed to be received and acknowledged. The fisheries are therefore ours, and the navigation of the Mississippi theirs, that is the British, as much as ever."[6]

Adams provided a powerful argument for Rush to use in negotiating American rights to fish in the coastal areas and bays of Nova Scotia, Labrador, and Newfoundland. But that same logic worked against Rush regarding the Mississippi River. Free access to the Mississippi and Columbia Rivers was England's primary concern in negotiating the boundary between the United States and Canada from the Great Lakes to the West Coast. Of primary concern to the United States (following the Louisiana Purchase) was total control of the Mississippi River and, to an increasing extent, control of the Columbia River farther west. Rush, therefore, needed to break with the past in asserting access to rivers while preserving the past in claiming American fishing rights. In both cases, he succeeded in getting more than he gave.

How did he pull this off? Regarding the northern border, he succeeded in part by agreeing to postpone agreement on that segment of the boundary west of the Rocky Mountains (affecting the Columbia River). For the segment from the Great Lakes to the Rockies, one element that contributed to Rush's success was yet another river, the St. Lawrence, 950 miles away. Rush explained in his memoirs:

> An attempt was made by the British plenipotentiaries to connect with this article a clause securing to Great Britain access to the Mississippi and right to its navigation.... We said that we could consent to no clause of that nature.... The United States have claimed, in a subsequent negotiation, the right of navigating the St. Lawrence, from its source to its mouth. The essential difference in the two cases is that the upper waters of the St. Lawrence flow through territory belonging to both countries.

Had England insisted on access to the Mississippi, it would have had no case for opposing American navigation on the St. Lawrence, an avenue of commerce that was as vital to Canada as the Mississippi was to the United States.

Why, then, the 49th parallel? Why not stick with the straight line established in the 1783 treaty? It commenced at the northwest corner of Lake of the Woods "and from thence on a due west course to the river Mississippi." The problem was that it didn't intersect the Mississippi. The headwaters of the Mississippi turned out to be south of that latitude. This error was known by the time Rush was renegotiating the boundary, which was why the British initially sought a border providing access to the river. Once England abandoned this issue, other waterways became crucial to British interests in this prerailroad era—those being the waterways that led to the Hudson's Bay Company's settlement at Winnipeg. From Winnipeg, waterways lead to Lake of the Woods and from there to Lake Superior. Once on the Great

Waterways leading to Winnipeg

Lakes, cargo could ship to the St. Lawrence River and the sea. While the precise latitude of Lake of the Woods was not yet known, it was known that Winnipeg was just below the 50th parallel. This knowledge may have accounted for the 1812 reference to the 49th parallel as the southern border of the Hudson's Bay Company, and for its use in stipulating the U.S.-Canadian boundary in the agreement Rush negotiated in 1818.

That agreement stated that the boundary extended from the northwest corner of Lake of the Woods "due north or south, as the case may be, until the said line shall intersect the said [49th] parallel of north latitude, and from the point of such intersection due west." Since, as it turns out, the 49th parallel is *south* of the northwest corner of Lake of the Woods, the U.S.-Canadian boundary in what is now Minnesota suddenly blips to the south before commencing its long straight line across the remainder of the continent.

Upon the election of John Quincy Adams as president, Rush set aside his diplomatic expertise to become the secretary of the treasury. In 1828 he was nominated to be vice president when Adams sought a second term, in a bitterly fought rematch with Andrew Jackson. This time Jackson won, and for the first time the White House was occupied by a president who had risen from among the common people, not from the patrician families of the Founding Fathers. Rush, however, was so esteemed for his skill at bridging differences that Jackson chose him to represent the United States in laying claim to an unusual and contested bequest of over half a million dollars to create an establishment for "the increase and diffusion of knowledge," whatever that meant. Rush succeeded in obtaining the funds left by a little-known British chemist named James Smithson. The funds were eventually used to create the Smithsonian Institution, with Rush serving as one of its first regents.

In 1846 Rush saw the boundary line he had negotiated in 1818 extended to the West Coast. The following year President James K. Polk appointed Rush ambassador to France—a particularly challenging post as the government of King Louis Philippe was overthrown during his tenure. Rush managed to maintain good relations with both the royal government and the provisional government that took its place. He duly participated in political and social events attended by the king, but Rush's fundamentally diplomatic character, which combined his father's political insight with detachment from his father's revolutionary zeal, served him well.

Rush's diary entry on February 23, 1848, began, "A revolution has come like a thunder clap."[7] Amid the turmoil and uncertainties, he recognized the symbolic importance of the United States being the first nation to recognize France's new democracy, known as the Second Republic. "Would it be right or expedient," he worried, "to wait for instructions before recognizing [the new government]? A month or more must elapse before instructions could reach me." Rush correctly anticipated the instructions of the Polk administration and established diplomatic relations with the new French government.

Rush's diplomatic career concluded at the end of Polk's presidency. But, after he returned to Pennsylvania, his name was increasingly mentioned as a possible nominee of the Democratic Party for the 1852 presidential election. Rush's skills as a diplomat, however, did not transfer to those of a presidential candidate. In an 1850 letter to a gathering of Pennsylvania Democrats, he addressed the issue of slavery by invoking the Founding Fathers:

I am of those who think that our Union is in danger from [the slavery issue]; not a visionary danger ... of a few ultras at each end of the Union, but a danger ... of constitutional obligations.... When a Southern man has ventured upon a claim for his fugitive slave ... men, otherwise good citizens ... have carried their opposition to the verge of treason.... Are the present philanthropists superior, as pure men, wise men, patriotic men, to Washington and his great associates—the Franklins, Adamses, Madisons, Jeffersons ... who signed or approved of the federal constitution with all its sanctions of slavery?[8]

Rush's suggestion of treason soon came back to haunt him. In September 1851 a Maryland slave owner and his two sons, accompanied by police officers, went to Christiana, Pennsylvania, to retrieve runaway slaves who were hiding there. The morning after their arrival, they were encircled by approximately eighty African Americans and whites who, on the prior advice of abolitionist leaders, demanded that the slave owner turn back. When the slave owner continued his effort (which had been made legal by the Fugitive Slave Acts of 1793 and 1850), shots were fired and a melee ensued in which the slave owner and one of his sons died. The grand jury indictments that followed were for treason, rather than murder, so that the charges could be (and were) brought against not only those who fired the fatal shots but also everyone else in the gathering and against those who had previously advised them. The antislavery press, citing Rush's earlier remarks, was not kind to the candidate. Boston's *The Liberator* wrote:

> Richard Rush mourns over the fact that his state is the only one in which treason has repeatedly been attempted against the United States.... Some [of those indicted] were merely present, looking on but taking no part in the affair. Some simply gave information in advance to the fugitives attempted to be arrested.... All these are indicted for treason, for "levying war"—for treason, according to the United States Constitution, "shall consist only in levying war" or adhering to the enemies of the United States, giving them aid or comfort.

The magazine *National Era* stated that "Mr. Rush is evidently not the man for the hour. He is timid, fearful, trembling. He does not counsel support of the Fugitive Slave Law because it is proper, just, and right; but [because] the 'eyes of the South' are upon Pennsylvania." In a separate article, the magazine even used Rush's success as ambassador to France to castigate him in the political arena: "We presume this humane ex-minister studied the philosophy of the guillotine when in Paris.... As cutting off peoples' heads has proven so efficacious in promoting a holy reverence for law and order in France, the venerable gentleman seems to be under the impression that strangling people must be equally beneficial in Pennsylvania."

Ultimately, none of those tried for treason at Christiana was convicted. In fact, no one was convicted of anything. When the Democrats convened in 1852 to select a presidential nominee, the ballot did not include Richard Rush.

Rush lived out the remainder of his life at his home in Philadelphia and his estate outside the city. Upon his death in 1859, obituaries appeared nationwide. Diplomatically, they made no mention of slavery or treason.

NATHANIEL POPE
Illinois's Most Boring Border

It is as plain as daylight that Wisconsin is about to be most flagrantly robbed of a large share of her rightful domain.... A fine strip of territory has been sacrificed.... Wisconsin is ... having her pockets picked!
—*WISCONSIN HERALD*, JANUARY 9, 1847

N athaniel Pope is responsible for the location of Illinois' most boring border, its straight-line northern boundary with Wisconsin. Had it not been relocated, the Land of Lincoln might have been the Land of Slavery. And what became the Civil War may well have had a different outcome. But try telling that to Wisconsin, which lost over 9,000 square miles in the deal.

Pope came to Illinois in February 1809, only days after Congress had created the territory. Born and raised in Kentucky, he was a twenty-two-year-old attorney when, in 1806, he began his career in the recently acquired Louisiana Territory, basing himself in the previously French town of Ste. Genevieve in present-day Missouri. The reason he then moved to Illinois, just as it was created, was that President James Madison had appointed him secretary of the new Illinois Territory, its number two position. The territorial secretary had the authority to act as governor should the appointed governor be absent. Pope received this appointment through the efforts of

Nathaniel Pope (1784–1850)

his brother, Senator John Pope of Kentucky.[1] Nepotism often results in the appointment of incompetents, but not this time. Nathaniel Pope was an able attorney and savvy politician. The northern border of Illinois proves it.

The legislation creating the Illinois Territory stipulated its boundaries to be the land east of the Mississippi River and west of both the Wabash River "and a direct line drawn from the said Wabash River and Post Vincennes due north to the territorial line between the United States and Canada." Thus the original Illinois included all of present-day Wisconsin and sections of present-day Michigan and Minnesota, though the legislation noted that these boundaries were only for the purposes of temporary government. Consequently, maps of Illinois prior to statehood anticipated the future state's northern border to be that established in the 1787 Northwest Ordinance, a line due west from the southernmost point of Lake Michigan.

Illinois's southern connections

Under the Northwest Ordinance, the introduction of slavery was prohibited in Illinois, as it was in the entire Northwest Territory. Not all residents of Illinois were happy about that fact. Illinois extended more deeply south than any other part of the Northwest Territory, and many of its original settlers were Southerners. Its connection to the South was strengthened by the fact that virtually all of its rivers flow into the Mississippi.

When, in 1816, Pope ran for Congress as the territory's nonvoting delegate, slavery was not yet a campaign issue. Statehood too was not a campaign issue, despite the fact that Illinois sought statehood only one year later. Pope was elected instead on a platform that emphasized road construction and education. The issue of slavery, however, was bubbling just beneath the territorial surface, and the skillful attorney in Pope understood that, when that surface turned into a state, a case could then be made to allow slavery based on a phrase in the same legislation that had prohibited it.

The Northwest Ordinance not only had proposed boundaries for future states in the Northwest Territory and banned the introduction of slavery, it also had stipulated the requirements for becoming a state. Critical in the case of Illinois were two elements in the clause that stated, "whenever any of the said states shall have sixty thousand free inhabitants therein, such state shall be admitted, by its delegates, into the Congress of the United States, on an equal footing with the original states in all respects." The phrase that caught Pope's legal-eyed attention was "on an equal footing with the original states." The original states had determined for themselves whether or not to permit slavery. Since, upon becoming a state, Illinois would exist on an equal footing with those states, it could attempt to claim the right to determine for itself whether or not to permit slavery.

The significance of this phrase helps explain Pope's reaction when, as a delegate to Congress, he unexpectedly received a resolution passed by Illinois's territorial legislature instructing him to propose a bill for statehood. To one congressional colleague he confided that he could not "suppress my regret that the application was made at this time."[2] The other element in the Northwest Ordinance that was problematic to Illinois's bid for statehood was the population requirement. Illinois was not yet sufficiently populated, and what population it did have resided primarily in its southern end, where pro-slavery sympathies predominated. "The only difficulty I have to overcome," Pope half-truthfully wrote in a letter to the *Illinois Intelligencer*, "is whether we have the population supposed by the legislature, no enumeration of the inhabitants having lately been taken.... If it were certain that we had even thirty-five thousand inhabitants, no objection I think would be made to our admission." While 35,000 is considerably less than 60,000, the number stipulated in the Northwest Ordinance, Pope knew of political tap dances that could step around that legal detail. But he also knew they wouldn't be easy.

A glimpse of Pope's anger at this unexpected task can be found in a letter he sent to Illinois's territorial governor, Ninian Edwards, under whom he had served when secretary of the territory and also as Edwards's adjutant during the War of 1812. "You are but a poor correspondent," Pope wrote sarcastically to his longtime political ally, "owing, I suppose, to being exclusively absorbed in mercantile speculations. It is, however, not a little surprising that upon the subject of [statehood] ... you should have withheld from me your own views—especially as, when I left home, it was not contemplated."[3]

Despite his misgivings, Pope pursued his assignment "with that candor and good faith becoming my station." Step one was to write a resolution enabling Illinois to hold a statehood convention. Pope included in that resolution a requirement that a census be taken. But what if the population turned out to be less than 60,000? The resolution stated that Illinois could become a state only if "it shall appear from the enumeration ... that there are within the proposed state, not less than ___ thousand inhabitants." Evidently, Pope was still working on this.

Step two was to do nothing. Pope simply sat and listened as Congress took up the topic of "internal improvements." It was an issue that, strange as it may seem today, was a hot topic in 1818. It also set the stage for Pope's next step. The debate on the floor regarded whether or not the federal government should provide funds to build internal improvements such as roads and canals. Unless amended, the Constitution prohibited almost all such expenditures. But the nation had doubled in size since the signing of the Constitution. New states were being created from the Northwest Territory and the Louisiana Purchase. Roads and canals (and soon railroads) could help strengthen the bonds of unity between these new states and the rest of the nation. The risk, however, was that Congress could favor certain states over other states—such as, say, Northern states over Southern states.

After his colleagues had talked themselves out, unable to reach agreement, Pope stood back up with his Illinois bill, to which he now, step three, urged a brilliantly crafted, perfectly timed amendment regarding its northern border. As originally proposed, the bill called for a northern border that was "an east and west line, drawn through a point ten miles north of the southern extreme of Lake Michigan." Though this boundary differed from that stipulated in the Northwest Ordinance (a line extending from the southernmost point of Lake Michigan), it was identical to the northern border Congress had recently created for neighboring Indiana. Why had Congress made this change? Why were ten miles of frontage on Lake Michigan more important in 1818 (or, in Indiana's case, 1816) than in 1787?

They were more important because, in 1817, New York had begun construction of the Erie Canal. In offering his amendment to a bill he himself had written, Pope addressed the issue that Congress had just debated—slavery:

> If [Illinois's] commerce is to be confined to ... the Mississippi ...
> there is a possibility that her commercial relations with the South
> may become so connected that, in the event of an attempted dis-

memberment of the Union, Illinois will cast her lot with the southern states. On the other hand, to fix the northern boundary of Illinois upon such a parallel of latitude as would give to the state the territorial jurisdiction over the southern shores of Lake Michigan, would be to unite [Illinois] ... to Indiana, Ohio, Pennsylvania, and New York. By the adoption of such a [boundary] line, Illinois may become, at some future time, the keystone to the perpetuity of the Union.[4]

Diversion of waterways in Illinois

Though access via the Great Lakes to the Erie Canal, which would further bind Illinois to the Union, was the primary reason Pope sought to relocate Illinois's northern border, he went on to discuss *another* canal. This was step four. He spoke of creating a canal that would connect Lake Michigan and the Illinois River. Combined with other canals being discussed in Illinois, the northern half of the state's waterways could be diverted from the Mississippi River and the South to the Erie Canal and the North. A potential harbor for this idea existed on Lake Michigan by having the canals connect to a small waterway called the Chicago River.

The land needed for these proposed canals was already included in the bill, by virtue of the northern border having been relocated ten miles north of the southern end of Lake Michigan. The amendment Pope proposed sought to relocate that border even further north—nearly sixty miles north of the tip of Lake Michigan. What, other than land, would Illinois gain?

It would gain people (step five). Pope needed all the people he could get to satisfy the population requirement for statehood—a figure that, as seen six months later in the *Annals of Congress*, he had managed to bargain down by the time Illinois had completed its statehood convention and submitted its proposed constitution to Congress for approval and admission as a state:

> MR. SPENCER, of New York, inquired whether it appeared from any
> documents ... that [Illinois] had the number of inhabitants required
> by the law....
>   MR. ANDERSON, of Kentucky, said that the committee had no infor-
> mation on that subject before them.... He had ... himself seen in the
> newspapers evidence sufficient to satisfy him of the fact that the pop-
> ulation did amount to forty thousand souls, the number required.

But Pope needed those people for more than just statehood. Statehood,
as he well knew, would enable Illinois to challenge its federally mandated
prohibition of slavery, based on the "equal footing" clause in the Northwest
Ordinance. Pope was opposed to slavery. He knew he could reduce the risk
of Illinois's seeking to permit slavery with the additional voters living in
the swath of land he sought to lasso into the state—particularly if this swath
became connected, via canals, to Northern commerce.[5]

It didn't take a genius to foresee these events. Even at the time Congress
voted on Illinois statehood, the handwriting was on the wall—or, more specifically, on Illinois's proposed constitution. New York Congressman James
Tallmadge Jr. objected to the fact that the proposed constitution permitted
the renting of slaves from residents of other states. The clause was subsequently deleted and, on December 3, 1818, Illinois became a state.

But four years later, Illinois residents sought to amend the state's constitution to permit slavery. Then as now, Illinois's constitution could only
be amended if, by referendum, a majority of voters opted to have a constitutional convention. The referendum took place in September 1824, with the
whole nation watching. Philadelphia's *National Gazette* soon reported, "Our
readers will recollect that ... the people of Illinois were to determine whether
they would have a convention for amending their state constitution, or in
other words, whether they would introduce slavery into that free state. The
question has been settled." The proposed convention garnered 1,410 votes
in favor; 2,593 opposed. At that time, the population of the region Pope had
added to Illinois was approximately 1,000. Their predominantly antislavery
votes were indeed needed.

Nathaniel Pope was by then Judge Pope, having been appointed to the
U.S. District Court for Illinois in 1819. He served in that capacity for the rest
of his life. Twenty years into that service, he saw the northern border of Illi-

nois back in the news. "We had a fine breeze in the House of Representatives on Tuesday last, growing out of the introduction of the Wisconsin resolutions ... to settle and ascertain the line between Illinois and Wisconsin," the *Milwaukee Sentinel* reported in February 1840. Wisconsin's nonvoting delegate had argued "that no change could take place [in the Northwest Ordinance boundary] without the mutual consent of [Wisconsin].... Consequently, the northeast corner of the state of Illinois is at the southerly bend or extreme of Lake Michigan." To say the border "is at," rather than "should be at," reflected the location of the newspaper. Congress, being located elsewhere, referred the question to the Judiciary Committee, which never responded—this being one of the traditional strategies of congressional committees. Meanwhile, many residents of Wisconsin continued to insist on what they viewed as their legal right to that land, threatening a Supreme Court challenge and even secession. Other residents told them to hush up, not wanting to rock Wisconsin's boat as it sought to navigate its own way to statehood. Ultimately, Wisconsin hushed up.[6]

Also ultimately, the union of states did rupture into the Civil War. Nathaniel Pope, however, did not witness that turn of events. He died on January 22, 1850.

Six months prior to his passing, Judge Pope received, as he often did, a request for a letter of recommendation:

> Dear Sir:
> I do not know that it would, but I can well enough conceive that it might, embarrass you now to give a letter recommending me for the General Land Office.... Having at last concluded to be an applicant, I have thought ... to show the influences which brought me to the conclusion.
>
> Your obedient servant,
A. Lincoln.

Abraham Lincoln did not get that job. In time he got a better one, in which he saved the Union, whose frail future Nathaniel Pope had sought to ensure. During the Civil War, the Union army was aided in no small part by more than 256,000 soldiers from the state of Illinois.

JOHN HARDEMAN WALKER
Putting the Boot Heel on Missouri

> The bill coming before the House for admitting us [Missouri] into
> the union ... lops off that part of the boundary ... between the White
> River and 36°30′ north latitude and west of the river St. Francis....
> The enemies to our prosperity ... [believe] the new state should have
> a pretty, geometrical appearance on the map.
>
> —*Jackson* [Missouri] *Herald*, September 4, 1819

No private citizen has left a more obvious irregularity in the shape
of a state than John Hardeman Walker, the man responsible for
the "boot heel" of Missouri. Not only did he succeed in altering the
southern boundary of Missouri that Congress was contemplating, but he did
so in his early twenties.

Already known as "the czar of the St. Francis River Valley," Walker owned
extensive amounts of land emanating
west of present-day Caruthersville,
Missouri. When Missouri was preparing for statehood, Walker realized
that the southern boundary being
proposed would put his land below
Missouri, in what would later become
the state of Arkansas. As the map
makes clear, he did not want that.

Why did Walker care? Slavery
would not have been his motive since
Missouri, which already had slavery, was seeking admission as a slave
state. Some historians have speculated that he may have been impatient

John Hardeman Walker (1794–1860)

The boot heel of Missouri

to be part of a state, with its attendant voting rights.¹ Indeed, the far less-populated region of Arkansas would not become a state for another fifteen years. He himself never said. But actions he took throughout his life reveal that John Hardeman Walker understood raw power.

Walker did not come from a powerful or wealthy family. His pioneering family had left Kentucky in 1809 and moved to a small village, Little Prairie, on the western bank of the Mississippi. Today Little Prairie no longer exists. "The bank of the river where the village stood," he later reminisced, "has washed away near three quarters of a mile back … so that the happy scenes of my boyish days are extinct."²

The Walkers were the only English-speaking family in Little Prairie. Their neighbors were French settlers from the days, only recently ended by the Louisiana Purchase, when France owned the land. Walker became close friends with a townsman named Jean-Baptiste Zegon. Together they would go on hunting expeditions, during the last of which Walker's land acquisitions were made possible.

On December 16, 1811, Walker and Zegon were hunting across the Mississippi River in the wilderness of western Tennessee. In the middle of the night, as Walker later recalled,

> We were awakened by a noise like distant thunder, and a trembling of the earth, which brought us both to our feet. The dash of the water against the bank of the lake, and rattling of the limbs in the tree-tops—now and then the falling of a dry branch in the water, or near us on the ground—all these things first led me to believe there was a storm approaching. But no. There was not a breath of air stirring.… It soon became still. My friend said, "May be, he is de shake of de earth."

It was indeed an earthquake, the first of several that, in 1811 and 1812, devastated parts of what are today Missouri, Iowa, Arkansas, Kentucky, and Tennessee.

Making their way through forests where no traces could be found of the paths along which they'd come, Walker and Zegon eventually arrived at the point on the river across from their village. There, Walker tells us, his friend's face "turned pale as death. The cause was soon visible. No smoke arose from the chimneys of our habitations, and not a single human being could be seen." After fashioning a raft and crossing, they discovered that all the homesteads lay in shambles and that everyone had fled. They encountered only a neighbor, returning to assess the damage, followed by Walker's father, desperate to find his son.

The French inhabitants of Little Prairie, determining that the structures were beyond repair, and knowing they were destined to become a minority now that their land had become part of the United States, opted to migrate to Canada. The Walkers returned to Kentucky, but John came back some months later, despite the fact that earthquakes and aftershocks were continuing. The unsteady ground presented a desolate landscape, absent of all but a few human beings, though evidence of their former presence remained scattered about—not the least of which was their cattle, now roaming free. In one of the greatest examples in American history of "Finders, keepers / Losers, weepers," Walker took possession of the land and the cattle, enclosing the herds in far-reaching barriers he fashioned using the rivers and streams. He was, in his own words, "the natural heir to Little Prairie."[3]

Land that Walker wanted but didn't "inherit" he purchased at rock-bottom prices from owners who had opted, like those of Little Prairie, to leave the area, or whose livelihoods had evaporated in their absence. Walker's holdings quickly spread west toward the St. Francis River.

Anyone who, as Walker demonstrated, so intuitively understood power would also have foreseen that Missouri would become the most powerful state in the region. It had access to the two most important rivers in the American hinterland (the Mississippi and the Missouri) and possessed the land where they converged: St. Louis. Not surprisingly, Walker's efforts to include his land in Missouri commenced immediately after its initial petition for statehood. This 1817 document, circulated and signed primarily by citizens in the vicinity of St. Louis, proposed a southern border that simply extended the line that ran across the bottom of Virginia and Kentucky at (with some irregularities) 36°30'.[4] Had it been adopted, this proposal would have put Walker's land in Arkansas.

The following year, Missouri's territorial legislature passed its own proposal for statehood. It sought far more extensive boundaries, includ-

Missouri legislature's proposal

ing the region where Walker owned land, along with additional land below 36°30′. Clearly, residents of those regions had persuaded the legislature to rethink the citizens' proposal. Yet between the time of the legislature's 1818 proposal and the enactment of statehood by Congress in 1819, the area below 36°30′ was reduced to include only Walker's region between the Mississippi and St. Francis Rivers.

Looking back some years later, Missouri Senator George W. Carleton spoke of how Walker had met with the people who would define the boundaries and so eloquently stated the reasons his region was more properly part of Missouri that he succeeded in persuading them.[5] Nonpoliticians remembered things differently. The *Kansas City Star* reported that, after convincing the territorial legislature to propose boundaries including his land, Walker went to Washington "with his old, muzzle-loading shotgun, not with any intention probably of ridding the country of any budding statesmen, but just to let them know at the capital that he was in earnest." More likely is that Walker relied on something other than a shotgun or eloquence to convince the lawmakers, something neither party would want recorded—such as money. Indeed, no record of this wealthy landowner's presence in Washington has been found in any newspapers or in any annals of Congress, despite the fact that shotguns in Congress were newsworthy even then, and eloquent reasoning is not something lobbyists keep private.

The debate in Congress over Missouri statehood suggests how Walker could have operated without attracting attention. It was highly emotional, touching on the nation's very existence. At issue was slavery in the states to be created out of the Louisiana Purchase. What ultimately resulted was the Missouri Compromise, prohibiting slavery in any new territory or state north of 36°30′, with the exception (this being the compromise) of Missouri. In the newspapers and the halls of Congress, attention was closely focused on this issue, thereby enabling Walker to go about his particular business unnoticed. Indeed, the only time the debate turned to the "boot heel" being appended to Missouri's southern border was when Rhode Island Senator

James Burrill Jr. declared, "With respect to the boundaries of the new state, I desire more definite information.... By a certain bill which has been laid on our desk by mistake, it appears that certain other boundaries have been thought of, and I wish to know the cause of this variation of boundaries." The record shows no response being provided.

Immediately after Missouri became a state, Walker made his first public appearance in the political arena. He became the sheriff in his neck of the woods, New Madrid County. He was just twenty-four years old. He went on to be the county's presiding judge and later created the city plan for the town of Caruthersville, close by where Little Prairie had been. There he lived out his days and is buried alongside the Methodist church.

JOHN QUINCY ADAMS
The Massachusetts Texan

Mr. Onis ... was willing that the boundary line with the United States should extend to the South Sea [Pacific Ocean].... [But] we would yield something of the western line we had proposed ... that she might have a barrier for Santa Fe. I told him ... if Spain had come to the determination ... to begin the line at the Sabine ... I could not express the disgust with which I was forced to carry on a correspondence with him upon subjects which it was ascertained that we could not adjust.

—SECRETARY OF STATE JOHN QUINCY ADAMS[1]

John Quincy Adams is widely remembered for the use of his middle name, distinguishing him from his more famous father, who is widely remembered for doing the things the Founding Fathers did. One thing the Founding Fathers indisputably did was to leave the next generation a tough act to follow. This challenge was vividly illustrated in the life stories of John Adams's three sons: one rose to become, like his father, a president; the other two failed to sustain successful careers and died as alcoholics.

As this second generation moved into the presidential ranks, the major rival to John Quincy Adams was Andrew Jackson. Adams was seen as representing the upper class from which all the previous presidents had come, and even as a bit monarchical, being the eldest son of a president. Jackson, on the other hand, represented the prototypical American, newly minted by democracy, whose citizens possessed no class (in both senses of the phrase). Both men, however, despite their differences, played key roles in establishing what is today the eastern border of Texas.

The event that ultimately resulted in today's eastern border of Texas was the Louisiana Purchase. When President Thomas Jefferson acquired this region from France in 1803, John Quincy Adams was a thirty-six-year-old senator from Massachusetts and Andrew Jackson, the same age, was a judge in Tennessee. The document conveying the land described its boundaries as being "the Colony or Province of Louisiana with the same extent that it has now." Other than the Mississippi River and the Gulf of Mexico, the extent of the "Colony or Province of Louisiana" was debatable at the time with both Spain to the west and England to the north. Sixteen years would pass before those borders were finally specified.

A primary reason for the delay was the fact that the young United States and England were still not on the best of terms, particularly when relations deteriorated into the War of 1812. Spain, therefore, was in no hurry to dicker, figuring it would do better if it waited, aided the British here and there, and then negotiated its border with a bruised and battered United States.

Adams and Jackson, meanwhile, were taking on increasingly significant roles in what would ultimately determine that Spanish border. Jackson, now a general, became a national hero for his victory during the war at the Battle of New Orleans. Technically, his victory was *after* the war since, unbeknownst to him, the war had ended two weeks earlier when American emissary John Quincy Adams negotiated the Treaty of Ghent.

Ironically, Spain was now far more battered and bruised. Between 1810 and 1819 (the year of the treaty creating the present-day eastern border of Texas), Spain lost control of Paraguay, Uruguay, Argentina, and Chile. More important, in terms of the United States, twice during this period the United States seized portions of Spanish Florida. At the outset of the war, the Florida Panhandle had extended all the way to the banks of the Mississippi River opposite New Orleans; by the time Adams had concluded the Treaty of Ghent, the Panhandle ended underneath Alabama, where it remains today.

John Quincy Adams (1767–1848)

With its empire in the Americas beginning to crumble, Spain decided the time had come to reduce the extent of its colonial claims in order to shore up what remained. Thus in 1818 it commenced negotiations over where the Louisiana Purchase ended and the Spanish colony of Mexico began. To give itself leverage in that negotiation while, at the same time, reducing its colonial claims, Spain also offered to sell Florida to the United States as part of the deal.

The United States, meanwhile, had emerged from the War of 1812 far less battered than Spain had hoped. Its new president, James Monroe, was even preparing to draw a boundary around *all* the Americas, in effect posting a sign—the Monroe Doctrine—saying "Europe Keep Out." The text of the doctrine would be written by the man with whom Spain was now to negotiate, Secretary of State John Quincy Adams.

Adams and his Spanish counterpart, Don Luis de Onís González Lopez y Vara, had barely said their hellos when Andrew Jackson came crashing through. General Jackson was in Florida, where he had just crushed a rebellion by the Seminole Indians. He had been authorized to cross into Florida, a Spanish possession, since the United States maintained that Spain had not lived up to its agreed-upon obligation to stop Indians in its colony from crossing into the United States to engage in attacks. Jackson now moved his troops to Pensacola—where there were no rebellious Seminoles but there *was* Spain's principal fortification—and conquered the fort. He then quickly took control of the Florida Panhandle, claiming it was necessary to keep the Seminoles subdued.

"Last night I received a note from the Spanish Minister," Adams wrote to President Monroe, "requesting an interview on affairs of the last importance to Spain and the United States."[2] Señor de Onís was furious: General Jackson's attack was an act of war. Spain demanded to know if the president had authorized the general's actions. If the president had not, Spain demanded to know what the president intended to do to General Jackson.

The diplomat in Adams viewed Jackson as a loose cannon. In his journal he wrote that the general's actions in Florida were "embarrassing." Still, the politician in Adams recognized shrewdness in those same actions, further noting in his journal that if one publicly criticized what Jackson had done, one would "give offense to his friends, [and] encounter the shock of his popularity." Most significant, the secretary of state in Adams noted a valuable nugget in the dustup: Spain, not having retaliated, was apparently weaker than the United States had thought.[3]

Adams consequently decided to stake out an ambitious opening bid in his negotiations over the border. "I would henceforth never recede an inch from the [Rio] Bravo," he wrote, referring to the river now known as the Rio Grande, which he proposed as the new southern boundary of the United States.[4] This boundary would follow the Rio Grande to its source in the Rocky

Mountains, then follow the Rockies north to the Colorado River, then follow the Colorado River to the Gulf of California. In 1848 all this would become part of the United States (with the exception of Baja California). In 1818, however, it was a hefty opening bid.

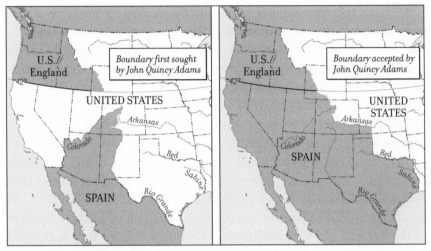

Adams-Onis Treaty, 1819

Amazingly, Onís did not immediately say no. Adams's reading of Jackson's actions in Florida and the reactions to them had been accurate. Realizing that the Americans perceived its weakness, Spain sought to cover up by claiming that when Adams had referred to the Colorado River, they had thought that meant the Red River. "How this mistake could have been made is inconceivable to us," Adams wrote, in conferring with the U.S ambassador in Spain, "inasmuch as we know of no maps which call the Red River of Natchitoches the Colorado."[5] The Colorado River and the Red River, being on opposite sides of the Rockies, would make for rather different borders.

Jackson, meanwhile, remained in hot water, facing a congressional investigation into whether or not he had disobeyed orders. Though he and Adams were both eyeing the 1824 presidential election, no personal enmity yet existed. Adams invited Jackson to dine at his home, an invitation Jackson declined, saying that he was accepting no social engagements during the investigation. Shortly thereafter, Jackson made a point of apologizing for declining the invitation.

Regarding the situation with Spain, Adams and Jackson continued not only to work well together but to see eye to eye. "I called on General Jackson,"

Adams wrote in his diary, "and mentioned in confidence to him the state of the negotiations with the Spanish Minister, and what we had offered him for the western boundary, and asked what he thought of it." The two men continued these discussions the following day at Adams's home, where they could speak more privately.

Adams and Onís proposed and counterproposed for another twelve months as they honed in on a boundary, much of which remains today in the eastern border of Texas. Adams's eventual success, which helped propel his nomination for president in 1824, was due in no small measure to the assist he had received from Jackson's adventure in Florida. Jackson's military successes likewise propelled his nomination in the same election. Still, their relations remained good—so good that Adams and his wife hosted a ball in Jackson's honor in January of that year, to help refute the view that Jackson was uncouth and slovenly. "It is the universal opinion," Mrs. Adams wrote afterward, "that nothing has ever equaled this party here, either in brilliancy of the preparation or elegance of the company."[6]

Two other candidates ran in the 1824 presidential election: Speaker of the House Henry Clay and Treasury Secretary William H. Crawford. As it turned out, none of the four received the necessary majority of votes in the Electoral College, so the decision went to the House of Representatives. Despite the fact that Jackson had won the plurality of electoral votes, the House chose John Quincy Adams.

The political manipulations behind this decision set the stage for an Adams-Jackson rematch in the 1828 election. This was a campaign that set a new low for mudslinging, stooping even to insinuations regarding Jackson's wife. Today's campaigns look tame by comparison. This time around, Jackson won.

Then as now, the candidates were hardly as evil as the opposition's claims. Likewise, the mudslingers were not necessarily in the control of the candidates. Adams disclaimed any connection to the accusations made about Mrs. Jackson. Jackson, however, knew for a fact that Adams was responsible, according to press reports quoting "an anonymous source."[7] As for the truth, Adams lamented in his diary, "In the excitement of contested elections and of party spirit, judgment becomes the slave of will. Men of intelligence, talents, and even of integrity on other occasions, surrender themselves up to their passions."

The bottom line in politics is always a complicated line. In this case, we can actually see that complicated line. It is the eastern border of Texas.

SEQUOYAH
The Cherokee Line

Se-Quo-Ya, who invented the alphabet of the Cherokee language ...
what has become of this remarkable man?... Is he still alive? Or
does his venerable head repose beneath some unknown clod of the
grand prairie? These are questions that we cannot now satisfacto-
rily answer.

—*Emancipator and Weekly Chronicle*, December 4, 1844

T he fact that only one state line preserves a treaty with American
Indians reflects both the absence of respect for their lands and the
special status those treaties accorded each tribe—not of independent
nations, as the Cherokees maintained, but of "dependent domestic nations,"
as the Supreme Court ruled in *Cherokee Nation v. Georgia* (1831). Thus the
boundaries in Indian treaties are unaffected by state lines. The one state line
that does preserve a treaty with an
Indian nation is the line (bent, as it
happens) separating Arkansas and
Oklahoma. Among those responsible for this line was Sequoyah,
a man most remembered for his
development of written symbols for
the Cherokee language.

Sequoyah and his fellow Cherokee leaders were, in a sense, the
Founding Fathers of today's Cherokee Nation, whose land is now
in Oklahoma but had been in the
southern Appalachians and upper
Tennessee River Valley. European

Sequoyah (ca. 1767–ca. 1843)

Americans' Founding Fathers emerged when the progress of the colonists led to their quest for independence from the British. A similar progression also led to American Indians' quest for independence. Like our Founding Fathers, the Cherokee leaders shared both a desire for freedom and profound disagreements. Sequoyah, like Thomas Jefferson, was not only politically involved but also had a scholarly and inventive mind. Highly revered today, Sequoyah was also, in his own day, like Jefferson, highly reviled.

Sequoyah was not, however, the Cherokee Jefferson. Though many aspects of Sequoyah's story have been challenged as having been mythologized, Sequoyah was not, by any account, the son of a prominent father, as was Jefferson.[1] Sequoyah's father is traditionally said to have been a white man, this being the reason he was also known as George Guess. If so, his father most likely died or moved on, since Sequoyah never learned English.[2] Some maintain, however, that Sequoyah was a full-blooded Cherokee who added to his name that of a white man he had killed. According to this view, to assume that Sequoyah's identity as George Guess indicates he had a white father implies that his great linguistic achievement was racially enabled.[3]

Unlike Jefferson's, Sequoyah's early political ambitions are uncertain. What is certain is that politics then were as convoluted as politics today. It was Jefferson who commenced a policy to relocate Indian populations out beyond the Mississippi River, in the newly acquired Louisiana Purchase.[4] The Cherokee leaders disagreed on the issue of migration. Recognizing this (having experienced several similar fundamental disagreements), Jefferson sent a message to the leaders, stating:

> I understand by the speeches which you have delivered me that there
> is a difference of disposition among the people of ... your nation;
> some of them desiring to remain on their lands, to betake them-
> selves to agriculture ... while others, retaining their attachment
> to the hunter's life, and having little game on their present lands,
> are desirous to remove across the Mississippi.... Those who wish to
> remove are permitted to send an exploring party to reconnoiter the
> country on the waters of the Arkansas and White rivers.

Benevolence or ethnic cleansing? Paradoxically, it was a joining of the two—which is to say: politics.

Jefferson's effort had only partial success. Following the War of 1812, Congress appropriated funds to induce more Cherokees to move. Sequoyah was among the delegation of Cherokees who received a written offer from General Andrew Jackson. Sequoyah had fought under Jackson in a Cherokee regiment (the Cherokees having placed their bets on the Americans in response to their enemy, the Red Stick Creeks, having bet on the British). Jackson did not know Sequoyah, who had only been a private during the war. Nevertheless Sequoyah knew something of Jackson and was sufficiently regarded in his tribe to have been included in the delegation to meet with him. Jackson discovered, however, that the delegates were not high-level leaders. He reported to the secretary of war that "as the Cherokee delegates seemed doubtful as to the extent of their powers, this treaty has been concluded subject to the ratification of the Cherokee nation."

A year later, Jackson returned with a more aggressive agreement. Though Sequoyah was not a party to this treaty, its acceptance altered his life. This 1817 treaty offered a land swap in which the United States would "give to that part of the Cherokee nation, on the Arkansas, as much land on said river and White River as [the United States] have or may hereafter receive from the Cherokee nation east of the Mississippi." To Sequoyah, it seemed like a relatively good deal. Under the leadership of Oolooteka, known also as John Jolly, Sequoyah relocated to the area of present-day Russellville, Arkansas. Other Cherokee chiefs opposed the treaty and bitterly resented that Oolooteka allowed the federal government to divide the Cherokee leadership openly and geographically.[5] They sent a delegation to Washington, instructing them:

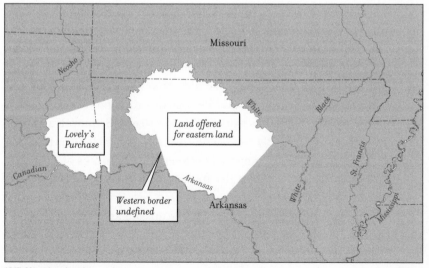

1817 Cherokee treaty

On your arrival at Washington city, you will deliver our letter to our elder brother, the Secretary of War.... You will state that ... we have of late years been subjected to the control of the minority of our nation.... Toolchair and others were sent to meet the commissioners with positive instructions to dispose of no lands but, contrary to his instructions, he entered into a conditional treaty ... [ratified] not by the whole Cherokee nation, as expressed by General Jackson in the ratification of that treaty but, on the contrary, there were six or seven headmen present who objected to the ratification of the treaty.[6]

The federal government, however, having achieved its objective, declared the treaty finished.

Sequoyah spent the next several years working, often with his daughter, on his longtime interest, the development of a set of symbols that would represent spoken Cherokee syllables. These efforts did not take place in a vacuum. During this era, missionaries were trying to develop a system that would transliterate the Cherokee language using Roman letters, as had been done by other missionaries with some Canadian and Alaskan tribes. Sequoyah too employed Roman letters, but in ways that bore no relation to their former role (indeed, they were often configured upside down or backward), and he invented additional symbols. Unlike the competing transliteration system of the missionaries, Sequoyah's syllabic approach was an instant success.

Except for the moment between "instant" and "success" when Sequoyah and his daughter were accused by their clan's shamans of fraudulently claiming magical powers—a serious offense. The two were placed in separate locations, and Sequoyah was told to use his magic pencil to make a particular statement. His interrogators then took this message to his daughter and asked her to tell them what it was. She did. After she wrote what they told her to, they took it to Sequoyah, and he repeated it. Then they demanded to be shown how the markings worked. Within weeks, Sequoyah's former accusers were teaching family and friends this new system for communication. Messages began being conveyed between the Cherokees of Arkansas and their brethren back east, who also immediately learned and taught each other to read.

Everyone was thrilled except, initially, the missionaries. While Sequoyah's creation clearly contributed to Cherokee literacy, it did so in a way that also contributed to Cherokee independence. "By the use of this alphabet," one missionary wrote, "so unlike any other, the Cherokees cut themselves from the sympathies and respect of the intelligent of other nations."[7]

As with the shamans, this pocket of dissension was quickly overwhelmed by an avalanche of admiration and support. By 1825 a report to the secretary of war stated that the Cherokees "are in advance of all other tribes. They may be considered as a civilized people. Their march has been rapid."

After acquiring special printing fonts, the Cherokees began churning out a tribal newspaper. Soon English-language newspapers were running stories about the new Cherokee alphabet. Sequoyah was now a national celebrity.

His fame coincided with increased conflicts with white settlers in the Arkansas land (to which they had agreed to migrate in order to escape such conflicts). Settlements were springing up in an area known as Lovely's Purchase. Years back, Indian agent William Lovely had bought land from the Osages (in a legally dubious transaction) to serve as buffer between the Cherokees who had accepted President Jefferson's invitation to migrate and the local, resentful Osages. By the time the 1817 treaty was signed, Lovely had passed away, but his widow, Persis Lovely, remained on their homestead. Hence, in the 1817 treaty, the United States promised that "all citizens of the United States, except P. Lovely, who is to remain where she lives during life, [will be] removed from within the bounds as above named." The federal government, however, was yet to fulfill its promise to remove the whites from within the stipulated boundaries.

Seeking enforcement of the treaty, the Cherokees sent a delegation to Washington in early 1828 that included, as a shrewd public relations move, their nationally known figure, Sequoyah. The delegates met in several sessions with the secretary of war and once with President John Quincy Adams. Sequoyah was a big hit. He was interviewed (via translators) by scholars and sat for his portrait. President Adams himself noted in his diary, "George Guess is the inventor of the Cherokee alphabet, by which, I told him, he had rendered a great service to his nation in opening to them a new fountain of knowledge." The only thing absent from everyone's good wishes to Sequoyah and his fellow Cherokees was any expression of enforcing the treaty.

Indeed, even when the government had been negotiating the 1817 treaty, plans were afoot for the future removal of the Cherokees from the land being promised. In 1816 Andrew Jackson's fellow negotiator, Jonathan Meigs Sr., wrote to the secretary of war:

> [The Cherokees] are aware, even if placed in the west of Arkansas, that they must probably make cession of lands to the United States in that

country, but they presume that they shall be less pressed on that subject there than here; and to guard against, or rather to provide for such
a contingency, it has been suggested to me by an intelligent Cherokee
that in allotting a tract of land for them ... to have only three definite
lines drawn to designate such allotment, leaving the boundary westward open as a wilderness, so that as they make cessions on the east
side, they may make proportionate advances on the west.

Quite possibly some Cherokees were aware of the government's plan; if not,
clearly the Arkansas chiefs suspected it, since they instructed the delegation
to Washington not to make any concessions of land.

Initially, President Adams advised his secretary of war as to how the
United States could squirm out of the treaty's obligations. He confided in
his diary:

[Secretary of War] Barbour called for a decision upon the application
of the Arkansas Cherokee Indians. Westward of the spot on which
they are located is a large tract which goes by the name of Lovely's
Purchase.... White people have discovered that the land is excellent and they are swarming thither like bees. They are covering
it with unlicensed settlements, and the people of the territory are
loudly claiming that the land should be offered for sale. This collision between the just and the reasonable demands of our own people
and the pledge seemingly given to the Indians is very embarrassing.
I observed, however, to Mr. Barbour that, as the pledge in its utmost
extent assured to the Indians only an outlet, or, in other words a right
of way, they might be informed that in the grants of lands upon Lovely's Purchase a right of peaceful way would be reserved for them.

The following week, Arkansas's territorial delegate (and future senator)
Ambrose Sevier complained to the president that the new treaty would be
the second time that the eastern end of Arkansas had been given to Indian
peoples. The first reduction, in 1824, had resulted from the fact that General
Jackson, making treaties right and left after the War of 1812, inadvertently
had granted to the Choctaws land upon which whites had already settled.
This second reduction resulted from a compromise that gave the Cherokees
the bulk of Lovely's Purchase. Under the proposed compromise, the upper
half of Arkansas's western border would shift eastward to the corner of Mis-

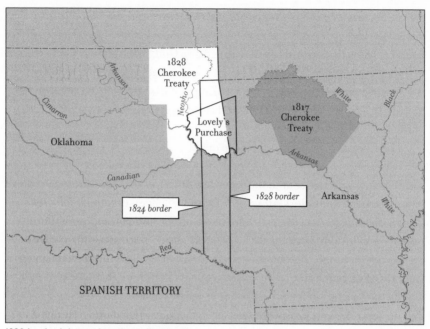

1828 treaty: Arkansas boundary adjustments

souri, then angle from that point through Lovely's Purchase to the Arkansas River (the southern extent of the Cherokee lands). The lower half of the Arkansas border would then also shift eastward to connect with the upper half, resulting in today's bent western border.

Arkansas's territorial delegate wasn't the only one who objected. The Cherokee delegates opposed the treaty as well. Their instructions were clear: get the government to abide by its promise to remove the whites from Lovely's Purchase and do not cede any land. But the government made it equally clear that it would only abide by that promise if the Cherokees moved further west.

Some of the delegates suggested that they simply go home. That too, however, had risks. The 1828 presidential campaign was in full swing. Jackson had been nominated for a rematch against Adams. Should Jackson win, the Cherokees would lose; Jackson was not a compromiser. If any of the English-speaking members of the Cherokee delegation read Washington's *Daily National Journal* while in town, they may have encountered its article on Jackson. Referring to the War of 1812 battle at Horseshoe Bend, when Jackson faced the British-allied Red Sticks, the article stated what the Cherokee delegates no doubt already knew: "The battle had ended—the poor untutored, misguided, and deluded savages had thrown down their arms and sued for mercy; but Jackson orders them to be exterminated; and keeps up the massacre until the shades of night stay the wave of human slaughter.... Cold is their bed of clay, while Jackson is worshipped as a God."[8] Many voters subscribed to the view of the *Carolina Observer* that Jackson had displayed patriotism "in the defense of his country ... controlling and directing the irregular valor of militia ... with which he chastised the cruelty and overawed the ferocity of the Indians."

The Cherokee delegates took the deal.

When news of the treaty reached the Arkansas Cherokees, the esteem in which Sequoyah had been held evaporated. To say that the Cherokees were upset would be an understatement. "Poles have been erected," the *Arkansas Gazette* reported, "in front of the houses of the delegation, on which their heads are to be exhibited as soon as they return." Learning of this, Sequoyah did not go home. He sought refuge among the Cherokees still living in Georgia.[9] By October there were news reports that, though anger still pulsed among the Arkansas Cherokees, some delegates had begun drifting back and had not been killed. Sequoyah, too, eventually returned and migrated west with his people to the land accorded them in the new treaty.

Sequoyah lived quietly from then on, venturing into political affairs only when the eastern Cherokees, forced to the reservation in 1838, vied with their western predecessors for dominance. He contributed to the drafting of an 1839 Cherokee constitution, hoping it—words on paper—would resolve the feud. It didn't. Only time did.

In the spring of 1842, the now elderly Sequoyah enlisted several companions to join him on a journey to Mexico. There he sought to find Cherokees with whom contact had been lost. This branch, having foreseen a future of loss in the United States, had migrated to land controlled by Spain, believing their chances there would be better. Age and illness pursued Sequoyah, but in August of the following year he and his companions found a Cherokee village near the present-day town of Zaragoza, Mexico, fifteen miles southeast of El Paso. There he connected with brethren who predated the rift between the eastern and western tribes and who welcomed him wholeheartedly. Several days later, he died among them. Shortly before he passed away, Sequoyah wrote a letter home. But his final message has been lost.

STEVENS T. MASON
The Toledo War

Never in the course of my life have I known a controversy of which
all the right was so clearly on one side, and all the power so overwhelmingly on the other.

—JOHN QUINCY ADAMS[1]

Michigan officially became a state on January 26, 1837, yet its state
seal bears the date 1835. The discrepancy represents the period
during which Stevens T. Mason led the self-declared state in what
has come to be called the Toledo War.

The seed of this dispute was inadvertently planted by Congress in 1787,
when it stipulated how the Northwest Territory would eventually be divided
into states. Among those boundaries was one that divided "the said [North-
west] territory which lies north of an east-and-west line drawn through the
southerly bend or extreme of Lake
Michigan." Unfortunately, Congress was using an inaccurate map.[2]
If an accurate map had been available, the stipulated line would have
put Toledo in Michigan, had Toledo
existed in 1787. As American commerce on the Great Lakes swiftly
increased, however, Toledo not only
came into existence, it brought Ohio
and Michigan to the brink of war.

In 1802 a hunter told delegates
to Ohio's statehood convention that
he believed Lake Michigan extended
considerably farther south, so much

Stevens T. Mason (1811–1843)

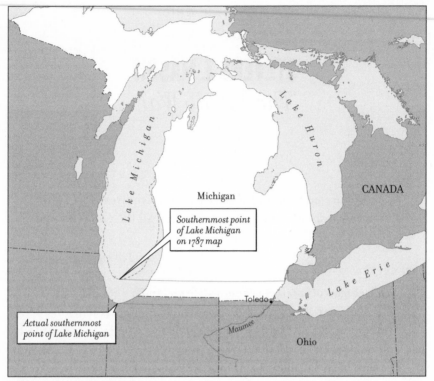

Toledo, Ohio, or Toledo, Michigan?

so that Toledo, whose first white settlers had arrived eight years earlier, might be in the territory to be created north of Ohio.[3] Since no one knew for sure the latitude at which Lake Michigan ended, or the latitude at which the Maumee River (known then as the Miami River) emptied into Lake Erie, the delegates defined Ohio's northern border slightly differently than in the 1787 Northwest Ordinance. They stipulated it as being "a direct line running from the southern extremity of Lake Michigan to the most northerly cape of the Miami Bay." Congress was aware of this alteration in wording, as was President Thomas Jefferson, who had authored the report that led to the boundaries specified in the Northwest Ordinance. Given the uncertainties, however, a report jointly issued by his administration and Congress concluded that it was "unnecessary to take it at this time into consideration."[4]

Meanwhile, Americans were beginning to migrate to the region above Ohio in larger numbers, and in 1805 Congress created the territory of Michigan. Yet twelve more years were to pass before Michigan challenged Ohio's boundary adjustment. Why so long? Possibly because of another event that took place in 1817, the year their boundary dispute commenced. Construction began that year on the Erie Canal.

Toledo, at the western end of Lake Erie, was now of such importance that Michigan's territorial governor, Lewis Cass, wrote to the surveyor general, "Report says that the line which has been recently run, purporting to be the line between the State of Ohio and this Territory, was not run [along] a due east course from the southern extremity of Lake Michigan to Lake Erie, but a course somewhat to the north of this, although how much I am unable to ascertain." Cass went on to cite the boundary mandated by the Northwest Ordinance, then said of the altered boundary in Ohio's constitution, "This proposition has never been acceded to by Congress … [and] no agreement, even by that body, without our consent, could alter these lines."[5]

The fact remained, however, that Congress had approved the constitution of Ohio with the boundaries it had stipulated.[6] But also a fact was that the Northwest Ordinance mandated that the "following articles shall be considered as articles of compact between the original states and the people, and states in the said territory, and forever remain unalterable, unless by common consent." Cass's letter resulted in a second survey of the Michigan-Ohio boundary. The first survey, to which he'd referred in his letter, came to be known as the Harris Line. It followed the boundary stipulated in the constitution of Ohio. The second survey, which came to known as the Fulton Line, conformed to the boundary stipulated in the Northwest Ordinance. Both surveys were then presented to Congress. It did nothing.

For nearly twenty years the issue remained an open wound before an infection entered, in the form of a second canal. "It will doubtless be gratifying to your readers," a correspondent for Washington, DC's *National Intelligencer* wrote, "to learn that another navigable communication between

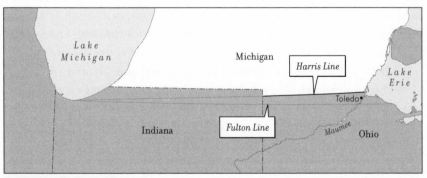

Conflicting federal survey lines

the Ohio River and the Northern Lakes has been commenced, and is now in progress of actual construction. This canal ... extends from the head of steamboat navigation on the Wabash River to the Maumee Bay."

The Wabash and Erie Canal would connect the Great Lakes to the Gulf of Mexico via the Maumee, Wabash, Ohio, and Mississippi Rivers. Its entry point on the Great Lakes was Toledo. During the commencement of its construction in the early 1830s, Michigan's population reached the point at which it could seek to become a state—a fact whose significance was not lost on Ohio. "This subject is particularly interesting at this time," Ohio's *Scioto Gazette* reported, "from the obvious necessity to Ohio that Maumee Bay, which will be the future termination of the Wabash and Erie Canal, should be included in the limits of this state."

Since Congress had never responded to the two conflicting surveys, Ohio's legislature upped its claim over the disputed region by enacting legislation in early 1835 (the year engraved in Michigan's crest) that created counties within the region. Six weeks later, Michigan's territorial legislature enacted the Pains and Penalties Act, making it a criminal offense for anyone other than officers of the Michigan Territory or the United States to exercise official functions in the disputed region.

The fight was on: Stevens Thomson Mason, Michigan's twenty-three-year-old territorial governor, versus Ohio's Governor Robert Lucas.

Mason came from a distinguished Virginia family. He was the great-grandson of Thomson Mason, who had been chief justice of the Virginia Supreme Court and whose brother, George Mason, was the author of the Virginia Declaration of Rights (the direct inspiration for the U.S. Bill of Rights). He had arrived in Michigan in 1830 after President Andrew Jackson appointed his father, John Mason, as secretary of the territory. John Mason resigned after a year to pursue a purported business venture in Mexico. The venture may in fact have been a secret mission for President Jackson, as it closely followed a meeting with Jackson (at which the younger Mason was present) and as Jackson then appointed Mason's then nineteen-year-old son to take his place.[7]

Whether or not the appointment was a political quid pro quo, the people of Michigan were not pleased. A citizens' committee passed a resolution stating that the "great responsibility and trust ... conferred on Stevens Thomson Mason, a minor, is ... derogatory to the freemen over whom he is thus attempted to be placed, and that we hold it to be our duty to take prompt measures with a view to his removal from office."[8] Jackson's appointment particularly galled the residents of Michigan because it coincided with Governor Cass's departure to become secretary of war and, as his replacement was yet to arrive, the teenage Mason would be in charge.

What the people of Michigan didn't know, but soon learned, was that young Mason was an extraordinarily talented individual. Public opinion changed as Mason deftly navigated the territory through difficulties involving the Black Hawk War during the absence of the new governor, George B. Porter. When Porter died in 1834, Mason became acting governor, now with considerable support as he led Michigan in its bid for statehood.

In 1835 Ohio Governor Lucas issued a directive to commence surveying in the newly created counties. In response, Michigan Governor Mason issued a directive, too. "The [Pains and Penalties Act] must be rigidly enforced," he directed the commander of Michigan's militia. "You are authorized to call to your aid, in the event that the *posse comitatus* of the sheriff should be insufficient, any assistance that may be required to resist the strength the military authorities of Ohio may bring against you."

President Jackson sought to dissipate the tension by submitting Michigan's Pains and Penalties Act to his attorney general for an opinion regarding the jurisdictional issues. Jackson's neutrality was suspect; the 1836 presidential election was just around the corner, and Jackson's favorite, Martin Van Buren, would need Ohio's electoral votes. Michigan, having no electoral votes, viewed Jackson's gesture as a clearly political gambit. But Michigan modified that view when Attorney General Benjamin Butler reported back that "the act of the legislature of Ohio extending the jurisdiction of that state over the Territory of Michigan is ... repugnant to the act of Congress."[9] Butler commented that Congress had the authority to determine the line, but that until it did so, "it will be the duty of the president to consider [the 1787 line] as the boundary of the Territory of Michigan."

The effect of the attorney general's opinion was to give Michigan the ammunition it needed to load—literally—the muskets of its militia. Three weeks later, Ohio's legislature, at the behest of Governor Lucas, appropriated $300,000 to equip and dispatch 500 troops to the disputed region.

President Jackson quickly dispatched two mediators to meet with the governors in April 1835, one of whom was the nation's preeminent diplomat, Richard Rush. The *Ohio State Journal* reported:

> Our last week's paper gave the gratifying intelligence, received at the hour of going to press, that all fears of disturbance in the disputed territory were for the present removed ... [due to] the advice

or instructions of the Commissioners, Messrs. Rush and [Benjamin C.] Howard.... But the scene has changed. On Wednesday night, at a late hour between twelve and three o'clock, a [Michigan] posse ... came to Toledo ... prowling about the streets and taking some of the citizens.... A number of the Toledians [*sic*] have been indicted for accepting office under Ohio law.

At this time Michigan began its self-declared statehood convention, amid continuing violence that included the stabbing death of a deputy sheriff.[10] The rhetoric of both governors reflected, if not abetted, the rage in the region. Ohio Governor Lucas declared to his legislature:

Some [residents of Toledo] have been driven from their houses in dread and terror, while others are menaced by the authorities of Michigan.... And for what? Is it for crime? No, but for faithfully discharging [one's] duty as a good citizen of Ohio.... The authorities of Michigan countenanced prosecutions against the citizens of Ohio ... with a degree of reckless vengeance scarcely paralleled in the history of civilized nations.

Governor Mason, for his part, declaimed:

Outrages of a most unjustifiable and unparalleled character have been committed by a number of persons at Toledo upon officers of the [Michigan] Territory.... A regular organization exists among these individuals for the purpose of resisting the execution of the laws of Michigan. If [Ohio] ... is permitted to dragoon us into a partial surrender of our jurisdiction ... the territorial government is at once annihilated. Criminals committing the highest offences are left at large.... All law is at an end.

Once again, President Jackson sought to defuse the situation. Twelve days after Mason's remarks, Jackson, abandoning any pretense of neutrality, fired him. In his place, Jackson dispatched John S. Horner. Like Mason, Horner came from Virginia and had never held political office. Once again, the people of Michigan were not pleased. The *Detroit Free Press* wrote in October 1836:

We have no hesitation in pronouncing what is almost the undivided sense of this community, that Mr. John S. Horner is utterly unqualified and unfit for the station in which he has been placed. We trust, however, that the forbearance of the people of Michigan will continue to be exercised for the few remaining days of their territorial existence. On the first Monday in next month, they become a state; they will then have their own executive, legislature, and other public officers. They will then take care of their own rights and interests, protect their territorial possessions, punish the transgressors of their laws and repel invasion.

Indeed, on the first Monday of the next month (November 2, 1835), voters in Michigan elected Stevens T. Mason governor of the state of Michigan—a state not recognized as such by the United States. Territorial Governor Horner and the new state government treated each other equally: he didn't recognize them, and they didn't recognize him.

Congress, at this point, finally took action. It approved statehood for Michigan with one big *if*: "Be it enacted that the constitution and State Government which the people of Michigan have formed for themselves be ... accepted, ratified, and ... declared to be one of the United States," the legislation stated, "provided always—and this admission is upon the express condition—that the said State shall consist of ... the following boundaries." The boundaries that followed conformed to Ohio's stipulated border—but they also included a peninsula extending eastward from what would later become Wisconsin. Michigan could take the deal, or hold out and remain a territory. If it held out, however, its boundary claim would now have an added hurdle: an act of Congress.

For Ohio, the issue was finished. Governor Lucas closed the book on the conflict, telling his legislature:

It is with peculiar pleasure that I announce to you the irrevocable establishment of the northern boundary line of Ohio, in accordance with what we have ever considered our incontrovertible right.... The assent of Congress has ... removed all grounds for contention, and put a final quietus to the clamorous pretensions of the authorities of Michigan.

In Michigan, Governor Mason said to his legislature:

No one can feel more deeply than myself the humiliation of the sacrifice we are called upon to make.... Were I to consult the first impulse prompted by the feeling which every citizen of Michigan must acknowledge, I might be led into a determination to resist the legislation of Congress. But as a public officer called upon to discard excited feelings ... I should violate my duty did I recommend to my fellow citizens to embark in a controversy offering so little hope of gain.

Accordingly, in September 1836, Michigan reconvened its constitutional convention. But the delegates rejected the offer from Congress. The "state" of Michigan seemed headed for a state of limbo. It didn't take long, however, for a sufficient number of Michigan's residents to recognize that they had painted themselves into a corner. In December a new constitutional convention accepted the terms demanded by Congress. Six weeks after that, Michigan entered the union.

As passions subsided, so too did the esteem in which Stevens T. Mason had been held. The legislature had voted to raise funds for roads and canals through the sale of bonds, for which Mason had entered into agreements with brokers just as the Panic of 1837 sent the nation into an economic depression. Funds had been committed based on the bonds, but with the sale of the bonds stalled by the depression, Governor Mason was held aloft as Michigan's leading scapegoat in the 1840 election and was not reelected.[11]

Months later, Mason moved with his wife to her hometown, New York City, where he practiced law. His career was cut short when he died of pneumonia at the age of thirty-one. But Stevens T. Mason was not to be forgotten. In the aftermath of the Civil War, the people of Michigan dusted off his reputation. His speech to the legislature when Michigan faced its ultimatum from Congress now conveyed its full meaning:

To preserve unstained the institutions of our country is one of the first duties of every citizen. Will we hazard these stakes now, or will we present to the world an example of compromise of opinion and feeling, dictated by a spirit of patriotic forbearance, even when injustice demands it? The federal government was the great work of a spirit of compromise, and it is only by the exercise of the same spirit by the states that it is to be perpetuated.

In 1905 Mason's remains were moved to Capitol Park in Detroit, where a statue was erected of Michigan's first elected governor.

ROBERT LUCAS
Ohio Boundary Champ Takes on Missouri and Minnesota

Ex-Governor Lucas [of Ohio] is one of the most deserving men in the party, and we doubt not will prove a good Governor of the new Territory [of Iowa]. He is far from being a brawling supporter of the administration. He is an old fashioned, honest, intelligent, western pioneer.
—CLEVELAND *DAILY HERALD*, JULY 16, 1838

When Colonel of the regiment and something younger than he is now, Lucas seduced a young lady, who sued him for breach of marriage contract and got judgment against him, and when he had put all his property out of his hands so that nothing could be got, he was put to jail for the debt, and then issued his orders for his regiment to come and rescue him from the custody of the law.
—LETTER TO THE EDITOR, *SCIOTO GAZETTE* (CHILLICOTHE, OH), SEPTEMBER 26, 1832

Robert Lucas (1781–1853)

Whether or not Robert Lucas was a wily scamp or an honest western pioneer—or matured from the one to become the other—this much is certain: he was a tough opponent. As governor of Ohio, he had led the state through its boundary dispute with the territory of Michigan and—despite the fact that Ohio claimed a boundary that violated what Congress had stipulated—Lucas won. When Lucas then became governor of the territory of Iowa, he inherited a nearly identical boundary dispute with Missouri—except that now *his* was the powerless territory challenging a formidable state. As if that contest were not enough, Lucas also sought a boundary with what would become Minnesota that triggered a conflict influencing the borders of seven future states.

The foot Lucas first set in Iowa in 1838 was the wrong foot. He and the territory's legislature were immediately at odds. "Strife has arisen between Gov. Lucas and the Iowa Territorial legislature on the question of power," the *Cleveland Herald* informed his former constituents in Ohio. "The Governor insists that all laws and resolutions must be approved by him before they are of any force. The Legislative body contests this position ... [and] all public business is delayed in consequence."

Lucas was not one to back down. But neither were Iowa's legislators. Six months after Lucas took office, an item in the *New York Spectator* revealed the progress these like-minded personalities had made: "The difficulties between [Iowa's territorial legislature] and Governor Lucas have resulted in an application from the former to the President of the United States, praying for the removal of the latter from office."

The brawl between Lucas and his territorial legislature subsided, however, when a bigger brawl presented itself in which they could join together: a boundary dispute with Missouri that was a mirror image of the dispute Lucas had faced with Michigan when he was governor of Ohio. What Iowa was disputing was Missouri's interpretation of the boundary stipulated by Congress in 1820. It defined Missouri's northern border as (fasten your seat belts) "the parallel of latitude which passes through the rapids of the River Des Moines, making the said line to correspond with the Indian boundary line; thence east from this point of intersection last aforesaid, along the same parallel of latitude to the middle of the channel of the main fork of the said River Des Moines."

Helpfully for readers (though not for Iowans), a line along these lines

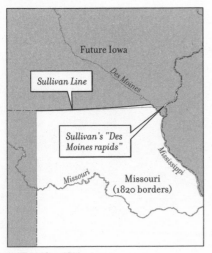

Sullivan Line, 1816

already existed. It had been surveyed four years earlier by John C. Sullivan. One can only call it "a line along these lines" because the boundary stipulated by Congress contained uncertainties. The first uncertainty was that a line starting at the point on the "parallel of latitude which passes through the rapids of the River Des Moines" be made "to correspond with the Indian boundary line," since the two were not necessarily the same. The second was the phrase "the rapids of the River Des Moines." While it clearly seems to mean the rapids in the Des Moines River, the fact is that there are no rapids in the Des Moines River. At the time, however, there were rapids in the Mississippi River as it met the Des Moines River. This segment of the Mississippi had long been known by river men as "the Des Moines rapids." Sullivan used these rapids in the Mississippi to determine his starting point at the western end, then surveyed eastward. As he proceeded, however, his line veered northward. Whether this deviation resulted from poor surveying or from making his line "correspond with the Indian boundary line" was yet another uncertainty, since no line in the vicinity had been stipulated in any American Indian treaty at or before 1816.

The Sullivan Line was not the line Governor Lucas challenged, but its uncertainties set the stage for the dispute. In 1836 Congress added to Missouri what is today the triangular region in its northwest corner. This region comprised all the land north of the Missouri River up to a westward extension of the state's northern border. Missouri then appointed Joseph C. Brown to survey the northern border of this new region. Unlike Sullivan, he interpreted "the rapids in the River Des Moines" literally. Though hard-pressed to

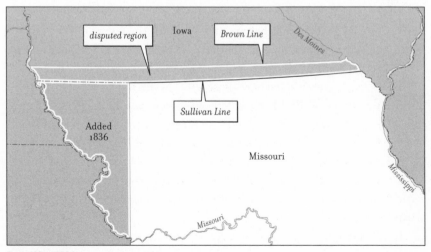

Brown Line, 1836

find anything resembling rapids in the Des Moines River, Brown ultimately decided that a point in the river known as "Big Bend" constituted the closest thing to rapids, and he used that point to determine the latitude of the border. He then marked off this updated border. Unlike Sullivan's, Brown's line was nice and straight. It was also considerably further north.

Two years later, Lucas arrived in Iowa and immediately challenged the boundary. His opening move was the same as that of his former boundary adversary, Michigan, in its failed challenge of Ohio. Lucas got Iowa's legislature to pass a virtually identical resolution:

> If any person shall exercise or attempt to exercise any official functions ... by virtue of any commission or authority not derived from this Territory or under the Government of the United States ... [he shall] be punished by a fine not exceeding one thousand dollars, or imprisoned ... not exceeding five years.... I do hereby enjoin ... all sheriffs, constables, Justices of the Peace, and other peace officers ... that they cause all persons ... attempting to violate any of the provisions of the act ... to be arrested.

But after enactment of the same kind of resolution, Lucas departed from Michigan's approach. Where Michigan's territorial governor, Stevens T. Mason, had remained confrontational, Lucas led the territory of Iowa in the opposite direction. "I know of no difficulty between the Territory of Iowa and the State of Missouri," he said to his legislature, then continued coyly, "Neither can the Territory of Iowa, as a territory, be party to a controversy. The territorial government being entirely under the control of the United States, the controversy about the southern boundary of the Territory of Iowa is between the State of Missouri and the General Government."

Lucas may have sounded here like a wily lawyer, but he was not an attorney. He was not even highly educated. Wily, however, he was. One of nine sons of pioneer parents who had migrated from Virginia to what would soon become Ohio, his schooling had consisted of what he learned from his family, augmented by basic lessons in mathematics and surveying from a tutor. Clearly, however, as he entered adulthood, Lucas continued to learn from those he encountered. Clearly, also, he had a lot of learning to do—particularly with regard to authority.

In 1810 an Ohio court had ordered the twenty-nine-year-old Lucas to pay damages emanating from a breach of promise to a young woman. Lucas sought to outfox the authorities by divesting himself of his assets and publicly dared the sheriff to arrest him. The sheriff thought it best to resign. The official to whom the task then fell also resigned, as did a third. Now, however, the issue was larger than Lucas; it was about the rule of law. A new group of Ohioans sought and won the vacated positions and collectively hauled Lucas off to jail. Lucas, a colonel in the state's militia, ordered his men to come rescue him. They didn't. He then quickly paid and, as he later stated, learned his lesson.

That Lucas had learned to obey authority was demonstrated during the War of 1812. He led a unit that was part of an effort to invade Canada. After the commanding general ordered the troops to pull back, Lucas obeyed, though he strongly disagreed with the order. He wrote to a close friend, "Never was there a more patriotic army ... that had it more completely in their power to have accomplished every object of their desire than the present—and it must now be sunk in disgrace for want of a General at their head." Such a letter carried considerable risk, were it to fall into the wrong hands, but evidently not enough risk for young Lucas, who added, "Neither was there ever men of talents as there are, so shamefully opposed by imbecile or treacherous commander."[1]

The Lucas Iowans now heard proclaiming, at age fifty-eight, "I know of no difficulty between the Territory of Iowa and the State of Missouri," was a far smarter Lucas. But underneath he was the same. What he had learned over the years wasn't simply how to cope with more powerful adversaries, but how to win.

How to win in this instance, however, involved considerable uncertainty. While the Articles of Confederation had stated that Congress was to issue decisions on boundary disputes, the Constitution (which replaced that document) said nothing on the subject. Today boundary disputes between states are routinely adjudicated by the Supreme Court, but by 1839 the court had heard only two such cases, neither providing much confidence about that approach.[2] Lucas, in a message to his legislature, opted to butter up Congress:

> Michigan contended that, as a Territory, she was a party to the controversy relative to the boundary between that Territory and the State of Ohio—she denied to Congress the right to act on the subject.... The Territory of Iowa, in the present controversy considers herself entirely under the control of the General Government and ... considers that Congress is the only competent tribunal to decide the controversy with the State of Missouri.

Lucas went on to stroke Congress in this message by saying he believed it had supremacy over the Supreme Court in rulings on such disputes.

On the other hand, he also silently sought to lay the groundwork for approaching the Supreme Court, urging Iowa's territorial legislature to seek statehood to redress "the unwarrantable and unjustifiable proceedings of the authorities of Missouri."[3] As a territory, Iowa could not take a dispute to the Supreme Court, since its boundaries, unlike those of a state, were not protected by the Constitution. Lucas, however, said nothing specifically about urging statehood to enable Iowa to approach the Supreme Court. If he privately shared such a strategy with Iowans, he failed to convince them. The legislature opted not to seek statehood, given that the territory was not yet sufficiently populated for the additional costs entailed.

This setback was not a problem for Lucas, since his first gambit was with Congress. One might wonder, however, what hope he had with this approach; Missouri had two senators and three representatives in that Congress, and the Iowa Territory had none. Lucas's hope was best expressed in Missouri itself, a slave state in which one of its senators, arguing that Congress did not have authority to decide the issue, fretted that "if Congress had settlement of this affair, I feel confident that all the free states would range themselves on the side of Iowa—and perhaps some of the slave states, from a feeling of jealousy created by the magnitude of our state."[4]

As it turned out, Lucas miscalculated. Though legislation was proposed stating that Congress had intended Missouri's northern border to be in accordance with the Sullivan Line, the bill failed to pass.[5]

Iowa became a state in 1846. Immediately, it took its dispute with Missouri to the Supreme Court. Lucas, however, was no longer the governor. Having been appointed by President Martin Van Buren, a fellow Democrat, he was replaced when William Henry Harrison, from the Whig Party, entered the White House in 1841. Lucas, however, had laid the groundwork for the legal challenge by having previously disputed the boundary and, with his early statehood proposal, having signaled plan B. In 1848 the Supreme Court issued its ruling. Iowa's *Burlington Gazette* reported that "the long existing difficulty between this State and Missouri is at last settled by the highest judicial tribunal known to the land—settled, too, we are happy to add, in favor of Iowa. The decision of the Supreme Court ... establishes the old Indian boundary line, as it is called, as the boundary of Missouri."

Most of those Iowans who had clamored for Lucas's removal at the outset of his governorship had come to the see him differently by the time he was replaced. "No man has ever been more true to his trust—none more faithful to the interests of the people over whom he governed," the *Gazette* now wrote. "The people of this Territory will be struck with astonishment to find that their old and trusted friend, Gov. Lucas, has been displaced."

Though he had been replaced, he was not so easily displaced. Lucas and his family remained in Iowa, and in 1844 he was elected as a delegate to the territory's statehood convention. Serving on its Committee on State Boundaries, Lucas continued an effort he had begun as governor regarding Iowa's border with its future neighbor to the north, Minnesota. In this instance, however, the boundary champ got knocked out.

Lucas had described the boundaries he envisioned for Iowa when he first urged its legislature to seek statehood. The lines he proposed were those of present-day Iowa, with the exception of its northern border. Lucas had sought a northern border composed of waterways leading to the Mississippi and Missouri Rivers (long-distance railroads still being two decades away). At the statehood convention, his committee again proposed such a border, but this time further north, being entirely framed by the Minnesota River (known then as the St. Peter River).

In Congress, Iowa's proposed northern border encountered unexpected and stiff opposition. Ohio Congressman Samuel F. Vinton, an influential member of the House Public Lands Committee, noted that Iowa's proposed boundaries resulted in a state similar in size to Illinois, Indiana, and Michigan. He pointed out that those states' borders were created for political reasons that violated Thomas Jefferson's vision for equitable representation in the Senate (see "Thomas Jefferson" in this book). Regarding Iowa (and other future states), Vinton argued:

> What has been the effect of this change? ... The vast and fertile region between the Ohio, the Lakes, and the Mississippi has been thus reduced from twelve to fourteen States to five at the most ... [that] can never have but ten votes in the Senate.... As an equitable compensation to the western country for this flagrant injustice, I would make a series of small States on the opposite bank of the [Mississippi] river.

Vinton then sought to move Iowa's proposed northern border from the Min-

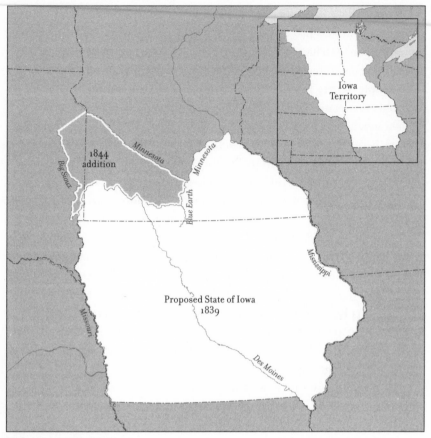

Borders proposed by Lucas

nesota River to the 43rd parallel. Iowa's nonvoting delegate, Augustus Dodge, strenuously but unsuccessfully opposed the shift, calling the new boundary "an artificial line."

Was it artificial? As ultimately passed, Iowa's northern border was a line set at 43°30′, resulting in the state having just under three degrees of height. Over the ensuing decades, Congress would go on to create a tier of prairie states just west of Iowa, each of which had three degrees of height (Kansas, Nebraska, South Dakota, and North Dakota). Just west of those states, Congress created a tier of states in the less populous Rocky Mountain region, each of which had four degrees of height (Colorado, Wyoming, and Montana).

Congressman Vinton's argument had been so powerful it not only affected Iowa's northern border but also brought Jefferson's underlying principle back into the equation for defining state lines. Iowa may have lost the boundary it sought, but it acquired the distinction of being the lynchpin in determining the next phase of the American map.

When Iowa became a state, Robert Lucas hoped to become its first elected governor. But he was now sixty-five years old, and a new generation had come of age. Iowa's Democratic Party instead nominated forty-one-year-old Ansel Briggs, who went on to win the election. Lucas's political career had come to its close, with one last exception. In 1852, the year before his death, he announced his departure from the Democratic Party, following its nomination of Franklin Pierce, a proslavery Northerner. The seventy-two-year-old Lucas, who had entered the Democratic Party as a young stalwart of Andrew Jackson, could no longer associate himself with the party when even its northern members veered further toward proslavery views for political purposes. Though Robert Lucas's tactics were wily, his principles were not.

DANIEL WEBSTER
Maine's Border:
The Devil in Daniel Webster

The [human] race, if it cannot drag a Webster along with it, leaves him behind and forgets him. The race is rich enough to afford to do without the greatest intellects God ever let the Devil buy.

—WENDELL PHILLIPS[1]

Those who know of Daniel Webster typically know of him only from being assigned to read "The Devil and Daniel Webster" or from having seen the film it spawned. Stephen Vincent Benét's fanciful short story posits Webster as the defense attorney for a man who has signed a pact with the devil; Webster wins the case even though the devil gets to pick the judge and jury.

Webster was indeed a great lawyer. He argued more than 200 cases before the Supreme Court and became the preeminent debater in the U.S. Senate. He was also a bit of a devil himself.

Those unfamiliar with Webster can take comfort in the fact that in September 1852 the *Daily Ohio Statesman* headlined an article on the then longtime political veteran, "Who Is Daniel Webster?" Everyone at that time knew his name, but few knew what—other than oratory—he had done.

Webster served for over twenty-three years as a senator from Massachusetts, was the secretary of state twice, and sought the presidency three times. While he never made

Daniel Webster (1782–1852)

it to the White House, his work as secretary of state is engraved on today's map in the boundary between Maine and Canada.

One might think that Maine's boundary would have been established in the treaty ending the American Revolution, thus defining the borders of this new nation England was relinquishing and recognizing. Americans thought it did, as the 1783 Treaty of Paris indeed devoted an entire section to boundaries. It divided Maine from Canada along "a line drawn due north from the source of St. Croix River to the highlands, along the said highlands which divide those rivers that empty themselves into the river St. Lawrence from those which fall into the Atlantic Ocean to the northwestern-most head of Connecticut River." Other than determining which rivers flow where, what was left to discuss?

Nothing ... until the War of 1812 caused England to rethink the line. The narrow strip of land it left between the American border and England's primary route into Canada, the St. Lawrence River, was highly vulnerable to attack—particularly in the winter when the river froze, closing off navigation.

Daniel Webster was a rookie congressman when England first sought to redefine Maine's boundary. In 1814, during negotiations to bring the War of 1812 to a close, British negotiators complained:

> With respect to the boundary of the District of Maine ... [we] regret that, although the American plenipotentiaries have acknowledged themselves to be instructed to discuss a revision of the boundary line, with a view to prevent uncertainty and dispute, yet by assuming ... an exclusive right to determine what is or not a subject of uncertainty and dispute, they have rendered their powers nugatory.

It being wartime, the British had called Americans all kinds of things. But "nugatory" was below the belt, and the Americans let them know it:

> The proposal of the British plenipotentiaries was not to ascertain, but to vary those lines in such a manner as to secure a direct communication between Quebec and Halifax, an alteration which could not be effected without a cession by the United States to Great Britain of all that portion of [Maine] ... intervening between the provinces of New Brunswick and Quebec, although unquestionably included within the boundary line.

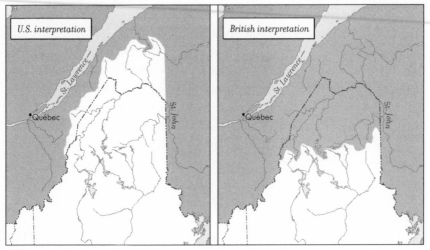

1783 treaty: border of Maine

The Americans allowed that, if the British wanted the two nations to survey the as-yet-unmarked line through the sparsely settled forests, any discrepancies could then be negotiated. Consequently, the line was surveyed in 1817, and indeed a discrepancy surfaced. The United States interpreted the 1783 treaty's phrase "highlands which divide those rivers that empty themselves into the river St. Lawrence from those which fall into the Atlantic" as the ridge separating the two watersheds. England interpreted the preceding phrase leading up to the word "highlands"—"a line drawn due north from the source of St. Croix River to the highlands"—as meaning a line due north to the *highest land*.[2]

The treaty ending the War of 1812 stipulated that boundary disputes could be arbitrated by a third nation agreeable to both sides. Most likely, the United States would have prevailed in arbitration, but it suddenly had cause to hesitate, owing to another glitch recently discovered elsewhere along the U.S.-Canadian border. "The line between New York and Canada on Lake Champlain," the *National Intelligencer* reported, "will leave Rouse's Point, on which the United States have expended between two and three hundred thousand dollars in fortifications, within the British province." The fort being built was located on a site long accepted as being on the south side of New York's border with Canada. But the surveys that followed the War of 1812 revealed the fort was actually on the border's north side.

"Fort Blunder," as it came to be called, was no minor military outpost. It commanded the northern entrance to Lake Champlain, a lake that

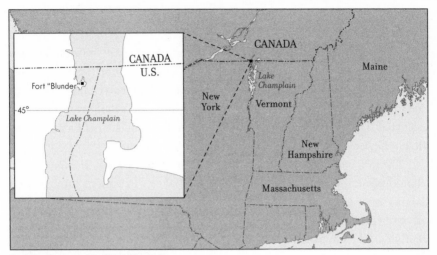

Fort Montgomery, aka "Fort Blunder"

extends far into New York and Vermont. The fort's importance for defense was equaled only by its importance as a danger if it were to end up in British hands. The Maine boundary negotiations were now profoundly changed. "A proposal has been discussed," the *Intelligencer* reported, "that the territory that would accrue to Maine be given as an offset for the fine military station on the Lake, which would be confirmed to New York. Our friends in Maine think the Commissioners have no right to run the line agreeably to the proposed compromise, and loudly protest against it."

From this point on, the reality was that the U.S. government was no longer negotiating with England; it was negotiating with the District of Maine. And Maine (which gained statehood in 1820) wasn't budging. Indeed, Maine became more militant, as a report from New Brunswick "to the King's Most Excellent Majesty ... humbly sheweth." The report informed British authorities that "a senator of the state of Maine ... came into this province and seized and marked a quantity of pine timber lying in the river St. John ... as having been cut on the river Restook, in the territory of the United States.... In the last year, 1825 ... [Maine issued deeds] to the settlers in this territory ... [for] one hundred acres each of the land by them possessed."[3]

Maine, in response, further sought to force the federal government to intervene on its behalf by ridiculing New Brunswick's appeal to its mother country. "Our neighbors in New Brunswick," Maine's *Thomaston Register* wrote, "feel quite warlike on the subject of the northeastern boundary.... They appear to think their masters in England have no other interest to protect.... But [England] ... has nothing to gain and much to lose by another contest with us."

Angered by this taunting, New Brunswick bit the bait. "John Baker, the citizen of Maine who was lately seized by the British authorities and carried to Frederickton [New Brunswick], was indicted ... on two charges amounting to Treason against the king of England," Vermont's *Burlington Messenger* reported. The acts of treason the newspaper cited consisted of Baker having flown the American flag and "resisted a British officer."

The U.S. government did not bite the bait. "Some young, discreet lawyer should be sent into New Brunswick to see Baker," President John Quincy Adams wrote in his diary, aware that there was more to the story than reported in the press. Baker, Adams noted, had been imprisoned "for stopping the British mail from passing over the land on which he was settled, within the disputed territory."

Baker wasn't the only American whose behavior was making life difficult for the president. The governor of Maine contributed, too, as Adams confided to this diary:

[April 28, 1827] A letter from Enoch Lincoln, Governor of the State of Maine ... is querulous, testy, and suspicious.... The tendency of all this is to multiply the difficulties of the negotiation.

[November 26, 1827] Lincoln's letters are absurd and provoking; and he is deeply infected with a disease which many of the Governors of the States are apt to catch—wanton assailing of the General Government, overweening zeal for the interests of the State.

When Maine's governor then activated the state's militia, Adams finally had no choice but to respond, and dispatched U.S. troops to Maine.

But Adams simultaneously made movements in the other direction as well, using the crisis to justify allowing the king of Holland to arbitrate the dispute. In 1831 King William I specified a compromise line that sought to split the difference between the American and British positions.

Maine responded by changing its strategy. It now maintained its boundary claims were part of a larger national issue: states' rights.[4] By aligning itself with slave states that were asserting states' rights to resist federal restrictions on slavery, Maine succeeded in getting the Senate to reject the Dutch king's decision. Consequently, the situation continued to smolder. Seven years later the smolders began to flame. In March 1839 the *Boston Atlas* reported:

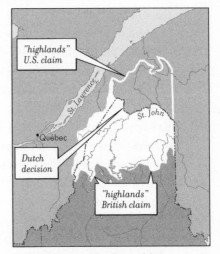

Northern Maine: arbitration decision

> A detachment of 26 [American] men, sent ... to break up a horde of trespassers on the Fish River has returned, having succeeded in their object.... [Maine] Gov. Fairfield is urging forward his militia with great zeal. In addition to the 700 enlisted men on the Aroostook, [militia] Gen. Hudson's brigade of 1000 men at Houlton, and Gen. Batchelder's brigade of 1000 who are on the march from Augusta, another 1000 are under orders to march.... It is rumored that 5000 British troops ... left Frederickton on the 23rd for the disputed territory.

Through the skillful intervention of U.S. General Winfield Scott and his British counterpart, no one died in what has come to be known as the Aroostook War (or, more incongruously, the Pork and Beans War). It did, however, result in two indisputable facts. First, a verdict on the boundary could no longer be postponed. Second, getting Maine to agree on a verdict would require a courtroom magician. The United States had one: Daniel Webster.

During the years that Maine's boundary dispute had been simmering, Webster had been orating his way to an 1836 presidential bid. Americans found him spellbinding. "No man has been found tall enough to overshadow him," Washington, DC's *National Intelligencer* exclaimed. "No man has been able to attract or intercept from him the constant regard of the nation, for he has been so conspicuous, so prominent, that whatever he has done, and whatever he has said, has been watched and understood throughout the borders of the land."

Webster's flair for speaking, however, was a component of an exuberant personality that also resulted in rumors of excessive drinking, of large sums of money having been given to him by wealthy merchants and bankers, and of womanizing.[5] Running in a field of five presidential candidates, Webster wound up with less than 3 percent of the vote.

In the next presidential election, candidate William Henry Harrison offered candidate Webster the vice presidency, in an effort to consolidate his bid. Webster declined, stating "I do not propose to be buried until I am really dead."[6] Still, rather than fruitlessly oppose Harrison in the 1840 election, Webster accepted the popular general's alternate offer of secretary of state. (Had Webster accepted the vice presidency, he would have become the president when Harrison died thirty-two days after his inauguration.)

In the wake of the 1839 Aroostook War, Maine's boundary with Canada became one of Secretary Webster's top priorities. England, equally anxious to end the dispute, sent Lord Ashburton to Washington as its negotiator. It was as shrewd a choice on England's part as Webster would prove to be on the American side. Lord Ashburton's family owned Barings Bank. Webster had performed legal services for Barings. The two men knew each other and liked each other. So informally did they proceed that, when the treaty they created was sent to Senate for ratification, Senator Thomas Hart Benton complained that he had never before seen a treaty accompanied by so little documentation.[7] The dearth of supporting documents, however, was not the result of a cozy relationship. Rather, it resulted from the fact that Webster was negotiating primarily with Maine—invisibly.

To tilt public opinion, Webster began with the press. The State Department budget set aside $17,000 for "secret service" regarding the boundary negotiations.[8] The money was used to fund a public relations campaign aimed at placing stories in newspapers and other publications.

It worked. In December 1841, as the nation awaited the arrival of Lord Ashburton, the *Christian Mirror* proposed a possible compromise that was extraordinarily detailed. After laying out what was purportedly its own proposal, the article pointedly concluded, "Is there a citizen of Maine who will not, upon careful meditation, pronounce such a compromise honorable to both parties, advantageous to both parties, and founded in a just regard for the wants and rights of the respective parties?"

The *National Intelligencer*, whose coverage of political events in Washington was often picked up by newspapers nationwide, published numerous editorials favoring a compromise. These editorials were rumored to have been written by Webster himself, a close friend of one of the paper's publishers. One such editorial, quite likely written by Webster, appeared in July 1842:

Rumors are afloat concerning the supposed terms of adjustment of the Northeastern Boundary question which we rather think—

indeed, we may almost say we know—are calculated to mislead the public mind.... It is not unlikely, we learn, that the line which the Dutch arbiter decided for ... will be agreed to. But then Maine gets what the Dutch king did not give her, the navigation of the [St. John] River, and this trebles the value of all her tall pine trees.

The editorial went on to detail other trade-offs, including:

England takes a tract of mountain land, untimbered and of no earthly value but as a boundary, and she relinquishes to the United States Rouse's Point, the key of Lake Champlain, and a large territory heretofore supposed to belong to New York and Vermont, but which turns out to lie north of the 45th degree of latitude and is therefore a part of Canada.

From the newspaper's point of view, it got a scoop. Webster got to dish it out.

In time, even Maine's *Augusta Age*, while remaining ardently opposed to any boundary compromise, was now conceding, "We do not deny that very many candid and honest men are numbered among the friends of the treaty; men, too, of the highest intelligence, and every way entitled to respect."

To persuade Maine itself, Webster employed a different approach: cartographic blackmail. Webster learned of two maps on which red lines had been drawn that conformed to the British interpretation of the Treaty of Paris. The lines had purportedly been drawn by Benjamin Franklin and John Jay, two of the key American negotiators. While questions could be raised as to whether Franklin and Jay had personally drawn the red lines, there was no question as to the maps' authenticity. One had belonged to Friedrich von Steuben, the Prussian general who had provided invaluable assistance to the Americans in the Revolutionary War; the other was in a French archive, also a nation allied with the Americans in that war.[9] Webster secretly sent word of the maps to Maine's governor, threatening that their existence would be made public if Maine did not accede to a compromise. Soon papers were reporting, along with the *New York Spectator*, "It is satisfactory to learn that the legislature of Maine is proceeding rapidly and judiciously in measures ... that will enable the general Government to effect an arrangement with Lord Ashburton."

Judiciously, perhaps. Rapidly for sure. Four months after Lord Ashburton arrived in the United States, the Senate ratified the Webster-Ashburton

Treaty, establishing the boundaries of Maine at their present-day location.[10]

Webster went on to make yet another bid for the presidency, this time in 1852. Because of the treaty he had managed to secure, he had reason to hope this election would be the one to put him in the White House. But he now had an additional liability: he was seventy, older than any first-term president ever elected. He lost the Whig nomination to Winfield Scott, who in turn lost in November to Franklin Pierce. By then, however, Webster was dead. In May 1852 he had sustained a head injury in a carriage accident. His recovery was hindered by cirrhosis of the liver.[11] Daniel Webster died in late October, nine days before the election.

Upon his death, the American philosopher Ralph Waldo Emerson, visiting the site of one of Webster's greatest speeches, wrote in his journal:

> Last Sunday I was at Plymouth.... I supposed Webster must have passed, as indeed he had died at three in the morning. The sea, the rocks, the woods, gave no sign that America and the world had lost the completest man.

Yet, on another occasion, Emerson had said of Webster:

> It was for his defect in moral perceptions, for the inequality of his moral to his intellectual faculty ... that hence came the sterility of thought.... It is a curious fact that though he wrote and spoke with an ability that impresses the world, there is not a single remarkable sentence, not a single valuable aphorism which can pass into literature from his writing.[12]

Both observations were true.

JAMES K. POLK
Fifty-Four Forty or Fight!

> On the nomination of Mr. Polk we hardly know what to say. A more
> ridiculous, contemptible and forlorn candidate was never put forth
> by any party.... Mr. Polk is sort of a fourth or rather fortieth-rate
> lawyer and small politician in Tennessee.
> —*NEW YORK HERALD*, MAY 31, 1844

W hat, if anything, is generally remembered about President James
K. Polk is that his campaign slogan was "Fifty-Four Forty or
Fight!" In fact, it wasn't. The issue (involving present-day Oregon,
Washington, and British Columbia) *was* central to his campaign, but there
is no evidence that the slogan existed at that time.[1]

During Polk's presidency, the American map changed dramatically, its
boundary expanding to include Texas, the Oregon Territory, and everything
in between, from the Rockies to the
Pacific. Many factors contributed to
the change, but a key element was
that, at critical moments, Polk was a
prodigious political poker player.

To follow how Polk's moves
resulted in these gains, we need to
know who else was at the table, since
each player's strategy affected the
others. Following his election in
1844, Polk found himself in a high-
stakes game already in progress
that included Mexico, Britain, and,
reflecting public opinion, Congress.
He also found himself having been

James K. Polk (1795–1849)

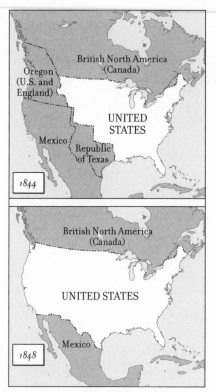

Oregon
(U.S. and
England)

British North America
(Canada)

UNITED
STATES

Mexico
Republic
of Texas

1844

British North America
(Canada)

UNITED STATES

Mexico

1848

United States when Polk entered office and when he left

dealt cards that were not particularly good.

In the case of Mexico, Polk began with a crisis over Texas. Texas had battled itself free from Mexico in 1836, though Mexico had not recognized its independence and therefore never agreed to particular borders. Texas claimed that its border with Mexico was the Rio Grande. But its southern border as a Mexican province had been farther north, at the Nueces River. Four days before Polk's inauguration, President John Tyler signed a congressional resolution admitting Texas to the Union, "subject to the adjustment by this government of all questions of boundary that may arise with other governments." Mexico, whose objections went considerably beyond "questions of boundary," recalled its ambassador during the first week of Polk's presidency, thus upping the ante on the prospect of war.

War with Mexico was not militarily intimidating, particularly since Mexico was in the midst of one of its many revolutions. War with Britain was another matter. And that possibility was another of the cards Polk had been dealt.

Until the presidential campaign that resulted in Polk's election, the United States and Britain had agreed to disagree about a boundary dividing the Oregon Country, a region far more vast than the present-day state of Oregon. Under an extension of a ten-year joint occupancy agreement included in the 1818 Anglo-American Convention negotiated by Richard Rush, Britain and United States shared the area bounded on the south by the 42nd parallel (below which, at that time, was Mexico), on the east by the crest of the Rocky Mountains, and on the north at 54°40' (the border with Russian Alaska that Britain negotiated in 1825). By the 1840s, the region's population had grown to the point that the United States and Britain picked up where they had left off in seeking to determine a boundary. The Tyler

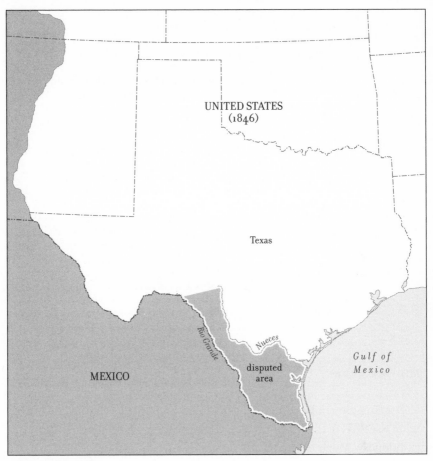

Texas: disputed border

administration proposed an extension of the 49th parallel—the line already in place from Minnesota to the Rockies. But the British sought a boundary farther south at the Columbia River.

Negotiations crept along cordially enough until the Democratic Party seized upon the issue as a possible means of defeating its formidable opponent in the upcoming election, Henry Clay. Clay's reputation was that of a creative compromiser, an invaluable skill in a nation fundamentally divided over the issue of slavery. The Democrats sought to outfox Clay by including in the party's platform a totally uncompromising position regarding Oregon. "Resolved, that our title to the whole of the Territory of Oregon is clear and unquestionable," it asserted, "that no portion of the same ought to be ceded to England or any other power."

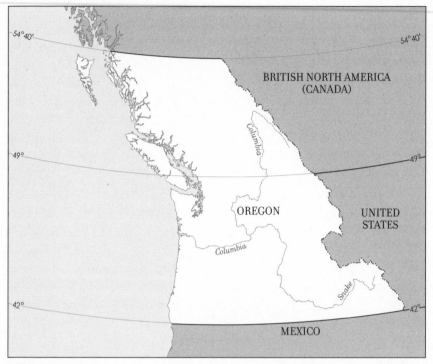

British-American Oregon

For this ploy to be effective, the public had to believe that the entire region was vital to the United States. Consequently, the Democrats beat this drum loudly. Much of the public responded to their alarm. To them, the Democrats had a clear vision regarding Oregon; Henry Clay's nuanced views were more ponderous. The Democrats won the White House.

But not the Democrat anyone expected. Seven candidates had vied for the party's nomination on the first ballot. Polk was not among them. Successive balloting failed to give any candidate a majority; none, however, would release his support to any opponent. Ultimately they chose to nominate someone who was no one's opponent (or hero), and who would publicly promise not to seek reelection if, by some fluke, he won. That candidate was former congressman and former Tennessee governor (twice defeated for reelection) James K. Polk. The fluke was the effectiveness of the Oregon issue.

Polk, for his part, had participated in the ploy and did believe expansion to the Pacific was vital to the nation's future. The ports provided by the Columbia River and, farther north, Puget Sound, would provide the nation with its only access to the Pacific Ocean (since California was still part of Mexico).

Polk thus took his seat at the table with Mexico threatening to go to war over Texas, and with an American public having provided him the seat through its support for his party's campaign to acquire the entire region of Oregon, which could mean war with Britain. In addition, he knew that the other players viewed him as a lightweight. The first thing Polk had to do, therefore, was change the way he was perceived. He needed to create the impression that he was somehow in possession of much stronger cards, or that he was wildly unpredictable. Either would do, since either would cause his opponents to take a step back. Polk made that first move in his inaugural address:

> The Republic of Texas has made known her desire to come into our Union.... I regard the question of annexation as belonging exclusively to the United States and Texas.... Foreign nations have no right to interfere.... Nor will it become in a less degree my duty to assert and maintain by all constitutional means the right of the United States to that portion of our territory which lies beyond the Rocky Mountains. Our title to the country of the Oregon is "clear and unquestionable."

That got Britain's attention, clearly fitting the category of wild and unpredictable. The *Liverpool Mercury* reported in April 1845:

> The Earl of Clarendon drew the attention of their Lordships to the inaugural address of the President of the United States respecting Texas and the Oregon territory, the language of which he described as characterized by a studied neglect of that courtesy and deference which governments were wont to observe when treating upon international affairs, and as leading to the inference that ... the only basis of negotiation was unconditional surrender by England of all that was claimed by America.

In achieving his initial objective with Britain, Polk limited his next move in terms of public opinion in the United States. "There has been an important debate in the British Parliament on the Oregon, disclosing the view of England on that subject," the *New York Herald* observed in April 1845. "We may now expect a serious difficulty between England and America. We do not see what is to prevent it. America has assumed her position, and England has now taken hers. Neither, therefore, can recede an inch."

Britain indeed did not recede but rather, turning to Mexico, raised the stakes by urging Mexico to go to war with the United States over Texas. "There are many considerations that militate in favour of the Mexicans," the *London Times* editorialized that same week. "Can anything exceed the dissatisfaction of the states of New England, or New York, or of Ohio, at having to meet the calls of war ... for the encouragement of slavery?... The military establishment of the United States is very well adapted to ... repel a foreign enemy.... But offensive and defensive war are two different things."

Mexico saw Britain's move and, three weeks later, added its chips. On May 7, 1845, its congress passed a resolution. "The unjust usurpation of which [the United States] sought to make Mexico the victim, makes it her duty to take up arms in her defense," it asserted, upping the ante by concluding, "The Mexican nation calls upon her sons to defend their national independence, threatened by the usurpation of the territory of Texas."[2]

It was Polk's turn again. What he needed now was room to maneuver, knowing he could not simultaneously take on two wars. In July he had Secretary of State James Buchanan make Britain an offer that gave him room to maneuver with U.S. public opinion, and time to do so by making it an offer Britain had to refuse. Polk achieved both with deceptive simplicity. He abandoned his campaign pledge (and inaugural address demand) that the United States was entitled to all of Oregon and returned to the previous administration's bid for a boundary that continued along the 49th parallel from the Rockies to the Pacific. Americans who preferred compromise to war were startled and impressed; Polk's militant supporters were startled and upset. Unnoticed by both groups was the absence, in Polk's proposal, of any mention of British access to the Columbia River. But the British noticed. The Columbia was a major artery of Britain's fur trade, conducted under the auspices of the Hudson's Bay Company. In addition, a line from the Rockies to the Pacific would divide Vancouver Island and its prized ports in the strait separating it from the mainland. Britain rejected Polk's proposal.

In the United States, Britain was now viewed as intractable. What wasn't viewed was the purpose of Polk's move—to make Americans view themselves as tractable. Polk had acquired the card he needed.

Later in the same month of July 1845, with Britain now pausing to reassess the U.S. president, Polk raised the stakes on Mexico. He ordered troops to cross the Nueces River, with those orders explicitly stating for the first time that the United States considered the Rio Grande to be the border between Texas and Mexico.

Britain, after considerable thought, opted to match this move. "In a short time," the *London Times* reported in November, "Admiral Seymour will be upon or near the coast of Oregon with one ship of 80, one of 50, one of 18, and one of 16 guns."

Within weeks Polk hedged his bet, sending Congressman John Slidell to Mexico with an offer to purchase Texas for as much as $40 million.[3] By hedging on Mexico, Polk caused Britain to ponder him yet again. Did war over Oregon amount to bluffing or not?

To make certain the British kept wondering, Polk used his December 2, 1845, State of the Union message (which he would later make further use of domestically) to ensure the uncertainty of his intentions. In speaking of Oregon, he repeatedly invoked the spirit of compromise while simultaneously raising the specter of war:

In consideration that propositions of compromise had been thrice made by two preceding Administrations ... and that the pending negotiation had been commenced on the basis of compromise, I deemed it to be my duty not to abruptly break it off.... A proposition was accordingly made which was rejected by the British.... All attempts at compromise having failed, it becomes the duty of Congress to consider what measures it may be proper to adopt ... for the maintenance of our just title to that territory.

Over in Britain, one thing was certain. It too had a militant faction that equated compromise with surrender. This faction was spearheaded by Lord Palmerston, a former foreign minister whose party no longer led Parliament. Prime Minister Robert Peel, like Polk, needed room to maneuver. In a parliamentary maneuver, Peel called Palmerston's bluff and won. Polk, in response to Peel's having marginalized Palmerston's opposition, sent word in January 1846 that if the British wished to make a counterproposal to his offer of the 49th parallel, he would send it to the Senate to hear its advice.

Meaning what? Britain, again having to contemplate this perplexing president, did nothing. One month later, Polk turned up the heat: the treaty of joint occupancy could be terminated twelve months after either nation served notice, and he urged Congress to serve notice.

The British Parliament was not the only legislature trying to figure out Polk. So was the U.S. Senate. If the clock ran out, what did the president plan to do? During a two-day period, Polk noted in his diary:

[March 4, 1846] Senator Hanegan of Indiana called.... He spoke of Mr. Haywood's speech in the Senate that day, in which he had undertaken to expound my views on the Oregon question, and seemed, without asking the direct question, to desire to know whether he was authorized to do so. I told him no one spoke *ex cathedra* for me, that my views were given in the annual message of the 2nd of December.... On going into my office I found Mr. Yulee & Mr. Lewis there and, as I anticipated, they had called to see me on the subject of Oregon. Unlike Mr. Hanegan, they expressed themselves to be greatly delighted at Mr. Haywood's speech in the Senate.... I repeated ... that my views were contained in my message of the 2nd of December.

[March 5, 1846] Senator Cass called this evening.... I told him my opinions on the Oregon question were contained in my annual message.

Louisiana Senator Alexander Barrow was among those who expressed befuddlement. To his fellow senators he declared:

We have before us a most extraordinary and, I must say, humiliating public spectacle.... We sit here as part of that great National Council which, along with the Executive, directs the affairs of this people.... Amongst us [the president] has a decided party majority, anxious to afford him support in all his measures. And yet ... his real purposes in the momentous questions before us ... are an enigma to his very adherents here, who cannot, for their lives, settle between them his true meaning and intention!

Like Prime Minister Peel, Polk had to outfox the leadership of his nation's militant faction. But for Polk that faction was in his own political party. Hence this move of asking Congress to start the clock ticking, while keeping them guessing his intentions if time ran out. As his White House encounters revealed, both sides assumed his ambiguity meant he was leaning toward them. On April 23 the Senate joined the House in voting to end the joint occupancy agreement.

It was not a moment too soon. Two days later, sixteen American soldiers were killed in a skirmish with Mexican troops. In early May Polk sent Congress a declaration of war.

The next move was Britain's. Which way would it go? The answer arrived on June 3. Britain would agree to the 49th parallel, but only from the Rockies to the main channel of the Juan de Fuca Strait, and only if the Hudson's Bay Company retained navigational rights to the Columbia River until the expiration of its charter in 1859.

Polk, as he'd promised, sent the proposal to the Senate but yet again flummoxed them by saying he planned to reject the proposal unless two-thirds of the Senate voted in its favor.[4] Polk then said nothing more on the subject, leaving the Senate to guess what that meant.

Militants in the Senate continued to oppose the proposed compromise, and those who had been opposed to war supported it. The critical votes would be from those less committed. Some, because of Polk's having just entered into a war with Mexico, voted for compromise, not wanting to fight two wars at once. Others opted for compromise, anticipating that Polk's silence and two-thirds request would tilt the field. The proposal thereby ended up being passed 37 to 12. Within weeks it became a treaty, which the Senate ratified 41 to 14.

Polk had not acquired all the Oregon territory his party had advocated in its campaign platform. But he had acquired all the territory that the previous president, also from his party, had unsuccessfully sought.

The Mexican War was brought to conclusion when the Treaty of Guadalupe Hidalgo brought what would become California, Nevada, Utah, and parts of what would become Wyoming, Colorado, New Mexico, and Arizona into the borders of the United States. The treaty was ratified on March 10, 1848, in the midst of the next presidential campaign.

James K. Polk, as promised, was not a candidate.

ROBERT M. T. HUNTER
Cutting Washington Down to Size

Virginia is ready to receive these people back into her bosom, and
they are ready and anxious to return. They desire to enjoy the rights
of men, the privileges of free men. Can the American Congress fail
to respect such a feeling?
                              —CONGRESSMAN ROBERT M. T. HUNTER[1]

In 1791 Andrew Ellicott and Benjamin Banneker marked off the boundaries of the District of Columbia: a square with ten-mile sides, straddling the Potomac River. It encompassed two municipalities (Georgetown and Alexandria), a federal enclave (Washington), and rural areas on either side of the Potomac (Alexandria County and Washington County).

Fifty-five years later, President James K. Polk signed away the entire section of the nation's capital on the Potomac's southern side, returning it to Virginia. In reaction, one newspaper in the North wrote:

District of Columbia, 1790–1846

The Senate has passed, by a
majority of more than two to
one, the bill which passed the
House the 8th of May, retroceding the city and county of Alexandria, D.C. to Virginia.

The Democrats of Maine
have nominated John W. Dana,
of Fryeburg, as their candidate
for governor.[2]

In the South, by comparison, a
Mississippi paper wrote:

In the Senate, on the 2nd inst., the bill taking the city of Alexandria from the District of Columbia and giving it to the State of Virginia passed.

In the House, on the 3rd, McKay's tariff bill passed.[3]

Hello? Was anyone paying attention?

This 1846 legislation was initiated by Virginia Congressman Robert M. T. Hunter. His success, however, culminated efforts that had begun more than forty years earlier. The seeming indifference of the press is misleading. It had been covering these efforts for decades. As early as 1803, Washington, DC's *National Intelligencer* reported on the problem of the federal government running the District of Columbia.[4] That year and the next, Congress vigorously debated the return of areas ceded to the federal government for the creation of a nation's capital. The *Annals of Congress* record that Virginia Congressman John Randolph "believed the interests of the several parts of the [District of Columbia] were as hostile as any in the Union, as it was manifest there was an Alexandria, a Georgetown, and a city interest.... He therefore thought it expedient to retrocede all the territory, excepting the City of Washington."

Robert M. T. Hunter (1809–1887)

While the preponderance of the speakers debated whether or not "retrocession" was constitutional, all agreed with Massachusetts Congressman John Bacon that "the exercise of exclusive legislation [for running the District of Columbia] would take up a great deal of time, and produce a great expense to the nation.... It was likely that as much time would be spent in legislating for this District as for the whole United States."

Years later, Hunter repeated Randolph's and Bacon's concerns, amplified now since they had become established facts:

We have three cities in this District, each aspiring to be great, and all desiring to open up communications to the sources of their trade.... They have shared unequally in the appropriations.... Go look at

[Alexandria's] declining commerce, her deserted buildings, and her almost forsaken harbor. Look to the waste of natural advantages and opportunities in that town, suffering not from the blight of God, but the neglect of man.... We have not done all that might have been done for those who depend upon us for the necessary care which this government alone can bestow.

Because Congress indeed had its hands full running the country, it had given scant and uneven attention to the District of Columbia. This, in turn, intensified the rivalry among the District's municipalities for congressional attention—particularly regarding commercial needs such as canals and bridges. "One of the early acts of this government ... was to throw a mole [dam] across from Mason's island to the south bank of the Potomac, and thus cut off the channel for boat communication between Alexandria and the water of the upper Potomac," Hunter cited as an example to his colleagues. "From the time this was done up to the completion of the canal, scarcely a boat was ever seen in Alexandria from the upper Potomac."[5]

Indeed, that earlier debate regarding a dam between Mason's Island (present-day Theodore Roosevelt Island) and the Potomac's south bank also reflected the rivalry of the municipalities, the inequities of congressional actions, and the resentment in Congress at having to devote time to the municipalities. In that 1804 debate, Virginia Congressman Randolph had declared:

[A] prompt rejection of the bill would serve as a general notice to the inhabitants of the District to desist from their daily and frivolous applications to Congress, to the great obstruction of the public business.

Andrew Gregg of Pennsylvania, however, pointed out that under the Constitution:

The House [was] bound to legislate for these people until it relinquished the claim to the jurisdiction either by authorizing them to legislate for themselves or retroceding them to the states to which they originally belonged.

Regarding the rivalry and inequitable treatment, North Carolina Congressman Nathaniel Macon argued:

The gentlemen in favor of this dam or causeway say it will do no harm.... On the other side, serious apprehensions are entertained of its injurious effects upon ... the Eastern Branch [the present-day Anacostia River] and its causing obstructions in the harbor of Alexandria.

In the years leading up to Hunter's 1846 effort, petitions seeking to detach the Virginia portion of the District of Columbia were repeatedly presented to Congress, resulting in bills that failed to pass in 1824 and 1840. Residents of Georgetown also periodically sought to have their area of the District returned to Maryland, most notably in an 1838 petition presented to Congress and in a bill that failed in 1856.

How, then, did Hunter succeed? Two overarching concerns account for Hunter's success—and also account for the continued failure of such efforts by District residents on the Maryland side. Over the years, one of those overarching issues diminished, while the other enlarged.

The issue that diminished regarded the location of the nation's capital itself. Differing visions among the Founding Fathers led to disputes as to whether the capital should be in Philadelphia or New York or a central location or in the South. Only after protracted negotiations between Thomas Jefferson and Alexander Hamilton was the Potomac River location accepted.[6] When Congress first debated retrocession in 1803, Delaware Congressman James A. Bayard voiced this ongoing concern. Should the land be returned to Virginia and Maryland, he worried, "What obligation is there in Congress to remain here? ... Unfix the Capitol and recede the District and believe me, Congress will soon take wings and fly to some other place." But compared to when the Founders had debated the capital's location, the issue now had an added dimension. President Jefferson was just then concluding the Louisiana Purchase, by which the United States suddenly became twice as large as it had been. If the legislative bolts locating the nation's capital were loosened, where might the expanded nation want its center of power?

As the Louisiana Purchase evolved, the development of railroads so greatly reduced the burdens of travel that the concerns of the new states and territories did *not* include relocating the nation's capital. The primary concern that emerged turned out to be the second overarching issue that contributed to Hunter's success: slavery.

It was during this era of national expansion that Robert Mercer Taliaferro Hunter grew up. The son of a prosperous landowner in Essex County,

Virginia, 100 miles south of the District, Hunter attended the University of Virginia, became an attorney, and in 1834 was elected to the Virginia House of Delegates. Three years later he was elected to the U.S. House of Representatives.

Hunter's personality was ideally suited for the period in which he served in the House. "Mr. Hunter is a conservative Democrat, a calm, quiet, undemonstrative, practical politician," the *New York Herald* wrote. "[He] speaks little and writes less.... Although strongly Southern in his sentiments ... he draws a glowing picture of the future of the republic."

Calm and undemonstrative he was, but not unfeeling nor without a sense of humor. He displayed both attributes as a college student in a letter to his widowed sister: "You seemed to be terribly in the dumps when you wrote. Are you still troubled with those thick-coming fancies, which are worse than real evils?... Have all the family feuds been appeased, so that you can no longer find amusement or occupation for your energies?... [If so] you may suppose me your opponent."

Shortly before Hunter went to college, an upheaval resulting from the Louisiana Purchase had threatened to undo the nation. At issue was whether or not slavery would be permitted in the states being created from its land. Though the dispute was resolved by the Missouri Compromise, no one in Congress wanted to endure such rancor again. Unfortunately, the nation did endure it again, and again. The next major upheaval involved the same question as applied to the land acquired in the Mexican War.

That war began within a week of Hunter's 1846 proposal for retrocession. Everyone in Congress knew that the United States would win the war and likely acquire vast territory.[7] And everyone in Congress knew that such a victory would raise the old question of whether slavery would be permitted in the newly acquired lands. Thus, when Hunter presented his resolution, it was during the calm before the storm. Members of Congress were inclined to do anything that could be done to mitigate the expected storm.

One thing Congress could do was to appease Virginia by giving back the land it had ceded to create the District of Columbia. Such an action, at that point in time, would help Virginia in two significant ways.

The first benefit would be Virginia's acquisition of additional proslavery voters electing representatives to its legislature. These votes were needed to counter those of the increasing population in Virginia's mountainous western region (present-day West Virginia), an area not suitable for the large plantations needed to support slave labor. When Hunter presented his proposal, Virginia's staunchly proslavery Democrats had recently lost their majority in the state's House of Delegates.

The second significant benefit had to do with the slave trade. As Hunter stated in Congress, Alexandria was suffering economically, in part because no federal facilities had been built on the Virginia side of the Potomac. To make matters worse, Congress had begun to contemplate a prohibition of the slave trade in the District of Columbia. Were that to happen, it would be yet another blow to Alexandria's economy.

Alexandria had been home to the nation's largest slave-trading firm, Franklin & Armfield. Though the company had dissolved by the time Hunter proposed retrocession, its partners had sold their interests to a number of local slave traders. The size of the market served even by these smaller Alexandria companies, and by other slave dealers in the District of Columbia, was evidenced on a daily basis in the local papers:

> CASH FOR NEGROES—I will give the highest cash price for likely NEGROES from 10 to 25 years of age. Myself or my agent can at all times be found at the establishment formerly owned by Armfield, Franklin & Co. at the west end of Duke Street, Alexandria.—GEORGE KEPHART

> NEGROES WANTED—The subscriber wishes to purchase any number of Negroes for the New Orleans market, and will give at all times the highest market price in cash in likely young Negroes. Those wishing to sell will find it in their interest to call at my establishment, corner of 7th Street and Maryland Avenue, where myself or agent can be seen at any time.—THOS. WILLIAMS[8]

While outlawing the slave trade would be an economic blow to Alexandria, if Congress returned Alexandria to Virginia and *then* outlawed the slave trade in the District, the prohibition would be a boon to Alexandria, since it would eliminate the competition. To achieve this boon required some delicacy. Hunter, with his calm, dispassionate manner, a Southerner who spoke glowingly of the future of the Union, was just the man for the job. The bill passed the House 96 to 65 (and the Senate 32 to 14).

The legislation stipulated that a referendum be held on the southern side of the Potomac to determine whether a majority of that area's voters (white males) wished to become Virginians. One group of Alexandrians particularly concerned about the vote's outcome were its African Americans, since

Virginia law prohibited teaching African Americans to read and write and required African American religious activities to be monitored by whites. Describing the day of the referendum, one free African American business-man in Alexandria wrote, "Whilst the citizens of this city and county were voting ... humble poor were standing in rows on either side of the court house and, as the votes were announced every quarter of an hour, the sup-pressed wailings and lamentations of the people of color were constantly ascending to God for help and succor."[9]

Today ghosts of the original District of Columbia remain on the map in the borders of present-day Arlington County, Virginia, and along the post–Revolutionary War segment of King Street in Alexandria.

As for Hunter, he was elected to the Senate later that year. While there, the anticipated storm erupted over slavery in the region acquired in the Mexican War. It blew away the Missouri Compromise. In its place, Congress cobbled together the Compromise of 1850 and then, four years later, took cover under the Kansas-Nebraska Act, which left the question of slavery to the states and territories (see "Stephen A. Douglas" in this book). Amid the bitter debates over the Kansas-Nebraska Act, Senator Hunter's calm demeanor and practical arguments provided influential support for the bill—so much so that, the following year, the *Cleveland Herald* noted, "Clubs are forming in [New York] for the support of Robert M. T. Hunter, at present U.S. Senator from Virginia, for President of the U.S."

Ghosts of old D.C. border

Though Hunter's presidential bid failed even to get his name on the ballot at the 1856 Democratic National Convention, it succeeded in calling attention to him as a candidate for the future. Indeed, four years later, a cor-respondent for the *Daily South Carolinian* reported:

I would respectfully suggest that a union of the Southern delegates might be effected upon the Honorable Robert M. T. Hunter of Vir-ginia.... Mr. Hunter is peculiarly fitted for the Presidency.... He is a man of superior natural abilities and thorough cultivation ... profoundly versed in the history of the rise and fall of empires.... However he is free from even the slightest tinge of pedantry and sentimentality. He is a plain, practical business man.

But the times no longer called for plain, practical men. The Compromise of 1850 and the Kansas-Nebraska Act had failed to mitigate the political storm over slavery. Inadvertently, they fed its escalation to hurricane force. In choosing a presidential candidate at the 1860 Democratic National Convention, the delegates were unable to coalesce after fifty-seven ballots. In each of those votes, Hunter placed a distant third among nine nominees. Ultimately the party shattered. Its splintered constituencies enabled the election of a visionary, Abraham Lincoln.

After Virginia's secession, Robert M. T. Hunter was elected to the Confederate Congress—but not for long. In July 1861, three months into the Civil War, Hunter became the Confederacy's secretary of state—also not for long. Individuals and factions were jockeying for power in the newly forming government, as San Francisco's *Evening Bulletin* observed in February 1862:

[Robert Toombs] was made Secretary of State for the Confederacy ... but resigned late in July, professedly that he might take the field [of battle].... Soon he was sent back to the rebel Senate, probably expecting to be chosen its presiding officer. But R. M. T. Hunter was too smart for him. That Virginian, rich in initials, was made Secretary of State after Toombs ... [then] resigned, was sent to the new rebel Senate, and has been elected its president *pro tem.*

Hunter served in the Confederate Senate for the duration of the war, but the center of action was on the battlefield. Near the war's conclusion, Hunter was one of three delegates selected to meet with President Lincoln at a peace conference held behind Union lines in Hampton Roads, Virginia.

The war left Hunter economically debilitated. In time, a government tidbit was thrown his way via an appointment as collector of the port of Tappahannock, Virginia. By then, Robert M. T. Hunter had become much like that section of the District he had restored to Virginia—a part of the government but hardly a participant, taking whatever opportunity came his way. Under the circumstances, however, there was no place to which he could retrocede himself.

SAM HOUSTON
The Man Who Lassoed Texas

Speaker of the House: Samuel Houston, you have been brought before this House, by its order, to answer the charge of having assaulted and beaten William Stanberry, a member of the House of Representatives of the United States from the State of Ohio, for words spoken by him in debate upon a question then depending before the House.... If you desire the aid of counsel ... your request will now be received.

Samuel Houston: Mr. Speaker, I wish no counsel.

—*REGISTER OF DEBATES*, 22ND CONG., APRIL 17, 1832

If you think Texas is big, take a look at the man whose name is now the state's biggest city: Sam Houston. He stood nearly six and a half feet tall, and that was the least of his outsized aspects. Houston, along with Stephen Austin, are the two people most associated with the fact that Texas is today part of the United States. While Austin followed a relatively direct path (continuing his father's founding of a colony in Mexico's sparsely populated region of Tejas), Houston's path was far more erratic. In retrospect, however, Houston's life seems inevitably to have led to Texas. Or to being shot dead.

Houston was born in Virginia, the son of a distinguished officer in the American Revolution. When his father died in 1807, the family moved to Tennessee, where fourteen-year-old Sam was enrolled in a Christian school run by his brothers. He played hooky so often the family put him to work in their farm-based trading post. Many of its customers were Cherokees from a nearby settlement. Sam was fascinated both by them and by the novels and literary classics he'd bring to the store from his father's library. The only downside to being a clerk was being a clerk. So Sam took off at age sixteen and headed into the woods to live with the Cherokees. Over the next several years, he learned their language and customs and found a second father. Houston was adopted by Oolooteka, known also as John Jolly, the leader of these Cherokees and, after their relocation, chief of the Arkansas Cherokees.

Following in the footsteps of both fathers, Sam Houston fought in the War of 1812, which involved the Cherokees, allying with the Americans in response to the fact that their enemy, the Red Stick Creeks, had allied with the British. Wounded at the Battle of Horseshoe Bend, Houston neverthe-less led a courageous charge when the battle seemed lost, only to discover that his comrades hadn't followed. Within moments Houston was again wounded, this time, it was believed, mortally. But he defied the doctors and lived, and also came to the attention of the commanding general, Andrew Jackson, who became yet another father—or, more accurately, godfather—to Sam Houston. "Old Hickory," as Jackson was known, appointed his young protégé to serve as the military's subagent to the Cherokees. In this capacity, Houston accompanied an 1818 delegation of Cherokees to Washington, DC, where, meeting with Secretary of War John C. Calhoun, Lieutenant Houston wore the blanket and loincloth of his adopted brethren. Calhoun was not pleased and, following the meeting, let Houston know it. Houston, equally displeased, resigned.[1]

Returning to Tennessee, Houston studied law and, for a brief time, was a local attorney. In rapid succession, he was appointed by the governor to the honorary post of major general in the Tennessee militia, elected to Congress in 1823, and reelected in 1825. In 1826 a flurry of gossipy newspaper items regarding one of Houston's numerous spats noted "information which may be relied upon has been received ...

that Gen. Houston and Gen. White had gone to Kentucky to fight a duel." This item, from Richmond's *Constitutional Whig*, included a curi-ously convoluted coda: "Gen. White accompanied Col. Smith when he bore the challenge from John P. Erwin, Esq. to Mr. Houston." One might think duels the most straight-forward way imaginable of resolving differences. Evidently not in this case: someone named Erwin, angry at Houston, got someone named Smith to deliver his challenge, in

Sam Houston (1793–1863)

response to which Houston ended up dueling someone named White, who accompanied Smith.[2] Honor among politicians, even then, had its intricacies.

The press reported on the duel as if it were the sporting event of the year, which, in effect, it was. The *New York Spectator* wrote in October 1826:

> The parties met on Thursday morning beyond the Kentucky line. They fought at the distance of fifteen feet only, and at the first fire Houston's aim took effect, striking White very near the center of the body, but, as he was in a walking position and the ball striking on a rib, it passed round the back and lodged on the opposite side, from which it was easily extracted. Had the ball passed directly through from the point of entrance to the point of extraction, it would have caused instant death.... They were accompanied by their friends on each side, who bear united testimony of the fair and chivalric conduct of the parties.

Clearly, Houston did not lack courage. But he could also tap-dance his way out of danger. Throughout his career, he was challenged to duels by numerous colleagues, including a naval commander and two of the presidents of the Republic of Texas.[3] Houston accepted none of their challenges. In fact, he never dueled again, possibly because the practice was coming to entail an additional risk: one could get arrested. Kentucky charged Houston with attempted murder following his duel with White. But he nimbly managed to stay one step ahead of the law, as revealed in an exasperated editorial in Kentucky's *Frankfort Commentator*:

> A grand jury at Nashville, Tenn. has presented Gen. Houston, of that place, for having lately fought a duel within the limits of this state with Gen. White, who was severely wounded—not as having been guilty of a violation of the laws of God and man, but as having performed a manly act, quite necessary and altogether proper for a gentleman, and which ought to have no unfavorable effect upon his election of Governor of Tennessee!!

That Houston managed to get a grand jury in Tennessee to consider an act he committed in Kentucky attests less to his guilt or innocence than to his ability to maneuver—as does Houston's subsequent use of the Tennessee grand jury's ruling as an asset in his bid to become the governor. With the duel having become a campaign issue, outgoing Tennessee governor William Carroll opted not to decide on a response to Kentucky's request for extradition. The decision then fell to the next governor, Sam Houston, who opted not to order himself to face trial in Kentucky.

While governor, an event took place that exploded Houston's political plans and landed him, badly damaged, facing Texas. That event was marriage. Three months after Houston wed Eliza Allen, she returned to her parents. The most likely cause was that Eliza had revealed to Houston her love for another man. Houston was twice the age of this eighteen-year-old girl, who may have yielded to her parents' pressure that she marry the more prestigious man.[4] Houston, for his part, said only that the matter was private. But he resigned as governor of Tennessee and went back into the woods, returning to his adopted father, Chief Oolooteka.

Oolooteka, now located in Arkansas, welcomed his prodigal son—though this prodigal son, as the astute chief knew, was closely connected to the new president of the United States, Andrew Jackson. Initially, Chief Oolooteka sent Houston on local missions to mediate intertribal disputes. Other relationships also occupied Houston's time—one in particular with a Cherokee widow named Diana Rogers Gentry. They soon married. How officially they were married depends on one's cultural customs, but among the Cherokees and in their own hearts, they were wed. Houston's relationship with the tribe also deepened as he formally became a full-fledged Cherokee.

Chief Oolooteka then sent Houston to Washington as part of a delegation working out details resulting from the Treaty with the Western Cherokee Nation of 1828. Houston was again in Cherokee garb, this time in the presence of the president. Old Hickory reacted with a grin and an embrace.

Houston's appearance in Washington as a Cherokee fooled no one—with the possible exception of Houston. His plans at this point were a mystery, perhaps even to himself. Speculation was rampant. Friends in Tennessee began setting the table for his return to elective office. Foes in Tennessee pulled the tablecloth off. In May 1830 the *Nashville Banner* reported:

> At a meeting of sundry respectable citizens ... it was resolved that a committee draw up a report expressive of the opinions entertained of the private virtue of Mrs. Eliza Houston, and whether her amiable character has received an injury among those acquainted with her in consequence of the late unfortunate occurrence between her and her husband, Gen. Samuel Houston.... It has been suggested that

... a belief has obtained in many places that he was married to an unworthy woman and that she has been the cause of all his misfortunes and his downfall as a man and a politician. Nothing is further from the fact.... The committee has no hesitation in saying that he is a deluded man; and his suspicions were groundless.

Tennessee was not Houston's only option. He had also been approached by friends in Texas, where the Anglo population had grown to the point that there was talk of separation from Mexico. Here too his enemies sought to undermine him, reporting that Houston planned to exploit rebellion in Texas by taking its helm. President Jackson wrote to his unpredictable protégé, laughing off the rumor "that you had declared you would, in less than two years, be emperor of that country by conquest." Jackson then mentioned that the military would suppress any such effort.[5]

Houston responded to these efforts to confine him by placing an ad in the *Nashville Banner*. Knowing that the press loved every aspect of his public and private controversies, Houston was assured his ad would soon appear as a news story nationwide. Worded as it was, it did:

> Now know all men by these presents, that I, Sam Houston, "late governor of the State of Tennessee," do hereby declare to all scoundrels whomsoever, that they are authorized to accuse, defame, calumniate, traduce, slander, or vilify and libel me, to any extent in personal or private abuse.... Be it known ... I do solemnly promise on the first day of April next, to give to the author of the most elegant, refined, ingenious lie or calumny, a handsome gilt copy (bound in sheep) of the *Kentucky Reporter*, or a snug plain copy of the *United States Telegraph* (bound in dog).[6]

Houston's humor concealed the dynamite around which it was wrapped. By detonating ridicule beneath the feet of his detractors, Houston obtained time to make a move. That move was to Texas, ostensibly as a business venture. To do so, however, Houston needed to clear the concerns of President Jackson. His move to Texas, therefore, was via Washington.

Jackson too, by dint of his flinty personality, was also an embattled man. Shortly after Houston's arrival in Washington, Congressman William Stanberry delivered a speech on the floor regarding Jackson appointees who had, or should have been, fired. Amid those he was listing, Stanberry declaimed, "Was the late Secretary of War removed in consequence of his attempt, fraudulently, to give to Governor Houston the contract for Indian rations?" The answer to that question was yes and no. No, that was not why Secretary of War John Eaton had left office. And yes, there had been fraud—but not in Houston's contract. The fraud was in the previous contract, the holder of which deprived the Cherokees of adequate rations while pocketing the surplus profits. Secretary of War Eaton awarded Houston the new contract knowing it would be administered honestly. In so doing, Eaton aroused the wrath of entrenched political interests.

Houston's anger at being wrongly accused of fraud was intensified by the fact that he had no legal recourse. Congressmen and senators have immunity from slander for anything they say in session. Houston did what any man worth his salt would do; he sent Stanberry a note. To which Stanberry replied:

> I received this morning, by your hands, a note signed Samuel Houston, quoting from the *National Intelligencer* of the 2nd a remark made by me in the House. The object of the note is to ascertain whether Mr. Houston's name was used by me in debate, and whether my remarks were correctly quoted. I cannot recognize the right of Mr. Houston to make this request.
>
>> Very respectfully yours etc.,
> > William Stanberry

One might wonder what Stanberry intended to achieve. Why not stand behind his statement, rather than imply the note might not be authentic (and therefore unfair to Houston) and then insult Houston? Elsewhere, Stanberry acknowledged that he knew the note was authentic and also knew the character of the man who sent it. "It was the opinion of one of my friends that it was proper that I should be armed," he stated on the floor of the House, "that, immediately upon the reception of my note, Mr. Houston would probably make an assault upon me. Mr. [Thomas] Ewing accordingly procured for me a pair of pistols."

Houston, however, did not assault Stanberry upon receiving his reply. He assaulted him ten days later. There could have been any number of reasons for the delay, including the "hot-headed" Houston's contemplation of the political chessboard.

One thing certain is that on the evening of April 13, 1832, Stanberry crossed the street from his boarding house and, as he later testified:

At the moment of stepping on the sidewalk, Mr. Houston stood before me. I think he called me by my name and instantly struck me with the bludgeon he had in his hand with great violence, and he repeated the blow while I was down.... Turning on my right side, I got my hand in my pocket and got my pistol and cocked it. I watched an opportunity while he was striking me ... and pulled the trigger, aiming at his breast. The pistol did not go off.... He wrested the pistol from my hand and, after some more blows, he left me.

Stanberry's testimony was not given in court. Houston's trial took place in the House of Representatives after it voted that its sergeant-at-arms should arrest Houston. Congressman James K. Polk strenuously opposed this action:

Was not the law of the District of Columbia open to the member? Was not the individual who had assaulted him ... guaranteed by the Constitution to a trial by jury?

But a counterargument was made by Congressman Daniel Jenifer:

The Constitution ... expressly declared that no member might be brought into question elsewhere for words spoken in the House.... Now, [I] would like to know, whether in the present case there had not been an attempt not only to question the words of the member assaulted, but to ... deprive him altogether of the power of exercising it.... Was it credible, was it possible, that ... in such a matter the House had no right to interfere ... that their fellow-member was to be left to the courts of the District of Columbia?

All of this behooved Houston. The attack on the snooty congressman became national news, as Houston likely expected. But the decision to try him in the House of Representatives was a bonus, adding constitutional importance to the story in a way that cast him in the role of victim.

During the trial, Houston's array of skills was in peak form. Courageously declaring that he wished no counsel, he then, without fanfare, obtained the most celebrated defense attorney of the day: Francis Scott Key. From April 14 to May 14, the House of Representatives devoted nearly all its time to Houston's trial, ultimately finding him guilty and sentencing him to hear an official reprimand.

Stanberry next chaired a special committee to investigate fraud in Houston's government contract and brought criminal charges against him in court. Houston was fined $500. Newspapers outside of Washington, DC, devoted no more than nine lines total to the trial—far less than their concurrent coverage of the official report from Stanberry's committee, which found no fraud.

Houston was now free to go. With his newly bolstered public esteem raising him above the rumormongers, he went where he had intended to go all along: Texas. His successful maneuver, however, was not without cost. Houston's Cherokee wife, Diana, was unwilling to part from her people. When Houston arrived in Nacogdoches, 165 miles southeast of present-day Dallas, he was alone.

All the rumors Houston's detractors had circulated about his ambition to lead a revolution in Texas proved true. No sooner had "businessman" Houston arrived than he wrote to President Jackson regarding American acquisition of Texas. "That such a measure is desired by nineteen-twentieths of the population of the province, I cannot doubt," Houston informed the president. "The course which Texas must and will adopt will render the transfer of Texas inevitable to some power, and if the United States does not press for it, England will most assuredly obtain it by some means."

Within two months, Houston was elected to be a delegate to a convention seeking Mexican statehood for Texas (then part of the Mexican state of Coahuila). While many at the convention urged independence from Mexico, Houston (contrary to his letter to Jackson) publicly sided with Texas patriarch Stephen Austin in urging loyalty to Mexico. Houston chaired the committee drafting a Mexican statehood constitution. Austin then delivered the document to the national government in Mexico City, where he ended up in jail.

With Mexican president Antonio López de Santa Anna threatening to send troops into Texas, Houston was chosen to head the militia in Nacogdoches. Skirmishes commenced between Mexican troops and the various Texas militias. After a year in prison (and no trial), Austin returned and resumed leadership. But his health had deteriorated during his confinement, and his brilliance was in creating, not destroying. Though Austin had misgivings about Houston, he recognized him as the man most able to lead the military. In 1836 Houston was given command.

In that same year, the two battles that stand out as mileposts in the Texas War of Independence took place: the Battle of the Alamo, a stunning defeat for the Texans, and the Battle of San Jacinto, a victory that marked the end of the war and commenced the independent Republic of Texas. Houston was not at the Alamo. He had, in fact, issued orders for its abandonment and destruction, upon learning of its vulnerability as Mexican forces approached. But his orders were not obeyed. Consequently, as the *New Orleans Commercial Bulletin* reported:

> On the 6th March about midnight, the Alamo was assaulted by the whole force of the Mexican army, commanded by Santa Anna in person. The battle was desperate until daylight, when only seven men belonging to the Texian garrison were found alive who cried for quarters but were told that there was no mercy for them; they then continued fighting until the whole were butchered.... The bodies of the slain were thrown into a heap at the center of the Alamo and burned.

Though the accuracy of this report is open to question, it was the version that "Texians" received. The same news report continued:

> Immediately after the capture, Gen. Santa Anna sent ... [a] servant to Gen. Houston's camp ... offering the Texians peace and general amnesty if they would lay down their arms and submit to his government. Gen. Houston's reply was, "True, sir, you have succeeded in killing some of our brave men—but the Texians are not yet conquered." The effect of the fall [of the Alamo] throughout Texas was electrical. Every man who could use a rifle and was in a condition to take the field marched forthwith to the seat of war.

Once again, an unfortunate affair ended up working in Houston's favor. Six weeks later, with the Texans' manpower boosted, events went differently. In May Washington's *National Intelligencer* reported:

> During the night of the 20th, after the skirmish between Mexican and Texian forces, Gen. Houston ... gained a position within rifle distance of the enemy before they were aware of his presence. Two discharges of small arms and cannon loaded with musket balls settled the affair.... The officers broke and endeavored to escape; the mounted riflemen, however, soon overtook all but one.... The pursuers ... searched the woods for a long time in vain, when it occurred to an old hunter that the chase might, like a hard-pressed bear, have "taken a tree." The

tree tops were examined, when lo! the game was discovered snugly ensconced in the forks of a large live oak. The captors did not know who their prisoner was until they reached the camp, when the Mexican soldiers exclaimed, "*El General! El Gefe! Santa Anna!*"

The captured Mexican leader signed a surrender. Though it did not include recognition of the Republic of Texas, for all practical purposes Texas was now an independent nation.

On September 5, 1836, Sam Houston became the second president of Texas, defeating the ailing Stephen Austin by a margin of nearly ten to one. Though Houston, like his mentor, Andrew Jackson, had earned a reputation for brash statements and acts, both men were capable of caution, as reflected at this politically critical moment. President Jackson's remarks on Texas called for moderation:

> My friend Sam Houston, after he thrashed Stanbery of Ohio, went to Texas…. Santa Anna said to Houston … "You must give up your arms." At this, Sam, whom I taught to fight, the rogue, stood straight up and told him, "Come and take them." On this Santa Anna … marched into Texas, passed the Rio del Norte and all the other rivers whose names I cannot remember, till he got as far as the San Jacinto. There Sam and his troops … attacked the Mexicans—routed, killed, chased, and captured the whole lot—pulled Santa Anna from a tree, up which he had climbed, and thus almost equaled—not quite—my victory at New Orleans. On this the Texians have established their independence…. I am informed that they want to be admitted into the Union, but we must not let that come yet. Let their recognition be openly made. Let Mexico and Europe be persuaded that it is no use to think of stopping Texas from going her own way.[7]

Houston echoed this view when addressing the Texas legislature on the subject of annexation to the United States. "It is not possible to determine what are to be [our] future relations," he stated. "Texas, with her superior natural advantages, must become a point of attraction, and the policy of establishing with her the earliest relations of friendship and commerce will not escape the eye of statesmen."

Houston devoted his presidency to the mundane tasks required to bring economic stability to his deeply indebted nation. Limited by law to one term,

Houston subsequently served in the Texas House of Representatives, where he counseled moderation regarding plans to expand into regions of Mexico that today include New Mexico, Arizona, and California. The initial target was an expedition to occupy Santa Fe, since the town was within the Rio Grande boundary that Texas declared to be its border. Houston declared the expedition foolhardy: the Hispanic population of Santa Fe would receive them as enemies, and the act of aggression would provide sympathy for, and justify military action from, Mexico. The bill was defeated.

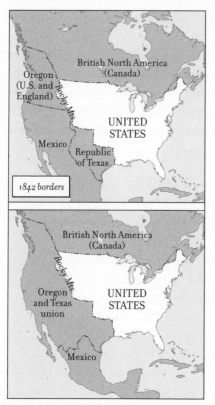

Houston's vision of United States without Texas

Still, Houston did not completely oppose expansion; his views were simply more pragmatic. After returning to the presidency in December 1841, Houston described to the U.S. minister to Texas an astonishing vision for the future if the United States did not offer it statehood:

The union of Oregon and Texas will be much more natural and convenient than for either separately to belong to the United States…. Such an event may appear fanciful to many, but I assure you there are no Rocky Mountains interposing to such a project. But one thing can prevent its accomplishment and that is annexation…. Most of the provinces of Chihuahua, Sonora, and Upper and Lower California, as well as Santa Fe, which we now claim, will have to be brought into the connection of Texas and Oregon. This you will see, by reference to the map, is no bugbear to those who will reflect upon the achievement of the Anglo-Saxon people.[8]

Such a map did indeed seem both fanciful and logical. The time had come for the United States to make up its mind about Texas.

On April 12, 1844, President John Tyler signed and sent to the Senate a treaty with the Republic of Texas that would convert the republic into an American territory. During the treaty's negotiations, public opinion was highly divided over whether or not the nation wanted Texas. Many in the North vehemently opposed the annexation of Texas, and not simply because it would be a slave state, but because Congress gave Texas the option of becoming as many as five states more equal in size with other states. Consequently, Southerners, envisioning ten additional proslavery votes in the Senate, vehemently supported its annexation. Texans, however, had developed such a strong sense of identify that they never considered subdividing the state. To remain a slave state, though, Texas had to relinquish its land north of 36°30' (the top of its Panhandle) to be in compliance with the Missouri Compromise.

Ultimately, a quest shared by Northerners and Southerners—expansion of the nation—prevailed over their slavery conflict, and Texas was admitted to the Union on March 1, 1845. Houston was elected to represent Texas in the U.S. Senate, where he participated in an additional boundary change. With the state still facing enormous debts from its days as a republic, Houston supported the $10 million sale to the United States of a large chunk of western Texas, which was then annexed to New Mexico.

More important was the context in which that sale took place: the Compromise of 1850, in which the central issue was slavery. Without the Compromise of 1850, the South would have seceded, as ten years later it nevertheless did. Though Sam Houston supported slavery, he opposed secession till the day he died in 1863, in the midst of the Civil War. Back during the debate in 1850, he had summoned all of his oratorical skills on behalf of loyalty to the Union. Those skills, like so many of Sam Houston's skills, were formidable. So formidable that a future president filched one of the lines from Houston's speech: "A nation divided against itself cannot stand."[9]

BRIGHAM YOUNG
The Boundary of Religion Revisited

The Mormons are, at present, eliciting considerable interest and inquiry in reference to the organization of a new State in the far West under the cognomen, State of Deseret.... Ought they be admitted without strict inquiry? For a starting point, Congress might appoint a committee to inquire into and report the facts ... relative to polygamy and, if the facts are unfavorable, that they be not ... styled "the State of Deseret but "the State of Whoredom."... And, further, to inquire whether the whole movement be more or less a mere Mormon church maneuver to create a Mormon church State, designed to be under Mormon church jurisdiction exclusively.

—*NATIONAL ERA*, JANUARY 24, 1850

Two hundred and fifty feet below the surface of Lake Mead is the town of Callville, Nevada, founded in 1858 at the behest of Mormon leader Brigham Young. Callville was the high-water mark of Young's efforts to create a Mormon state. The high-water mark for Callville itself (or, as it turned out, its second highest water mark) was in October 1866, when the first ocean-going steamship arrived at its dock. Its highest-water mark was in 1936, when it was inundated by the Colorado River upon completion of the Hoover Dam. By then, however, it had been abandoned for more than fifty years, despite having played a key role in establishing the present-day boundary between Nevada and Arizona—a boundary far from Utah, the state predominated by Mormons. That distance reflects the scope of Brigham Young's dream.

Young was a thirty-year-old carpenter and blacksmith when he joined the Mormon Church in 1832. The church itself had only recently been organized by Joseph Smith, who published the *Book of Mormon* in 1830. Through the energy Young devoted to the church, and his charismatic personality, he rose in its ranks over the next decade, surfacing in the national press in 1842 when the *New York Herald* mentioned him among the leadership of the Mormons. That article, however, was a report on the nation's animosity toward Mormons. "The fights and quarrels in Mormon country promise to be much richer than anything that has occurred here since the days of the Revolutionary War," it began, relating that Missouri "has charged Joe [Smith, founder of the church] with instigating the man who attempted to kill Gov. Boggs."

The nation's antagonism emanated from the Mormons' firm belief in traditional marriage—biblically traditional marriage, which is to say polygamy. But the hostility grew to include other matters. Joseph Smith had prophesied that God would soon bring "a full end of all nations." In view of the Mormon disregard of state laws prohibiting polygamy, Smith's proclamation on "the end of nations" got Washington's attention. Smith sought to mitigate these fears in 1838 by publishing *The Political Motto of the Church of Latter-day Saints*, which praised the U.S. Constitution as being "founded in the wisdom of Almighty God." But not everyone believed him. Later that year he was arrested for treason. Lacking sufficient evidence, authorities in Missouri struck a face-saving deal in which Smith was allowed to escape. He relocated in Illinois, but the conflicts followed him and in 1844 he was assassinated.

A leadership crisis ensued. "There has been a feud and division among the Mormons," South Carolina's *Southern Patriot* reported. "When Joe Smith, the head imposter, was killed, there was a struggle for ascendancy. Sidney Rigdon thought that he ought to be next in command.... Emma Smith, the widow, seemed disposed to be the spiritual leader.... Wm. Smith, the brother of Joe, set himself up as Patriarch....

Brigham Young and the Council of Twelve then took upon themselves the spiritual and temporal government of the Mormons."

Despite the venom in the article, it reported two facts that proved to be significant. It noted that the Brigham Young faction proposed "to remove all the Saints beyond the Rocky Mountains" and that the "mass of the Mormons appear to be disposed to adhere to Young and his party." Indeed, the majority did opt for the path proposed by Young. The

Brigham Young (1801–1877)

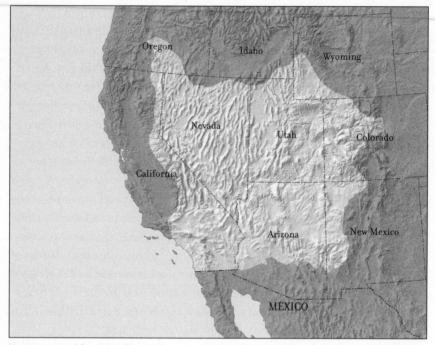

Mormon proposal for state of Deseret

area around the Great Salt Lake had the advantages of being sparsely populated and outside the United States (the Southwest then still belonged to
Mexico). Just as the Mormons were resettling, however, the United States
won the Mexican War, and Young's followers found themselves back inside
the boundaries of the United States. Less than a year after that, gold was discovered at Sutter's Mill in the Sierra Nevada Mountains to the west. Suddenly
it was rush hour on the Mormon Trail. Before the year was out, California
had become a state.

In response, Young organized a predominantly Mormon convention that
sent Congress a proposal for a state of Deseret. It stipulated boundaries that
encompassed all of the Great Basin between the Rockies and the Sierras and
extended to include Southern California with its Pacific ports.

Congress gave it a different border and a different name. Suspicion of
the Mormon agenda had only increased with their migration outside the
boundaries of the United States. With the U.S. acquisition of this land, the
vast boundaries of the Mormons' proposed state of Deseret further fed the
fear that they might eventually declare independence and establish their
own nation—right between California and the rest of the United States.

In lieu of the state of Deseret, Congress created the Utah Territory. Its northern and southern boundaries are those that Utah possesses to this day, but at the time they extended westward from the crest of the Rockies to California. Because Utah was designated a territory rather than a state, its governorship became a presidential appointment rather than an elected office. President Zachary Taylor, however, prudently appointed Brigham Young.

Fear that the Mormons might create a separate nation was not, however, as preeminent a national security concern as fear that slave states might create a separate nation. The town of Callville illustrated the connection between both controversies.

In the years just before Callville was founded, the Democrats had been losing ground to a newly formed abolitionist party known as the Republicans. In 1854 Democratic Senator Stephen A. Douglas sought to cope with slavery (and propel himself to the presidency) by convincing Congress to enact a policy known as "popular sovereignty." It removed the federal government from deciding where slavery would or would not be allowed, leaving the decision to the individual states and territories. The Mormons seized upon this principle to defend Utah's right to allow polygamy (the practice was eventually abandoned in 1890 by the church's main branch). The Democrats responded by, first, disagreeing, and second, making Mormon polygamy a campaign issue in the 1856 presidential election. In so doing, they hoped to disentangle themselves from the Mormons' inconvenient logic and, by fanning fears regarding marriage and morality, to divert attention from their party's highly nuanced position regarding slavery.

They succeeded. The shift in attitudes was reflected in the nationwide publication *The Saturday Evening Post*. In 1849 the magazine published positive commentary regarding the proposed state of Deseret:

> The progress of the Mormon sect in this country, when duly considered, must be regarded as an extraordinary phenomenon of the times. From small beginnings they have gone on increasingly steadily, in spite of persecutions and hardships.... But the strangeness of the thing consists in the wonderful and rapid extension of a faith of which so little is known, and which had its origin in stories and devices apparently the most absurd that ever made mockery of human credibility. The converts to this faith, moreover, do not appear to belong to that class of enthusiasts that give way to hallucinations. The Mormons are a practical people; they are industrious,

temperate, orderly. Wherever they plant themselves in the wilderness, the aspect of a cultivated region is soon visible.

Following the 1856 election, the same magazine sounded the alarm:

The accounts from Utah—or as the "saints" now insist on its being called, "Deseret"—are chock-full of fight.... It will be noticed by the threat relative to Jackson County, Missouri, that some of these fanatics really cherish the delusion of ultimate success, in the case of war with the United States.... It's a pity that proper measures were not taken years ago to remove this cancer, when it was comparatively small and powerless.

After the Democrats won the White House in 1856, newly elected President James Buchanan had to make good on the moral outrage his party had exploited. He did so by replacing Young with a non-Mormon governor and by dispatching 2,500 troops to Utah to erect a permanent fort.

Young, in turn, prepared for war. Among those preparations, he directed Anson Call to locate a settlement on the farthest navigable point of the Colorado River. With Callville as the terminus of a string of Mormon settlements leading from the Salt Lake Valley to the Colorado River, landlocked Utah now had access to the sea via the Colorado to the Gulf of California to the Pacific.

Callville soon became a landing for food and mining supplies. It also served as a portal for immigrants recently converted to Mormonism by missionaries who had traveled to Europe, Latin America, India, Australia, and the Pacific Islands. These foreigners, arriving out of devotion to the Mormon Church as opposed to the United States, contributed to government concerns regarding an eventual Mormon nation.

Though the 1857–58 Utah War, as it became known, never erupted into full-fledged combat between the Mormon militia and the U.S. Army, over a hundred civilians died in various armed confrontations, and enormous amounts of public and private property were destroyed. Ultimately the Mormons accepted Buchanan's governor in return for amnesty regarding destruction of government property. The federal troops soon left to deal with the *actual* present danger to national security: the formation of the Confederacy and the Civil War it triggered.

Continued growth and progress in Callville enabled the first steam-

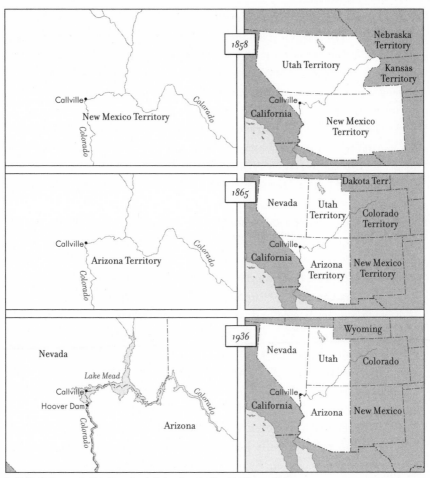

Callville before and after Nevada statehood, and after the Hoover Dam

ship to arrive one year after the Civil War ended. Not coincidentally, that same year Congress redrew the boundary between the Arizona and Nevada Territories.

When Nevada became a state in 1864, it inherited the southern border of the Utah Territory—the straight line continuing to California. To its south, the Arizona Territory also extended west to California, and thus encompassed the navigable lower end of the Colorado River. In 1866, Congress gave Nevada that portion of the Arizona Territory west of the Colorado River, including Callville (and a region in this otherwise arid environment that Spanish explorers had called "Fruitful Plains"—or, in Spanish, Las Vegas).

Congress may have been seeking to create future states more equal in natural resources. At the time, Nevada had recently exhausted its efforts to claim the crest of the gold-rich Sierras as its rightful boundary with California. It may have also been payback time for Arizonans, who, during the Civil War, had first created Arizona (extending across the southern half, as opposed to western half, of the New Mexico Territory) and been granted territorial status by the Confederacy.

Arizona was officially outraged and baffled by the land transfer. Its outrage was expressed in a resolution passed by its territorial legislature. "By this great river the Territory receives the most of its supplies," it protested, "and lately it has become the channel of a large part of the trade of San Francisco with Utah and Montana." The phrase "lately it has become" referred to the recently commenced steamship traffic at Callville. Its bafflement was expressed by state historian Thomas Edwin Farish when he later wrote, "For some reason, to this day unexplained, the greater portion of the land in this Arizona county [Pah Ute County] was ceded to the State of Nevada by the Congress of the United States under an act passed on May 5, 1866."

Nevada, on the other hand, viewed the land transfer as perfectly logical. In its official state history, Beulah Hershheiser blandly noted that "the desired tract was a mining district; that Nevada was a mining State; and that the interests of the two sections were therefore identical."

To guard the important landing on the Colorado from these controversies, the Army erected Fort Callville. It was occupied only briefly, since the town soon began to lose population. Commerce dried up owing to the arrival of railroads and, more literally, because the Colorado River was increasingly being drained for irrigation. By 1869 Callville was a ghost town.

Though the dried-up town was later drowned by progress, Callville's underwater ruins represent important American struggles—including those of a state (Utah) whose boundaries purposely never included it. Indeed, the boundary imposed on Brigham Young's vision reveals a critical insight: national security became a boundary of religious freedom, a boundary extendable to other freedoms as well.

JOHN A. SUTTER
California: Boundless Opportunity

The hat must come off before the military general, the flag staff, and the church, and I preferred a country where I could keep mine on ... where I should be absolute master.

—JOHN A. SUTTER[1]

On January 24, 1848, gold was discovered in California at Sutter's Mill. The discovery determined the way California would be shaped. Had it not been for John A. Sutter, gold would still have been discovered. Sutter was just lucky—or, as it turned out, unlucky.

Like a moth to a flame, Sutter was attracted to fragile boundaries: geographic, social, and contractual. Born in northern Switzerland, he served in the Swiss military, married, and went into the dry goods business. By the time he was thirty, he had five children, was deeply in debt, and had lost control of his business to his mother-in-law, who had financed it. With the help of his wife, Sutter secretly sold off the store's inventory and fled, arriving in Missouri in 1834. There he established a similar business, became an American citizen, fell deeply into debt, and fled the day before he'd been summoned to appear in court.

During the Missouri years and in the year that followed, Sutter's business pursuits took him to Santa Fe, Oregon, Hawaii, and California. Taken together, these destinations tell us something of his instincts. At

John A. Sutter (1803–1880)

the time, none of these locations was within the United States (though it shared, and disputed, Oregon with England). All of them, however, became part of the United States within the next ten years. Sutter, of course, could not have known this. What he could have known was that they were jurisdictionally weak.

Arriving in California in 1839, he sought permission from the Mexican government to establish an agricultural colony. "Governor [Juan Bautista] Alvarado ... was very glad to hear that ... I intended to settle in the interior on the banks of the river Sacramento, because the Indians ... would not allow white men, and particularly of the Spanish origin, to come near them," Sutter recorded in his diary. "I got ... permission to select a territory wherever I would find it convenient."

He selected territory at and around the juncture of the Sacramento and American Rivers, building his settlement's initial structures slightly to the southeast, above the flood plain, and naming it New Helvetia (New Switzerland). Governor Alvarado may have been pleased about the location, but Mexico's regional military commander, General Mariano Vallejo, was not. The area was too far in the interior for Vallejo's forces to assert control. That fact suited Sutter, who sought a place where he need not remove his hat to anyone. It also suited him that the location was ripe for business, perched along a route used by pioneers heading to the Oregon Territory.

Adding to General Vallejo's concern was the fact that Sutter's initial colony was non-Hispanic, consisting of five American and German men, eight to ten Hawaiians (two of whom were, according to Sutter, wives), one bulldog, and three cannons. The bulldog and cannons provided a measure of security from hostile Indians, but Vallejo knew they could also provide protection from Mexican forces.

Sutter became well known even before gold was discovered at his mill. His importance rated inclusion in an 1844 report to the State Department. "Augustus Sutter, *alcade* of the new town of New Helvetia ... is a Swiss, and now a citizen of Mexico, and obtained from the government a large tract of land," the U.S. consul in Mexican California informed his superiors. "All parties by land from Oregon or from the United States to California touch at this establishment."[2]

An alcade was the Mexican government's chief executive and judicial officer for a municipality. Sutter did not possess this authority. He did, however, possess a personality ideally suited for commerce with travelers. A March 1849 item in the magazine *Home Journal* reveals a good deal of his gregarious character:

Captain Sutter ... was one of the officers of the Swiss Guard in the Revolution of July during the reign of Charles X. After this Revolution, he emigrated to the United States.... Capt. Sutter is kind, hospitable, and generous.... Surrounded as he was, on his first settling in this country, by tribes of wild Indians, he has by kindness and just dealing, attached them to his interest.... They, for their food and a pay from four to six dollars per month, man his fort, work his farms and mills, and do all the labor generally required in the new settlement.

Actually, Sutter had been neither a captain nor a Swiss Guard. He had been a sublieutenant in the local reserves. He also appears to have misled the correspondent regarding labor-management relations. He may have paid his Indian workers $4 to $6 a month during the Gold Rush, when labor was scarce in every enterprise other than mining. Before that, however, American dollars were a rarity in what was still Mexican California. So too, for that matter, were pesos in tribal transactions, since payment was generally made in goods.

Still, as the correspondent reports, Sutter did have a character befitting a lord of the manor. To one Indian caught stealing, he imposed a sentence of twenty-fives lashes, which was duly carried out, despite the fact that Mexican law prohibited private citizens from exercising judicial functions.[3] Mexican law enforcement, however, was 90 miles downriver in San Francisco.

In 1841 Sutter purchased the Russian-American Company's coastal trading post known as Fort Ross (near present-day Jenner, California). He transported its movable goods and livestock to New Helvetia and held the distant Pacific Coast land as an investment. To finance the purchase, he borrowed from the Russian-American Company, using New Helvetia as collateral. He subsequently took out loans to finance his agricultural, ranching, fur-trapping, and distilling enterprises by putting up portions of his land as collateral, despite the fact that all his land was now mortgaged to the Russian-American Company. The common denominator in these and later transactions was the boundaries that contracts were written to stipulate. Sutter was not big on boundaries.

Loyalty, too, is a boundary, dividing certain actions one will and will not do. Sutter's political loyalties were just as supple regarding that boundary. At the time, Mexico's control of California was being challenged both by native-born *californios* (under the leadership of José Castro, General Vallejo, and Governor Alvarado) and by the United States. After Mexican President

Antonio López de Santa Anna replaced Governor Alvarado with Manuel Micheltorena, the new governor sought to secure his authority by offering Sutter clear title to all his land in return for a vow of loyalty to Mexico. Sutter avowed it. When General Vallejo confronted Sutter regarding his action, Sutter avowed his loyalty to Vallejo.

After the Mexican War commenced in 1846, Sutter kept the Mexican military informed of events that came to his attention—until events tilted in favor of the U.S. forces. Sutter then sent a letter of support to General John C. Frémont. By adjusting his sails to the prevailing winds, Sutter spent the war years expanding his enterprises. For one such project, the construction of a lumber mill, he partnered with James Marshall, with Sutter providing the financing and Marshall overseeing construction. In Sutter's diary entry for January 28, 1848, he wrote in his less than perfect English, "Marshall arrived in the evening. It was raining very heavy but he told me he came on important business. After we was alone in a private room, he showed me … specimens of gold. That is, he was not certain if it was gold or not, but he thought it might be."

Four days later, Sutter traveled to the site to see for himself. This may seem blasé, but there had been discoveries of gold before in California and each had turned out to be insignificant. By the time he arrived, continual findings of gold suggested that this one could be big.

But there was a hitch. The mill was not on Sutter's land. He and Marshall promptly leased the land and surrounding area from the Yalisumni Indians, making no mention of the gold. The Yalisumnis made no mention of not being the tribe to whom Mexico had accorded the land.

Over the next year, more than 80,000 people flooded into the region. Sutter's debts had left him poorly positioned to profit from the gold or from providing supplies to the prospectors. To make matters worse, their arrival caused Sutter's lax attitude toward boundaries to boomerang, as evidenced by an announcement he published in July 1849:

NOTICE TO SQUATTERS
All persons are hereby cautioned not to settle without my permission on any land of mine in this territory. Said land is bounded as follows:

What followed was a lengthy and precise stipulation of boundaries. But Sutter's notice went unheeded due to jurisdictional weakness—the very element that had drawn him to this region. With the Mexican War just ended, Con-

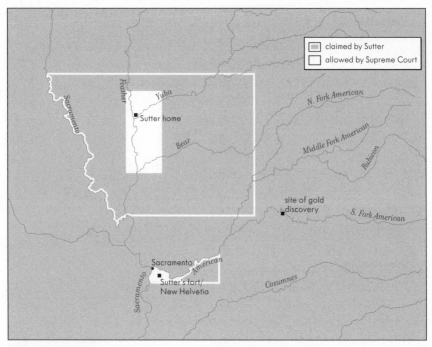

Sutter's land claims

gress had not yet established a territorial government, and the military's forces were depleted by soldiers deserting for the gold fields.

Unfortunate as the squatters were for Sutter, something worse was arriving in their wake: jurisdictional strength. California's statehood convention in 1849 marked the imminent establishment of state and federal courts that would become the arena of his undoing.

The statehood convention also established California's borders, and the debates regarding those borders were intense. Two big issues were at stake. Slavery was the more urgent of the two, and its advocates sought to create two states: a Northern and a Southern California—one free, the other slave. The second issue was water. California had very little of it in its south unless it located its border at the Rocky Mountains in order to include the Colorado and Gila Rivers. Such a border, however, would create a huge state. Opponents advocated a border just beyond the gold-filled Sierra Nevada Mountains, extending south to the Colorado River and along that river to the Gulf of California.

Among the delegates to the convention was Sutter, at whose mill all this had begun. Now out of his element, he spoke briefly only once during the

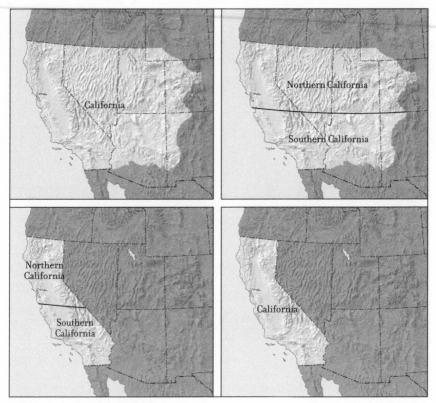

Defining California: four proposals

proceedings, adding his support to the majority preference: a single state with the more modest eastern border.

Meanwhile, the Russian-American Company commenced legal action to foreclose on New Helvetia owing to Sutter's many missed payments. The crisis was averted by the arrival of Sutter's eldest son, August (soon followed by the rest of the family, from whom Sutter had been apart for twenty years). To delay foreclosure, Sutter transferred title to all his property to August. August proceeded to have plans drawn up for a town in the squatter-populated area at the juncture of the rivers. He named it Sacramento. Sutter objected vehemently to the plan, both because it was in a floodplain and because he had been trying to sell lots for a town of Sutterville, located on higher ground three miles below the juncture.[4] But demand was so high for real estate at the point of entry, August was able to pay off all his father's debts. Sutter then invested in gold mines, using as collateral property that was now in his son's name.[5]

Sutter's tangled title claims soon became a gold mine for lawyers, representing or suing not only Sutter but also those who had bought land from him to which his title was dubious. The *Chicago Tribune* reported in July 1858:

Judge Hoffman, of the United States District Court, rejected the claim of Milton Little for 22,197 acres of land opposite Sacramento City. This claim is founded on an alleged grant from Mexico, and among the papers offered in evidence were two certificates signed by [John A.] Sutter and dated in 1845. Judge Hoffman declares himself satisfied that one of these was written in 1857 and ante-dated, and he expresses a suspicion of the good faith of the other. This is the second case in which Judge Hoffman has declared certificates of Sutter dated previous to the American conquest to have been written since and ante-dated.

Not only in the courts but in the streets, the forces of organization were increasingly challenging Sutter's claims. The squatters now formed themselves into a political association:

Whereas, the evidence that the land in Sacramento County belongs to the United States is becoming clear and more positive everyday....

Resolved, that we will hold our hold [*sic*] peaceably, if we can—forcibly, if we must—till a decision shall be had upon this question in the Supreme Court of the United States.

Resolved, that if the bail of an arrested squatter be refused, simply because the bondsman is not a landholder under Capt. Sutter, we shall consider all executions issued in consequence thereof as acts of illegal force and shall act accordingly.[6]

Sutter's claims ultimately made their way to the U.S. Supreme Court, the decorum of which was also disrupted by his disregard for boundaries. Two attorneys claimed to be his representative. Once resolved, the legal arguments—involving "conveyances," "petitions for surplus," and "parol evidence"—decorously masked the fact that they had been the cause of bloodshed and death in Sacramento. In February 1859 the Supreme Court announced its ruling. It affirmed Sutter's claim to his original land grant by Governor Alvarado but rejected his second (and twice as large) claim. That claim was based on Governor Micheltorena having sweepingly cleared any rival claims, in return for Sutter's vow of loyalty to Mexican President Santa Anna.

The decision caused the collapse of Sutter's shaky finances. His remaining hope was to find a means of keeping his home and the farmland on which it sat. Relief came in 1864, when California provided him with a pension of $250 per month.

Through it all, Sutter remained unchanged. In 1865 a discharged soldier whom he had hired to do odd jobs was caught stealing. Sutter, ever the lord of the manor, ordered the man flogged—as illegal under American law as it had been when he'd done the same under Mexican law. This time Sutter paid a price, similarly without regard to the boundaries of law. "The old adobe residence of General Sutter ... together with its valuable contents, was destroyed by fire on Wednesday morning, the 21st," San Francisco's *Evening Bulletin* reported. "The fire was the work of an incendiary [arsonist], supposed to be a discharged soldier, who had been hanging about the premises the past few days."

With everything in ashes, the Sutters left California, relocating in Lititz, Pennsylvania. Sutter spent his remaining years seeking to salvage something of the fortune that had slipped through his fingers. Shuttling between Lititz and Washington, DC, he had entreaties to Congress prepared on his behalf. "Now in his old age, and in a state of absolute penury," one such plea stated, "he asks not for one cent for such aid as he rendered to his adopted and profoundly honored government in the extension of its domain to the borders of the Pacific Ocean, and ... the untold treasures of California. He asks only that the government shall secure to him so much of its unsold public lands as it has caused to be unjustly taken from him, or its equivalent in money."[7]

Every new Congress, over a period of fifteen years, considered another of his appeals. While in Washington continuing his efforts in 1880, Sutter died at the age of seventy-eight. Congress no longer had to decide what it thought about John A. Sutter.

JAMES GADSDEN
Government Aid to Big Business

If the Union is to continue to be bounded as it has been extended, from the Atlantic to the Pacific … measures must be adapted to bring nearer together the extremes, by these iron highways which, in stimulating social and commercial intercourse, constitute the strongest bonds of political harmony.
—JAMES GADSDEN, PRESIDENT, SOUTH CAROLINA RAILROAD COMPANY

The life of James Gadsden reveals that there is nothing new about powerful lobbyists winning government funds to support their special interests. Nor is there anything new about individuals leaving high-level government jobs for corporate positions from which they operate as influential lobbyists. Gadsden was an adjutant general in the U.S. Army who left government service and became a railroad president—a railroad president later appointed by President Franklin Pierce to purchase land from Mexico for the purpose of building a railroad. The Gadsden Purchase, which the United States acquired in 1853, also resolved a lingering boundary dispute between the two countries. It now forms the southern end of Arizona and southwestern New Mexico.

James Gadsden was born in 1788 to a distinguished South Carolina family. His grandfather had been a delegate to the Continental Congress and, later, a brigadier general in the war itself. After graduating

James Gadsden (1788–1858)

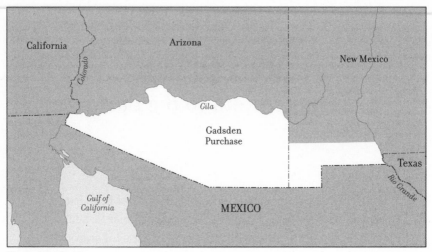

The Gadsden Purchase

from Yale and serving in the military, Gadsden became the president of the South Carolina Canal and Rail Road Company. In that capacity, he saw opportunities to connect the South via rail to gold-rich California and ports on the Pacific. A firm believer in slavery, he also saw in the newly acquired western lands the opportunity—indeed, the necessity—to secure its continued legality through additional congressional votes from new slave states. Toward that end, Gadsden joined an effort under way to divide California in two, with slavery permitted in the southern half. To encourage the legislature via the prospect of bringing development to sparsely populated (mostly by Mexican Americans) Southern California, he sent a petition in 1852 bearing 1,200 signatures of people seeking permission to establish a district that would be farmed by "African Domestics."[1] Slavery was a hotly contested issue in California. Gadsden's plan aroused debate but went nowhere.

When President Franklin Pierce decided the United States should seek to purchase land from Mexico, Gadsden was ideally situated for the appointment—just as appointments today often go to corporate executives whose resumes include previous government positions and powerful politicians as references.

The reason the southern railroads said they needed this Mexican land was that it contained mountain passes that did not exist elsewhere in the region. One such pass, in the area still under dispute, was so important that the town where it was situated had been named after it: El Paso.

Still, the purchase of land for the purpose of building a railroad triggered a three-way clash of political power, ideals, and pork. Abolitionists believed the government should not actively promote the economy of the slave-holding South. Southerners responded with outrage, though others in the South who were troubled by slavery argued that promoting industry in the region would help build an economy that need not depend on slavery to be financially viable.

Ideals and pork also came into conflict. Southerners' commitment to states' rights had previously led them to oppose federal expenditures for road and bridge construction. Such projects, they believed, were the responsibility of the states. Once the federal government entered in, they argued, it would open the door to ever-increasing centralization of power. Indeed, history has proven them right.

But in this instance most leaders left their ideals on the campaign trail and reached for the pork. Railroads, after all, were beginning to shift the flow of commerce through the north, rather than along the waterways leading to the Mississippi River. Moreover, even if the Southern states could have afforded the $10 million price tag for the Gadsden Purchase, they were barred by the Constitution from negotiating a treaty with another country.

Faced with these realities, the South's two foremost advocates for states' rights, Jefferson Davis and John C. Calhoun, found ways to justify federal involvement in the building of a southern transcontinental railroad. Davis, at the time secretary of war in the Pierce administration, maintained that federal expenditures to enable such a railroad were legitimate because it might be needed for national defense.[2] And while Calhoun, in his keynote address to the 1845 Memphis Commercial Convention, asserted that building railroads was beyond the purview of Congress, he allowed as to how the government, as owner of the land on which such a railroad would be built, could grant alternate sections of the land to the railroads, since such grants would raise the value of the land the government retained.

Gadsden was also present at that convention. It was there that he proposed two possible routes for such a railroad—one terminating in San Diego and the other in Mazatlán, a port on the Mexican coast opposite the southern tip of Baja California. San Diego, at that time, was also in Mexico. Since federal investment, not an agreement with Mexico, was the issue at hand, how were the Memphis conventioneers planning to pull this off? War with Mexico?

Less than a year later, that's exactly what happened. What they were thinking in 1845 may be suggested by what surfaced in 1853 when Gadsden received his instructions regarding the purchase. He was authorized to

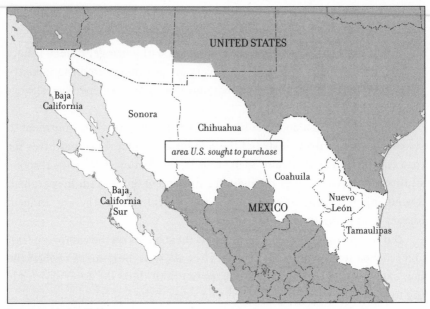

Gadsden's mission, 1853

spend up to $65 million to acquire a region that included most of what are now the Mexican states of Baja California, Coahuila, Chihuahua, Sonora, Nuevo León, and Tamaulipas.

Gadsden's mission sparked a new voice of opposition in the person of Senator Thomas Hart Benton, whose doubts began with the underlying premise that the land was necessary in order to build a southern railroad through the Rockies:

> We have a fine ... route on the parallels of 34 and 35, by Albuquerque, corresponding with the center of the southern states. The route gained by the [Gadsden] treaty is not even a sectional route. It is too far south to be southern. It is not only beyond the center, but beyond the limits and latitudes of the southern states; and is besides ... through country so utterly desolate, desert, and God forsaken that Kit Carson says even a wolf could not make his living upon it.

Benton went on to speculate regarding a darker causes for locating a railroad so far south:

> What is the reason of this strange deflection? I will tell you.... The

city of New San Diego. Here it is—[holding up a map]—here it is, and with explanatory notes showing that it is a "port." ... New San Diego, then, is the governing point in the southern proposed railroad route to the Pacific Ocean. And who owns this city on the map which has suddenly become a governing point in our legislation and diplomacy? It is said to belong to the military.

To Benton, a railroad located so far south, when considered with the fact that Gadsden had been authorized to acquire far more of Mexico, suggested that proslavery interests sought to expand the South—through purchase, if possible; through military actions, if necessary—and consequently increase the number and influence of slave states.

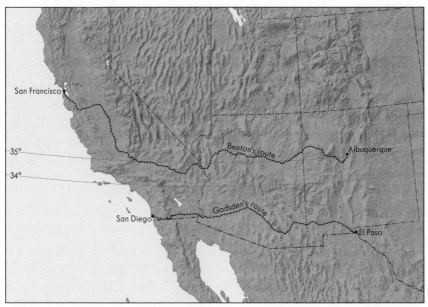

Benton's claim of an alternate southern rail route

Why then would Mexico be willing to sell? Not because it wanted to. The United States was its greatest threat. Even as Gadsden was in Mexico City seeking to purchase a wide swath of territory, a privately raised army of Americans under the leadership of William Walker illegally invaded sparsely populated Baja California and briefly declared it an independent republic before being chased out by local Mexicans. Fortunately for Gadsden, however, Mexico was burdened by $17 million of debt from its recent war with the

United States. President Santa Anna therefore grudgingly agreed to sell only enough land to raise sufficient funds to enable his military to defend against further incursions by the United States.

The agreement was sent to Washington for approval. Gadsden then pursued the purchase of the rest of the land the United States sought by not so privately meeting with revolutionary elements in Mexico. To further unsettle Santa Anna, he told the Mexican president "the spirit of the age" was such that these northern regions of Mexico would eventually secede to join the United States, so he might as well sell them now.[3] Santa Anna responded by having his ambassador in Washington demand that President Pierce recall Gadsden. Pierce expressed his understanding and respect to the ambassador and did nothing. Later, when the agreement was being finalized by the U.S. Senate, Gadsden offended virtually every Mexican by telling Americans living in the country to ignore a call to illuminate all homes in celebration of Mexico's Independence Day.[4] President Pierce then sent word to Gadsden to come home.

James Gadsden did not live to see the railroad for which he had labored so long. He died in 1858. The railroad was delayed by the approach and outbreak of the Civil War. Only after Union troops secured the Southwest in 1862 did planning and construction begin. As it turned out, Senator Benton had been right. Adequate passes did exist through the mountains north of the Gadsden Purchase, and in laying out its main line, the Southern Pacific Railroad did not pass through the Gadsden Purchase.

STEPHEN A. DOUGLAS
The Line on Slavery: Erasing and Redrawing

The issues between Mr. Lincoln and myself ... are direct, unequivo-
cal, and irreconcilable. He goes for uniformity in our domestic
institutions, for a war of sections, until one or the other shall be subdued. I go for the ... right of the people to decide for themselves.
—FROM THE LINCOLN-DOUGLAS DEBATES

Illinois Senator Stephen A. Douglas established more present-day state
lines than any other individual. Two of those borders later resulted in
the location of even more state borders than he had directly established.
In addition, because of his role in creating the present-day boundaries of
Texas-New Mexico, Oklahoma-Kansas, and Kansas-Nebraska, Douglas twice
prevented the United States from
breaking apart over slavery. What
more must one do to become president? (Answer: Run against someone other than Abraham Lincoln.)

Actually, Douglas beat Lincoln
in their 1858 Senate race. That was
the election during which the famed
Lincoln-Douglas debates took place.
It was also after Douglas had created the boundaries that temporarily
averted the Civil War. Illinois voters
loved Douglas for this achievement,
since the state was economically
connected to both North and South.

Stephen A. Douglas (1813–1861)

It was connected to the North through the Great Lakes to the Erie Canal. It was connected to the South through its rivers, virtually all of which flow to the Mississippi.

As a towering figure in the struggle to avert the Union's breakup, Douglas, a short man, was known as "the Little Giant." Like the towering Lincoln, he rose from difficult circumstances. Born in Vermont in 1813, Douglas was only three months old when his father died. After his schooling, he relocated to Illinois at the age of twenty—again, much like Lincoln, who migrated to Illinois at twenty-one. Both men undertook the study of law.

Within two years of his arrival, Douglas was elected to the state legislature, where he served with another newly elected young legislator. (Need I say who?) Douglas looked back at those days (through politically tinted glasses) during the 1858 Lincoln-Douglas debates:

> Lincoln is one of those peculiar men who perform with admirable skill everything which they undertake.... He was just as good at telling an anecdote as now. He could beat any of the boys wrestling, or running a foot-race, in pitching quoits or tossing a copper; could ruin more liquor than all the boys of the town together; and the dignity and impartiality with which he presided at a horse-race or fist-fight excited the admiration and won the praise of everybody that was present and participated.

The Lincoln-Douglas debates, stripped of their backhanded compliments and oratorical ornaments, were about slavery. More precisely, they were about Douglas's record in the U.S. Senate regarding slavery: his coauthorship of the Compromise of 1850 and sole authorship of the Kansas-Nebraska Act in 1854. Today these laws are mainly names memorized for tests. Back then they tested the nation's ability to survive. The Compromise of 1850 created a crack in America's largest political dam; the Kansas-Nebraska Act caused the dam to collapse.

That dam was the Missouri Compromise, enacted in 1820 to settle the slavery disputes that had flared anew after the Louisiana Purchase. It stipulated that no new state or territory north of 36°30′ could have slavery, with the exception of Missouri. It blocked the conflict well enough for the Louisiana Purchase, and even when Texas later joined the nation. But after the vast acquisition of lands in the Mexican War, the South could see that continuing the dividing line at 36°30′ would no longer maintain parity between free states and slave states. Added to

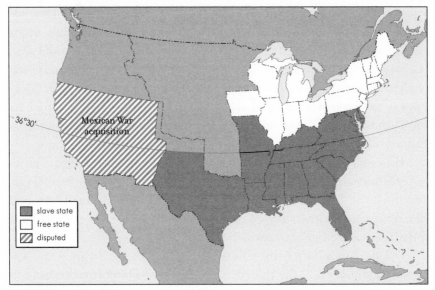

Slave and free states, 1848

the South's concerns were California (filled with gold) and New Mexico (filled with Mexicans). These three issues created an explosive political mix.

California had organized its own boundaries without waiting for congressional authorization—boundaries so large that they crossed the Missouri Compromise line. But Congress had yet to vote on whether or not to accept those boundaries.

The region now known as New Mexico was populated by people who had not sought to join the United States. Minimizing their potential animosity was crucial, since their population was centered in Santa Fe, easily accessible to Mexico. The Polk administration assured the region's residents that, unless their local laws violated the Constitution, their laws would remain in force. Their laws prohibited slavery.

Both the events in California and the emerging territory of New Mexico raised hopes in the North and caused alarms in the South. A new level of intensity infused editorials in Southern newspapers. "It was to be hoped that the rapacity of the ... North would have been satisfied with having monopolized the whole of California," Georgia's *Savannah Morning News* commented, "and that for the sake of appearances at least, they would for a time have abstained from any interference with the territory lying contiguous to, and belonging to, the slave states."

Stephen Douglas was now the chairman of the Senate Committee on Ter-

ritories, which had responsibilities for proposing where territorial boundaries would be located and for structuring territorial governments. If his
committee chose to deviate from the Missouri Compromise, it could send
such legislation to the Senate floor. Because the Missouri Compromise was
the lynchpin in the dispute over slavery in new territories, Chairman Douglas was sitting in a highly precarious chair. It was the chair in which he
most wanted to sit; if he could sufficiently satisfy both North and South, his
chances of winning the presidency would be greatly enhanced.

He sought to achieve that goal through the Compromise of 1850, a pack-
age of bills dealing with California statehood, the creation of the New Mexico
Territory, the Texas-New Mexico boundary, slave trade in the District of
Columbia, and fugitive slaves. Taken together, they were designed to coun-
terbalance each other in terms of the slavery dispute.

Douglas himself wrote the bills involving New Mexico. In his Texas-New
Mexico boundary bill, the United States purchased land from Texas (still
greatly in debt from its years as a republic) and annexed that land to New
Mexico. In his bill creating the New Mexico Territory, its citizens were allowed
to decide for themselves whether or not to permit slavery. The same choice was
also given to California. The Missouri Compromise was set aside.

Douglas believed the Missouri Compromise was more than set aside; he
believed it was eliminated. Most important, he believed the nation's inabil-
ity to reach agreement on slavery had now been resolved by a larger issue on
which the nation *did* agree: democracy, whereby the people decide. "It was
one of the great merits of the compromise measures of 1850," Douglas told his
fellow senators, "that they furnished a principle ... to prevent any strife, any
controversy, any sectional agitation in the future.... A geographical line had
been abandoned and repudiated by the Congress of the United States and,
in lieu of it, the plan of leaving each territory free to decide the question for
itself was adopted."

Indeed, Douglas's approach to ending the nation's division over slavery
succeeded in 1850, though it did so by dividing the divisions. Some on both
sides accepted it; others on both sides did not. The editors of Georgia's *Macon
Weekly Telegraph* were shocked and offended that the legislation had given
New Mexicans the right to decide for themselves whether or not to allow
slavery, declaring in September:

> Is there any outrage, is there any farce, too gross to be perpetrated
> on any Southern right, or to be approved under ... [the] new-found

discovery of the inherent right of a people of a territory to sovereignty? ... The submission of the South will soon find that, although their sense of honor and their regard for right is extinct, yet the position they have assumed of being kicked by the North indefinitely is quite as uncomfortable even to timid servility.

In October, up in Vermont, the editors of Brattleboro's *Weekly Eagle* were equally outraged:

There is joy in Washington ... over the "Settlement of our Slavery Difficulties." ... The consent of certain citizens to forego their purpose of dissolving this Union ... is deemed an occasion suited to these demonstrations of joy and thankfulness. We infer from the nature and magnitude of the concession made to slavery, that free men have been greatly in the wrong. We have been guilty of some grave offence for which severe atonement was demanded.

Amid the clamor, the public failed to notice that the new Texas-New Mexico boundary, for which Douglas was responsible, set the stage for future states in a way that transcended the issue of slavery. Time would show that Douglas had located the boundary precisely for the future division of the New Mexico Territory into two states, virtually equal in size, thus providing a maximum buffer for New Mexico's Hispanic citizens, who greatly feared Texans (see "Francisco Perea and John Watts" in this book). It is one of the three most brilliant straight lines on the American map.

The other two equally brilliant straight lines were drawn by the same man. They resulted from the fact that the Compromise of 1850 did not, as Douglas had hoped, end the debate over slavery. It flared up yet again in December 1853, when Douglas sent to the Senate floor his committee's bill for the creation of Nebraska. Ironically, what reignited the debate was that aspect of Douglas's bill that he thought had settled the argument: popular sovereignty. In this instance, however, popular sovereignty had the opposite effect than it had had in the Compromise of 1850. It now raised hopes in the South and alarms in the North. A Mississippi newspaper claimed that Douglas's Nebraska bill "will put to the test professions which have been made by the Northern men," while an Ohio paper described the bill as "a crazy, dangerous, and dishonorable effort to break down the Missouri Compromise."[1]

Douglas was not discouraged. He believed he had the key; the problem had

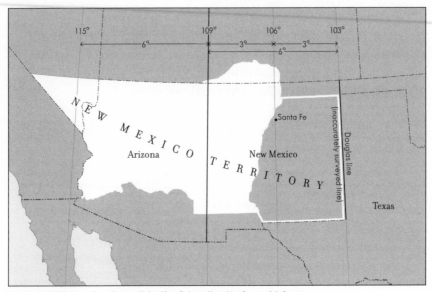

Douglas's 1850 boundary line anticipating future New Mexico and Arizona

to do with the door. The nation needed *two* doors: one opening on Nebraska, the other on a territory called Kansas, carved from the southern end of his original Nebraska proposal. Creating the two territories simultaneously made it possible that one would choose slavery and the other would not.

Douglas introduced the revised bill in January 1854, and indeed it did make a difference. Although Northerners continued shaking their fists, they now added insults aimed at Douglas. "Year after year we have warned those who have been disposed to yield much to the South for sake of harmony," an editorial in New Jersey's *Trenton State Gazette* declared, disparaging the Little Giant of the Senate by adding, "Now we find the Missouri Compromise, always regarded with religious faith by its great originator, Henry Clay, attacked by a pygmy statesman."

Douglas's addition of Kansas also made a difference in the South. They now *resumed* shaking their fists. But, unlike the North, they did not shake them at Douglas. They shook them at the North for continuing to shake *their* fists, even after Douglas's two-state response to northern fist shaking. The conflicts were becoming increasingly complex. Each camp, however, believed the matter was becoming increasingly clear. "We have never read speeches which more completely and irrefragably established what [the Kansas-Nebraska Act] proposed to do, than have the efforts of the friends of Mr. Douglas' Bill," the *Macon Weekly Telegraph* asserted. "The enemies of the measure have in every instance been ... forced to take some poor pitiful shift of abolition, maudlin cant, or irrelevant discussion."

As with the Compromise of 1850, the furor over slavery in the Kansas-Nebraska Act diverted attention from the significance of Douglas's boundary lines. Though he originally proposed that Kansas's southern border be located, quite logically, adjacent to Texas at 36°30′, shortly after the bill was introduced he shifted the border to 37°. This shift left a gap of one-half of one degree. Today that gap is the Oklahoma Panhandle. Why did Douglas do this? "The southern boundary of the proposed territory ... is on the line of 36°30′," Douglas noted when introducing the amendment to shift the boundary, explaining, "[My] attention has been called, by the chairman of the Committee on Indian Affairs, to the fact that that boundary would divide the Cherokee country; whereas, by taking the parallel of 37° north latitude as the southern boundary, the line would run between the Cherokees and the Osages."

That sounded plausible ... except for the fact that American Indian boundaries were unaffected by state lines. Two weeks later, Senator William Sebastian, the committee chairman to whom Douglas referred, revealed the truer reason when he stated on the floor of the Senate, "[My] committee is maturing a policy which ... directly affects the terms and conditions upon which the title of the Indians to the lands guaranteed to them by treaty, within the proposed limits of these territories, is to be extinguished." Shifting the line simplified the task of extinguishing various Indian treaties.

In addition, the shift enhanced the geometry for future states—though it left that pesky gap. With a boundary at 37° as a baseline, two tiers of equally spaced future states emerged. One was a tier of prairie states: Kansas, Nebraska, South Dakota, and North Dakota, each having three degrees of height. Just to their west was a tier of mountainous states: Colorado, Wyoming, and Montana, each with four degrees of height.

Did Douglas envision this? His Kansas-Nebraska Act stipulated Kansas's northern border at precisely the height that, if replicated, would yield the tier of states that resulted. Yet he never expressed this geometric logic in the Senate debate. Likewise, if he foresaw the future Arizona and New Mexico by virtue of where he located the Texas-New Mexico boundary, he never expressed that either. Perhaps for good reason. Both debates were filled with suspicion regarding future slave and free states. For Douglas to add projected states to the debate would have added fuel to the fire he was seeking to tamp down. Though his intentions for future boundaries cannot be ascertained

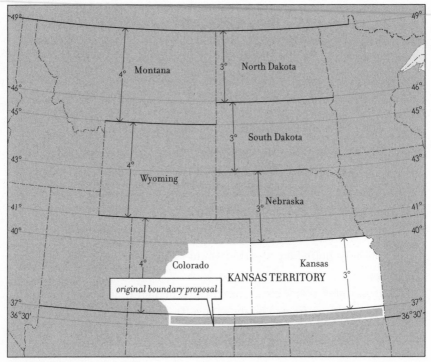

Kansas: southern boundary shift

from what he didn't say, a pattern emerges from the added facts that he also made no mention of his colleague's plan to extinguish Indian treaties, and that his prized policy of "popular sovereignty" was never expressed as such in the 1850 legislation that initiated it.

While Douglas was successful in winning popular sovereignty in the Kansas-Nebraska Act, popular sovereignty proved less than successful in Kansas. Proslavery settlers drafted a Kansas constitution at Lecompton; antislavery settlers drafted an opposing Kansas constitution at Topeka. Both constitutions were sent to Washington for approval. Congress approved neither, but Senator Douglas favored the antislavery Topeka constitution over its proslavery rival from Lecompton:

> Is there a man within the hearing of my voice who believes the Lecompton constitution does embody the will of a majority of the bona fide inhabitants of Kansas? ... We are told that it ... has been submitted to the people for ratification or rejection. How submitted? In a manner that allowed every man to vote for it, but precluded

the possibility of any man voting against it. We are told that there is a majority of about five thousand five hundred votes recorded in its favor under these circumstances.... On the other hand, we have a vote of the people, in pursuance of law, on the 4th of January last, when this constitution was submitted by the Legislature to the people for acceptance or rejection, showing a majority of more than ten thousand against it.

Though he could not know it at the time, Douglas had just ended his chances to become president. As the 1860 campaign neared, the cost of Douglas's choice surfaced. Southerners denounced Douglas along the lines stated by former congressman and diplomat William Stiles of Georgia:

In 1854, Mr. Douglas, to curry favor with the South ... brought forward his measure for the repeal of the Missouri [Compromise] restriction. The South was enchanted and shouted paeans to the "Little Giant." ... But would they have shouted those paeans ... had they supposed it covered, as Mr. Douglas now claims, his odious squatters sovereignty doctrine? Never! Never!! Has not Stephen A. Douglas, then, cruelly deceived and wantonly betrayed the South? Did he not bring forward a measure which he induced us to believe was for our benefit, and does he not show us now and boast that it was for our ruin![2]

The Democrats split into two parties during their 1860 convention, both claiming to be the true Democratic Party. The Northern party nominated Douglas; the Southern party chose John C. Breckenridge. By dividing its supporters, the Democrats enabled Republican Abraham Lincoln to win the White House with less than 40 percent of the popular vote.

One month after Lincoln's election, Southern states began seceding from the Union. Douglas made a final plea to avert the hemorrhage. "Are we prepared for war?" he beseeched his colleagues. "I do not mean that kind of preparation which consists of armies and navies, and supplies, and munitions of war; but are we prepared in our hearts for war with our own brethren and kindred? I confess, I am not."

The long fuse leading to the Civil War detonated at Fort Sumter in April 1861. Whichever side won, Douglas had lost. On the Sunday following the firing on Fort Sumter, he (after some coaxing from his wife) went to the White

House to speak with President Lincoln. The two longtime rivals exchanged pleasantries, then Lincoln read to Douglas his draft of a speech summoning the nation to war. Douglas offered only one criticism, recorded by a mutual friend who was present. "Instead of the call for 75,000 men," Douglas advised, "I would make it 200,000. You do not know the dishonest purposes of those men as well as I do."[3] He then asked to see a map. Standing next to the president, the man who knew the American map as well as anyone—and who had sought to avoid war as much as anyone—pointed out the geographic weak points in the South.

Six weeks later, he was dead, having fallen ill with typhoid fever. A large monument marks his grave in Chicago. But perhaps the most meaningful monument to Stephen A. Douglas is on the map itself: the equally spaced lines in the middle of the nation. They, and the gap that became Oklahoma's Panhandle, are enduring monuments to a visionary who dreamed of equality but accepted imperfection.

JOHN A. QUITMAN
Annexing Cuba: Liberty, Security, Slavery

I believe that the institution of slavery is not only right and proper, but the natural and normal condition of the superior and inferior races, when in contact.... That the preservation of the institution of slavery in Cuba ... is essential to the safety of our own system.... That it is consistent with the designs of Providence, and our right and duty, not to restrain but to encourage the white Caucasian race to carry humanity, civilization and progress to the rich and fertile countries south of us, which, now in the occupation of inferior and mixed races, be undeveloped and useless.

—JOHN A. QUITMAN[1]

During the early 1850s Mississippi Governor John A. Quitman raised a private army for the purpose of invading Cuba and offering it to the United States. His primary reason was to preserve slavery on the island (ruled, at the time, by Spain) and thereby add an additional slave state to the Union.[2]

Quitman's involvement commenced in 1850, when he was introduced to Narciso López, leader of a group of Cuban revolutionaries. López and his followers were wealthy landowners and merchants who turned against Spain when a key element of their wealth—slavery—was threatened by changes in colonial policy.

John A. Quitman (1798–1858)

211

Spain, greatly weakened by the loss of nearly its entire empire, was seeking to ally itself with the nation whose empire was most rapidly growing: England. England, for its part, was seeking to undermine the nation whose borders were most rapidly growing: the United States. By allying with Spain, England could establish a naval presence in Cuba, thereby dominating the intersection of commerce between the Gulf of Mexico and the sea.

The United States, needless to say, was well aware of these moves. Two years before Quitman met López, Senator Lewis Cass stated, "Doubts have been expressed here as to the designs of England upon Cuba.... It has been repeatedly said that she has demanded the island, either in absolute conveyance, or as a mortgage for the payment of the debts due to her people." Cass avoided domestic controversy by not mentioning another aspect of England's maneuver. If England could get Spain to end slavery in Cuba, the island would become a beacon to American slaves—if nothing else, as a haven of escape; possibly, as encouragement to revolt. No matter how it played out, emancipation in Cuba might well derail the American express.[3]

Governor Quitman knew the impact it would have on his and all other slave states if Cuba came under British domination. Still, when approached by López in 1850, he did not accept the offer of command. Having risen to the rank of major general in the Mexican War, the governor recognized both the political and the military risks. So too had Jefferson Davis and Robert E. Lee, other distinguished veterans of the Mexican War, both of whom had already rejected López's offer.

Narciso López (1797–1851)

While Quitman did not accept the offer, neither did he completely reject it. Rather, he cited his current commitments as governor. In addition he told López that he could only come to his aid after a revolution had commenced under Cuban leaders. This stipulation reflected Quitman's concern about violating the Neutrality Act of 1818, which prohibited any person "within the territory or jurisdiction of the United States ... to set on foot, or provide or prepare the means for any military expedition or enterprise to be carried on from then against the territory or dominions of any foreign prince or state or any other colony, district, or people with whom the United States are at peace."

López was indeed on the verge of launching the revolution Quitman stipulated. Or something similar—because Cuban forces were hard to come by (nearly half the island's young men being slaves, disinclined to fight for slavery), he had been recruiting Americans to fight for Cuban independence from Spain. The same month when he met Governor Quitman, Washington's *Daily National Intelligencer* reported, "[An] invasion of Cuba is contemplated. This new expedition we are told is to rendez-vous somewhere in the island of Haiti, under Gen. Lopez, and attempt a landing at some port on the south side of Cuba.... Our information from Havana is that the government there has been made aware of every movement." Two months later, the Cuban revolution began. A correspondent for the *Missouri Courier* ably covered the historic event:

> The expedition ... landed at Cardenas on the 19th [of May 1850], lost some in landing ... entered the town, [and] attacked the jail, supposing it to be the barracks. The jail was guarded by 15 men who stood the fire well.... After this, some soldiers went to the Governor's house.... The house was well defended.... The invading troops, having lost time in getting off their wounded and procuring fuel for the steamer, *Creole*, which was to return for reinforcements, became disheartened and insisted on going to Key West. They were closely pursued by the Spanish war steamer *Pizarro* but happily escaped.

The invaders were home in time for dinner.

Confirming Quitman's legal concern, López was arrested for violating the Neutrality Act. But he had become so popular with Americans as a "freedom fighter" that, after three hung juries in the trial of a coconspirator, the government opted not to pursue the case. The fact that politics had trumped the law on this issue was not lost on Governor Quitman.

The political landscape shifted further in this direction when López launched another invasion of Cuba the following year. On August 12, 1851, he successfully landed and entered the interior of the island with, according to his records, 400 troops—forty-nine of whom were Cubans. The following morning, Spanish soldiers in the vicinity attacked a contingent of López's recruits. But the recruits not only repelled the Spaniards, they pursued them—right into a much larger force of Spanish soldiers. That same morning, other recruits, with whom López himself was based, were also attacked by a Spanish division. Many managed to retreat with López into the mountains, but they were left nearly depleted of supplies and weaponry. By August 16 those still alive were either captured or, like López, surrendered.[4]

Once again, the fate of Cuba fired up Americans. Though López had failed, he remained a hero in the United States—front-page news in the September 8, 1851, *Boston Daily Atlas*:

> General Lopez was condemned to be garroted on Monday, the 1st of September ... at the entrance of the [Havana] harbor, directly opposite the Moro [old Spanish castle]. There were on the ground at the time 5,000 troops, 3,000 infantry, and 1,000 cavalry, and about 8,000 citizens.... Lopez was brought forward and ascended a platform, about fifteen feet high, on which was the chair of execution.... His last words were, "I die for my beloved Cuba." He then took his seat, the machine was adjusted, and at one turn of the screw his head dropped forward.

Because most Americans believed public execution was barbaric, wresting Cuba from Spain was now elevated to an even loftier plane. The death of Narciso López also left only one credible commander at that time: John A. Quitman.

The political landscape shifted further in Quitman's favor when Franklin Pierce was elected president in 1852. Pierce made plain from the outset his expansionist views. "The policy of my Administration will not be controlled by any timid forebodings of evil from expansion," he stated in his inaugural address. "Indeed, it is not to be disguised that our attitude as a nation and our position on the globe render the acquisition of certain possessions not within our jurisdiction eminently important for our protection."

Four months later, Quitman agreed to organize an invasion of Cuba. His efforts took him to New York, where he sought funds from business interests connected to cotton, tobacco, and other Southern products. He then headed to Washington to secure the private political support needed for his venture. There he met not only with influential Southern politicians but also with Illinois Senator Stephen A. Douglas, whose backing, as chairman of the Senate Committee on Territories, would be vital to the annexation of Cuba. The meeting went well, as Quitman likely expected, since Douglas's views on Cuban annexation were well known:

> Whenever the people of Cuba shall show themselves worthy of freedom by asserting and maintaining their independence and

establishing republican institutions, my heart, my sympathies, my prayers, are with them for the accomplishment of the object.... When that independence shall have been established, if it shall become necessary to their interest or safety to apply as Texas did for annexation, I shall be ready to do by them as we did by Texas, and receive them into the Union.[5]

In Cuba, meanwhile, Spain sought to preempt American designs by issuing a number of decrees regarding slavery and race. One freed those slaves illegally imported from the United States. Another established a procedure enabling slaves to purchase their freedom. A third allowed Cubans of any color to join the militia. And a fourth legalized interracial marriage. Journalists in the United States referred to these decrees as the "Africanization" of Cuba.

With Quitman recruiting troops, stockpiling armaments, and raising funds through the issuance of Cuban bonds bearing his signature as "Commander-in-Chief," the Senate took up consideration of a proposal to suspend the Neutrality Act. The legislation was sent to the Foreign Relations Committee, but Quitman's quest suddenly became an uphill effort when Senator Douglas proposed the Kansas-Nebraska Act. Because Douglas's bill would end federal regulation of where slavery could and could not exist, the annexation of Cuba became embroiled in rumors that the Kansas-Nebraska Act was part of a grand Southern conspiracy. Senator Thomas Hart Benton brought those rumors out in the open:

I must now ... look out for [the bill's] real object—the particular purpose for which it was manufactured, and the grand movement of which it is to be the basis. First, the mission of Mr. Gadsden to Santa Anna. It must have been conceived about the time that this bill was. Fifty million dollars for as much Mexican territory on our southern border as would make five or six states.... Secondly, the mission of [Ambassador] Soulé to Madrid—also a grand movement in itself ... two hundred and fifty million dollars for Cuba.... I only call attention to them as probable indexes to this grand movement ... and my own belief [that] this Nebraska bill is only an entering wedge to future enterprises—a thing manufactured for a particular purpose—a stepping stone to a grand movement which is to develop itself in this country of ours.

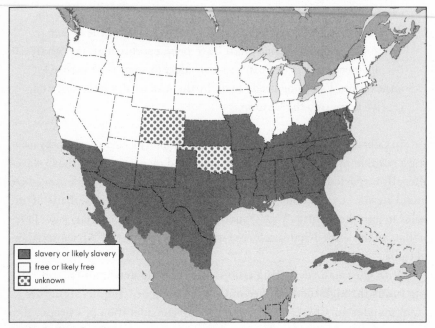

Senator Benton's fear

The "grand movement" that Benton suspected consisted of Cuba being annexed as a slave state, Kansas becoming a slave state, James Gadsden acquiring the regions of Mexico he sought, a slave state being created from the southern half of the New Mexico Territory, and a slave state being created from the southern half of California. Taken together, these possibilities would have made the slave-holding South indomitable. Such a movement had in fact been suggested by López in a letter to Governor Quitman the day after their initial meeting. López had linked the annexation of Cuba to a "union of the Southern States ... [that] could never be broken."

Despite Senator Benton's misgivings, President Pierce signed the Kansas-Nebraska Act and, the following day, sought to mitigate Northern anger by issuing a proclamation regarding Cuba:

> Whereas information has been received that sundry persons, citizens of the United States and others residing therein, are engaged in organizing and fitting out a military expedition for the invasion of the island of Cuba; and
>
> Whereas the said undertaking is contrary to the spirit and express stipulations of treaties between the United States and Spain,

derogatory to the character of this nation, and in violation of the obvious duties and obligations of faithful and patriotic citizens....

I do issue this proclamation to warn all persons that the General Government ... will not fail to prosecute with due energy all those who ... presume thus to disregard the laws of the land and our treaty obligations.

Privately, Pierce confided to Louisiana Senator John Slidell and others that he would not seek to enforce the Neutrality Act if Quitman's expedition could be kept under wraps. But Quitman's luck was running out. Eleven days after the presidential proclamation, the *New York Express* revealed that "many of the Northern members [of Congress], and several from the slaveholding states ... are convinced that there is plan on foot to get Cuba—peaceable or otherwise.... The Administration, it is believed, will favor the scheme." As rumors mounted in the press, Supreme Court Justice John A. Campbell ordered that a grand jury be presented with charges against Quitman for violating the Neutrality Act. The grand jury, however, refused to issue an indictment for a crime not yet committed. Judge Campbell then sought to torpedo the commission of the crime by ordering that Quitman be held in prison until he had posted bond as assurance that he would not enter Cuba. The order triggered widespread condemnation as unconstitutional, given that Quitman had not been charged with any crime.

While his lawyers navigated the legal obstacle course, Quitman struggled with other obstacles. Many of his recruits and backers were now having second thoughts in the wake of the court's actions. Seeking to bolster their commitment, he traveled again to Washington in April 1855, hoping he could somehow obtain a meeting with President Pierce. In a case of fact being stranger than fiction, a correspondent for the *New York Herald* witnessed the president and Quitman unexpectedly encountering each other on Pennsylvania Avenue. "During the past six weeks, [President Pierce] has been seen but once on the avenue," the correspondent wrote. When Pierce next ventured out for a rare stroll, "in front of the Milkwood house he met General Quitman.... There was no chance to dodge, and they stood face to face.... With slight tremor in the voice, I heard him say, 'General, why haven't you been to see me? Call in the morning.'"

The following morning, Pierce shared with Quitman intelligence he had received regarding Spain's military buildup in Cuba. Troop levels were being increased, fortifications upgraded, and its naval presence bolstered.

With Quitman's recruits and dollars dwindling, the bottom line was clear: he had no chance. Six weeks later, Quitman resigned as revolutionary Cuba's commander in chief.

Though he gave up the title, he did not abandon the dream. Six months after resigning from the Cuban expedition, Quitman won election to the U.S. House of Representatives, where he sought further opportunities to pursue his agenda. The opportunity presented itself when William Walker, who had previously raised a private army that he unsuccessfully led into Mexico, raised another private army that he more successfully led into Nicaragua. Like Quitman's venture, Walker's acts violated the Neutrality Act. Upon Walker's arrest, Congressman Quitman resumed his quest. "A resolution calling upon the President for information relative to the arrest of Gen. Walker ... has passed the House by a large majority, and Gen. Quitman made an attempt to introduce his bill for the repeal of certain sections of the neutrality laws," the *New York Herald* reported in January 1858.

Quitman's efforts, however, were cut short. The following month, the press reported on a disease that only affected patrons of the National Hotel in Washington. In July the *Charleston Mercury* wrote, "The telegraph announces the decease of General Quitman.... [T]he intelligence is not a surprise; for, under the effects of the mysterious National Hotel disease, his vital powers have been slowly but surely failing." The mysterious disease turned out to have resulted from backed-up sewage in the hotel's basement, emitting toxic bacteria.

Though John A. Quitman failed to put Cuba on the U.S. map, he himself is on the map. His name is preserved in the towns of Quitman, Mississippi, Georgia, Louisiana, Missouri, and Texas.

CLARINA NICHOLS
Using Boundaries to Break Boundaries

The debate [on women's rights] was quite an animated one on the various modes to dispose of it.... Motions were made to hear Mrs. Nichols before the Convention or before the [elective franchise] committee. The hall was finally granted to Mrs. Nichols on Wednesday evening, to discuss this "vexed question."
—*NEW YORK HERALD*, JULY 20, 1859

In the states created after the Revolutionary War, proposals for boundaries often originated at statehood conventions, embedded in the state constitution being drafted for approval by Congress. At the Kansas statehood convention, Clarina Nichols spearheaded the first effort to dispute certain boundaries *within* a proposed state boundary, among them the boundary around the voting booth that kept women (and African Americans, American Indians, and Chinese Americans) out.

Delegates to the 1859 convention at Wyandotte, Kansas, received, among the numerous citizens' petitions submitted to such bodies, one that began with the usual frilly phrasing, but in this case lured the reader to a most unfrilly point:

We, the undersigned citizens of Kansas Territory, do respectfully submit to your honorable body that, whereas the women of the State have individually an evident common interest with

Clarina Nichols (1810–1885)

its men in the protection of life, liberty, property and intelligent
culture ... and whereas, in virtue of these common interests and
responsibilities, they have pressing need of all the legal and constitutional guarantees enjoyed by any class of citizens; and whereas,
the enjoyment of these guarantees involves the possession of equal
political rights: Therefore we, the undersigned, being of full age, do
respectfully petition and protest against any constitutional distinc-
tions based on difference of sex.[1]

As the representative of Kansas's Women's Rights Association, Clarina
Nichols sat among the spectators at the convention, dutifully knitting during each session and, during any recess, collaring delegates. What brought
this woman, who had lived happily and prosperously with her husband and
children in New England, to this place at this point in time? Was it that, as
she said, "I commenced my life with the most refined notion of women's
sphere.... But I could, even then, see over the barriers of that sphere, and
see that, however easy it might be for me to keep within it, as a daughter, a
great majority of women were outside its boundaries."[2] Perhaps. But it was
not until Nichols found herself outside the boundaries of "women's sphere"
that she became an activist on behalf of equal rights.

She was born Clarina Howard in 1810 to a family that lived modestly,
despite being among the wealthiest in West Townshend, Vermont. Her parents adhered to strict Baptist beliefs that included opposition to slavery and
abstinence from alcohol. During her childhood, these two tenets formed
into separate organized social movements: abolitionism and temperance.
The early feminist movement in the United States was, in many respects,
a result of women's becoming involved (and politically educated) in these
two movements. But a third issue provided the catalyst, one that affected all
women: the absence of equal rights regarding property and child custody.
Not all American women sympathized with the abolitionist or temperance
movements. But the more a woman subscribed to one or both of those movements, the more likely she was to perceive a pattern of empowerment that
favored white men over all others.

Nichols's first husband, Justin Carpenter, who came from a family of
similar values and affluence, did not seem to fit that pattern when she married him. He and his bride settled in Brockport, New York, where Carpenter
partnered with a like-spirited man to open a private school and lending
library. There they became deeply involved with the Temperance Society of

Brockport. But it was also there that she found herself facing the dilemmas all women of that era faced when their husbands turned out to be different persons than they had at first appeared. Clarina never revealed the causes of her failed marriage, although she once described their love as "one-sided."[3] What is known is that Carpenter suddenly ended his business partnership and later closed his school. When he then left his wife, he took the children. Doing so, at that time, was his legal right.

Fortunately for Clarina, Carpenter's father secured her children's return to her. Carpenter then opted to have no further contact with his children, nor to provide support. The injustice of this law became her primary concern. "I have asked learned judges why the state decrees that the father should retain the children, thus throwing upon the innocent mother the penalty which should fall upon the guilty party only," she stated in an address to a women's rights convention. "Say they, 'It is because the father has the property; it would not be just to burden the mother with the support of his children.'"[4]

Clarina was fortunate not only to have had sympathetic in-laws to help her regain her children, but also parents who had previously provided her with an education and self-esteem and who later offered a home to which she could return. All this support enabled her to get back on her feet. Soon she was making a living for herself and her children through her skills as a seamstress and by writing articles for the local newspaper. Her gifts for writing and public speaking quickly propelled her to the front ranks of the newly forming women's movement. Her talents also drew the attention of the paper's publisher, George Nichols, who became her second husband.

Twelve years into their marriage, the second precursor of the women's movement, abolitionism, propelled George and Clarina Nichols to move to Kansas. The 1854 Kansas-Nebraska Act had replaced the Missouri Compromise with "popular sovereignty," allowing a state or territory to decide for itself whether or not to allow slavery. As a result, among the droves of people moving to Kansas and Nebraska for economic opportunity, many opted for Kansas in an effort to create a majority vote for or against slavery. A key reason Kansas was more inviting to slaveholders was its adjacency to the slave states of the South. Though its immediate neighbor to the south, present-day Oklahoma, was then the Indian Territory, there were slave owners among the Cherokees and among the region's sparse white population.

The droves arriving in Kansas for the purpose of creating a proslavery majority were followed by droves seeking to counter this effort. George and Clarina Nichols were among this second wave of arrivals, though Clarina, being female, had no vote. When not establishing their homestead or coping with a near-fatal accident that befell one of her sons, or her husband's illness and subsequent death in 1855, Nichols worked as a journalist and activist. As the Moneka Woman's Rights Association strategized for the statehood convention, Nichols opposed the suggestion that they attach their quest for equality to the more formidable quest for racial equality. Doing so, she feared, could result in more harm than good for both.

Reflecting the turmoil over the question of slavery in Kansas, the Wyandotte convention was the territory's *fourth* constitutional constitution. The geographic boundaries of the proposed state were not at issue; the demographic boundaries were. The lines defining the status of human beings collided in the efforts to create Kansas. Finally, at Wyandotte, a bloodied and exhausted territory produced a constitution that both the territory's voters and Congress approved.

The boundary barring women from the voting booth was only one of several boundaries Nichols sought to eliminate in the proposed constitution at Wyandotte. More immediately important to her were the boundaries that preserved child custody and all property for men. As in the later civil rights movement, Nichols kept her eyes on the prize, but she focused her initial efforts on these specific, indisputable injustices. In her 1841 speech, she explained:

> Now, my friends, you will bear me witness that I have said nothing about woman's right to vote or make laws.... When I listen to Fourth of July orations ... tributes of admiration paid to our fathers because they compelled freedom for themselves and sons from the hand of oppression and power ... I have faith that when men come to value their own rights as means of human happiness, rather than of paltry gain, they will feel themselves more honored in releasing than in retaining the "inalienable rights" of woman.[5]

With custody and property rights as her priorities, Nichols was able to persuade the men at the Wyandotte convention to embed in the constitution equality regarding these two issues. Article 15 stated, "The Legislature shall provide for the protection of the rights of women in acquiring and possessing property, real, personal, and mixed, separate and apart from the husband; and shall also provide for their equal rights in the possession of their children." The same article also provided protection for a woman's home (or a man's, for that matter) by declaring it to be "exempted from forced sale under any process of law, and shall not be alienated without the joint consent of husband and wife." These two clauses rendered the Kansas constitution a historic document in the American struggle for women's rights.

The abolitionist and feminist movements scored partial victories at the Wyandotte convention. In addition to gender-neutral property and custody protections, the delegates voted to prohibit slavery in the state. But both African Americans and women lost when it came to voting rights.

The outbreak of the Civil War resulted in a hiatus for the women's movement, as its members turned their attention to the crisis at hand. Nichols moved to Washington, DC, where she worked in the Army Quartermaster Department and, with the end of the war, became the matron of a home operated by the National Association for the Relief of Destitute Colored Women and Children. She returned to Kansas in 1866, then moved in 1871 to California, where her grown children had migrated.

Nichols did not live to see voting rights extended to women. Throughout her life, women's influence resided primarily in their persuasive skills or, for some, the power of their beauty. Nichols's persuasive skills combined her keen wit and her ability to reveal (in the words of her petition) "common interest" with those she sought to persuade. One such common interest—surprising, perhaps, in an ardent feminist—was her valuing of feminine beauty. But Nichols's sense of beauty was beautifully insightful:

> Can it be that we have no more lasting claims to admiration than that beauty and those accomplishments which serve us only in the springtime of life? Surely our days of dancing and musical performances are soon over, when musical instruments of sweeter tone cry, "Mother."... Has not God endowed us with some lasting hold upon the affections? My sisters ... cultivate your powers of mind and heart, that you may become necessary to his better and undying sympathies.... Then will his soul respond to your worth, and the ties that bind you endure through time, and make you companions in eternity![6]

Clarina Nichols passed away in Mendocino, California, in 1885. Her viewpoints continue to be passed on.

LYMAN CUTLER'S NEIGHBOR'S PIG
The British-American Pig War

Lyman A. Cutler, being duly sworn, deposes and says ... that on or about the 15th of last June he shot a hog belonging to ... Mr. Griffin, and immediately informed him of the fact, stating it was done in a moment of irritation, the animal having been at several times a great annoyance, and that morning destroyed a portion of his garden.... That same afternoon, Mr. Griffin, in company with [Alexander Dallas, of the Hudson's Bay Company] came to his house.... Mr. Dallas stated this was British soil, and if Cutler did not [pay] ... one hundred dollars he would take him to Victoria ... for trial.
—DEPOSITION OF LYMAN CUTLER, SEPTEMBER 7, 1859[1]

In 1859 Lyman Cutler affected a border in today's state of Washington by shooting a pig. Because it was a particular pig, at a particular place, at a particular time, its demise brought the United States and Great Britain to the brink of war.

This particular pig lived on an island whose possession was disputed by the United States and Britain. The San Juan Islands, named by Spanish explorers prior to the arrival of British settlers, are a cluster of small islands between Canada's Vancouver Island (then under British rule) and the state of Washington. Possession of the islands was unspecified in the 1846 treaty that divided the Oregon Country, a region mutually claimed by the United States and Britain. The land was divided by an extension of

The pig (image based on available data) (ca. 1856–1859)

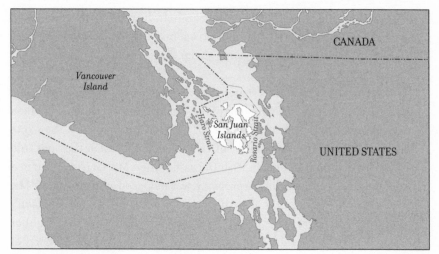

Disputed San Juan Islands

the 49th parallel from the crest of the Rocky Mountains "to the middle of the channel which separates the continent from Vancouver's Island, and thence southerly through the middle of the said channel" (see "James K. Polk" in this book). Though the negotiators were informed that islands in the waterway could result in ambiguity regarding "the middle of the channel," neither side knew the geography well enough, nor wanted to wait for information that might crack a fragile treaty that had taken decades to negotiate.[2]

As it turned out, there were two comparable channels. The Haro Strait passed between the San Juan Islands and Vancouver Island; the Rosario Strait passed between the San Juan Islands and the United States. A British–American boundary commission was formed, but its members were unable to agree as to which channel constituted the boundary and thus which nation possessed the islands. The reason they couldn't agree was because the islands were of strategic value to both nations.

That the particular *time* was significant is borne out, first, by the fact that there had already been an event similar to that involving the pig—this one involving sheep—which did not escalate to the brink of war. It had occurred in 1853–54, when the Hudson's Bay Company landed 1,300 sheep on San Juan Island to provision its personnel on the mainland and Vancouver Island. The company assumed that the island was part of Britain's Canadian territory under its proprietorship. When the Hudson's Bay Company was informed by the Territory of Washington that it had failed to pay the tariff for the sheep it had imported into the United States and that the company owed property tax for the land it used on the San Juan Islands, Britain disputed the Americans' claim to jurisdiction. In response, the Washington Territory sent a sheriff, who seized thirty some sheep that were then sold to recover the unpaid taxes.

Not surprisingly, Britain's regional governor, James Douglas, had some words for Isaac Stevens, the governor of the Washington Territory. "A person named Barnes, who styles himself Sheriff of Whatcomb County," he wrote to Stevens, "did abstract a number of valuable sheep, which they put into boats, and were about to depart with the same when Mr. Griffin returned and, demanding restitution of his property, was menaced with violence."[3] Mr. Griffin turned up again in the 1859 dispute. Charles J. Griffin, the Hudson's Bay Company's manager of the livestock on San Juan Island, was the neighbor whose pig Lyman Cutler shot. Like the sheep, Griffin's pig was the property of the Hudson's Bay Company. The element that had prevented the sheep incident from spiraling out of control surfaced as Governor Douglas's letter proceeded to calm down: "Wisdom and sound policy enjoin upon us the part of leaving the question to the decision of the supreme governments, and of abstaining from enforcing rights which neither party is disposed to acknowledge."

Five years later, however, the parties involved did not calm down. This difference resulted in large part from the arrival, in 1858, of General William S. Harney as the new commander of the U.S. military in the region. General Harney had shown himself to be effective in war, but, as an earlier news report illustrates, he was not a man disposed to calm down. "A fellow by

the name of Harney ... murdered a Negro woman [his slave, Hannah] by whipping her to death in St. Louis," the *Boston Liberator* reported in September 1834. "It has been stated by ... the coroner's inquest that, from the circumstantial evidence and the testimony of individuals to Harney's own confessions to them, that this horrible act was committed ... for successive days.... Harney is ... an officer connected with the army and has fled to Washington." Over the course of his military career, Harney was court-martialed four times:

General William S. Harney (1800–1889)

twice for insubordination, once for refusing to return a stolen horse, and once for maliciously flogging a soldier.[4]

Harney learned of the pig incident three weeks after it had happened and even then by chance. In early July 1859, having paid a courtesy call on Governor Douglas at Vancouver Island, Harney noticed an American flag flying on nearby San Juan Island. Knowing the island's possession to be under dispute, he went to investigate. It turned out that the flag had not yet been lowered from the American residents' Fourth of July celebration—but not entirely by accident. There was considerable excitement among the islanders, Harney discovered, about a recent dustup over a pig. Harney was told about Cutler, the produce-poaching pig, the confrontation with Griffin, and the Hudson's Bay Company bigwig who had threatened to have Cutler arrested and put on trial.

Harney knew that such a trial, if it took place uncontested by the United States, would undermine American claims to the San Juan Islands. He therefore issued orders to his aide, Captain George Pickett, stating that he was to land a company of men on San Juan Island:

> First: to protect the inhabitants of the island from the incursions of the northern Indians.... Second: ... [T]o afford adequate protection to the American citizens ... and to resist all attempts at interference by the British authorities.... This protection has been called for in consequence of the chief factor of the Hudson's Bay Company, Mr. Dallas, having recently ... threatened to take an American citizen by force to Victoria for trial by British laws.

On July 27 Pickett landed on the island with sixty men. But Harney's orders hadn't stopped there:

> The steamer *Massachusetts* will be directed to transport your command.... [T]ake into consideration that future contingencies may require an establishment of from four to six companies retaining the command of San Juan harbor.

Meanwhile British Governor Douglas also knew that, if no effort were made to prosecute Cutler or to object to the presence of American troops, it would undermine Britain's claim to the San Juan Islands. He therefore issued orders to his aide, John de Courcy, to arrest Cutler.

Upon Courcy's arrival on the island, he and Pickett drew their lines in the sand and reported back to their respective superiors. This time Governor Douglas did not calm down, most likely because, this time, the USS *Massachusetts* was lurking in the harbor with additional troops. Consequently, Douglas matched that move and upped it. He ordered the arrival of two warships, with a combined total of fifty-two guns, and a third ship with a detachment of troops.

General Harney responded by ordering the arrival of additional American ships and troops. Within eight weeks, one man's shooting of a pig had escalated to sixty heavily fortified American troops, backed by 400 offshore reinforcements, facing British battleships aiming 167 cannons at them and transporting some 2,000 troops.

Hotheadedness, however, was only one of the elements that had turned Cutler's bullet into a diplomatic bomb. Another difference between the 1854 and 1859 incidents was that in 1859 the United States was on the verge of its Civil War. Though General Harney was a slave owner, and a brutal one at that, he strongly opposed secession. There is reason to believe that, with the nation on the brink of implosion, he saw both political and military value in the San Juan Islands.

Militarily, if the United States possessed the San Juan Islands, it could control the shipping channels between Vancouver Island and the mainland of Canada. With that control, commerce in western Canada would be at the mercy of the United States. Should the United States seek to acquire Canada, taking possession of the San Juan Island would provide an excellent military wedge.

Harney may have sought to drive that wedge of conquest at that point in time for political reasons as well. Historians have speculated that he hoped to divert Southern secessionist passions into American expansionist passions.[5] This view is buttressed by his selection of Captain Pickett to lead the landing force on San Juan Island. George E. Pickett came from a long-prominent Virginia family. His buoyant personality added popularity to prominence. In the years ahead, Pickett would become a Confederate general most known to posterity for Pickett's charge at Gettysburg, that charge being the high-water mark of the Confederacy. If this wild idea of invading Canada was Harney's intention, he would not have been the only high-ranking government official to entertain it. Secretary of State William Seward would soon propose it to President Lincoln as a last-ditch effort to avoid the Civil War.

Once Harney's reports arrived in Washington, cooler heads prevailed. President James Buchanan dispatched Adjutant General Winfield Scott to assess the situation firsthand, with the aim of preventing war. "Harney considers San Juan Island as part of the Washington Territory," General Scott reported to his superiors. "If this does not lead to a collision of arms, it will again be due to the forbearance of the British authorities, for I found both Brigadier General Harney and Captain Pickett proud of their 'conquest' of the island." In response, the secretary of war sent General Scott a one-sentence message: "The Adjutant General will order Brigadier General Harney to repair to Washington city without delay."

The War Department officially censured General Harney. The Washington Territory, on the other hand, nominated him for president of the United States. General Scott, meanwhile, working with British governor Douglas, stabilized the military situation by agreeing to a troop presence by both nations on the island.

With the military standoff carefully managed, diplomats were able to take control of the dispute. As they did so, the number of British and American troops was steadily reduced to a token presence. Those remaining came to exchange pleasantries, play cards, share adult beverages, and even celebrate Christmas together at a large dinner while waiting for the diplomats to complete their task.[6]

The wait lasted twelve years. In 1872, under arbitration headed by Germany's Kaiser Wilhelm, the San Juan Islands were deemed to lie within the boundaries of the United States. The decision was based on the records of the original 1846 boundary negotiations, during which England had sought to have the boundary along 49th parallel turn south through the channel only to keep Vancouver Island in British possession, never mentioning any possession of the San Juan Islands.

Today this segment of Washington State's boundary remains on the map, an artifact of Lyman Cutler's triggering the Pig War, the only casualty of which was the pig.

ROBERT W. STEELE
Rocky Mountain Rogue?

Gov. Steele informs his constituents ... that "the eyes of the Union are upon them." ... The eyes of the Union, we venture to say, have not even discovered the Territory.... Not one man in five hundred, we presume, in the country at large, is aware of the existence of any such political community as the Territory of Jefferson. In point of fact, it has as yet no legal existence.
—*NEW YORK TIMES*, NOVEMBER 26, 1859

In the winter of 1859, a group of gold prospectors and miners in the Pikes Peak region of the Rocky Mountains idled away the time until the snow melted by deciding to take the law into their own hands and form a territory. No matter that they were already in a duly constituted U.S. territory, that being Kansas (which at the time extended west to the crest of the Rockies).

The boundaries the mining men stipulated for their "Territory of Jefferson" went beyond the western region of Kansas, extending into the Nebraska Territory, Utah Territory, and New Mexico Territory.[1]

The idea had originated a year earlier and spread rapidly among the men working in the gulches and ravines. Spending the upcoming winter making their own territory would be a welcome alternative to drinking, brawling, and shooting each other. When the snows began, they held a convention, sent a pro-

Territory of Jefferson, 1859–61

230

posal to Congress, and, when Congress did nothing, elected as their
governor Robert W. Steele, a man
who had been in the region less than
a year. He and the legislature elected along with him then proceeded
to write themselves a constitution
and laws. Legally speaking, it was
all very woolly.

Were these just a bunch of
bewhiskered varmints thinking
they could simply take control? One
need only glance at their legislation. Take, for example, their law for
evicting some scoundrel or squatter

Robert W. Steele (1820–1901)

from one's property. "Judgment of forfeiture and eviction," it began, "may be
rendered against the defendant whenever the amount of damages so recovered is more than two-thirds the value of the interest such defendant has in
the property wasted, and when the action is brought by the person entitled
to the reversion." That sounds like lawyer talk, and indeed it was. Steele *was*
a lawyer, and he had been a member of the Nebraska territorial legislature.[2]
While he was serving in that legislature, word came of gold in the foothills of
Pikes Peak. After his term expired, Steele set out for the region, established
a stake and a homestead, and was soon joined by his wife and children.

Steele was clearly not a woolly varmint. Indeed, he and his cronies were
trying to rein in the woolly varmints. Being hundreds of miles from the
nearest Kansas sheriff, the region's bandits, disputants, and liquored-up
miners were misbehaving with impunity in the settlements that had sprung
up in a matter of months. In lieu of threats, assaults, murders and vigilantes,
Steele and his cohorts sought to substitute due process of law.

The Territory of Jefferson, which at first glance appears to have been a
wild and rebellious creation, was actually the opposite. Its founders were
seeking to create a government only because the established governments—
both in Kansas and Congress—had failed to do so.

In fairness to Kansas, only a year earlier this western region of its
sprawling territory had been nothing but desolate hills, described in an
earlier military exploration as "uninhabitable by a people depending upon
agriculture for their subsistence."[3] When the discovery of gold suddenly

brought hordes of inhabitants, Kansas, itself only four years old, had its hands full with the much bloodier issue of slavery.

Kansas struggled during its first four years to decide whether or not to permit slavery, as permitted in the Kansas-Nebraska Act. Among the thousands of advocates, pro and con, who entered the state to vote on this issue, many joined paramilitary armies that attacked each other's settlements in pitched battles. Flattered as Governor James Denver may have been to have a gold rush town named after him, deciding whether to deploy his overwhelmed resources toward the suppression of paramilitary armies close to home or brawlers and gun slingers in the western mountains was a no-brainer.

Congress too could have stepped in by acting upon the proposal sent by the men who had convened at Denver. Indeed, Congressman Alexander Stephens proposed the creation of a Territory of Jefferson in January 1859. But Stephens, a Southerner, had been the floor manager for approval of Kansas's first proposed constitution, which was proslavery. That effort failed. This one was relegated to a committee. Slavery continued to paralyze Congress.

The mining men responded by simply declaring themselves a territory and holding their first election. Governor Steele deftly navigated the legal white water. To avert conflict with Kansas or Congress, should they seek to act upon their jurisdictions, his administration always included the word "provisional" in its territorial documents. Although its provisional laws specified the taxes it would levy and the salaries it would pay, Steele received no compensation nor authorized payments to anyone. Likewise, his administration collected no taxes, since Steele knew that any revenue they received could be challenged—probably successfully—in federal court.[4] When elections for the legislature were held again the following year (after Congress again failed to act), Steele cautioned the candidates, "All persons who expect to be elected to any of the above offices should bear in mind that there will be no salaries or per diem allowed from this territory."[5]

Steele and his colleagues also averted conflict regarding the ad hoc miners' courts that had previously sprung up in various camps. While the provisional laws of the Jefferson Territory established county courts, district courts, and a supreme court, they also included the miners' courts. This provision limited the miners' courts to disputes regarding "mining claims and miners' interests." But no effort was ever made to assert the jurisdiction of a county court over a miners' court—though litigants often disputed which of the two illegally created venues was the appropriate venue.[6]

On January 3o, 1861, Congress again took up a motion to create the Jefferson Territory. This time, rather than being relegated to a committee, the motion was subjected to debate, with ensuing arguments over whether to name the territory Jefferson or Idaho or Colorado. Colorado won out, and three weeks later President Buchanan's signature turned the less-than-legal Jefferson Territory into the fully official Colorado Territory.

Why was it suddenly so easy? Earlier that month, Mississippi, Florida, Alabama, Georgia, and Louisiana had seceded from the Union and were no longer participants in the issue. South Carolina, too, was gone, having left in the previous month.

Steele had achieved his goal, but it cost him his job. The national crisis caused by secession, which enabled Congress to create Colorado, also caused outgoing President Buchanan, a Democrat, to put country above politics and leave the appointment of a territorial governor to his Republican successor, Abraham Lincoln. President Lincoln appointed William Gilpin, a Republican, to replace Steele, a Democrat. Party affiliation, however, was only one element in the decision. Though Steele had legal and governmental expertise, that contribution was now in place. Gilpin had a military background and a wide-ranging knowledge of the western territories. If war commenced, his military skills would be of more value.

Steele, for his part, recognized this. He issued a proclamation dissolving the Jefferson Territory and urging the citizens of the Colorado Territory to remain "loyal and true" to the U.S. government.

Robert W. Steele's days in the limelight were over. He returned to his work in the mining industry and, four years later, moved with his family to Iowa to secure better educational opportunities for his children. But he had been a father of Colorado as well, and he later returned to his out-of-wedlock territory, living to see it become the nation's thirty-eighth state. He passed away in Colorado Springs in 1901 at the age of eighty-one, surrounded by his family.

FRANCIS H. PIERPONT
The Battle Line That Became a State Line

The consent of the legislature of Virginia is constitutionally necessary to a bill for the admission of West Virginia becoming a law. A
body claiming to be such legislature has given its consent. We cannot well deny that it is such, unless ... [it] was chosen at elections in
which a majority of the ... voters of Virginia did not participate. But
it is a universal practice ... to give no legal consideration whatever
to those who do not choose to vote.

—ABRAHAM LINCOLN[1]

I n the U.S. Capitol's Statuary Hall, Francis H. Pierpont stands com-
memorated in marble as "the Father of West Virginia." Yet, technically,
he never lived in West Virginia until five years after it became a state.
"Technically," however, is no small matter in this instance. It is what gave
birth to West Virginia: a technical-
ity discovered, and put to use, by
Francis Pierpont.

West Virginia became a state in
the midst of the Civil War. Previously, it had been part of Virginia, which
encompassed the Tidewater region
(its flat coastal lands), the Piedmont
(its rolling hills leading west to the
Blue Ridge mountains), the Shenandoah Valley (between the Blue Ridge
and the Alleghenies), and western
Virginia (the Alleghenies and the
land beyond to the Ohio River).

One could say that after Virginia

Francis H. Pierpont (1814–1899)

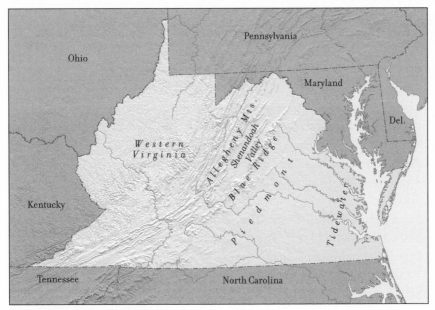

Virginia at the onset of the Civil War

seceded from the Union, western Virginia seceded from Virginia. Legally, that was precisely what it did *not* do. Since the federal government considered it illegal to secede from the Union, it would have also considered it illegal for western Virginia to secede from Virginia. Thus, for western Virginia to secede from Virginia, it had to devise an approach rooted in the illegality of secession.

But why would western Virginia have wanted to secede from the revered and influential Old Dominion? The short answer is that the region opposed slavery, but there was more to it than that. Most of its residents did oppose slavery, though their righteousness was likely buttressed by the fact that most could not afford them. The region's mountainous topography was poorly suited to agriculture. Its mountains, moreover, were ideally suited for escape.

But western Virginia's wish to secede resulted more directly from an issue at one remove from the slavery conflict. Slaves in Virginia were counted as three-fifths of a person for purposes of apportioning representation in the state legislature (though, of course, slaves could not vote). This formula reflected that which had been used in the U.S. Constitution, and it resulted in slave regions having greater representation than nonslave regions. Western Virginians repeatedly sought to abolish the use of that formula in the Virginia state constitution.

Disproportionate representation was made even more disproportionate by the fact that the authors of Virginia's constitution (among them, Thomas Jefferson, James Madison, and George Mason) had embedded a property-value requirement for voting in the document. Because many western Virginians barely eked out a livelihood in their hardscrabble terrain, this requirement created a further disparity in representation.

The anger of western Virginians would have been among Francis Pierpont's earliest memories. As far back as 1817, when he was a three-year-old on the family farm and tannery, the region's discontent was surfacing in newspapers. Washington, DC's *National Advocate* quoted one of the region's residents: "Western Virginia is ruled with a rod of iron; and unless ... we can obtain a change in some manner, our castigation will be so severe that we shall not be able to bear it. We are treated ... as a deserted step-child, instead of the legitimate offspring of Virginia."

Virginians who supported the property requirement for voting feared that giving voting representation to those without a certain level of wealth would "transfer power into entirely new hands," resulting in "many evils and inflict crying injustice."[2] In 1830, however, the mounting discontent in western Virginia over the issue of representation caused the state to hold a new constitutional convention. Ironically, the property requirement for voting resulted in western Virginians being as underrepresented at the convention as they had been in the legislature. As a result, only marginal changes were made in the 1830 constitution, and they backfired. As the *National Journal* commented, "That section of the state will never be satisfied to remain a portion of the Old Dominion unless there shall be a still further extension of the right of suffrage."

Ten years later, the 1840 census introduced a new element into the equation—one that riveted the attention of the nation's antislavery movement. The *Liberator* reported in March 1842:

> The recent census develops the fact that a majority of the white population [of Virginia] lies west of the Blue Ridge, in the free labor part of the State. Yet the eastern counties have nearly three-fourths of the political power by the amended constitution.... The subject is now before the legislature, and the [antislavery] *Richmond Whig* advises the Western Virginians to demand either concession to their demands or the formation of a new State, bounded east by the Blue Ridge.

Though the abolitionist press focused exclusively on the slavery aspect of the dispute, underrepresentation continued to spark complaints among western Virginians regarding inequitable schools, roads, and railroads.[3]

Pierpont was, by this time, a successful attorney in western Virginia. With only intermittent months of education available at a local one-room school, his parents had encouraged him to read what books they had and to seek a college education. But no college existed in western Virginia until after Pierpont had entered Allegheny College in northwestern Pennsylvania. After graduating with honors, he became a schoolteacher near his home in Fairmont. Many Americans were migrating westward at the time, and Pierpont too chose to relocate. He, however, went south, becoming a teacher in Pontotoc, Mississippi, for reasons no longer known. Whatever the reasons, the choice displayed a recurring pattern in Pierpont's life: his willingness to embark with others on a major move, yet moving in his own direction.

During his years as a teacher, Pierpont was also learning law. After returning home in 1841, he became a licensed attorney. His keen legal mind won him the Baltimore and Ohio (B&O) Railroad as a client, representing its interests in nearby counties. After the Virginia legislature yielded in granting the B&O permission to lay track in western Virginia, the railroad's main line ended up passing through Fairmont, near to which he opened a coal mine. By the early 1850s he was a wealthy and prominent man, married to a well-bred, abolitionist wife from the North.

Also by the early 1850s, the next census had shown that over 10,000 more whites now lived in western Virginia than in the rest of the state. At the same time, the conflict between western Virginia and the rest of the state regarding slavery had also grown by leaps and bounds (as it did nationwide following the tumultuous Compromise of 1850). In 1851 presidential aspirant Daniel Webster cast his strongly pro-Union gaze on western Virginia, in a speech closely followed nationwide. "Ye men of Western Virginia ... what course do you propose to yourselves by disunion? If you secede, what do you secede from, and what do you secede to?" Webster asked, imploring the people of the region to consider that their economy was more connected to the nation's hinterland than to the rest of Virginia. "Do you look for the current of the Ohio to change, and bring you and your commerce to the tide-waters of eastern rivers? What man in his senses can suppose that you will remain part and parcel of Virginia a month after Virginia should have ceased to be part and parcel of the United States?"[4]

Four months later, Virginia sought to consolidate the loyalty of its western residents by ratifying yet another constitution, this one extending voting rights to all white male residents over twenty-one, regardless of whether or not they owned any property. But it was too late. Though it resolved the conflict over representation, the conflict over slavery now dominated the political landscape, and the new constitution did not move that mountain.

The equation changed yet again on November 6, 1860, the day Lincoln was elected president. One month after his inauguration, Virginia voted to secede. Pierpont, a delegate to that April 1861 convention on secession, hurried home with the news. His longtime friend Alston G. Dayton later recalled:

> The people stood and listened dumbfounded.... They gathered in knots on the streets and corners in the towns and villages, at the country stores and crossroads, and with bated breaths whispered to each other, "What does it mean?" ... [But then] they began to ask ... why should they be menaced, devastated, destroyed, because the seashore planters will it so? ... Their anger rose to fever heat.... They would protest. They would have another convention.... They would secede from the seceding Virginia.[5]

Within a month, western Virginians did indeed convene in Wheeling to decide upon a course of action. Leading the effort to secede from Virginia was John S. Carlisle. Pierpont opposed Carlisle's proposal. He pointed out that, because the federal government maintained that states could not secede from the Union, it could not then recognize a state that had seceded from its parent state. Moreover, he cited the clause in the U.S. Constitution that declares, "no new States shall be formed or erected within the jurisdiction of any other State; nor any State be formed by the junction of two or more States, or parts of States, without the consent of the legislatures of the States concerned as well as of the Congress." Since Carlisle's proposal would erect a new state within the jurisdiction of Virginia, Virginia would have to consent, and that was not going to happen.

Pierpont's insights shattered the unity at the Wheeling convention. Anger and recriminations replaced determination during subsequent sessions, until Pierpont himself discovered a way to thread a legal needle that would repair the damage and create the state. His scheme was later recounted by Dayton:

> Virginia was still in the Union; only her officers had abandoned

their trust.... Virginia was entitled to her representatives in Congress, to elect her legislative agents.... If a legislature thus elected
under the law saw fit to grant permission to the counties west of the
Alleghenies to form a new State, then the requirement of the federal
Constitution would be fully and legally met. If the counties east of
the Alleghenies did not want this permission given, let them ... elect
their accredited membership to the legislature and vote the proposition down.... It was plain sailing after Pierpont had found the way.

Whether the delegates to the convention reacted with stunned silence
or with chortles is not recorded. Pierpont was proposing a four-step legal
maneuver. Step one entailed declaring that, since Virginia's elected officials
had (from the federal government's perspective) abandoned their offices,
a new election would be held in Virginia to replace them. Voters throughout the state could, as in any election, choose to vote or not. Unspoken, but
obvious to all, was that those voters who supported secession would not
invalidate their claim by voting in an election for a Virginia that claimed
to be part of the United States. In addition, the Confederate army, present
throughout nearly all of the slave-holding regions of Virginia, would never
permit such an election. In effect, only western Virginia (where the Union
army had already established itself) would vote. Step two would be to get
the U.S. Congress to recognize and seat those elected as the duly authorized
replacement representatives of Virginia. Once thus recognized, step three
consisted of creating the new state by complying with the U.S. Constitution.
To do so, the replacement legislature of "Virginia" would pass a resolution
calling for a statewide referendum on whether or not to allow western Virginia to form itself into a separate state. As with the election of replacement
officials, the referendum would be, theoretically, statewide—though here too
it was obvious that only voters in western Virginia would participate. Once
statehood was approved by those who voted, step four consisted of completing
the constitutional requirement by formally seeking acceptance of the new
state from the U.S. Congress.[6]

It was fiendish, it was brilliant, and it worked. In May 1861 Pierpont
was elected governor of what was called "the replacement government of
Virginia," and in June Congress officially seated its representatives to the
House and Senate. In August the new "Virginia" legislature passed a resolution enabling the state to hold a referendum on whether or not to allow a
new state to be created from Virginia's western region. The referendum took

place in October. As before, voting took place only in western Virginia. Since Virginia's constitution required voting to be done by voice, not by secret ballot, the referendum was overwhelmingly approved. Consequently, another convention was held, this one to write a constitution for the new state. That constitution was then sent to Congress for final approval.

Here, however, the plan began to unravel. While Congress had played along with the charade of seating representatives from "Virginia," recognizing "Virginia's" approval of West Virginia's creation was another question. Kentucky Senator Lazarus W. Powell put the cards on the table:

> I do not believe it was ever contemplated by the Constitution of the country, that less than one-fourth of the people constituting a State should, in revolutionary times like these, form themselves into a legislature and give their consent to themselves to form a new State within the limits of one of the States of this Union. It is inaugurating a principle that, in my judgment, is dangerous.

Ohio Senator Benjamin Wade was unimpressed. In his view, because the South had abandoned the Union, Congress was not playing with a full deck:

> If all was calm, if all was peace, if all was just as it should be, then to tear old Virginia asunder might cause a commotion that would induce men to hesitate.... Now is the time for great events, when you can see that a commotion in the land has brought it within the compass of your power to do a great and mighty good, to perform it. To treat the fact of that commotion as a reason why you should not do it is the narrowest statesmanship in the world.

The times were such that paradoxes—and brute force—ruled. The Senate ultimately passed an amended statehood bill by a vote of twenty-three to seventeen; the House passed it ninety-six to fifty-five. The amendment stipulated that the West Virginia Constitutional Convention insert language into the document explicitly ending slavery.

The reason such language was not already in the proposed constitution was that two of the counties that had voted in favor of creating West Virginia were at the northern end of the fertile and slave-holding Shenandoah Valley, where the presence of Union troops had enabled a vote to be taken. Some in Congress questioned the logic of including these counties, separated by

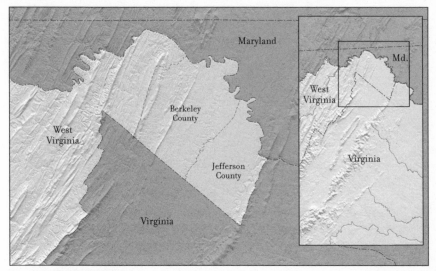

Top of the Shenandoah Valley

mountains from the rest of western Virginia. But it wasn't just those two Shenandoah Valley counties western Virginians dreamed of possessing. "Virginia" Senator John Carlisle maintained that *all* the land west of the Blue Ridge mountains should compose the new state.

Western Virginians were not alone in urging Congress to include the Shenandoah Valley in the new state's boundary. The B&O Railroad, another powerful interest (closely connected to Pierpont) urged it as well. The North's southernmost railroad was a Confederate target no matter what, boundaries being meaningless in wartime. But the B&O, looking ahead to the postwar period, knew that it would be better off having none of its track under Virginia's jurisdiction.[7] Senator Carlisle spoke for both parties when he beseeched the Senate to locate West Virginia's eastern boundary farther east, "including the counties in the valley, which properly belong, in a commercial aspect, to the same trading community that we do. But we can at least do this: we can secure the counties through which the Baltimore and Ohio Railroad passes." West Virginia, as it turned out, did not get everything it wanted, but the B&O did.

West Virginia's statehood convention modified its proposed constitution as directed by Congress, and President Lincoln signed the legislation. Come June 20, 1863, West Virginia would officially become a state. Meanwhile, the Confederate army was approaching in full force. General Robert E. Lee and all of his corps—the commands of Generals James Longstreet, Richard

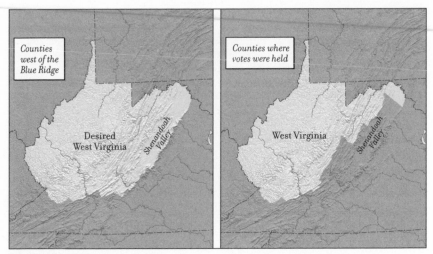

West Virginia: idealism versus realism

Ewell, A. P. Hill, and J. E. B. Stuart—were moving up through much of what was scheduled to become West Virginia. "We direct particular attention to the following dispatch from Governor Pierpont of Virginia.... The rebels are advancing in force, and are only about nineteen miles distant from this city [Wheeling]," a Pennsylvania newspaper reported one day before the state's official creation. "If ever there was a time for the citizens of western Pennsylvania to awaken in earnest, before the horrors and civil war are actually thrust upon their homes and firesides, now is the time."[8]

As it happened, the storm clouds did not burst until two weeks after West Virginia's birth. When they did, it was indeed in Pennsylvania, at the previously sleepy town of Gettysburg. During that military hurricane, Francis Pierpont was unpacking documents in Alexandria, Virginia. The father of West Virginia was still the governor of "Virginia." He opted to remain in that post, in the hope that he could better serve the Union in that capacity.[9] At the moment, however, there was only one place in what now remained of Virginia where he could safely locate his "government." The town of Alexandria, just across the Potomac River from Washington, DC, though Confederate in sympathies, was heavily occupied by Union troops protecting the nation's capital.

With the end of the Civil War, Pierpont's hopes of serving the Union by remaining in office were given the boot. Authority now resided with General John M. Schofield, who oversaw Virginia during Reconstruction. In effect, Pierpont went from being the governor of "Virginia" to being the "governor" of Virginia. But the lawyer in him continued to act on behalf of those he represented. He sought to have voting rights restored to Virginians who had served in the Confederate army, while at the same time he advocated the creation of schools for newly freed slaves. His commitment to equal justice eventually angered enough people—from ex-Confederates to progressives—that he was removed from office by General Schofield in 1868.

Returning to his hometown, Pierpont lived for the first time in the new state he had done so much to create. Virginia, meanwhile, had commenced a constitutional challenge by suing West Virginia over its possession of Berkeley and Jefferson Counties. In 1871 the Supreme Court rejected Virginia's challenge. As significant as the decision itself was the extent to which it was covered in the press, which was precious little. Americans now had, and for many decades would continue to have, little interest in revisiting the issues of the Civil War—be it the constitutionality of West Virginia or the constitutionality of racial segregation.

Francis Pierpont lived out the rest of his life quietly. He passed away in 1899 at the age of eighty-five and was buried alongside family members in his hometown of Fairmont, now in West Virginia. Though West Virginians too did not wish to revisit the past, they did wish to revisit Francis Pierpont. An obituary in Utah's *Salt Lake Tribune* noted that his "remains lay in state in the [family's] church, and were viewed by thousands of people. The casket was almost buried in flowers."

FRANCISCO PEREA AND JOHN S. WATTS
Two Sides of the Coin of the Realm

Mr. Perea of New Mexico Territory: I ask the unanimous consent of the Convention to allow the delegates from New Mexico to record their votes for President and Vice-President of the United States.
Chairman: The motion is not in order.
Mr. Watts of New Mexico Territory: Mr. Chairman, we are ready to pour out our life-blood in carrying your glorious heaven-born banner wherever the honor of our country requires it to be carried. We feel as patriotic and as much disposed to sustain it as any other portion of the country, and I hope that we shall not be denied the privileges which have been granted to other sister Territories upon this floor. I want an opportunity to record our votes for Abraham Lincoln and Andrew Johnson.

—REPUBLICAN PRESIDENTIAL CONVENTION, 1864

Francisco Perea and John S. Watts, sixteen years apart in age, had only recently gotten to know one another when they jointly sought to have the Republican Party include New Mexico's vote. Yet prior to their relationship, both played key roles in defusing an explosive situation that followed the United States' 1848 acquisition of New Mexico (and a great deal more) in the Mexican War. The danger was that, in acquiring the land, the United States had also acquired people

Francisco Perea (1830–1913)

who spoke another language and had not sought to become Americans.

Watts and Perea's leadership had little to do with the fact that one was Anglo and the other Hispanic. Neither group was of one mind regarding New Mexico's future. Their leadership resulted from the fact that both men comprehended those complexities. Their success as leaders can be seen today in the seemingly simple straight line dividing New Mexico and Arizona.

New Mexico's complexities were embedded in the orders General

John S. Watts (1816–1876)

Stephen Kearny received after capturing Santa Fe in the opening year of the Mexican War. "In your whole conduct you will act in such a manner as best to conciliate the inhabitants," the secretary of war had instructed, "and render them friendly to the United States." Hardly complex orders in theory, but in practice they entailed considerable complexity. The first complication surfaced when the general issued a set of laws to govern New Mexico. Collectively known as the Kearny Code, they adhered to the secretary of war's orders by leaving in place the region's Mexican laws and guaranteeing freedom of religion, freedom of speech, the right to assemble—indeed, everything in the Bill of Rights with one exception: the right to bear arms.

The part of the Kearny Code that proved to be dicey—and that later affected Perea, Watts, and the Arizona boundary they sought—was its opening statement. "The country heretofore known as New Mexico," it benignly began, "shall be known hereafter and designated as the territory of New Mexico, in the United States of America." Sounds simple enough ... unless one should ask (and many did): what *was* "the country heretofore known as New Mexico"?

To New Mexicans, the answer was clear and important. Nuevo Méjico had been a province in Mexico that extended north along the Rio Grande valley from what is now the Mexican border. But after Tejas won its independence from Mexico in 1836, becoming the Republic of Texas, it claimed the Rio Grande valley on the Texas side of the river. Mexico never accepted this claim. When Texas later joined the United States, Congress stipu-

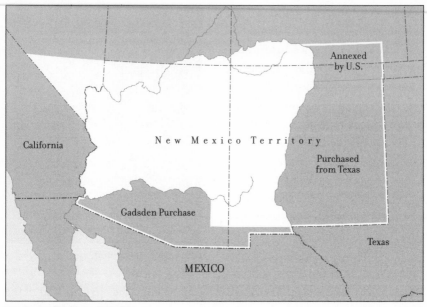

New Mexico Territory, 1848–50

lated the Rio Grande as its western border, and the Mexican War began.

While the implication in General Kearny's statement might go unnoticed today, Congress and President James K. Polk spotted it at once and rejected it, since it was unconstitutional to create a new jurisdiction that altered an existing state line without the consent of that state. Nevertheless, four years later Congress found a way to grant New Mexico's wish via the nation's enduring curse: slavery.

The Compromise of 1850 was delicately held together in part by adding an additional issue to the deal: the Texas-New Mexico border. Texas had acquired enormous debt during its days as a republic. Under the compromise, Congress enabled Texas to pay off its debt by purchasing a large block of its western region, which it then gave to the New Mexico Territory. For some reason, New Mexico's new boundary, the 103rd meridian (later found to have been inaccurately surveyed), was considerably farther east than the Rio Grande Valley. Though unstated, the reason was not lost on a newly appointed territorial judge being sent to New Mexico, John S. Watts.

Watts had recently arrived from Indiana, where he had spent his youth, become a lawyer, and served for a term in the state legislature. He got along well with the New Mexicans and did well for himself, too. After a few years as a judge, he resigned to go into private practice, specializing in Hispanic land claims. His clients were not the campesinos scratching out a meager living on parched parcels; they were the grandees, the wealthiest families with Spanish land grants that encompassed thousands of acres. In some instances, Watts did work for no money, accepting land instead. He soon became both wealthy and well connected with the region's leading families.

When Watts had first headed to Santa Fe, young Francisco Perea, who came from a prominent Nuevo Mexicano family, was heading to St. Louis. He had just finished college in Manhattan at the Bank Street Academy. During the years that Perea was away, a new fuse was lit in New Mexican politics. In 1853 James Gadsden purchased a region of Mexico on behalf on the United States. The region, which was added to the New Mexico Territory, was needed to build a second transcontinental railroad through the South. Northern states believed such a railroad would provide new economic opportunities in the South and help wean it away from slavery. Southern states believed such a railroad was vital for slavery to survive. They saw it as linking the slave state of Texas to the slavery-still-possible state of California. The only territory in between was New Mexico.

Slavery had been abolished in Mexico in 1820, and Mexican law had been preserved in New Mexico. This was the new fuse that Congress lit when it officially created the Territory of New Mexico as an adjunct to the Compromise of 1850. In return for granting New Mexico's dream of regaining its former land, it loosened the bolts on its inherited law by saying this particular territory could decide for itself whether or not to permit slavery.

Few if any Hispanics aspired to become slave owners. But all remembered that their nemesis, Texas, had begun organizing its War of Independence when Mexico had banned slavery. The same thing was now happening again. "A large number of delegates from different parts of the Gadsden Purchase assembled at Tucson for the purpose of taking into consideration the measures necessary for the organization of a Territorial government," the *New York Herald* reported in November 1856. "Many emigrants from Texas this year have stopped in the Purchase, and doubtless if the new territorial government were formed it would soon fill up with a hardy, industrious American population." The boundaries the Anglos in the Gadsden Purchase had in mind for "Arizona," as they called it, encompassed the southern half of the New Mexico Territory—thereby bordering both Texas and California.

Hispanics in New Mexico liked the idea of creating a separate territory composed primarily of the Texas transplants. But dividing the territory horizontally would put the planned transcontinental railroad in Arizona. In seeking a vertical division, many New Mexicans thought it wise to espouse nonconfrontational views on slavery so as to minimize Southern support for the "Arizonans."

Though Watts was an Anglo, his career was based in the Hispanic community. And though he hailed from Indiana, where slavery had never been permitted, he too adopted less-than-abolitionist views regarding slavery—though he joined the new Republican Party, which came into existence primarily for the purpose of opposing slavery.

All these elements accelerated with the candidacy of Abraham Lincoln in 1860. Perea was in San Francisco the night Lincoln was elected. He later recalled, "The occasion was celebrated by immense processions of men and boys marching through the principal streets to the music of many brass bands, the firing of cannon, and the discharge of anvils. It is needless to say all of us New Mexicans heartily joined in to swell the throng."[1]

Perea now returned to New Mexico just as Watts was leaving it. Watts was headed to Washington, having been elected the territory's delegate to Congress. In letters to President Lincoln, he urged him to choose New Mexicans for the territory's appointed positions, despite the fact that New Mexico's leading citizens were ambivalent about slavery. He warned that appointing outsiders would offend New Mexicans, pointing out that slavery was not their foremost concern (Texas was). By choosing New Mexicans, the president would win their hearts and, should war erupt, their loyalty.[2] Lincoln heeded this advice, though he took a lot of heat for it. Watts's insights proved to be right. The man who proved it was Francisco Perea.

Perea had returned to discover that his birthplace was in crisis. As Southern states began seceding from the Union, Anglos in the Gadsden Purchase began seeking the establishment of a Confederate Territory of Arizona. Traveling throughout the Rio Grande valley, Perea visited the leading Hispanic families and urged them to commit their loyalty to the United States. His efforts succeeded. Hispanic New Mexico produced a greater percentage of volunteers for the Union army than any other state or territory.[3]

Perea's success validated not only Watts's advice regarding appointments but also Watts's insight regarding New Mexico's fear of Texans. Perea's most effective argument for loyalty to the Union was that if the Confederacy accepted Arizona as a territory, it would send Texan troops to defend it.

And indeed they did. In July 1861 the Second Regiment of Texas Mounted Rifles entered the Gadsden Purchase. Perea had enlisted in the Union army, where he commanded one of the brigades assigned to oust the Texas troops. Over the course of several battles, Union forces finally prevailed.

Watts, meanwhile, was fighting the battle of the boundary. He introduced a bill in Congress for the creation of an Arizona Territory that would be divided by a vertical line along the 109th meridian. New York Congressman William A. Wheeler argued that dividing the territory was unnecessary, noting that the only logic for the location of the proposed Arizona-New Mexico border was that it continued the line dividing Utah and Colorado. When Watts responded with the reason for its location, he also shed light on why the Texas-New Mexico line had been located so far east of the Rio Grande valley. Because of the location of that Texas-New Mexico line, Watts pointed out that his proposed Arizona-New Mexico line "divides the Territory of New Mexico into two equal parts."

The boundary battle, however, was about more than geographic equality. It was also about ethnic equality. Watts knew that this moment, on the floor of the House of Representatives, was the time and place to attack this head on:

> There may be a well-grounded dispute in the minds of some people as to who are white and who are black. [Laughter] There are many men in the Territory of New Mexico who, by living constantly in the open air and exposed to the rays of a burning sun, have become bronzed in complexion.... Whatever may be their color, the treaty stipulations between the United States and the republic of Mexico have invested them with all the privileges and immunities of American citizens.... [T]he first duty which the government owes to its people is to give both military and civil protection. In this case, the government is under a double obligation.... [Mexico was] compelled to relinquish her right to a portion of her territory and her right to protect a portion of her people, endeared to her by ten thousand pleasant memories and hopes, and doubly endeared by ten thousand painful forebodings for the future.

Watts linked this understanding of the Hispanic population's experience with the issue of boundaries:

> I know how the people of New Mexico felt—I know how I felt—when a preceding Congress, merely for the purpose of beautifying the

lines of the new Territory of Colorado, took sixty miles broad and two hundred and fifty miles in length from the Territory of New Mexico. Yes sir, Congress took those people and put them with a people alien in laws, alien in language, alien in association.

On February 24, 1863, Congress created the Territory of Arizona, stipulating the boundaries advocated by Watts on behalf of his Hispanic constituents.

Though Watts remained active in Republican politics, he chose to return to his law practice. Following that year's November elections, John C. Watts introduced President Lincoln to New Mexico's newly elected territorial delegate, Francisco Perea.

SIDNEY EDGERTON AND JAMES ASHLEY
Good as Gold

Gov. Edgerton was not a member of the Committee on Territories, and I never heard of his having anything to do, directly or indirectly, with the organization of the territory of Montana or with fixing its western boundary.

—JAMES M. ASHLEY

I had many interviews with Gov. Ashley, who was a strong supporter of the bill [to create Montana] and, as chairman of the Committee on Territories, had a great influence.

—SIDNEY EDGERTON[1]

Clearly, one of these men had a faulty memory. The fault line dividing their recollections can be seen on the map. It is the boundary between Montana and Idaho—a border that often raises questions, since Montana would be quite a large state even if it didn't overflow its straight lines as it barrels into the Rockies, pushing Idaho every which way until only a thin panhandle remains.

Sidney Edgerton was an Ohio congressman from 1859 to 1863. James Ashley was an Ohio congressman from 1859 to 1869. Both were abolitionists who assisted escaped slaves via Ohio's Underground Railroad. They were good men, but not perfect, as hinted in their divergent recollections regarding Montana's western border.

Following Edgerton's second term in Congress, President Lincoln appointed him to a judgeship in the newly formed Idaho Territory. This first territorial incarnation of Idaho was very different from today's state. It encompassed present-day Idaho, Montana, and Wyoming. Edgerton and his family set off for the arduous journey to the territorial capital at Lewiston. But they stopped short of their destination. "It is difficult to understand what it meant in 1863 to undertake a journey from Ohio to Lewiston, the capital of Idaho," Edgerton's daughter later recollected. "News of the recent gold discoveries at Bannack, together with the fact that the [winter] season was somewhat advanced, brought about the decision to go [to Bannack]."[2]

Another reason for not continuing to Lewiston was the fact that it was not in Edgerton's judicial district. Some historians believe that territorial governor William H. Wallace was demonstrating his well-known opposition to imported judges by assigning to this Ohioan a vast and sparsely populated district east of the Rockies. Others believe that Wallace's insult motivated Edgerton's efforts the following year to push the western border of the Montana Territory as far as he could into the original Idaho Territory. And others, such as eminent Idaho historian Merle W. Wells, maintain that, because of the gold discoveries at Bannack, "Edgerton's district had far greater importance than the one containing the temporary capital, and because of his financial interests in the district to which he was assigned, Edgerton had no great desire to make the long, hard trip to Lewiston."[3]

Financial interests? Perhaps Judge Edgerton would have recused himself from any cases in which he would have had a conflict of interest. At it happened, he never presided at any trials because, before the snows had melted, he had accepted the task of returning to Washington to represent this region in the creation of the Montana Territory.

Whatever his motive, time was of the essence. James Ashley, chairman of the House Committee on Territories, was about to set the boundary ball in

Sidney Edgerton (1818–1900)

James Ashley (1824–1896)

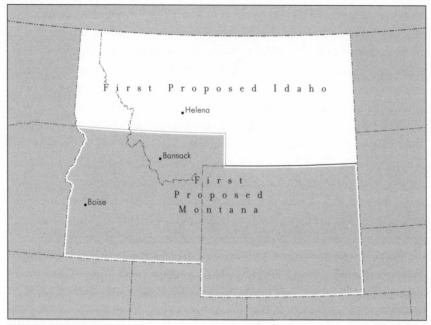

Ashley's original proposal

motion. During the previous Congress, Ashley had proposed radically differ-ent—and far more equal—borders for Idaho and Montana. Ashley's plan was to divide the region horizontally, with Montana occupying the southern half and Idaho occupying the north. The proposal was then sent to committee.

Word arrived in Bannack shortly after Edgerton's arrival that Ashley was now planning to bring the bill back to the House floor. To rank-and-file min-ers, the boundary made little difference. But to those with financial interests in the mines, Ashley's horizontal division would dilute their political clout in their respective territories by dividing the mountainous mining region and combining it with soon-to-be agricultural and ranching regions. Mine owners in Idaho could maintain more clout with a vertical division, since it would result in an agricultural region limited to the Snake River Valley in what would then be its south. In Montana, however, limiting the vast agricul-tural regions was not an option, no matter how you sliced it. Consequently, it was imperative for the mine owners that they acquire a western border with as much of the gold-rich mountains as possible.

The logical choice to make the case for Montana was Edgerton. Not only had he served in Congress, but he had done so from the same state and political party (Republican) as Ashley, the territorial committee chairman.

Moreover, Edgerton was personally acquainted with President Lincoln. And he knew what to wear and how to pack. "Ingots were quilted into the lining of my father's overcoat," his daughter recollected, "and he carried in his valise immense nuggets wherewith to dazzle the eyes of Congressmen and to impress upon their minds by means of an object lesson some adequate idea of the great mineral wealth of this section of the country."

While members of Congress may have been familiar with the quantities of gold being mined in the region, Edgerton's daughter was quite right that the object itself would have dazzled their eyes—and possibly ethics. "Arriving safely in Washington, the gold was exhibited, Congressmen interviewed, and at length the desired end was accomplished," her recollection continued, concluding, "Judge Edgerton saved to Montana all of her rich territory lying west of the summit of the Rockies."

Idaho's representative, William H. Wallace (the man who, as territorial governor, had assigned Edgerton his judicial district) joined Edgerton in supporting the vertical division over Ashley's horizontal proposal. Wallace, however, sought a vertical boundary along the Continental Divide, whereas Edgerton sought a boundary that shifted to the more westerly crest of the Bitterroot Range. Edgerton won (though the northernmost segment of the border departs from the Bitterroots, preserving the Kootenai River Valley for Idaho).

Who, among those congressmen Edgerton "interviewed," as his daughter put it, might have been both persuaded by his "object lesson" and sufficiently influential to change Congressman Ashley's proposed borders so radically? The ideal person, of course, would have been Congressman Ashley himself. But could a man so committed to the most progressive issues of his day (abolition of slavery, the right of women to vote) have been influenced by the sight of gold? It doesn't seem unlikely; in April 1869 the *New York Times* devoted four articles to Ashley, detailing "abundant evidence of his public corruption."

Edgerton left Washington not only with the boundary he had sought for Montana but also with the governorship of the new territory. He soon discovered, however, that the line he purchased failed to take into account other lines that divided the region, such as the interests of farmers and ranchers. He was unable to govern the various groups opposed to his personal interests. He left the territory before his term expired and was replaced by an interim governor until—small world—James Ashley was appointed.

Learning of Ashley's appointment, Montana's congressional delegate,

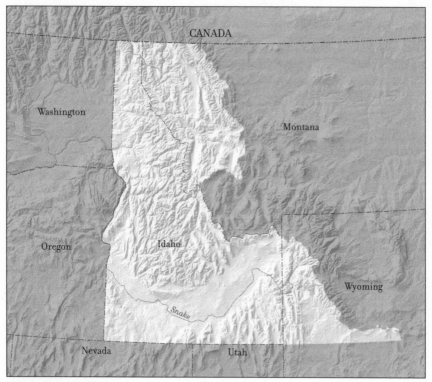

Idaho's border proposal

James M. Cavanaugh, stated on the floor of the House that he "never solicited [Ashley] to come among us." Cavanaugh (who, unlike a territorial governor, was elected, not appointed) characterized Ashley as "having been spewed out at the mouth" and protested that the territories were "being made receptacles for political convicts."

Like Edgerton, Ashley proved unable to govern the tough, pugnacious people of Montana. He was dismissed by the president before his term expired. Together, Sidney Edgerton and James Ashley demonstrated that all that's gold does not glitter.

WILLIAM H. SEWARD
Why Buy Alaska?

Seward appeared before the Committee and made a long explanation
of the status of affairs in Alaska and the reasons which induced him
to make the purchase.... The discussion which followed was decid-
edly spicy, and somewhat acrimonious.

—*NEW YORK TIMES*, MARCH 19, 1868

On a map, Alaska looks like it ought to be part of Canada. How and from
whom did the United States obtain it? Not from the Canadians, since it
never belonged to them, nor to their colonial predecessors, the British.
Since the Battle of Sitka in 1804, it had essentially belonged to Russia (although
indigenous peoples such as the Tlingits, Aleuts, and Yupiks would have begged
to differ). In 1867 the United States acquired Alaska when Secretary of State
William H. Seward negotiated a treaty with Russia for its purchase.

At the time, Alaska was popularly derided as "Seward's folly" and "Seward's
icebox." Even the *New York Herald*, which supported the purchase, couldn't resist
Alaska laughs. Its November 12, 1867, edition contained an abundance of what
purported to be classified ads, among them:

> Cash! Cash! Cash!—Cash paid for cast off territory. Best price given
> for old colonies, North or South. Any impoverished monarchs retir-
> ing from the colonization business may find a purchaser by address-
> ing W.H.S., Post Office, Washington, D.C.

Aside from its coastline, Alaska was viewed by many as little more than
a mammoth stretch of barren tundra and ice. It is indeed a lot of land—over
twice the size of the nation's second largest state, Texas. Virtually no public
opinion was expressed leading up to the treaty's signing, since only a select
few knew that it was in the wind. The purchase of Alaska was not revealed,

even to Congress, until the day the treaty was signed. At that point, it became headline news.

Typical of the initial press reports was that of the *San Francisco Bulletin*, whose March 30, 1867, front page story trumpeted:

Important Treaty With Russia
She Surrenders Sovereignty
to all Russian America
British Excluded From the Ocean

The President has communicated to the Senate a treaty with Russia. The latter surrenders to the United States sovereignty over all Russian America and adjacent islands, and especially includes a strip of 400 miles down the coast, excluding British America from the ocean. British diplomats are highly excited.

Britain was indeed "excited" but not, as first reported, excluded from the ocean. British Columbia, with its bustling port at Vancouver, remained between Alaska and the rest of the United States.

How could—and why would—such a huge purchase be pulled off so secretly? The answer can be summed up in two words: William Seward.

Seward had been raised in Orange County, New York, the son of a prosperous doctor. As a young lawyer, he became a protégé of Thurlow Weed, a political boss from whom he learned his way around back rooms. He was elected to the state senate in 1830 and later became New York's governor and then senator. In 1860 he was the odds-on favorite to become the Republican nominee for president. But he lost out to a relative newcomer from Illinois named Abraham Lincoln. Lincoln chose Seward to be his secretary of state. It was a smart choice.

Though the purchase took place after the Civil War, Seward's reasons for purchasing Alaska were rooted in that war's underlying element. Before, during, and after the war,

William H. Seward (1801–1872)

Seward's greatest political fear was that the United States might disunite.

Seward first voiced this fear in 1849 when California sought statehood. That suddenly populated gold rush region presented Congress with proposed boundaries that were outrageously large. Many members of Congress sought to create two states—in effect, North and South California—and to push back the proposed eastern boundary to the crest of the Sierra Nevada range, thereby sharing its gold with the neighboring states yet to be created. Seward opposed these adjustments. Pointing out that the U.S. military had no direct access by rail or sea, if it were needed to prevent California from declaring itself a separate nation, he argued in the Senate, "Are we so moderate, and has the world become so just, that we have no rivals and no enemies to lend their sympathies and aid to compass the dismemberment of our empire?"

Seward's remarks on California reflected his insight into foreign affairs, which he viewed as a multidimensional chess game. As secretary of state he demonstrated this view in the way he went about the purchase of Alaska and, prior to that, in the way he urged Lincoln to avert the Civil War. In April 1861, with Southern states seceding and war appearing inevitable, he sent Lincoln a memo entitled, "Some Thoughts for the President's Consideration." Among those thoughts were such notions as, "I would demand explanation from Spain and France [regarding intervention in Mexico to retrieve unpaid debts].... And if satisfactory explanations are not received from Spain and France, would convene Congress and declare war against them." In a letter to governors of those states bordering the Great Lakes, Seward suggested going to war to acquire Canada. With the nation on the verge of Civil War, such actions were not the kind of recommendations one would expect from the nation's premier diplomat.

But these were not actions, they were words, and the key to understanding Seward's words is to ask what he was *doing* by saying them. In this instance, Seward was suggesting a "chess move" to create fear of an imminent war with outsiders, in the hope that it would rally enough Americans to forestall the crumbling of the Union. He had no intention of France or Spain mistakenly interpreting such saber rattling as a genuine threat.[1]

When it suited his purpose, Seward readily admitted that his words should not be taken at face value. Shortly before his appointment as secretary of state was made public, he told a British diplomat that he would soon be in a position that would require him to insult Great Britain. Years later it was discovered that, five weeks before Seward's private memo to Lincoln, the British foreign secretary recorded in his diary that he'd received information indicating that the United States might create a quarrel with Britain in an effort to prevent the nation from dividing.[2]

Seward believed that Alaska was of vital importance to strengthening the bond securing the West Coast (whose residents relied on Alaska for imports of fish, timber, and fur) to the rest of the nation. Further securing that bond was also embedded in Seward's other main reason for purchasing Alaska: to promote and protect American commerce with China and Japan.

Buying Alaska revealed Seward's diplomatic skills; selling to the public the buying of Alaska required his political skills. He knew he was investing in a huge amount of territory about which most Americans knew nothing. Other than Americans on the West Coast, awareness of Alaska's significance was limited primarily to a few intellectuals. But even these citizens did not know that diplomatic signals regarding Alaska's potential sale to the United States were in the works, and had been for over a decade. In 1854 Russia, at war with Britain, offered the Americans a "treaty of purchase." Being an act of diplomacy, the words did not necessarily mean what they said; the treaty was actually a fake. The Russians' idea was to leak the treaty's existence to avert a British attack on Alaska.[3] As it turned out, Russia and the United States decided not to release the phony agreement. But Tsar Alexander II's advisers increasingly viewed Alaska as more of a liability than an asset, and American political figures increasingly broached the purchase of Alaska with members of the cabinet and Russian ministers.

The Civil War slowed the frequency of these winks and nods but did not end them. Nor did the assassination of President Lincoln end Seward's tenure as secretary. By 1867 he and Russian ambassador Eduard Stoeckl were exchanging offers and counteroffers. On the evening of March 29, Stoeckl called upon Seward at his home to inform him that his government had accepted the deal, and to ask for time the next day to begin drafting the actual treaty. Seward, wanting to keep the agreement under wraps, suggested they start now. The family's dinner table was cleared, secretaries were summoned, and at four o'clock in the morning, a treaty was ready to take to the White House. President Andrew Johnson signed it the following day, sending word of his action to Congress.

The treaty now needed Senate ratification. That debate took place in executive session, away from public scrutiny. Nevertheless, the debate commenced immediately in the press. Most newspapers initially touted the purchase's virtues in nearly identical language.[4] Clearly, someone had prepared a public relations campaign timed to the release of the treaty. Given that the treaty had just been written the night before in Seward's dining room, only Seward himself could have masterminded such a campaign.

The need for this public relations blitz quickly became evident. Opposition to the purchase commenced as soon as it was made public. On the East Coast, some papers such the *New York Times* supported the purchase while others such as the *New York Tribune* opposed it. Midwestern newspapers were likewise divided.[5] West Coast newspapers, not surprisingly, vigorously endorsed it. And Southern newspapers—hardly fans of the man whose diplomacy had helped prevent European aid to the Confederacy—urged the Senate to vote no.

The Senate, as it turned out, was less divided. Emerging from private deliberations, it voted thirty-seven to two in favor of ratification. Constitutionally, once the Senate ratifies a treaty, that's that. In this instance, however, the treaty required the United States to pony up $7,200,000, and that appropriation required approval by the House of Representatives. In effect, it too would have to ratify the treaty.

The House debate was public, and so heated one might think the purchase of Alaska entailed some master plan for the future. In fact, it did. The *New York Herald* wrote in March 1867 that the purchase of Alaska was "an important step toward the absorption of the whole continent by the United States." Seward himself believed that, with the purchase of Alaska, the United States would inevitably come to acquire the land separating Alaska from the lower forty-eight states: the Canadian province of British Columbia. Those opposed to the purchase worried that the United States would expand too far—geographically and racially.[6] Ultimately, however, over a year after the signing of the treaty, the House of Representatives sent to the Senate a bill containing the funds for the purchase of Alaska.

William Seward, meanwhile, had continued his efforts to expand America both westward and eastward. He sought to purchase the Dominican Republic and the Virgin Islands. He sought to gain a privileged American connection with Hawaii. And he acquired another barely habitable territory: a tiny group of islands in the Pacific, mid-distance between the American West Coast and Asia, and thus named Midway. The strategic importance Seward foresaw in this forlorn little atoll was borne out in World War II, when it became the scene of a critical battle between the United States and Japan.

STANDING BEAR V. CROOK
The Legal Boundary of Humanity

Webster describes a person as "a living soul; a self-conscious being: a moral agent; especially a living human being; a man, woman or child; an individual of the human race." This is comprehensive enough, it would seem, to include even an Indian.

—JUDGE ELMER S. DUNDY, 1879[1]

Geneneral George Crook was not a crook. He was not even an opponent of Standing Bear. Only in legal terminology were they at odds. Also in legal terminology, an American Indian (according to the U.S. government) was not a person. Ponca chief Standing Bear, supported by General Crook and an increasing cadre of others, changed that. In the process, the boundary of Nebraska changed too. Also changed were the lives of every American Indian—though not necessarily in a way that they, or Standing Bear, may have hoped.

In the 1870s Standing Bear was one of a number of chiefs of the Ponca Nation. The Poncas were a small, peaceful nation that occupied land—repeatedly reduced by treaty—between the Missouri and Niobrara Rivers, today a region along Nebraska's northern border. Standing Bear raised livestock, grew vegetables, often wore Western farm clothes, and lived in a two-story home. Like many of the Poncas, he was a practicing Christian.[2] The tribe had long coexisted amicably with nearby

Chief Standing Bear (ca. 1834–1908)

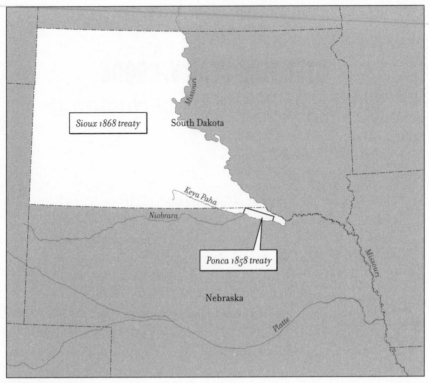

Conflicting treaties

white settlers. Their only enemy was the Sioux, who lived to their north and vastly outnumbered them.

Standing Bear's troubles began, unbeknownst to him, in 1868, when the Sioux signed a treaty with the federal government redefining the boundaries of their land. Neither the American negotiators, nor anyone in Washington, noticed that the treaty gave land to the Sioux that had belonged to the Poncas. The error provided the Sioux with a new excuse for a series of raids on the Poncas. The federal government, finally reacting to its error in 1877, did so in ways that revealed the complex web in which all Indian tribes were caught.

Standing Bear and his fellow Ponca leaders were called to a meeting with Commission on Indian Affairs inspector Edward Kemble and the government's local Indian agent. Kemble had been directed by his superiors in Washington to tell the Poncas that "their interests have been carefully considered, and that it is very desirable that they should be established in a country where the circumstances are more favorable."[3] The more favorable country was in the Indian Territory (present-day Oklahoma).

Although resistant to giving up their ancestral land, the Ponca leaders ultimately agreed and went to look at available areas. *Or:* Although resistant to giving up their ancestral lands, the leaders ultimately agreed to look at available areas. Kemble, claiming the first version, later testified in a Senate investigation:

> Most undoubtedly, they could not be removed without relinquishing their land there, and the next step after such relinquishment, or such agreement to relinquish, was to take a delegation to the Indian Territory to select some other home for them.

Standing Bear, claiming the second version, testified:

> He told us he would take us to see this land down there first, and if we were suited we could come to Washington and tell the President so, and if not we could tell the President so.

One could be telling the truth and the other lying, or the truth could "lie" in language itself. None of the Ponca leaders spoke English, so a translator had been employed. Kemble testified, however, that he had hired the best man available:

> *Q:* You had Charlie Le Claire as interpreter?
> *A:* Yes, sir....
> *Q:* Was that before or after he had been driven out of the territory for fomenting trouble?
> *A:* I had no information on that....
> *Q:* There did not seem to be any objection to him as interpreter?
> *A:* He was the only one we could get.

Ten of the Ponca leaders, including Standing Bear, went with Kemble to look over the land being offered. When a Senate committee later questioned Kemble, words again proved to be problematic:

> *A:* A great many wanted to go, but the instructions I had received ... limited the number to ten.... Big Snake, Standing Bear's brother, head soldier of the tribe, gave me a great deal of trouble. He wished

to go…. But these ten men were insisted upon, and—

Q: Who insisted upon these ten men?

A: Myself and the agent.

Q: You picked out the men?

A: I did not say that….

Q: Did you not say that you insisted that these ten men should go?

A: Subsequently I did, but that was after objection had been raised by Big Snake.

Even among the ten men selected by Kemble, none liked what they saw. "I said to him, 'We have seen the land; we have told you we do not like it,'" Standing Bear recalled to the Senate committee. "'You said you would take us to Washington to see the President.' … Then he said, 'The President did not tell us to take you to Washington.' 'Well then,' we said, 'take us back to our own land that we came from.' And he said, 'The President did not tell us to take you back to your own home.' … He had given us two alternatives: either to take the land or … walk home."

They walked. All but the two eldest, who could not do the 400-mile winter trek.

Six weeks later, Standing Bear arrived home to find Kemble. Having traveled by train, Kemble arrived ahead of them and now had new orders from the Commissioner on Indian Affairs. "Removal of Poncas will be insisted upon," he was instructed. "[Sioux Chiefs] Spotted Tail and Red Cloud must move this summer to Missouri River. Their presence will render further stay of Poncas at old location impossible." No ambiguity there, except in logic. If the Poncas were being moved from their land (south of the Missouri River) to protect them from the Sioux, why was the government now limiting the movement of the Sioux to the Missouri River? The answer would surface five years later, when Nebraska's boundary changed.

Standing Bear found his people in panic, with Kemble demanding they pack at once and threatening to use force if they did not. Meanwhile, Standing Bear's brother, Big Snake, was demonstrating why he was the tribe's head soldier, having begun to organize resistance. Now that Standing Bear had returned with negative views about the land being offered, Kemble called for the military. He ordered the soldiers to take Standing Bear and Big Snake into custody.

By the time the brothers were released, the forced removal was commencing. Soldiers compelled the Poncas to journey without pause through a spate of horrific weather. The lack of sufficient shelter and rest took the lives of many of the tribe's oldest, youngest, and otherwise weakest members—including Standing Bear's tubercular daughter, Prairie Flower, herself the mother of two young children. The death toll did not abate when they were released in the new land, since the government had failed to provide sufficient food, lumber, wagons, and horses. In their first two years in the Indian Territory, one-third of the tribe died. Among them was Standing Bear's teenage son, Bear Shield.

Following the death of his son, Standing Bear embarked on a plan to lead his people back to their ancestral home. In January 1879 he and twenty-nine carefully selected comrades quietly left the reservation, setting off as the vanguard of what they hoped would be a Ponca exodus. The local Indian agent wired Washington to alert agents posted with other tribes to be on the lookout for Standing Bear and, if seen, to have him returned to the Indian Territory.

Two months after their departure, Standing Bear and his cohorts turned up at the Omaha reservation. They were welcomed by the Omahas and by their government agent. But the agent's words were deceiving. He contacted the region's military commander, General George Crook, who promptly sent men and arrested the Poncas.

What happened next, from Standing Bear's perspective, was difficult to fathom, as he later recalled to the Senate committee:

A: They put us in where the soldiers were, in the fort.... We stayed there all winter.... The soldiers said, "We do this because we were ordered to do so." ...

Q: What did you then suppose they were going to do with you?

A: I supposed they were going to take us back to the Indian Territory.

Q: What did the soldiers actually do?

A: Somebody got the soldiers to let us go. There were three men in Omaha that helped get us away from the soldiers.

Q: You don't know how?

A: No, sir.

One of the men who helped

General George Crook (1828–1890)

Standing Bear get away from the soldiers was the assistant editor of the *Omaha Herald*, Thomas Tibbles. In a book published a year later, Tibbles (masked behind a pseudonym, Zylyff) recalled, "On the 29th of March, 1879, at about eleven o'clock at night ... the city editor came in and informed [me] that he had just returned from Fort Omaha ... where there was a band of Ponca Indians under arrest for running away from the Indian Territory." It was not, however, the city editor who came into Tibbles's office. Tibbles attributed the tip to the city editor to protect his source. It was General George Crook, the commanding officer of Fort Omaha, who came to his office that night.[4]

Tibbles knew a good story when he saw one, and at Fort Omaha he saw one. He wrote it up for the *Omaha Herald*, then telegraphed it to papers nationwide:

> Gen. Crook held a formal council with the Ponca Indians this morn-
> ing ... Standing Bear, hitherto in citizen's clothes, in full Indian cos-
> tume [said] ... "Before I went to the [Indian] Territory, I had a good
> house and a barn.... I had cattle and hogs and all kinds of stock, and
> somebody came and took all my things away.... If a white man had
> land and someone should swindle him, that man would try to get it
> back, and you would not blame him. Look on me! ... I need help." ...
>
> Gen. Crook, turning to Standing Bear, said, "It is a very hard
> case, but I can do nothing myself. I have received an order from
> Washington and I must obey it."

To describe Tibbles as a journalist is to give his résumé short shrift. As a teenager in Kansas, he had joined the ranks of abolitionist John Brown in the bloody confrontations in which Brown (who later attacked the U.S. Army arsenal at Harpers Ferry, Virginia) was then engaged. After serving in the Civil War—possibly as a Union spy—Tibbles became an itinerant preacher, then a journalist, and eventually an impresario. After seeing his story picked up in Chicago, St. Louis, and three New York newspapers, he knew it would behoove him to keep it going. But how?

Tibbles reasoned that if *he* were being held by the government, his reaction would be to get a lawyer. He therefore took the case to a lawyer. His keen instincts led him to John L. Webster, a boyhood friend who, much like himself, had substantial ambitions. (Webster later became active in Nebraska politics, unsuccessfully seeking a U.S. Senate seat and the Republican nomination for vice president.) Where Tibbles saw a potentially big news story, Webster saw a potentially big legal issue—so big that, to help assure it got attention, he sought a cocounsel, former Omaha mayor Andrew J. Poppleton. The legal bombshell they spotted was a writ of habeas corpus, a procedure to have a person in custody brought before a judge. It takes place every day in courtrooms across America. But it had never before been applied for an American Indian.

Because Standing Bear was in the custody of General Crook, the petition was presented in court as *Standing Bear v. Crook*. General Crook, the nominal defendant, did not testify in the proceedings for reasons that, in his memoirs, become crystal clear. "[I] stated bluntly that [my] interest in the case was official, that personally [I] sided with the Poncas," he wrote, adding, "The Poncas were ... simply another case of injustice to the Indians, a subject with which [I] was becoming increasingly familiar."

As Tibbles had hoped, the court case quickly commanded the attention of the nation's press. "At Omaha yesterday, Judge Dundy of the United States Court granted a writ of *habeas corpus* commanding General Crook to show cause why he has in custody Standing Bear and other Ponca Indians who fled from the Indian Territory," the *New York World* reported in August 1879. "The United States District Attorney has been directed to ... endeavor to have the writ dismissed. He takes the ground that ... the Indians stand as wards of the government, as minors are to their parents."

The U.S. attorney's legal argument matched the attitude of many Americans at that time, as expressed by Kemble in his later Senate testimony:

> *A:* If the Senator will permit me to say, in dealing with Indians, we must sometimes do as we do in dealing with children ... and may have to decide for them what is best ... in order to bring them to see things correctly.
>
> *Q:* To see things as you see them?
>
> *A:* To see things correctly.
>
> *Q:* As you see them?
>
> *A:* As white men see them.

On May 12 Judge Elmer Dundy ordered that Standing Bear and the other Poncas, having committed no crime nor having been charged with committing any crime, be released from custody. In rendering his decision, Dundy rejected the U.S. attorney's claim that Indians had no legal right to a writ of habeas corpus. "The district attorney ... claimed that none but American citizens are entitled to sue out this high prerogative writ in any of the federal courts," he ruled. "The habeas corpus act describes applicants for the writ as persons or parties who may be entitled thereto. It nowhere describes them as citizens."

The significance of the judge's decision detonated in the pages of the press. "The decision of Judge Dundy ... virtually declares Indians citizens of the United States, with the right to go where they please, regardless of treaty stipulations," Boston's *Daily Advertiser* reported in May 1879. "The district attorney at Omaha has been instructed to take the necessary steps to carry the case to ... the Supreme Court, if necessary. It is felt that to surrender this point is to surrender the whole Indian system."

The ruling also detonated in the halls of government. Secretary of the Interior Carl Schurz, whose department included the Commission on Indian Affairs, wrote in his memoirs that President Rutherford B. Hayes, in meeting with his cabinet, ultimately opted not to appeal the decision:

> The judge's decision opened up an alarming vista of ... restless braves and ambitious attorneys [who] could ... thwart the government in its efforts to control the movements of the Indians. Despite this prospect, however ... [it was] decided not to take an appeal to the Supreme Court.... [W]rong had been done to the Poncas ... but far greater wrongs would result if ... [the Supreme Court were] to undo the action of Congress.

Technically, Dundy's decision applied only to Standing Bear and his companions. If, however, the Supreme Court upheld his decision, it would apply to American Indians nationwide. The Hayes administration feared that, because of the wrongs done to the Poncas, not to mention the legal basis for Standing Bear's case, the Supreme Court might well uphold Dundy's decision.

The case reverberated in other directions as well. It stirred public sentiments regarding the treatment of Indians. The Senate launched an investigation into the manner in which the Poncas had been relocated (at which no one testified about the Senate having ratified a treaty with the Sioux that conflicted with a treaty with the Poncas). At these hearings, the most significant reverberation of Dundy's decision was voiced by Interior Secretary Schurz. Asked about the future security of tribal lands in the Indian Territory, he answered:

> I have no doubt that, in the course of time, the land in the Indian Territory not occupied by Indians, will be occupied by whites. But there are certain things that ought to precede that development. The title to the lands occupied by the Indians ought to be ... divided

among the Indians in severalty ... each upon his own farm, like the
white people, and get individual titles.... When such an arrangement as this has once been made, the question whether that part of
the Indian Territory not occupied by Indians shall be open to occupation by whites changes entirely.

To shift Indian land from tribal ownership to individual ownership—
and with it, the right of each Indian to sell his land—would end the tribal
way of life in all but its spiritual aspects (the dismantling of which was being
handled by missionaries and their schools). On the other hand, as tribes had
increasingly been forced to relinquish good land for desolate land in return
for payments, rations, and supplies, the tribal way of life had become vulnerable to massive graft and fraud on the part of government agents, their
suppliers, and on occasion the Indians' own leaders.

Among the committee members hearing this suggestion was Massachu-
setts Senator Henry L. Dawes. Quite likely, Dawes played a role in getting the
suggestion into the record, for seven years after the 1880 hearings, the Dawes
Act mandated exactly the change in land ownership that Schurz had described.
For better or for worse, Indian life would never be the same (see "Alfalfa Bill
Murray, Edward P. McCabe, and Chief Green McCurtain" in this book).

For journalist Tibbles, the news event ended with Dundy's decision ...
unless a new event were to occur. Tibbles therefore replaced his reporter's hat
with that of an impresario and undertook arrangements for a speaking tour
for Standing Bear—a challenging project, since the speaker spoke no English.
To serve as a translator, Tibbles arranged for an appealing young woman from
the Omaha tribe, Susette LaFlesche, whose uncle was one of the Ponca chiefs.
Miss LaFlesche spoke impeccable English, having recently graduated from
the Elizabeth Institute for Young Ladies in New Jersey. Tibbles introduced
her to the American public using the English translation of her Omaha name,
Bright Eyes. Five months after the court case concluded, the trio spoke at a
church gathering in Omaha; in October 1879 they began a nationwide tour.
The *Chicago Inter-Ocean* found it to be a highly polished performance:

Last evening at the New England Congregational Church ... Bright
Eyes, a comely young Indian maiden ... attired in Indian costume
... [detailed] the wrongs committed by the federal authorities ... in
simple but forcible style.... Mr. Tibbles, who seems to be a sort of a
manager for the Indian troupe ... gave a bragging account of what he

had done for the Poncas.... Standing Bear, the Ponca Chief, was then introduced and spoke in his own language, which was translated by Bright Eyes. The chief ... wore a bright blanket in sash form and a heavy necklace.

Meanwhile, back among the Poncas in the Indian Territory, life continued as if nothing had ever happened. The *St. Louis Globe-Democrat* reported in early November:

Some time ago, a report was received by [Indian] Commissioner Hayt from the Ponca Reservation ... that Big Snake ... who last summer caused his arrest and imprisonment for a month at Fort Reno for brutal and disorderly conduct, was making himself a terror to the Indians as well as the agency employees. His rearrest was ordered.... Big Snake, resisting arrest, was shot dead by a soldier. The occurrence caused considerable excitement among the Indians, but it was soon quieted.

Despite the death of Standing Bear's brother (and, days later, the death of Tibbles's wife), the show went on. The tour made its way to Boston, where standing-room-only audiences energetically responded. Carefully choreographed or not, the event made its point: Indians were people with the same inalienable rights as other Americans to life, liberty, and the pursuit of happiness. That point became ironic as they arrived at their final destination, New York City. In the Fifth Avenue hotel where they were staying, Standing Bear mentioned to Tibbles that he was going to the hotel's barber shop to get a haircut. Tibbles was aghast; he insisted that Standing Bear keep his braids. The day after the tour ended, Standing Bear got a haircut and changed into his normal clothes.[5]

Standing Bear returned to his ancestral land, but it was now desolate. The Poncas were gone. The Sioux had never settled there. The homes and structures had been demolished on government orders.

But big things were about to happen, beginning with the arrival of the Central Pacific Railroad. The only thing in its way, from Nebraska's point of view, was the state line. The now extraordinarily valuable land was in the Dakota Territory. To remedy this, Nebraska Senator Alvin Saunders sought to relocate that segment of his state's border northward to the Missouri River. Dakotans were not happy, but in 1882, lacking voting representation

Relocation of Nebraska border

in Congress, they had to rely on others to speak on their behalf. None spoke, though some asked:

> *Sen. Plumb:* What is the feeling of the people of Dakota about it? We are taking away what is apparently valuable property from the Territory of Dakota, which is here seeking admission as a state. It seems to me we ought to have regard for the wishes of those people....
>
> *Sen. Saunders:* This bill was before the Senate more than a year ago....
>
> *Sen. Hale:* Is there any population there?
>
> *Sen. Saunders:* There is no population....
>
> *Sen. Teller:* I should like to inquire if the Indians are not affected by it?...
>
> *Sen. Dawes:* The Indians have all been removed to the Indian Territory.
>
> *Sen. Edmunds:* At the point of the bayonet.
>
> *Sen. Dawes:* They have been removed at the point of the bayonet, so that the bill does not affect them.

Congress relocated the boundary.

Standing Bear lived out his remaining days on his ancestral land along the Niobrara River. Thomas Tibbles and Bright Eyes married each other in 1882 and continued to write on Indian issues. Other Poncas returned to what, by then, were their individually owned plots of lands. Most of the tribe, however, now settled and adjusting to the Indian Territory, opted to remain where they were. Standing Bear died in 1908 and was buried on his allotment of land in Nebraska. In the 1920s the property was sold to a white farmer who plowed the land, with the result that the location of Standing Bear's remains is now unknown.

LILI'UOKALANI AND SANFORD DOLE
Bordering on Empire

They were followed by her Majesty the Queen, dressed in a light colored silk which tended to add somewhat to her dark complexion and negro-like features, and more plainly exhibiting in the facial outlines a look of savage determination.... Next came four homely ladies-in-waiting, dressed in the loud colors so much admired by all dark-colored races.... And then the dignified [white] justices of the supreme court, whose manly bearing and intellectual appearance gave a relief to what had preceded. One of them, Mr. Dole, afterwards became President of the Republic.

    —LUCIEN YOUNG, *THE REAL HAWAII*, 1899

O f all the American boundaries, Hawaii's is, far and away, the most far and away. How and why did the United States extend its border to such an extreme?

In 1893 citizens in Hawaii overthrew Queen Lili'uokalani, replacing the island chain's monarchy with a democratic republic. Being a small, remote nation, the new Hawaiian government sought the protection of a powerful but like-minded democracy, the United States, in the form of annexation.

Or one could say: In 1893 a cabal of wealthy white people living in Hawaii overthrew Queen Lili'uokalani and established a government in which representation was gerrymandered to ensure that the white population would rule. The first president of this new government was Sanford Dole. Since Hawaii's white population—composed primarily of Americans or descendants of Americans—was a small minority in this remote chain of islands, Dole and his associates sought increased protection and control through annexation to the United States.

Both of these versions of events are true. But there are *buts* in both. Numerous white people in Hawaii, including some wealthy owners of sugar plantations, opposed the overthrow of the monarchy; others opposed annexation to the United States. Multiple issues were involved. Each of those issues remains a major factor in American politics today: involvement in foreign affairs, cheap immigrant labor, racism, and an issue that was new at the time: the power of Japan.

American annexation of Hawaii had first been proposed in the mid-nineteenth century by Hawaiians. King Kamehameha V feared that his realm was being eyed by Europe's colonial empires, particularly France. Since Hawaii had only scant experience with foreign governments, its king turned to the few whites living on his islands for advice. They urged numerous changes, including an elected legislature to advise the king and a cabinet to administer government functions, and suggested that the king ask the United States for protection since that nation shared Hawaii's value of self-rule. Kamehameha initially resisted this last idea, but in 1851, fearing that a French attack was imminent, he sent a formal request to the United States seeking cosovereignty in the event that France invaded.

But the United States declined. Secretary of State Daniel Webster told Kamehameha that while "the government of the United States was the first to acknowledge the national existence of the Hawaiian government … acknowledging the independence of the Islands, and of the government established over them, it was not seeking to promote any peculiar object of its own … or to exercise any sinister influence itself over the counsels of Hawaii."[1] Even as Webster wrote those words, Americans 3,000 miles from his desk were developing a coastal region the nation had only recently acquired: Califor-

Queen Lili'uokalani (1838–1917)

Sanford Dole (1844–1926)

nia. Its highly populated port city of San Francisco constituted both a market for, and a direct connection with, Hawaii. While American missionaries had lived in Hawaii since 1820, a new motive sent a second wave of Americans and, to a lesser extent, Europeans. Hawaii's climate and soil were perfect for growing sugarcane. Big money could be made.

Because it benefited everyone, sugar production quickly grew to the point that, in 1855, a free-trade agreement was negotiated by President Franklin Pierce and Hawaii. But sugar producers in the United States successfully lobbied the Senate to reject the treaty. In 1867 California sugar refiners lobbied the Senate to ratify a more limited free-trade treaty. That same year the purchase of Alaska reflected the fact that the nation's attitudes about boundaries were expanding beyond the continental United States. President Andrew Johnson expressed the new view in his statement to Congress on the proposed trade agreement with Hawaii:

> I am aware that upon the question of further extending our possessions it is apprehended by some that our political system cannot successfully be applied to an area more extended than our continent; but the conviction is rapidly gaining ground in the American mind that, with increased facilities for intercommunication between all portions of the earth, the principles of free government ... would prove of sufficient strength and breadth to comprehend within their sphere and influence the civilized nations of the world.

Though attitudes were changing, they were not completely changed. The Senate again rejected the treaty.

An additional reason for the Senate's reluctance to ratify either treaty can be inferred from its third time at bat. In 1873 the Senate did ratify a trade agreement with Hawaii ... and Britain immediately protested. Quite likely, until this time, the Senate had not thought it wise to risk military conflict in the middle of the Pacific Ocean with the world's preeminent empire.

Once the United States and Hawaii had established this free-trade agreement, the islands' sugar industry expanded exponentially. Not everyone in Hawaii was thrilled, however. "Some foresaw that this treaty with the United States might become the entering wedge for the loss of our independence," Queen Lili'uokalani later reflected in her memoirs. "What would be the consequences should the Islands acquire too great a commercial attraction, too large a foreign population and interests?"

The fear of too large a foreign population soon took on an additional dimension. The sugar plantations could produce far more sugar than Hawaii had natives to provide the labor. Workers would have to be imported. The white plantation owners were as cognizant of the risk they were taking by importing foreign workers as Hawaii's king had been in entering into the free-trade treaty. Initially the plantation owners paid for immigrants from Portugal, which had a surplus labor supply. (China and Japan, too, had a surplus of workers, but the planters considered the Portuguese, being Europeans, to be a more "desirable for permanent settlement.")[2] Providing transportation from Portugal, however, proved to be so costly that planters began opting for Chinese and Japanese workers. As feared, these immigrants came to constitute half the population over the next fifteen years. Native Hawaiians now made up roughly 45 percent of their nation, with the white population, which controlled nearly all the wealth, constituting the remaining 5 percent.[3] While political power remained in the hands of the monarch, the rapid change—and lack of change—led to racial, religious, and political friction.

By the summer of 1887, white residents had acquired influence with a sufficient number of King Kalākaua's advisers that the king, not knowing whom among those closest to him he could trust, acceded to what became known as the "bayonet" constitution. It provided for voting representation by the people, while preserving power for the nobility in a creatively revolutionary way. To be or vote for a representative, a citizen had to be a Hawaiian or white male, thereby excluding the nation's 25,000 or so Chinese and Japanese residents. To be or vote for a noble, however, one had to be a Hawaiian or white male with an annual income of at least $600 or $3,000 in property. Few Hawaiians had that.

Kalākaua's heir to the throne was his sister Lili'uokalani, who opposed these changes, despite the fact that she was steeped in Western culture. Born in 1838, Lili'uokalani had been educated at elite Hawaiian boarding schools run by missionaries. She was well versed in history, literature, science, and math, and a gifted pianist and composer. Nevertheless, when she ascended the thrown in 1891, Lili'uokalani embarked on an effort to restore power to— depending on one's point of view—Hawaii's natives or herself:

> I inquired at the opening of the cabinet meeting what was the business of the day, to which reply was made that it was necessary that I should sign without any delay their commissions, that thus they might proceed to the discharge of their duties. "But gentlemen," said I, "I expect you to send in your resignations before I can act." My rea-

soning was that, if they were new cabinet ministers, why should they appeal to me to appoint them to the places that they already filled?

Lili'uokalani's position was legally sound, and she won the right to nominate new ministers. Since, under the "bayonet" constitution, the monarch could not dismiss a cabinet member after the nominee had been approved by the legislature, Lili'uokalani chose carefully those who would, in effect, run the country. She and her advisers also began to draft a new constitution that would extend greater voting rights to nonwhite citizens. That task was sidetracked, however, when the legislature rejected her cabinet nominees. A tug of war began, ostensibly over nominee negotiations but, as Lili'uokalani knew, really over something far more profound. Hawaii's wealth had enriched and empowered the white population, but, as Lili'uokalani wrote, "sooner or later [it will] … also elevate the masses of the Hawaiian people into a self-governing class."

Indeed, Lili'uokalani's struggle roused the nation's nonwhite residents. In response, the white residents formed a Committee on Public Safety, which approached the U.S. commissioner to Hawaii for protection. He in turn instructed the commander of the USS *Boston*, at anchor in Pearl Harbor, to dispatch its Marines. Lili'uokalani later recalled:

> At about 2:30 PM, Tuesday [January 17, 1893], the establishment of the Provisional Government was proclaimed, and nearly fifteen minutes later Mr. J. S. Walker [president of the Legislative Assembly] came and told me "that he had come on a painful duty; that the opposition party had requested that I should abdicate." … Since the troops of the United States had been landed to support the revolutionists by the order of the American minister, it would be impossible for us to make any resistance.

Later that day, the chairman of the Committee on Public Safety declared to a mass gathering outside the government building that Lili'uokalani had abdicated and that a provisional government would rule until union with the United States was completed.[4] Sanford Dole had been selected as president of the provisional government.

Dole, the son of missionary parents, had been born in Honolulu in 1844. Though he left Hawaii to attend Williams College in Massachusetts and was, for a brief time, an attorney in Boston, he returned to practice law and was elected to the legislature in 1884. Three years later, he participated in the delegation that had maneuvered King Kalākaua into signing the "bayonet" constitution, transferring power to the white minority. Dole became a justice of the Hawaiian Supreme Court that same year.

Not all white people in Hawaii supported Dole and his colleagues in their quest for annexation, since the 1882 U.S. prohibition of Chinese immigration would be applied to Hawaii, thus ending a main supply of imported labor. On the other hand, the United States had not restricted Japanese immigration. And Japan, as newspapers were beginning to report, was becoming a force to be reckoned with—and was already the nation Hawaii most feared. "The Hawaiian government is now endeavoring to check further Japanese immigration," the *New York Times* reported in September 1897, noting that Dole's government feared "Japanese influence and numbers may become too powerful and possibly overthrow the republic and bring about Hawaiian annexation to Japan." Previously, the November 1896 issue of *Harper's Monthly* had included an article entitled "The New Japan." It coincided with news reports regarding Japan's formal protest of American efforts to annex Hawaii.

But Japan declared it had no intention of annexing Hawaii. "I am instructed by the imperial Government to state most emphatically and unequivocally that Japan has not now and never had any such design, or designs of any kind, against Hawaii," its foreign minister stated.[5] (The United States, when Daniel Webster was secretary of state, had said the same thing.)

Most likely, opinions in Japan were mixed, as they certainly were in the United States. The *New York Times* expressed the views of those Americans who opposed the annexation of Hawaii, many of whom also deplored Hawaii's coup d'état. Three editorials appeared in 1893 alone bearing headlines such as, "To Convey a Stolen Kingdom," "A Case of Government by the Few," and "A Shameful Conspiracy."

Many other Americans, however, supported annexation. Voicing their views that same year was the *Chicago Tribune*, arguing in a February editorial:

> The objections made nearly a century ago to the purchase of Louisiana were similar to those made now to the annexation of Hawaii. It was asserted that that territory was a great ways off, that its [Louisiana's French-speaking] inhabitants were un-American ... that it would be impossible to defend in case of war with a foreign country. All those were as naught when weighed against the fact that it was necessary for the United States to own the mouth of the Mississippi. It is necessary now that the United States should have Hawaii for the safety of its oceanic commerce.

Even at the highest level of leadership, Americans were of two minds about this unprecedented extension of the country's borders. President Benjamin Harrison had supported it. But he had been defeated in 1892 for reelection by the man he himself had defeated for reelection, Grover Cleveland. President Cleveland opposed Hawaiian annexation. Moreover, he ordered an investigation into U.S. military involvement in the coup d'état, raising the possibility that he might support the return to power of Lili'uokalani.

Given these uncertainties, Dole expected that the American debate would be long and drawn out. Consequently, he proceeded to turn the provisional government into an official republic, the first step of which was writing a constitution. This entailed defining how Hawaiians would elect their leaders, and that entailed confronting Hawaii's underlying conflict: power versus race.

Dole sought guidance from an American constitutional scholar at Columbia University, John W. Burgess, to whom he described the delicate issue:

> Under the monarchy there were two classes of legislators who sat together and who were elected by voters having different qualifications. There are many natives and Portuguese, who had had the vote hitherto, who are comparatively ignorant of the principles of government, and whose vote from its numerical strength as well as from the ignorance referred to, will be a menace to good government.[6]

Burgess replied: "I understand your problem to be the construction of a constitution which will place the government in the hands of the Teutons, and preserve it there, at least for the present." He recommended separating the legislature into a system similar to the American Senate and House of Representatives, but tailored to Dole's concerns. In addition to maintaining the current voting restrictions, Burgess suggested that the new Hawaiian republic "elect your president by a college of electors, … that one half of those electors should be elected by the voters for the members of the lower house of the legislature, and the other half should be elected by the voters for the upper house of the legislature." By this method, white residents would garner yet another advantage in determining the nation's leadership. Burgess closed his letter with some added advice: "Appoint only Teutons to military office."

Meanwhile, President Cleveland adjudged that, despite legitimate grievances and policy disputes, the coup d'état that had ousted Lili'uokalani was made possible through the use of American troops that had been deployed without presidential or congressional authorization. Consequently, he sent

Kentucky Congressman Albert S. Willis to Hawaii to commence efforts to reinstate the queen, provided she grant amnesty to those who had participated in her ouster. Lili'uokalani was less than enthusiastic about this proviso. "There are certain laws of my government by which I shall abide," she stated. "My decision would be, as the law directs, that such persons should be beheaded and their property confiscated to the government."

After a month of meetings with Willis and her advisers, the dethroned queen revised her view. "I must forgive and forget the past," she now officially declared. One day later, Willis sent a message to Dole demanding his resignation, along with that of all others in the provisional government. After conferring with his cabinet, Dole sent Willis an official response saying, in effect, come and get us. It was a shrewd move, since even President Cleveland was reluctant to invade Hawaii and oust an ostensible democracy headed by white people in order to restore a dark-skinned monarch. Cleveland opted to punt; he submitted the question to Congress.

Rather than drag on, however, the decision was made rather quickly, following the explosion of an American battleship at anchor in Havana. The sinking of the *Maine* in February 1898 triggered the Spanish-American War. Three months later, Admiral George Dewey destroyed the Spanish fleet defending the Philippines, a Spanish colony, in the Battle of Manila Bay. Dewey's victory demonstrated the need for a permanent American military presence in the Pacific. Eight weeks later, on July 4, 1898, Congress enacted a resolution offering annexation to Hawaii. The islands' white-dominated government readily accepted.

In April 1899 President William McKinley appointed Dole to be Hawaii's first territorial governor. In November Dole's twenty-two-year-old cousin, James Dole, arrived in the islands and purchased sixty-four acres of government land on which he grew and canned pineapples. Sanford Dole left the governorship in 1903 to accept a presidential appointment as the territory's federal judge. When he retired in 1915, his cousin James had expanded his operations and was now exporting roughly $10 million of canned pineapples per year.[7] Sanford Dole died in 1926, not long after his eighty-third birthday.

Lili'uokalani remained in Hawaii. The former queen urged her people to accept their future as American citizens. Annexation to the United States brought one immediate improvement for native Hawaiians, in that the Fifteenth Amendment to the Constitution prohibited the denial of voting rights based on race or color. Periodically Lili'uokalani traveled to Washington, DC, unsuccessfully seeking government compensation for the loss of her family's property. She died in 1917 at the age of seventy-nine.

ALFALFA BILL MURRAY, EDWARD P. McCABE, AND CHIEF GREEN McCURTAIN
Oklahoma's Racial Boundaries

> I have no doubt that today there are half a million people in the Indian Territory.... A small fraction are full-blooded Indians, another portion are mixed bloods, and a large share of them are white people who are members of the tribe simply by marriage or adoption....
> Then, in connection with that, there are a number of negroes.
> —SEN. KNUTE NELSON, OKLAHOMA STATEHOOD DEBATE, 1903

O klahoma came close to being two states. The western half, whose residents were primarily white, would have been the state of Oklahoma. The eastern half, whose residents were primarily Indians, would have been the state of Sequoyah—named in memory of the Cherokee who had devised the first American Indian alphabet and, not, presumably, in memory of the fact that a pole had once been erected to display his head because of boundaries he had helped negotiate (see "Sequoyah" earlier in this book).

In addition, another effort was made to create a different racial boundary. When Indian lands were made available for settlement, a movement was initiated among African Americans to migrate to the new territory (named Oklahoma) in sufficient numbers to constitute a majority of the population. Had the effort succeeded, Oklahoma would have become, in effect, an African American state. But the movement triggered a countereffort to embed white supremacy in the Oklahoma constitution.

Green McCurtain, "Alfalfa Bill" Murray, and Edward P. McCabe were

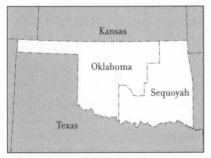

Proposed states of Oklahoma and Sequoyah

three of the principal participants in
these different efforts to create, in
effect, racial boundary lines. Of the
three, only McCurtain, a Choctaw, was
born and raised in present-day Oklahoma. At the time of his birth in 1848,
Oklahoma was part of a region known
as the Indian Territory. The Indian
Territory was not composed of U.S.
citizens with a governor appointed
by the president but rather of American Indian reservations, each with its
own tribal leadership. McCurtain was
forty-four, married, and treasurer of
the Choctaw government when his

Chief Green McCurtain (1848–1910)

career was profoundly altered by events in Washington. Aspiring settlers seeking land in the West had been pressuring Congress to open up unassigned lands
in the western half of the Indian Territory. Americans rich and poor, along with
railroads and other corporations, recognized the opportunities available with
this land. "Fully a hundred thousand people are intending to rush into Oklahoma, as soon as it is opened for settlement," the *Atchison Daily Champion* reported
in February 1889. As arrangements with the tribes were completed, the gates
opened, and settlers poured into the new Territory of Oklahoma.

McCurtain first surfaced in outside news accounts as a result of his
tribe's agreement with the federal government. The Choctaw Nation bore
little resemblance to the tribe that had arrived from Mississippi some sixty
years before, as could be gleaned from an 1891 *Dallas Morning News* article on
the land transfer: "Some of the members [of the Choctaw Council] could not
speak Choctaw and some could not speak English…. Appointed delegates to
Washington to watch the interests of the Choctaws … are Gov. W. N. Jones,
Treasurer Green McCurtain, and Thomas D. Ainsworth."

The final paragraph of the same news item contained an omen regarding the state of Sequoyah: "It is frequently suggested that the Five Civilized
Tribes [the Cherokees, Chickasaws, Choctaws, Creeks, and Seminoles] should
form a federation for their mutual protection. This is not likely to be done for
some time on account of local jealousies. When it is done it will be too late,
and only precipitate the transfer of that country to the control of the whites."

As it happened, the Five Tribes set aside their jealousies less than two years later when Congress added a clause to its 1893 appropriation for the Office of Indian Affairs. Inserted into the bill in the last few hours before Congress adjourned, the amendment gave the consent of the United States for tribes to divide and deed their lands to individual members. In addition, those Indians who acquired ownership of their share of land would become citizens of the United States. The option was accepted with virtually no debate.

The seemingly benign amendment regarding land deeds enabled a geographic shift of politically epic proportions. Transferring ownership of Indian land from a tribe to its members would shift the authority to sell the land. From the perspective of Indian leaders, such a shift would be nothing short of divide and conquer.[1] In 1896 McCurtain, now the elected chief of the Choctaw Nation, called for a convention of the Five Tribes to plan their opposition. When they met in November of that year, the delegates ultimately agreed to relinquish their tribal form of government and to divide their lands among each tribe's individual members—on condition that the Indian Territory be admitted as a state.

It was not a decision easily reached. Very few, in fact, of the delegates who voted in favor of the resolution fully agreed with it—including the man who had initiated the summit, Green McCurtain. "It has come to the point where the Indian must take a decisive step forward or forever be swallowed up and lose his identity," he agreed, but he opposed the demand for immediate statehood. "Today the Choctaw Indian—and what I say applies equally to the other tribes— is not prepared to have a state or territorial government.... It will result in the red man being outvoted by the white occupants of the territory."[2] McCurtain preferred a gradual implementation of the land shift, to buy time for American Indians to learn how the levers of power worked in white America. Once acclimated, he hoped, Indians would be able to maintain their hold on those levers when the land transition was completed and statehood conferred.

Even that, he knew, was a huge hope, since those levers of power weren't always securely fastened. When a proposal for Oklahoma statehood first came before Congress in 1905, the *Dallas Morning News* showed how they could become unhinged.

A circumstance in this statehood controversy worthy of remark is the beautiful faith of the Indians that Congress will redeem the promises ... made as far back as 1839.... These agreements between the government and the Indians ... were not intended to express a fixed policy for all future time but were designed to meet the exigencies of the period in which they were made.

McCurtain put it differently:

> No Indian can get the better of a paleface.... Two Oklahoma palefaces once hunted in my camp. They spent the evening with me and over the fire.... Bill said, "Sam, let's trade horses—my bay for your roan."
>   "It's a go," Sam agreed. "Shake on it, partner."
>   They shook hands. Then Bill said with a loud laugh, "I've bested ye this time. My hoss is dead. Died yesterday."
>   "So's mine," Sam said, "Died this morn'n. And what's more, I've took his shoes off."[3]

Despite his misgivings, when the Sequoyah Convention for statehood was convened in August 1905, McCurtain joined in, serving as one of its vice presidents. A fellow vice president, representing the Chickasaw Nation, was William H. Murray, soon to be widely known as "Alfalfa Bill" for his urging Oklahomans to grow alfalfa. Murray, however, was not of Chickasaw descent. Born to a poor family in Toadsuck, Texas in 1869, he had arrived in the Indian Territory in 1897 as a young lawyer and became involved in the successful election campaign of Chickasaw governor Douglas Johnston. Not long after, he married Johnston's niece—a social event in Indian society which so emulated white high society that Oklahoma's *Daily Ardmoreite* headlined the wedding announcement as "Prominent Young Attorney Secures a Chickasaw Queen."

Though Murray was a fellow vice president at the Sequoyah Convention, he privately doubted the effort would succeed. He was not alone. "There is not the faintest chance to get the Indian Territory admitted separately," Idaho's *Daily Statesman* asserted. "If it were necessary to create a state where Indians would exercise such great influence the experiment might be tried, but in this case it is not necessary and the country will never consent." Murray, for his part, was not aiming to create an Indian state. His goal was to organize future voters in the Indian Territory in order to strengthen that

"Alfalfa Bill" Murray (1869–1956)

constituency in the future state Murray anticipated—one that would combine the Oklahoma Territory and the Indian Territory.[4]

The effort to create a state of Sequoyah was ultimately torpedoed by President Theodore Roosevelt. "I recommend that Indian Territory and Oklahoma be admitted as one state," he had told Congress in his 1905 State of the Union message. That the boundaries of the Indian Territory would thereby be obliterated did not concern him. "There is no obligation," he told Congress, "to treat territorial subdivisions, which are matters of convenience only."

With the president endorsing a state that combined the two territories, the action moved to the Oklahoma statehood convention in Guthrie in 1906. At this venue, the delegates elected "Alfalfa Bill" as the convention president. Murray's opening address praised Green McCurtain and the other chiefs as "great men," then went on to paint the colors, as it were, of the state he foresaw. "We must provide the means for the advancement of the negro race, and accept him as God gave him to us and use him for the good of society," he declared. "As a rule, they are failures as lawyers, doctors and in other professions. He must be taught in line with his own sphere as porters, bootblacks, and barbers.... It is an entirely false notion that the negro can rise to the equal state of a white man."

While many states had enacted Jim Crow laws, Murray sought to embed white supremacy in the Oklahoma constitution. Other white delegates disagreed—not with Murray's racial views, but with the political wisdom of including them in a constitution that would require approval by Congress and the signature of President Roosevelt. Ultimately, the delegates, including Murray, opted to avoid a confrontation. They contented themselves with a resolution stating "it is the sense of this body that separate coaches and waiting rooms be required for the negro race ... [but] consider this a legislative matter rather than a constitutional question."

Oklahoma became a state on November 16, 1907. On the legislature's opening day, it enacted Senate Bill No. 1, mandating segregated railroad coaches and waiting rooms as its first order of business.

In thus privileging white people, Oklahoma faced the issue of its red people, whose political support was essential, given the state's demographics. Anticipating this need, the Oklahoma constitution included a section devoted to the definition of race. "Wherever in this Constitution and laws of this state, the word or words, 'colored,' 'colored race,' 'negro,' or 'negro race' are used," Article 23 stated, "the same shall be construed to mean or apply to all persons of African descent. The term 'white race' shall include all other persons." Legally speaking, American Indians were now white people in Oklahoma.

Edward P. McCabe was one of several thousand African Americans who had migrated to Oklahoma since the 1890s. Most of these settlers were from the South, seeking economic opportunity and escape from persecution. Unfortunately for them, many poor Southern whites (such as Murray) had also migrated to Oklahoma for economic opportunity.

Compared to Murray, McCabe came from an economically advantaged background. Born in Troy, New York, in 1850, he had been raised in Newport, Rhode Island, and educated at a boarding school in Maine. As a young man, he became an attorney in Chicago and then moved to Kansas where, in 1882, he became the first African American elected to state office, serving as the Kansas auditor.

McCabe became involved in the Topeka-based Oklahoma Immigration Association, part of the larger movement to encourage African American migration to Oklahoma. In 1890 he himself relocated there and, with landowner Charles Robbins, founded the town of Langston. He started a newspaper, the *Langston City Herald*, which trumpeted the town's existence as "a Negro city."[5] Other newspapers sounded a bugle: "The blacks, it appears, are preparing themselves to try the experiment, not merely of the equality, but of the supremacy of their race," the *New York Times* alerted its readers in March of that year. It warned that a "secret society of negroes which has undertaken this work in Oklahoma has a candidate of its own for the Governorship of the Territory." Though there was no secret society, there was such a candidate, and he was Edward P. McCabe. With the imminent creation of the Oklahoma Territory, McCabe had gone to Washington at the behest of the Oklahoma Immigration Association to seek support for his appointment as governor. "There is much bitterness over the candidacy of Edward P. McCabe, colored, for governor of [the Oklahoma] Territory," the *Times* reported, citing an unnamed Oklahoman who "declares emphatically that if President Harrison appoints McCabe governor, the latter will be assassinated."

Opposition to McCabe's appointment—and to an African American—majority state—was not, however, universal. "A partial solution of the Southern negro question ... is now

Edward P. McCabe (1850–1920)

at hand," *Chicago Tribune* columnist William H. Thomas wrote. "A governor is soon to be appointed to preside over [the Oklahoma Territory] and a reliable, capable colored man should be placed in that position. That would mean a home for the colored man in the South."

President Benjamin Harrison, concerned with the potential for violence, ultimately chose a man with military experience, former Indiana congressman George W. Steele, to be governor of the Oklahoma Territory. Even after this appointment, however, articles in the press continued to sound alarms about a conspiracy to make Oklahoma a black-majority state. "Few people here seem to realize the possibility of Oklahoma becoming a Negro State," a correspondent for the *Chicago Tribune* told its readers in 1891, "so quietly, yet so constantly, have the blacks been coming into the territory." (In point of fact, the African American population in the territory was less than 9 percent.)[6]

A *New York Times* editorial in 1892, entitled "Not Ready for Statehood," joined the chorus of concern. "Oklahoma contains more conflicting elements than does any other Territory in the Union," it began. "With allotment comes citizenship to the Indian, ill prepared for the privileges that go with that state.... Then comes the negro race, which is a considerable factor in Oklahoma, a factor determined to maintain its rights according to its own peculiar ideas."

The *Chicago Tribune* noted that Oklahoma's racial conflicts were not as simple as white people versus red and black. "Another cause for excitement," it commented in September 1891, "is the hatred of the Indians for the negro.... They know that they themselves cannot prevent the negroes from settling on the land, but they hint in unmistakable terms that they will make it very uncomfortable for the 'black man' if he settles among them."

The racial boundary between African Americans and American Indians was, in fact, even more complicated. Prior to the Civil War, some wealthy members of the Five Civilized Tribes had been slave owners—these slave owners typically being of mixed Indian-white descent. On the other hand, runaway slaves frequently took refuge among these same tribes, and (further blurring the boundary) intermarried, resulting in a growing population of African American Indians.[7]

Oklahoma's part-white Indians and part-black Indians had separate misgivings about the influx of African American settlers. Part-black Indians feared the influx might cause "pure" Indians to discriminate against their tribal claims, particularly claims of land allotments. Indeed, the Chickasaws did create a "colored committee" to determine the validity of tribal claims by part-black Chickasaws, with none other than "Alfalfa Bill" Murray among its panelists. At the other end of the spectrum, part-white Indians were concerned that the influx of African Americans might negatively impact their own tenuous status with the white ruling class.

Oklahoma's statehood convention in 1906–7 marked the success of the combined opposition of whites and American Indians over African Americans. Soon after statehood became official, Edward McCabe returned to Chicago. There, however, he immediately set his sights on undermining Oklahoma Senate Bill No. 1 by suing the Atchison, Topeka and Santa Fe Railway for not providing equal accommodations for black passengers. He lost, but his appeal of the decision eventually made its way to the U.S. Supreme Court. He lost there, too. During these defeats, McCabe's extraordinarily energetic career began running out of steam. By 1911 Oklahoma's *Ada News* reported that he had become a waiter in a Chicago area restaurant. He died quietly in 1920, so quietly that the event appears to have been noted only in the city where he was buried. "Mr. McCabe was a highly educated scholarly gentleman," the *Topeka Plaindealer* wrote. "He never bartered or catered to the white man the rights of the colored race and always stood up for his people. For this we reverence and honor his name.... It is to be regretted that he died in needy circumstance and a charge on the public."

Green McCurtain's career had sputtered to an end as well. In 1910 Congress investigated charges of bribery involving McCurtain. He testified that he had ultimately rejected the bribe, and no evidence to the contrary was found. He passed away later that year. A wire-service obituary sent to newspapers nationwide began, "Green McCurtain, chief of the tribe of Choctaws Indians, who sprang a sensation before a congressional committee by swearing he had been offered one-fourth of the profits of a $10,000,000 deal after the sale of Indian lands, died yesterday. He was 62 years of age." Fourteen paragraphs followed, all dealing exclusively with the bribery accusation.[8]

"Alfalfa Bill" Murray's career did not sputter. He went on to become an Oklahoma congressman and governor. Upon his death in 1956, a wire-service obituary also appeared in newspapers nationwide. "William H. (Alfalfa Bill) Murray, one of the principal framers of Oklahoma's constitution ... died today at the age of 86," it began, going on to recount his career as governor, his short-lived presidential bid in 1932, his feud with President Franklin Roosevelt over "constitutional safeguards of liberty," and the election of his son, Johnston, as Oklahoma governor in 1950.[9]

These contrasting obituaries sum up the complex racial boundaries that came into conflict with the emergence of Oklahoma. The result of that conflict, however, was not complex. The whites won.

BERNARD J. BERRY
New Jersey Invades Ellis Island

Ellis Island is to be put up for sale for private commercial use. The
little island ... which for fifty years had been "God's twenty-seven-
and-a-half acres" for at least 15,000,000 immigrants, is scheduled
to be sold to the highest bidder.... The decision to dispose of Ellis
Island by sale put an end to the hope that the historic spot might be
preserved as a public area. New York and New Jersey had each sought
to obtain the island.

—*NEW YORK TIMES*, SEPTEMBER 14, 1956

N
ine months prior to this decision to sell Ellis Island, the efforts of
New York and New Jersey to obtain the island had taken a bold new
turn. January 4, 1956, had been foggy in the New York metropolitan
area. As reported in the *New York Times*, the fog presented ideal conditions to

land an expeditionary force of New Jersey officials on Ellis Island.
New Jersey wants the island even though New York contends it is within its own territorial limits and will fight for it to the last lawyer. The
three federal government employees on the island yesterday put up no
resistance. In fact, it took about fifteen minutes to find them. There
were no casualties, although Mayor Bernard J. Berry of Jersey City got
separated from the main party and for a while was listed as "lost."

Once found, Mayor Berry suggested that they plant a New Jersey flag in
the ground, but no one in the raiding party had thought to bring one. After
some discussion about going back to the office to get one, they decided to let
that go, since by the time they could return some New Yorkers might have
heard about their foray, and the middle-aged officials did not think a rumble
would aid their purpose.

What *was* their purpose? Boundary disputes between states were settled by the Supreme Court even in the early years of the Republic, when invasions by militias did happen. What, then, were the New Jerseyans up to, and why were they up to it at this point in time?

The purpose of the "raid" was publicity—as evidenced by the excerpt above, in which the nature and degree of detail suggest the presence of the reporter. The purpose of the publicity was to create greater awareness of New Jersey's claim to Ellis Island, since the famous immigration portal had always been known as Ellis Island, New York. And the reason for doing so at this moment was that, just more than a year earlier, the federal government had closed the island.

In response to the closure, New York prepared a proposal to use some of the island's now aban-doned buildings to house the home-less and treat alcoholics, and to use the remaining buildings as part of the Department of Corrections—not a place to take the family. New Jer-sey proposed using the island and its structures for an ethnic museum

Bernard J. Berry (1913–1963)

and park. Since the federal govern-ment owned the land, it could lease it for either project. But New Jersey's proposal would stand a far better chance politically if the land it sought to lease was in New Jersey, which is what Mayor Berry and his troops in gray flannel suits maintained.

Nor were they the first to do so. Disputes over the boundary of Ellis Island dated back to 1893, just after the island was put into service as an immigration station. In that initial challenge, it was not New Jersey that brought suit but a defense attorney for an immigrant charged with com-mitting perjury in the statements he made when being processed at the new facility. The case was assigned to the federal court for the Southern District of New York, but the defendant's attorney wanted his client to be tried in the federal court in New Jersey.

The defense attorney based his argument on the unique boundary lines that divide that segment of the two states. The division is marked by two simultaneous boundary lines. Nowhere else in the country has such a boundary ever been implemented. But nowhere else was there such a valuable harbor, particularly at the time the boundary was negotiated in the early years of the Republic. One of the boundary lines is where the water meets the mainland, thus giving all of the Hudson River and Upper New York Bay—and the islands in those waters—to New York. The other boundary line is under the water along the middle of the channel. This second boundary enabled New Jersey to build a structure on its land, extend it over the water and secure it in the ground under the water—in other words, to build piers.

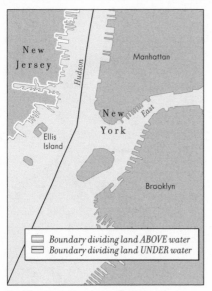

Dual New York–New Jersey borders

When the federal government decided to use Ellis Island for an immigration portal, the facility it planned required that the island be enlarged, which was done with landfill. Because the added acreage was built up from land on the New Jersey side of the underwater border, the argument could be made that the newly added land belonged to New Jersey.

The issue of federal court jurisdiction in the 1893 criminal case was ultimately decided without ruling on the boundary issue, since neither state was a litigant. Neither was the issue resolved in 1903–4, when New Jersey sued the U.S. Immigration Commission on behalf of the descendants of the colonial proprietors of Ellis Island. In this instance, the claim was based on a deed issued by the Duke of York, whose ownership was based on a deed issued by his brother, King Charles II. The government opted to sidestep this head-scratching challenge by simply buying Ellis Island from New Jersey. The deed for this purchase was therefore issued by New Jersey, but that fact did not constitute a definitive decision on the boundary, since such a ruling could only be issued by the U.S. Supreme Court.

These were the historical reasons why Bernard Berry and his merry men temporarily occupied Ellis Island, but a more contemporary issue further motivated them. In the 1950s Americans had begun moving from densely populated cities to suburbs. Shopping centers, some with branches of downtown department stores, were cropping up in the suburbs as well. Not far behind were office buildings. If the trend continued—and it did—urban centers would find themselves increasingly depleted. Berry's raid was part of a larger effort to attract commerce to New Jersey's older urban areas.

In 1954, for example, Berry had sought and received commitments from Jersey City businesses to contribute to the renovation of nearby Newark's old Center Market as part of an effort to lure the New York Stock Exchange to relocate in New Jersey. The following year, Berry commenced a major effort to lure the Brooklyn Dodgers to Jersey City. In 1956 the Dodgers played seven league games and one exhibition game at Jersey City's Roosevelt Stadium. Mayor Berry again displayed his quirky publicity skills when *Time* magazine wrote that the Dodgers had "crossed the Hudson to Jersey City for a second 'opening game,' the first of seven regular-season 'home' games they will play there this year," and went on to note that "somebody gave Jersey City Mayor Bernard J. Berry a ball to throw out. Came time for the historic throw. 'Mr. Mayor, the ball,' an aide prompted. 'The ball?' echoed His Honor with surprise. 'I gave it to some kid.'"

The Dodgers left Brooklyn after the following year's season, but not for Jersey City. Team owner Walter O'Malley opted for the nation's burgeoning "suburbanopolis," Los Angeles, where the population had doubled since the beginning of World War II and was still expanding without end in sight. Undaunted, Berry unsuccessfully offered the stadium the following year to the Philadelphia Phillies, the Pittsburgh Pirates, and the Cincinnati Reds.

Berry's efforts to keep Jersey City and its neighboring urban centers economically viable were coupled with efforts to prevent them from becoming what he did not want them to be. Toward this end, he ordered the confiscation of the film *The Moon Is Blue* and the arrest of a movie theater manager, who was charged with violating state and city obscenity laws. Berry's act in October 1953 drew national attention because *The Moon Is Blue* was not some low-budget porn film but a comedy directed by Otto Preminger, with a cast that included William Holden and David Niven. Critic Bosley Crowther, in his *New York Times* review, wryly noted the film's prerelease hype regarding its "decency" and observed that several thousand people had jammed the two Manhattan theaters showing the film, which dealt with "such things as whether a nice young lady who has let herself be lured to a pleasant young bachelor's apartment should frankly inquire of him as to his romantic intentions, whether she should ask him about mistresses and such, and whether she should candidly acknowledge a healthy but cautious interest in sex." After a grand jury refused to issue an indictment, the Jersey City theater manager again scheduled the film. Again the theater was raided—this time during the film's first show. The squadron of police, not wanting to disturb (or confront) the adult-only audience of more than 400, sat and watched with them before arresting the manager.[1]

During this same period, Berry also sought to have bookstores in Jersey City voluntarily cease selling James Jones's popular novel *From Here to Eternity*. The novel's language was more explicit than the Academy Award–winning film, which was currently in release.

While these actions may sound outrageous today (and were controversial and derided at the time), they shared a common denominator with Berry's other efforts, and in particular with his adventure on Ellis Island. They all bespoke a desire to preserve Jersey City as it was—or as Berry believed or wished it was. Ironically, Jersey City had been one of the most politically corrupt cities in America when ruled by Mayor Frank Hague and his nephew, Mayor Frank Hague Egger, from 1917 to 1949. But that was not the Jersey City Berry longed to preserve. His vision, real or imagined, was captured in the town's *Hudson Reporter* in 2007, forty-five years after his death. "Prior to the large malls, there were many neighborhood stores," a letter to the editor remembered. "Totaro Hardware, Stegman Tavern, Stanley Bakery.... The candy stores on Jackson Avenue would remain open until after 10 PM.... The City, under Bernard J. Berry, conducted nightly basketball games at Audubon Park (starring Vinny Ernst), art shows, handball games and an open playground with outdoor showers for the children in the summertime."

Bernard Berry was unable to stop the cultural and economic forces of the 1950s. But one effort that succeeded was his Ellis Island raid. It raised awareness of New Jersey's ownership claim, thereby helping prepare the way for the state's subsequent legal efforts. The legal challenge, far less theatrical and far more time-consuming, culminated in 1998, when the U.S. Supreme Court finally ruled that the landfill acres of the island were indeed in New Jersey. Today Ellis Island is officially Ellis Island, New York/New Jersey.

But Berry's publicity stunt achieved even more. His vision of an ethnic museum and park—yet another of his efforts to preserve and respect the past—prevailed when Ellis Island became part of the National Park Service's Statue of Liberty National Monument in 1965. Since 1990, following a $150 million restoration effort, its main buildings have served as a tremendously successful immigration museum and records center.

LUIS FERRÉ
Puerto Rico: The Fifty-First State?

Puerto Ricans have served with distinction in all the wars in which the U.S. has been involved [since 1898].... Several, such as Fernando Luis Garcia ... have been decorated with the Congressional Medal of Honor. Among other distinguished leaders is Admiral Horacio Rivero, in 1968 the Chief of NATO Forces in Southern Europe.... Our great actors, like José Ferrer and Raul Julia, have been American favorites.... Roberto Clemente has been included in the Hall of Fame.... The time has come for Congress ... to do justice to more than 3.6 million disenfranchised American citizens.

—Luis Ferré[1]

P uerto Rico became an American possession during the Spanish-American War when, in 1898, U.S. troops landed on the island and met the welcoming arms of its residents, delighted to be liberated from Spain. Congress conferred citizenship on Puerto Ricans in 1917, followed one month later by draft notices. In 1947 Congress allowed Puerto Ricans to elect their own governor. Statehood, however, repeatedly faced resistance ... from the majority of Puerto Ricans.

Luis Ferré was the leading voice of those Puerto Ricans who sought statehood. He founded and led the New Progressive Party, whose central platform was Puerto Rican statehood.

Luis Ferré (1904–2003)

This quest had commenced much earlier, dating back to the very beginning of American sovereignty and emanating from both Americans and Puerto Ricans. One month before the ceasefire that ended the Spanish-American War, a letter to the editor in the *New York Times* described the "triumph of democracy." The letter stated that the United States "is capable of ruling men of different habits, religions, and modes of life; and [if] the United States is to be the exemplar of this doctrine ... the time is ripe for action. It is certain that Spain must part with Cuba and Puerto Rico, the former to become, perhaps, independent ... the latter to be, as indeed Cuba should be, brought ultimately into the Union."

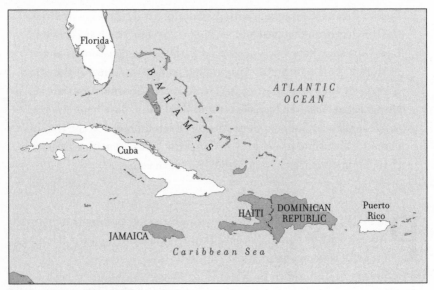

Spanish-American War: two future states?

With the signing of the peace treaty, the U.S. military governor of Puerto Rico called for a convention of representatives from the island's various regions to draw up a list of concerns. The issues they raised pertained to trade with the United States, education, and voting rights. Those same issues have remained the underlying elements in Puerto Rico's debate over statehood. They came to be joined, however, by an additional element: doubt among Puerto Ricans regarding U.S. awareness of problems in Puerto Rico and its commitment to fixing them.

The origins of these doubts can be found in statements made by the first two presidents to follow American acquisition of the island. William McKinley, in his 1899 State of the Union message, spoke of Puerto Rico's future solely in terms of an improved postal service. Theodore Roosevelt, in his 1901 State of the Union, contentedly declared that Puerto Rico "is thriving as never before, and it is being administered efficiently and honestly. Its people are now enjoying liberty and order under the protection of the United States, and upon this fact we congratulate them and ourselves."

Soon, however, Roosevelt was obliged to recognize that Puerto Rico's economy was not, in fact, "thriving as never before." Federal government policies aimed at thwarting exploitation of Puerto Rican workers turned out also to thwart U.S. business investments. "We cannot afford to put our people at a disadvantage," Roosevelt declared in his 1905 State of the Union. "We have been paying all possible heed to the political and educational interests of the island but, important though these objects are, it is not less important that we should favor their industrial development." Puerto Ricans were finding such statements difficult to decipher. One element, however, remained consistent in all of Roosevelt's remarks on Puerto Rico: he repeatedly urged Congress to grant its residents U.S. citizenship.

It was into this Puerto Rico that Luis Ferré was born in 1904. His father, Antonio Ferré, had emigrated from Cuba in 1894 and founded the Puerto Rico Iron Works, which became highly profitable.[2] Between the First and Second World Wars, Puerto Rico, like the United States, was affected by the aftershocks of the Russian Revolution, the rise of organized labor, and the Great Depression. Puerto Rico, however, was far more profoundly affected, because of its greater disparity between rich and poor. During this era, Luis Ferré earned his bachelor's and master's degrees in engineering from MIT. Returning to Puerto Rico to help run the family's iron works, he witnessed social and political conflicts intensifying to the point of violence.

In October 1935 four people were killed and many more injured in a melee between police and members of the Nationalist Party, which sought independence from the United States. Four months later, members of the Nationalist Party assassinated the American in charge of the Puerto Rican police. The assassins were arrested and, during interrogation, shot dead. For the United States, Puerto Rico was becoming an unpleasant possession.

Two months after the assassination of the police chief and the assassination of his assassins, a bill to provide independence for Puerto Rico was unsuccessfully introduced in Congress. The *New York Times* noted in its coverage that "Luis Munoz Marin, leader of the Liberal Party in Puerto Rico, which has consistently advocated independence, has been in Washington for some time." Muñoz Marín soon became Puerto Rico's foremost politician.

Luis Muñoz Marín (1898–1980)

His foremost rival was Luis Ferré. The rivalry between Ferré and Muñoz Marín commenced in the years following World War II. With the war's end, Puerto Rican leaders resumed their efforts to get the attention of Congress. Violence had, for the time being, been replaced by flight. "Puerto Ricans are swelling this city's population by 1,500 new arrivals a week," the *New York Times* reported in January 1947. "The migration of Puerto Rican natives to New York is a 'bloodletting' of the 2,200,000 residents of the over-crowded island." Economic studies showed that emigration alone would help, but not solve, the problem of poverty in Puerto Rico.[3]

Ferré believed the solution was statehood. The statehood option was supported primarily by wealthy Puerto Ricans and those professionals who perceived themselves as easily adaptable to becoming American.[4] Socially, for example, one would be hard-pressed to imagine anything more American than membership in a businessmen's club—which is where one could find Ferré in 1947. "The International Association of Lions Clubs closed it four-day annual convention today," California's *Oakland Tribune* reported. "Members of the new executive board of governors elected during this week's convention were: Jack Peddycord … Luis A. Ferre …"

The following year President Harry Truman set aside his authority to appoint Puerto Rico's governor and permitted Puerto Ricans to elect the candidate of their choice. They chose Muñoz Marín. He was now a member of the Popular Democratic Party, which did not support independence but instead sought a uniquely defined status. In that election, Ferré's prostatehood party finished second and the independence party third.

In the United States, the greater autonomy that President Truman had granted to Puerto Rico and the gubernatorial election that followed cloaked the intensity of the island's conflicting visions for its future. On November 1, 1950, that cloak was removed, right across the street from the White House. "Two members of the revolutionary Puerto Rican National party were shot down this afternoon while attempting to blast their way with pistol fire …

with the expressed purpose of shooting President Truman," the *Chicago Tribune* reported. "One of the assassins was slain. The other was wounded. One White House policeman was wounded fatally.... The gunman who was killed ... carried in his pocket a letter from Pedro Albizu Campos, Harvard educated leader of the Puerto Rican revolution."

Four years later, with Puerto Rico now having written and ratified its own Constitution, syndicated columnist John Dixon wrote that "the party for independence ... isn't taken too seriously, except for a fanatical few." The day after this column appeared on March 1, 1954, the "fanatical few" were front-page news:

> Five members of [the United States] Congress were shot today, one of them wounded critically, when three Puerto Rican men and a Puerto Rican woman whipped out pistols and sprayed the assembled House [of Representatives] with bullets.... When it ended, the automatic pistols empty, five members of the House were left sprawled on the floor. First aid was administered ... first by physician members [as] ... members shouted to the press gallery to summon other physicians.... The gunmen were part of the same group which attempted to assassinate President Truman.[5]

Columnist Dixon next focused on Ferré:

> The main fight now is between the statehood forces led by Luis Ferre ... and the leave-well-enough-alone forces headed by Gov. Munoz Marin.... I spent an exceedingly entertaining, if not informative, couple of hours with each of the two leaders. I wound up as confused, undecided, and dizzy with contradictory notions as nearly every U.S. legislator and bureaucrat who has poked into Puerto Rico's problem.

Ferré challenged Muñoz Marín for the governorship in Puerto Rico's 1956 election. He lost. In 1960 he challenged him and lost again. One key factor contributed significantly to the victories of Muñoz Marín: he had been navigating Puerto Rico's relationship with the United States in ways that, over time, had made Puerto Rico more prosperous than any independent island in the Caribbean. Still, it remained poorer than any of the fifty states.[6]

A separate key factor worked against Ferré: Puerto Ricans feared that statehood would cost them their culture. Ferré learned this in no uncertain terms when he testified before a Senate committee in 1966. "The unity of our federal-state structure requires a common tongue," Senator Henry "Scoop" Jackson told him. "A condition precedent to statehood must be the recognition and acceptance of English as the official language."

Ferré disagreed. "To be an American does not mean to speak English," he stated at a later time. "For Puerto Ricans, to be American ... is to be true to the principles of democracy which are set forth in the Constitution, and to feel one with other American citizens in the protection of our freedoms."[7]

Congress voted to let Puerto Ricans decide their political status for themselves. In 1967 a plebiscite was held in which they could choose independence, statehood, or commonwealth status. Commonwealth meant, in this instance, having the same autonomy (and constitutional limitations) as a state. Commonwealth residents could not, however, vote in presidential elections or have voting representation in Congress.

Ferré knew that the opportunity for Puerto Ricans to choose their political status would not come again in his lifetime, and he urged his compatriots to take a frightening but important step:

> During the last twenty years, there has been a revolution in communications media.... But in spite of this easier communication, we have made precious little progress in comprehension and understanding. That is the new dimension which we must add to progress.... The Puerto Rican, because of his understanding of the two cultures of America, has the ability and also the obligation to serve in achieving the ... dream of a united America.... History has proven ... that diversity, not assimilation, is the nerve and essence of the new American culture.... This is the moment for diversity within the unity of the great American nation. Let us make our contribution at this precious moment in history![8]

More than 65 percent of Puerto Rico's voters came to the polls. Emerging from the years of confusion, complexity, mismanagement, and violence, they made their wishes clear. Statehood received 273,315 votes, compared to only 4,205 for independence. Commonwealth status, with 425,081 votes, surpassed the other two choices combined.

Clearly the majority of Puerto Ricans did not want statehood. But they did want Luis Ferré. The year after the plebiscite, he was elected governor of Puerto Rico.

DAVID SHAFER
When the Grass Is Greener on the Other Side

In the spring of 1818 the States of Georgia and Tennessee, by their commissioners, ascertained and marked the dividing line.... The 35th parallel of north latitude constitutes that boundary and there was nothing more to do than to trace and mark that parallel on the surface of the earth.... The result of the observations made on that occasion differs from that of those contained in this report.

—JAMES CAMAK, REPORT TO THE GEORGIA SECRETARY OF STATE, 1827

O n February 10, 2008, members of the Georgia State Senate sang "This land is your land, this land is my land" as Senator David Shafer stood to propose a bill authorizing the governor "to initiate negotiations with the Governors of Tennessee and North Carolina for the purpose of correcting the flawed 1818 survey erroneously marking the 35th parallel south of its actual location and to official-ly recognize the State of Georgia's northern border with the States of Tennessee and North Carolina as the precise 35th parallel as was intended when both states were created." The Senate passed the resolution unan-imously. Georgia's House of Rep-resentatives followed suit, and the governor signed.

"I would offer to settle this dis-pute over a friendly game of foot-ball," one Tennessee state senator replied, "but that would be unfair to

David Shafer (1965–)

the state of Georgia." "I think they're embarrassing themselves," said another. "Absurd and laughable," said a third. One Tennessee official went before the press in a coonskin hat as a colleague proclaimed, "Davy Crockett is not going to give up the fight." David Shafer was not amused. When a prominent member of the Tennessee legislature joked (or half joked), "I think we need to have our militia down there," Georgia's Senator Shafer replied that they were welcome, so long as the troops didn't go below the 35th parallel.[1]

Emotions were turning serious on both sides of the line. Fingers began to be pointed, and not just across the state line. When, in proposing a resolution rejecting Georgia's call for a boundary commission, a Tennessee legislator included the phrase "legal precedent favors the Volunteer State, just as good fortune often smiles upon the righteous," he was criticized by a fellow legislator who declared, "I don't take this as a tongue-in-cheek matter."[2] The language regarding the righteous was dropped.

In Georgia, too, the debate regarding the state line was causing other lines to surface. A February 2008 editorial in the *Athens Banner-Herald* began, "As one man's quixotic quest, the effort to get Georgia's northern border moved one mile farther north was an entertaining diversion from the more routine motifs of pettifoggery and pandering that dominate the annual sessions of the Georgia legislature. But now that the whole Senate has bought into Sen. David Shafer's legislative proposal, it has crossed the line from the merely entertaining to the more than mildly troubling."

The same editorial, however, observed, "That's not to say Shafer ... doesn't have a point."

What *was* the point of resurrecting a 190-year-old surveying error? Water. Tennessee had it; Georgia needed it. Georgia had been suffering an extreme drought since the spring of 2007. The drought sorely exacerbated an ongoing problem in Atlanta, where rapid population growth had outpaced the region's water supply. If the northern border of Georgia had been accurately surveyed in 1818, the state line would pass through the Tennessee River.

But it would not have in 1818. Only after the federal government built Nickajack Dam in the mid-1960s did the river back up enough to cross the 35th parallel. Still, prior to the original surveying of the line in 1818, Georgians assumed there was no question that the river crossed below the 35th parallel. This assumption is revealed in Georgia's 1802 Act of Cession, the legislation in which Georgia released to the federal government its western land from colonial days (present-day Alabama and Mississippi). The act described Georgia's northern border as commencing at the point where its newly defined western border ran "in a direct line to Nickajack on the Tennessee River; then crossing the last mentioned river, and thence running up the said Tennessee River and along the western bank thereof to the southern boundary line of the State of Tennessee." The southern boundary of Tennessee had previously been established by Congress as the 35th parallel. That Georgia's Act of Cession described the boundary as going *up* the river to the southern border of Tennessee reveals that no one at the time knew exactly where the 35th parallel was. Including, as it turned out, the 1818 surveyor, who located the line just over a mile south of where it should have been. Tennessee ratified the 1818 survey. Georgia did not.

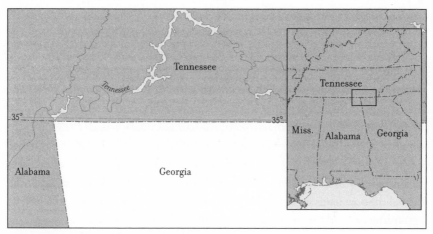

Erroneously surveyed Georgia-Tennessee border

Two centuries later, Shafer's concern was the same as the state's leaders in the early years of the Republic. "Georgia must increase its water supply," he stated, echoing the objective stated in the Act of Cession. "I am more concerned about securing riparian [river bank] rights to the Tennessee River than obtaining the entire disputed area."[3]

Though the intent of his resolution was to obtain water, the resolution itself concerned a boundary. As it happened, Tennessee's lieutenant governor, Ron Ramsey, was a professional surveyor. Ramsey cited "adverse possession," a technical term that refers to a legal precedent regarding inaccurately surveyed lines. "If this line has been there that long," he told the *Chattanooga Times Free Press*, "almost 200 years, or 190 years, that's the line now."

Adverse possession … riparian rights…. Out with the jokesters, in with the experts. The lawyers were about to have a field day—particularly since both water rights and boundary rights are areas with complex legal histories. In Georgia's corner was Atlanta-based attorney Brad Carver, whose specialization included both land use and water use law. In a report Carver helped prepare for the Georgia legislature, he described numerous instances in which Georgia *had*, in fact, challenged the incorrectly surveyed state line.

As far back as 1887, Georgia had passed a resolution much like Shafer's, seeking Tennessee's cooperation in correcting the boundary location. Georgia went on record again in 1941, when its legislature created a committee to look into means of correcting the error. In 1947 Georgia acted yet again, this time authorizing its state attorney general to bring suit, if necessary, before the U.S. Supreme Court. That got Tennessee's governor to meet with the boundary committee Georgia's legislature had created, but ultimately the issue went nowhere. And in 1971 Georgia had passed a resolution calling upon the two states to create a boundary line commission. Again, no such commission was created.

But Tennessee had experts, too. While it was true that Georgia had disputed the boundary's location as far back as 1887, it had known about the discrepancy since 1826. That was when surveyor James Cemak discovered it while locating the northern border of Alabama. Cemak was also the surveyor who had made the error, and he was also not surprised to discover it. He had known back in 1818 that the equipment provided by the state of Georgia was ill-suited to the task. Upon discovering the inadequacy of the equipment, Cemak had written to Georgia's governor, asking him "to procure such an apparatus as would be necessary to enable me to perform my duties with the greatest possible accuracy." But, as Cemak later recounted, "The shortness of the time would not admit of sending abroad for them."[4]

Not only did Georgia instruct its surveyor to continue despite his concerns about accuracy, but after the inaccuracy was discovered by Cemak during his 1826 survey of Alabama's border, Georgia did nothing for sixty years. Tennessee pointed out that these facts had previously been the basis of a conclusion by a University of Georgia professor that Georgia had thereby lost any rights to the land.[5]

Tennessee's experts also cited an 1893 Supreme Court decision in a case where Virginia had challenged a faulty survey of its boundary with Tennessee nearly a century after the error was made. The court had rejected Virginia's challenge. Likewise, in a boundary dispute between Georgia and South Carolina, the Supreme Court had stated that "long acquiescence in the practical location of an interstate boundary and possession therewith, often has been used as an aid in resolving boundary disputes."[6]

Other than periodic resolutions passed by its legislature, Georgia had never filed suit, never sought to collect property taxes in the disputed region, and never offered residents of the region in-state college tuition or state-sponsored scholarships. It had, however, published official state highway maps and voting district maps, all bearing the governor's signature, and all showing the disputed boundary in its current location.

One month after Shafer's resolution was passed, Tennessee passed a resolution rejecting it. Anticipating this, Shafer's resolution had authorized the Georgia attorney general to file suit before the U.S. Supreme Court in the event that the two states could not reach an agreement. Shafer believed Georgia could win.

But Georgia's governor wasn't so sure. *"Authorize* means to give the ability to do so," his spokesperson said. "It doesn't mean *shall*."

To date, no suit has been initiated.

ELEANOR HOLMES NORTON
Taxation without Representation

Congress legislates in all cases directly on the local concerns of the District [of Columbia]. As this is a departure, for a special purpose, from the general principles of our system, it may merit consideration whether an arrangement better adapted to the principles of our Government and the particular interests of the people may not be devised, which will neither infringe the Constitution nor affect the object which the provision in question was intended to secure.

—PRESIDENT JAMES MONROE[1]

I n 1990 Eleanor Holmes Norton was elected to the U.S. House of Representatives as a nonvoting delegate from the District of Columbia. She and others maintain that the status of the District, whose local laws can be repudiated or imposed by Congress, replicates that of the colonists for whom taxation without representation ignited the American Revolution. The similarity can be seen in a 1774 resolution of New Hampshire colonists, expressing support for the Boston Tea Party. "To send us their teas, subject to a duty [tax] on landing here," the resolution stated, England "testified a disregard to the interests of Americans.... This town approves the general exertions and noble struggles ... for preventing so fatal a catastrophe as is implied in taxation without representation."[2]

Some Americans, however, disagree with this comparison. They maintain that the status of the District of Columbia is embedded in the Constitution. Among the powers given to Congress in Article I is the authority to "exercise exclusive Legislation in all Cases whatsoever, over such District (not exceeding ten Miles square) as may, by Cession of particular States, and the acceptance of Congress, become the Seat of the Government of the United States." Implicit in this clause is the fact that the nation's capital is not a state.

How did this predicament come to be? Its underlying cause was reported in the *Philadelphia Gazetteer* in 1783, prior to the existence of Washington, DC:

> Several of the disbanded [Revolutionary War] soldiers have, for some days past, been clamorous for this pay.... On Saturday last, about two or three hundred of them hostilely appeared before the State-house [present-day Independence Hall] and handed in ... their demands in writing, accompanied with a threat.... The Congress ... hastily resolved to exchange their old sitting place for the more salubrious air of Princeton, in the State of New Jersey ... having received no satisfactory assurances for expecting adequate and prompt exertion of the State [of Pennsylvania] for supporting the dignity of the federal government.

Five years later, when Congress replaced the Articles of Confederation with the Constitution, it penned Article I, Section 8, reserving for itself exclusive jurisdiction over the District of Columbia to assure it would never again be at the mercy of a state for its own protection.

Even at the time, however, the status of the District of Columbia was controversial. The record of the debate over the proposed Constitution states:

> Mr. George Mason thought there were few clauses in the Constitution so dangerous as that which gave Congress exclusive power of legislation with ten miles square.... It is an incontrovertible axiom that, when the dangers that may arise from the abuse are greater than the benefits that may result from the use, the power ought to be withheld. I do not conceive that this power is at all necessary, though capable of being greatly abused.

No less a figure than James Madison disagreed:

> How could the general government be guarded from undue influence of particular states,

Eleanor Holmes Norton (1937–)

or from insults, without such exclusive power?... If this commonwealth depended, for the freedom of deliberation, on the laws of any state where it might be necessary to sit, would it not be liable to attacks of that nature, and with more indignity, which have already been offered to Congress?

Patrick Henry—most remembered for declaring "Give me liberty or give me death!"—brought that same fervor to the debate over the status of the District:

Will not the members of Congress have the same passions which other rulers have had? They will not be superior to the frailties of human nature.... Show me an instance where a part of the community was independent of the whole.... This sweeping clause will fully enable them [members of Congress] to do what they please.... I have reason to suspect ambitious grasps at power.

To which James Madison replied:

Mr. Chairman, I am astonished that the honorable member should launch into such strong descriptions.... Were it possible to delineate on paper all those particular cases and circumstances in which legislation by the general legislature would be necessary, and leave to the states all the other powers, I imagine no gentleman would object to it. But this is not within the limits of human capacity.

Not by accident, then, or unaware of the risks, did the Founding Fathers create the dilemma faced by the citizens in the District of Columbia. From that time to the present, its residents and Congress have repeatedly struggled to untangle these issues. As of this writing, that effort is being led in Congress by DC delegate Eleanor Holmes Norton. Without a vote, however, what influence can she wield? After two hundred years of effort, what hope can she have? Norton has sought to use the influence of hope itself, much as had two of the nation's most influential figures. "George Washington was the paradigm unifying figure, the first American of the new republic; [Martin Luther] King was a profoundly unsettling figure, who challenged the republic," she wrote in a 1986 *Washington Post* column commemorating Martin Luther King Day. "Yet King and Washington are not odd fellows thrown together by the fickle if democratic process that produces national holidays. Different as the two men were, they have been honored for the same reason. They managed to draw out the best in the American character."

Hope drove those who risked their lives to found the nation and has remained the nation's most influential force. It has also defined Norton's life. One such pivotal moment occurred in high school. "We heard the chime that told us there would be an announcement," she later recollected. "I remember the voice of the principal, Mr. Charles Lofton, interrupting class to tell us news of major importance. We had the right to go to any school now. We were stunned, then elated. And I remember believing that the world had changed, literally had changed."[3]

Norton graduated in the last segregated class of Dunbar High School in Washington. Among the city's segregated schools, Dunbar was reserved for academically gifted "colored" students. Its graduates went on to the nation's premier black colleges and universities, such as Fisk, Tuskegee, Howard, Morehouse, and Spelman. Norton, however, chose predominantly white Antioch College, an Ohio school with a reputation for being politically left-wing.

Norton herself did not come from a politically radical family. Her father, a third-generation Washingtonian, was an attorney whom she described as a "died-in-the-wool" Democrat. Her mother, a teacher who had migrated from the South, brought with her the traditional customs of southern African Americans. But both parents embraced the spirit of Norton's great-grandfather, Richard Holmes, who had been the first member of the family to move to Washington. He did so in the dead of night, escaping slavery in Virginia. The Washington into which he had arrived in the early 1850s was risky terrain for an escaped slave. While it had many free African Americans, it also had slaves, and under the Fugitive Slave Act, runaway slaves could be reclaimed at any time. Though the stakes were considerably less for young Eleanor, her venturing to Antioch echoed her great-grandfather's spirit of risk.

In 1963 the soon-to-become Yale law student ventured into terrain every bit as dangerous as her great-grandfather's. She traveled to Greenwood, Mississippi, to participate in that summer's historic effort to register African American voters. Arriving in Jackson, she met with the field secretary for the state's NAACP, Medgar Evers, who briefed her on the situation she would be encountering, then dropped her off at the bus station for her trip to Greenwood. That night Evers was shot and killed.

As a young lawyer, Norton worked for the American Civil Liberties

Union, where she first began to get national attention. *Ebony* magazine wrote of her in 1969:

> In her Afro hairstyle, her dangling earrings and her multi-colored striped dress ... Eleanor Holmes Norton hardly looks like what she is—an astute constitutional lawyer who has argued controversial cases before the Supreme Court and won. But there is a certain irony in a number of her victories.... [S]he has ... defended the free speech of George C. Wallace, the segregationist National States Rights Party, and individual klansmen.

For Norton, civil rights transcended race and political views. Rather, she saw them as inseparably connected to humanity's inalienable rights. This deeply held conviction drew the attention of New York Mayor John V. Lindsay. "Eleanor Holmes Norton, a civil liberties lawyer, was appointed chairman of the city's Commission on Human Rights yesterday," the *New York Times* reported in 1970. "As head of the city's principal antidiscrimination agency, Mrs. Norton, who is 32 years old, will also be the highest ranking Negro woman in Mr. Lindsay's administration." Norton's achievements during her seven years in New York brought her to the attention of others as well. In 1977 President Jimmy Carter chose Norton to head the Equal Employment Opportunity Commission.

In 1990, when Washington, DC's delegate to Congress retired, Norton (now a law professor at Georgetown University) sought and won election to the position. Once in office, she took up the torch that had been carried by a long line of predecessors: equal representation for the District of Columbia.

Following President Monroe's 1818 call to rectify the status of the District, its residents had created a committee to propose solutions. "The Committee confesses that they can discover but two modes in which the desired relief can be afforded," it reported back to Congress in 1822, continuing "either by the establishment of a territorial government ... restoring them to equal rights enjoyed by the citizens of the other portions of the United States, or by a retrocession to the States of Virginia and Maryland of the respective parts of the District which were originally ceded by those States to form it."[4] Neither idea was new, ideal, or favorably received.

The problem then went dormant until 1841, when it was picked up again by President William Henry Harrison. "It is in this District only where American citizens are to be found who ... are deprived of many important political privileges," he declared in his inaugural address. "The people of the District of Columbia are not the subjects of the people of the States, but free American citizens. Being in the latter condition when the Constitution was formed, no words used in that instrument could have been intended to deprive them of that character." Unfortunately for District residents, Harrison died one month later.

In 1846 the issue was resolved for those District residents living on the Virginia side of the Potomac. That year, Congress returned that portion of the city to Virginia (see "Robert M. T. Hunter" in this book).

In 1888 New Hampshire Senator Henry W. Blair proposed an amendment to the Constitution to provide voting representation for the District of Columbia. The Senate voted it down. He was followed in 1918 by Illinois Senator James Hamilton Lewis. "The United States is the only country in the world that exiles it own National Capital," Lewis wrote in a *Washington Post* column proposing statehood for the District. "The federal government could reserve a sufficient area for all federal buildings and reserve governmental control over all the area, just as it does now over military posts." Senator Lewis's efforts went nowhere as well. His statehood proposal was followed by that of Texas Representative Hatton Sumners in 1940. Sumners's was followed by that of another Texas congressman, Henry Gonzalez, in 1967. Gonzalez's was followed by that of Iowa Senator Fred Schwengel in 1971; Schwengel's by Massachusetts Senator Edward Kennedy's in 1984, 1985, and 1987.[5]

This field of failures was the terrain into which Norton ventured in 1990. Over the years, the struggle had become further complicated by the terrain dividing into various battlefields: statehood, retrocession to Maryland, territorial status, and limited voting rights. But risky terrain for fundamental rights had always attracted her. Though a rookie in Congress and, as a nonvoting delegate, batting without a bat, she made her play within months of her election. The *Washington Post* reported:

Delegate Eleanor Holmes Norton ... acknowledging that statehood faces an uphill battle, introduced legislation that would create the state of New Columbia.... Under Norton's bill, the boundaries of the new state would be the same as the District's, excluding the Mall and other federal landmarks such as the White House. These would be made part of a federal enclave that would remain under direct congressional control.... Critics have long contended that the Constitution would have to be amended to achieve statehood.

Over the years, neither the Republicans nor the Democrats have consistently opposed or supported DC statehood. During his 1991–92 presidential campaign, Democrat Bill Clinton supported DC statehood despite having opposed it as the governor of Arkansas.[6] Likewise, among present-day Republicans there are some who maintain that Congress can extend voting representation to DC residents without having to amend the Constitution. Two of the most prominent of such Republicans are Utah Senator Orrin Hatch and Kenneth Starr, a former federal judge appointed to the bench by President Ronald Reagan, then appointed solicitor general by President George H. W. Bush, and later selected to be the independent counsel investigating misconduct by President Clinton.[7] In his 2004 testimony before Congress, Starr pointed out:

The judiciary has rightly shown great deference where Congress announces its considered judgment that the District should be considered a "State" for specific legislative purposes.... In 1949, the Supreme Court's *Tidewater* decision ... confirmed what is now the law: the Constitution's use of the word "State" in Article III cannot mean "and not of the District of Columbia." Identical logic supports legislation to enfranchise the District's voters: the use of the word "State" in Article I cannot bar Congress from exercising its plenary authority [over the District] to extend the franchise to the District's voters.

Despite the fact that Starr and Hatch agreed that the Constitution need not be amended to provide voting representation to the District, politicians from both parties continued to invoke the need for a constitutional amendment in order to cloak other concerns. "Del. Eleanor Holmes Norton bristled several times when witnesses contended that the proposed statehood legislation is unconstitutional," the *Washington Post* reported in March 1992, when her bill was under consideration by the House Committee on the District of Columbia. The following month, the committee sent Norton's bill to the floor of the House. With every (nonretiring) member of the House having to face the voters in November, opponents of representation for the District now uncloaked their actual concerns. "President Bush recently criticized a District law expanding homosexual rights," the *Post* reported in a May 1992 article headlined, "Statehood Stirs Up Opposition." The article quoted a mass mailing by Senator Jesse Helms that told voters, "I've already got my hands full fighting the far-left, ultra-liberals in Congress. And the last thing I need is having to battle Jesse Jackson." (At the time, African American leader Jesse Jackson lived in the District of Columbia.)

This opposition effort, which its backers ratcheted up as the November election approached, succeeded. "Citing recent overwhelming defeats for the District on issues such as the death penalty and gay rights, Del. Eleanor Holmes Norton said she will not ask lawmakers to vote on statehood before they adjourn," the *Post* announced in October. "Norton said she remains upbeat about statehood's chances for several reasons, including the chance that Bill Clinton might be elected President."

Following the election of President Clinton, Norton again introduced a proposal for DC statehood. The bill's supporters emphasized that the population of the District exceeded those of Alaska, Wyoming, and Vermont, that District residents paid taxes and served in the military just as other Americans did, and that the Constitution did not prevent Congress from granting voting rights to the District. Norton spoke to the issue's core. "We are debating whether at last to grant full citizenship to a group of people on whom every duty of citizenship has been imposed," she stressed on the House floor. "This nation was formed precisely because Americans paid taxes to a sovereign who afforded them no representation. The animating principle of American democracy has been no taxation without representation."

Michigan Representative John Dingell, one of the most powerful Democrats in the House, spoke in opposition to DC statehood. "I have heard many, many complaints about people being denied constitutional rights," he responded. "There is no constitutional right whatsoever that is being denied to the citizens here. If they do not like the way the government is run, they can pack up and move out."

Dingell was not the only Democrat opposed to DC statehood. Though the Democrats constituted a majority of the House of Representatives, the measure failed 277 to 153.

This defeat was followed by another. The era's political winds were propelling the Republican Party into increasingly conservative positions and, via those same winds, increasing popularity. In the 1995 congressional elections, the Republicans won a majority of the seats in the House and maintained that majority for the next twelve years. During this time, Norton knew she needed to adjust her tactics. Since a core belief of the Republicans was that the nation benefited from tax relief, Norton sought to persuade her Republican colleagues via that aspect of the District's status. The *Post* reported this shift in February 1995:

Del. Eleanor Holmes Norton, the District's representative on Capitol Hill, has long advocated D.C. statehood by arguing that the city's situation constitutes "taxation without representation." ... Norton has come up with a new plan: no representation, no taxation. This week, she introduced legislation to exempt District residents from paying federal taxes.... Norton's plan probably won't become reality soon. The federal government ... is not likely to give up $1.6 billion in revenue.

This effort failed, as the *Post* had predicted.

In addition to the challenges in Congress, Norton has also faced challenges from those residents in the District who believe she should pursue other avenues toward representation. "Eleanor Homes Norton is a 10-term delegate to the U.S. House of Representatives.... Douglass Sloan is a Ward 4 advisory neighborhood commissioner.... He wants her job," a neighborhood newspaper reported in 2010, quoting her challenger: "She's been there 20 years ... and she hasn't gotten anywhere." Despite an energetic campaign, Sloan won only 9 percent of the vote in the 2010 Democratic primary, and Norton again triumphed in the general election.

Eleanor Holmes Norton may or may not eventually succeed in achieving statehood for the District of Columbia. What is certain, however, is that if she does not, others will take up the torch—for it is the same torch that has been carried by every individual in this book. It is a torch that illuminates the lines *inside* us, that define who we are. The lines on the American map are also our *interior* portraits. Americans don't always find each other attractive, but each of us desires to be acknowledged, to count. In this nation, that desire is a right. The quest for that right is the torch carried by Eleanor Holmes Norton.

Notes

Roger Williams

1. Letter from Roger Williams to the Town of Providence, in *Publications of the Narragansett Club*, 1st series, vol. 6 (Providence: Narragansett Club, 1874), 279.

2. Williams's religious basis for the separation of church and state was not rooted in acceptance of other religions; he actively sought to convert non-Christians. His views were rooted in Puritan tenets. From these he derived the belief that, since mankind is comprised of those who are bestowed with Divine Grace and those who are not, and since we cannot know who among us has been bestowed with Grace, forced worship brings suffering to those bestowed with Grace by empowering others—whom we have no way of knowing whether or not they are bestowed with Grace—to impose laws regarding a realm where only God has jurisdiction. See Roger Williams, *The Bloudy Tenent of Persecution for Cause of Conscience*, ed. Richard Groves (Macon: University of Georgia Press, 2001); Alan Simpson, "How Democratic Was Roger Williams?" *William and Mary Quarterly*, 3rd series, 13, no. 1 (January 1956): 53–67.

3. Simpson, "How Democratic Was Roger Williams?"; Mauro Calamandrei, "Neglected Aspects of Roger Williams' Thought," *Church History* 21, no. 3 (September 1952): 239–58; Sidney V. James, "Ecclesiastical Authority in the Land of Roger Williams," *New England Quarterly*, 57, no. 3 (September 1984): 323–46.

4. LeRoy Moore Jr., "Roger Williams and the Historians," *Church History* 32, no. 4 (December 1963): 432–51; Sacvan Bercovitch, "The Typology of America's Mission," *American Quarterly* 30, no. 2 (Summer 1978): 135–55.

5. Roger Williams, "Mr. Cotton's Letter Examined and Answered," in *Publications of the Narragansett Club*, 1st series, vol. 1 (Providence: Narragansett Club, 1866), 325.

6. LeRoy Moore, "Roger Williams and the Revolutionary Era," *Church History* 34, no. 1 (March 1965): 57–61.

7. Edmund J. Carpenter, *Roger Williams: A Study of the Life, Times and Character of a Political Pioneer* (New York: Grafton, 1909), 126.

Augustine Herman

1. Samuel Hazard, ed., *Annals of Pennsylvania* (Philadelphia: Hazard and Mitchell, 1815), 281.

2. Francis Vincent, *A History of the State of Delaware* (Philadelphia: John Campbell, 1870), 320.

3. James McSherry, *History of Maryland* (Baltimore: Baltimore Book Company, 1904), 246–49.

Robert Jenkins's Ear

1. Thomas Carlyle, *History of Friedrich the Second, called Frederick the Great*, vol. 2 (New York: Harper, 1868), 503.

Robert Tufton Mason

1. *Collections of the New Hampshire Historical Society*, vol. 8 (Concord: New Hampshire Historical Society, 1866), 264.

2. Letter from the General Court of Massachusetts to Oliver Cromwell (1651), in Thomas Hutchinson, *The History of the Massachusetts Bay*, 2nd ed. (London: M. Richardson, 1765), 521.

3. Letter from New England Ministers to Oliver Cromwell (1650), in *Collections of the Massachusetts Historical Society*, 4th series, vol. 2 (Boston: Massachusetts Historical Society, 1854), 118.

4. Petition of Robert Mason, in Albert Stillman Batchellor, ed., *State of New Hampshire Documents Relating to the Masonian Patent*, vol. 29 (Concord, NH: Edward Pearson, 1896), 101–3.

5. Gov. John Endicott to Charles II (1661), in Albert Bushnell Hart, ed., *American History Told by Contemporaries*, vol. 1 (New York: Macmillan, 1917), 454–55.

6. Opinion of Sir Geoffrey Palmer, Nov. 8, 1660, in Batchellor, *State of New Hampshire Documents*, 106–7.

7. A. H. Buffinton, "The Isolationist Policy of Colonial Massachusetts," *New England Quarterly*, 1, no. 2 (April 1928): 161.

8. Charles II to Massachusetts Government, March 10, 1675, in Batchellor, *State of New Hampshire Documents*, 111.

9. *Publications of the Prince Society: Capt. John Mason* (Boston: Prince Society, 1887), 104–5.

10. Royal Commission on New Hampshire (1679), in William Forsyth, *Cases and Opinions of Constitutional Law* (London: Stevens and Haynes, 1869), 136.

11. Charles II to Massachusetts Government (1682), in Batchellor, *State of New Hampshire Documents*, 123.

12. Jeremy Belknap, *The History of New Hampshire*, vol. 1 (Dover, NH: S. C. Stevens and Ela & Wadleigh, 1831), 114–15.

13. Allen's daughter was married to Massachusetts Governor John Usher. Under Usher's leadership, Massachusetts bought Gorges's claim to Maine, finalizing its annexation of the territory. Why Massachusetts did not also purchase the Mason claim is unknown. See John Gorham Palfrey, *History of New England*, vol. 4 (Boston: Little, Brown, 1897), 207; Belknap, *History of New Hampshire*, 1:252.

14. Isaac W. Hammond, ed., *State of New Hampshire, Miscellaneous Provincial and State Papers: 1725–1800*, vol. 18 (Manchester: John B. Clarke, 1890), 72.

Lord Fairfax

1. Worthington Chauncey Ford, ed., *The Writings of George Washington*, vol. 1 (New York: Putnam, 1889), 4.

2. William Hand Brown, ed., *Archives of Maryland: Letters to Governor Horatio Sharpe* (Baltimore: Maryland Historical Society, 1911), 15.

3. James V. L. McMahon, *Historical View of the Government of Maryland*, vol. 1 (Baltimore: Lucas, Cushing, 1831), 64–65.

Mason and Dixon

1. Anonymous, "The Rights o' Man," *Punch* 38 (January 28, 1860): 41.

2. Edwin Danson, *Drawing the Line: How Mason and Dixon Surveyed the Most Famous Border in America* (New York: John Wiley, 2001), 54–55.

3. H. W. Robinson, "Jeremiah Dixon (1733–1779): A Biographical Note," *Proceedings of the American Philosophical Society* 94, no. 3 (June 20, 1950): 273.

4. Charles Mason and Jeremiah Dixon, *Field Notes and Astronomical Observations* (autograph manuscript), in *Report of the Secretary of Internal Affairs of the Commonwealth of Pennsylvania* (Harrisburg, PA: Edwin H. Meyers, 1887), 145.

5. Thomas D. Cope, "Some Contacts of Benjamin Franklin with Mason and Dixon and Their Work," *Proceedings of the American Philosophical Society* 95, no. 3 (June 12, 1951): 238.

Zebulon Butler

1. Williamson, James R., and Linda A. Fossler, *Zebulon Butler: Hero of the Revolutionary Frontier* (Westport, CT: Greenwood Press, 1995), 14.

2. Albert Henry Smyth, ed., *The Writings of Benjamin Franklin*, vol. 10 (New York: Macmillan, 1907), 215.

3. Williamson and Fossler, *Zebulon Butler*, 61.

4. Robert J. Taylor, ed., *The Susquehannah Company Papers*, vol. 7 (New York: Cornell University Press, 1969), 245–46.

Ethan Allen

1. *Connecticut Courant*, June 1–June 8, 1773.

2. Walter Hill Crockett, *Vermont: The Green Mountain State*, vol. 1 (New York: Century History, 1921), 182.

3. Ibid., 338.

4. Ibid., 341.

5. Ibid., 370.

6. Hugh Moore, *Memoir of Col. Ethan Allen* (Plattsburgh, NY: O. R. Cook, 1834), 48–62.

7. Prentiss C. Dodge, *Encyclopedia Vermont Biography* (Burlington, VT: Ullery Publishing, 1912), 12.

8. Ibid., 15.

Thomas Jefferson

1. Thomas Jefferson to James Monroe, in *The Jeffersonian Cyclopedia*, ed. John P. Foley (New York: Funk & Wagnalls, 1900), 940.

2. H. Hale Bellot, "Thomas Jefferson in American Historiography," *Transactions of the Royal Historical Society*, 5th series, vol. 4 (1954): 135–55.

3. Robert F. Berkhofer Jr., "Jefferson, the Ordinance of 1784, and the Origins of the American Territorial System," *William and Mary Quarterly*, 3rd series, 29, no. 2 (April 1972): 231.

4. Jefferson to Monroe, July 9, 1786, in Berkhofer, "Jefferson, the Ordinance," 257.

5. J. M. Keating, *History of the City of Memphis, Tennessee* (Syracuse, NY: D. Mason, 1888), 72–78.

6. Congress did not officially adopt Jefferson's proposed surveying method until it enacted the Land Ordinance of 1785.

John Meares

1. J. Richard Nokes, *Almost a Hero: The Voyages of John Meares, R.N., to China, Hawaii, and the Northwest Coast* (Pullman: Washington State University Press, 1998), 9–11.

2. John Meares, "Memorial to the House of Commons," in *London Daily Advertiser*, May 20, 1770.

3. *Public Advertiser* (London), May 31, 1790; November 10, 1790.

4. "[There is a] settlement at the Columbia River ... formed before the late war [of 1812] and broken up by the British ... in the course of it.... As the British government admit explicitly their obligation under the first article of the treaty of Ghent to restore the post, there can be no question with regard to the right of the United States to resume it." Worthington Chauncey Ford, ed., *Writings of John Quincy Adams*, vol. 6 (New York: Macmillan, 1916), 402–3.

5. John Meares, *Voyages Made in the Years 1788 and 1789 from China to the North-West Coast of America* (1790; repr., New York: Da Capo Press, 1967).

6. *London World*, February 23, 1791.

Benjamin Banneker

1. Davis S. Shields, ed., *American Poetry: The 17th and 18th Centuries* (New York: Penguin, 2007), 574.

2. Sylvio A. Bedini, *The Life of Benjamin Banneker* (New York: Scribner, 1972), 17.

3. Martha E. Tyson, "Banneker: The Afric-American Astronomer," in *The Posthumous Papers of Martha E. Tyson, edited by Her Daughter* (Philadelphia: Friends' Book Association, 1884).

4. *Pennsylvania Mercury*, October 15, 1791.

5. Michael Hardt, ed., *Thomas Jefferson and the Declaration of Independence* (New York: Verso, 2007), 85.

6. Ibid., 86.

7. Bedini, *Life of Benjamin Banneker*, 238.

Jesse Hawley

1. Jesse Hawley [pseud. Hercules], *Genesee Messenger* (New York), January 1807, in David Hosack, *Memoir of DeWitt Clinton* (New York: J. Seymour, 1829), 311.

2. Ibid., 323.

3. Cadwallader Colden, *The History of the Five Indian Nations of Canada Which Are Dependent on the Province of New York in America and Are the Barrier Between the English and French in that Part of the World* (1724), in Ibid., 234.

4. John Lauritz Larson, "'Bind the Republic Together': The National Union and the Struggle for a System of Internal Improvements," *Journal of American History* 74, no. 2 (September 1987): 363–87; Pamela L. Baker, "The Washington National Road Bill and the Struggle to Adopt a Federal System of Internal Improvement," *Journal of the Early Republic* 22, no. 3 (Autumn 2002): 437–64.

5. Hosack, *Memoir of DeWitt Clinton*, 347.

6. Gerard Koeppel, *Bond of Union: Building the Erie Canal and the American Empire* (Cambridge, MA: Da Capo Press, 2009), 7.

7. William Cooper, *A Guide in the Wilderness, or the History of the First Settlements in the Western Counties of New York with Useful Instructions to Future Settlers* (Dublin: Gilbert and Hodges, 1810), 21–22.

8. *Daily National Intelligencer* (Washington, DC), May 19, 1813; Roy I. Wolf, "Transportation and Politics: The Example of Canada," *Annals of the Association of American Geographers* 52, no. 2 (June 1962): 176–90; Don C. Sowers, "The Financial History of New York State from 1789 to 1912," *Studies in History, Economics, and Public Law*, vol. 57 (New York: Columbia University, 1914), 61.

9. *Rochester Democrat*, repr. in *Cleveland Daily Herald*, January 17, 1842; *Albany Evening Journal*, repr. in *New York Spectator* (New York City), January 19, 1842; *Milwaukee Journal*, February 2, 1842.

James Brittain

1. Robert Scott Davis Jr., "The Settlement at the Head of the French Broad River or the Bizarre Story of the First Walton County, Georgia," *North Carolina Genealogical Journal* 7, no. 2 (May 1981): 65.

2. In addition to Davis's "Settlement at the Head of the French Broad River," Brittain is named in Alexia Jones Helsley and George Alexander Jones, *A Guide to Historic Henderson County, North Carolina* (Charleston, SC: History Press, 2007); Harry McKown, "December, 1810: The Walton War," *This Month in North Carolina History* (December 2006), http://www.lib.unc.edu/ncc/ref/nchistory/dec2006/index.html; Jim Brittain, "History Corner," *Mills River, North Carolina Newsletter* 5, no. 2 (Summer 2008): 2.

3. Theodore Davidson, *Genesis of Buncombe County* (Asheville, NC: Citizen Company, 1922), 78.

4. Ibid., 119. The name of the grand jury foreman, William Whitson, also appears with Brittain's in the list of dismissed commissioners. Whitson was also Brittain's commanding officer in the state militia.

5. John Preston Arthur, *Western North Carolina: A History from 1730 to 1913* (Raleigh, NC: Edwards and Broughton, 1914), 19, 33.

6. Martin Reidinger, "The Walton War and the Georgia-North Carolina Boundary Dispute" (unpublished manuscript), North Carolina Collection, University of North Carolina at Chapel Hill, 1981, cited in "State's First Walton County Caused Ruckus," *Atlanta Journal-Constitution*, December 3, 2007.

7. Cal Carpenter, *The Walton War and Tales of the Great Smoky Mountains* (Lakewood, GA: Copple House Books, 1979), 26; *Atlanta Journal-Constitution*, December 3, 2007.

8. Jim Brittain, "History Corner," *Mills River, North Carolina Newsletter* 1, no. 1 (Winter 2003): 3.

9. Lucian Lamar Knight, *A Standard History of Georgia and Georgians*, vol. 1 (New York: Lewis, 1917), 456. Similarly, a history of Georgia coauthored by a former governor states, "A number of minor controversies concerning the boundaries have occurred at different times, but they were mostly local in character and have been settled by the mutual agreement of the state authorities. Between 1803 and 1818 several of these disputes arose between Georgia and North Carolina. In the fall of 1881 ..." The transition to 1881 is a considerable leap. See also Allen D. Candler and Clement A. Davis, *Georgia: Comprising Sketches of the Counties, Towns, Events, Institutions, and Persons, Arranged in Cyclopedic Form*, vol. 3 (Atlanta: Georgia State Historical Association, 1906), 207.

10. Arthur, *Western North Carolina*, 33.

Reuben Kemper

1. Andrew McMichael, "The Kemper 'Rebellion': Filibustering and Resident Anglo American Loyalty in Spanish West Florida," *Louisiana History: The Journal of the Louisiana Historical Association* 43, no. 2 (Spring 2002): 136.

2. Isaac Joslin Cox, *The West Florida Controversy, 1798–1818* (Baltimore: Johns Hopkins Press, 1918), 152.

3. McMichael, "The Kemper 'Rebellion,'" 149.

Richard Rush

1. Richard Rush, *Residence at the Court of London*, 3rd ed. (Philadelphia: Lippincott, 1872), 77–78.

2. *National Intelligencer* (Washington, DC), July 28, 1812.

3. *National Intelligencer*, October 19, 1813; November 30, 1813; March 31, 1815; March 29, 1815.

4. Letter from Charles Bagot to Lord Binning, Sept. 26, 1818, in George Canning, *George Canning and His Friends*, vol. 2 (New York: E. P. Dutton, 1909), 85–86.

5. Rush, *Residence*, 314.

6. John Adams, *The Works of John Adams*, vol. 10 (Boston: Little, Brown, 1856), 160–61.

7. Rush, *Residence*, 437.

8. Letter from Rush to Democratic Citizens of Penn District, in *Daily National Intelligencer*, November 16, 1850.

Nathaniel Pope

1. William A. Meese, "Nathaniel Pope," *Journal of the Illinois State Historical Society* 3, no. 4 (January 1911): 7–8.

2. Pope to New York senator Rufus King, in James A. Edstrom, "'Candour and Good Faith': Nathaniel Pope and the Admission Enabling Act of 1818," *Illinois Historical Journal* 88, no. 4 (Winter 1995): 244.

3. Ibid., 246.

4. J. Seymour Currey, *Chicago: Its History and Its Builders*, vol. 1 (Chicago: S. J. Clarke, 1912), 118. In the nineteenth century, the same wording had appeared as a description of Pope's argument in Congress, in John Moses, *Illinois: Historical and Statistical*, vol. 1 (Chicago: Fergus Printing, 1889), 227. Pope is recorded as saying that access to Lake Michigan "would afford additional security to the perpetuity of the Union, inasmuch as the state would thereby be connected with the states of Indiana, Ohio, Pennsylvania and New York through the Lakes." *Annals of Congress*, 15th Cong., 1st sess., 1678.

5. Alexander Davidson and Bernard Stuvé, *A Complete History of Illinois from 1673 to 1873* (Springfield: Illinois Journal, 1874), 295–96.

6. William Radebaugh, *The Boundary Dispute between Illinois and Wisconsin* (Chicago: Chicago Historical Society, 1904).

John Hardeman Walker

1. Robert Sidney Douglass, *History of Southeast Missouri*, vol. 1 (Chicago: Lewis Publishing, 1912), 242.

2. Samuel Cummings, *The Western Pilot* (Cincinnati: G. Conclin, 1848), 138–42; "Account by John Hardeman Walker," transcription and notes by Susan E. Hough, U.S. Geological Survey, July 2000, http://pasadena.wr.usgs.gov/office/hough/walker.html.

3. Ibid., 142.

4. Floyd Calvin Shoemaker, *Missouri's Struggle for Statehood: 1804–1821* (Jefferson City, MO: Hugh Stevens Printing, 1916), 39.

5. H. Dwight Weaver, "Bootheel Politics, Frontier Style," *Missouri Resources Magazine* (Winter 1999–2000), 21.

John Quincy Adams

1. John Quincy Adams, *Memoirs of John Quincy Adams*, ed. Charles Francis Adams, vol. 4 (Philadelphia: Lippincott, 1875), 208–9.

2. Worthington Chauncey Ford, ed., *Writings of John Quincy Adams*, vol. 6 (New York: Macmillan, 1916), 384.

3. Adams, *Memoirs*, vol. 4, 108–10, 115.

4. Ford, *Writings*, vol. 6, 346.

5. Ibid., 306.

6. William Graham Sumner, *American Statesmen: Andrew Jackson* (Boston: Houghton Mifflin, 1899), 104.

7. Adams, *Memoirs*, vol. 8, 484.

Sequoyah

1. Two notable critics of Sequoyah historiography are John B. Davis, "The Life and Work of Sequoyah," *Chronicles of Oklahoma* 8, no. 2 (June 1930): 49–180, and Traveller Bird, *Tell Them They Lie: The Sequoyah Myth* (Los Angeles: Westernlore Press, 1971).

2. Samuel C. Williams, "The Father of Sequoyah: Nathaniel Gist," *Chronicles of Oklahoma* 15, no. 1 (March 1937): 3–20.

3. Traveller Bird, *Tell Them They Lie*, 45–46, 113.

4. S. Charles Bolton, "Jeffersonian Indian Removal and the Emergence of Arkansas Territory," *Arkansas Historical Quarterly* 62, no. 3 (Autumn 2003): 253–71.

5. Thomas Valentine Parker, *The Cherokee Indians* (New York: Grafton, 1907), 13.

6. *American State Papers: Indian Affairs*, vol. 2 (Washington, DC: Gales and Seaton, 1834), 145.

7. George E. Foster, *Se-quo-yah, the American Cadmus and Modern Moses* (Philadelphia: Indian Rights Association, 1885), 106.

8. *Daily National Journal* (Washington, DC), May 5, 1828; Harold D. Moser et al., *The Papers of Andrew Jackson*, vol. 3 (Knoxville: University of Tennessee Press, 1991), 52–53.

9. Charles Russell Logan, *The Promised Land: The Cherokees, Arkansas, and Removal, 1794–1839* (Little Rock: Arkansas Historic Preservation Program, n.d.), 21.

Stevens T. Mason

1. Quite possibly John Quincy Adams did make this statement, or something much like it. The bill was highly controversial and strongly opposed by Adams, who had returned to Congress after his presidency. Adams's statement of outrage at the beginning of this chapter has previously been cited in Thomas M. Cooley, *Michigan: A History of Governments* (Boston: Houghton Mifflin, 1905), 219; Henry M. Utley and Byron M. Cutcheon, *Michigan as a Province, Territory, and State*, vol. 2 (New York: Publishing Society of Michigan, 1906), 358; Willis F. Dunbar and George S. May, *Michigan: A History of the Wolverine State* (Grand Rapids, MI: Eerdman, 1980), 257; and other sources. None of these sources, however, is a history of Ohio. Ohio historians may be censoring Adams, or they may have excluded the statement because there is no evidence that he said it. Adams did say, "The report of the committee of the Senate simply declares that the committee had no doubt of the right of Congress to settle the disputed boundary conformably to the claim of Ohio. That report, I think I have seen qualified in one of the official documents from the State of Ohio, as a very able report. Yes sir, and this great ability consisted in a simple declaration … of the power of Congress to settle the boundary—but not one iota of argument, nor one single allusion, to any ques-

tion of right between the parties." See *Congressional Globe*, 24th Cong., 1st sess., 2095.

2. The map used was by John Mitchell, *Amérique septentrionale avec les routes, distances en miles, villages, et etablissements françois et anglois* (Paris: M. Hawkins, Brigardier des armées du roi, 1776).

3. Don Faber, *The Toledo War: The First Michigan-Ohio Rivalry* (Ann Arbor: University of Michigan Press, 2008), 25.

4. *Report of the Committee on the Business of the State of Ohio* (Feb. 4, 1803), in the *Scioto Gazette* (Ohio), February 2, 1804.

5. Lewis Cass to Howard Tiffin, November 1, 1817, in T. C. Mendenhall and A. A. Graham, "Boundary Line between Ohio and Indiana, and between Ohio and Michigan," *Ohio Archaeological and Historical Publications*, vol. 4 (Columbus: Ohio Historical Society, 1895), 161.

6. Over a century later, it was discovered that Congress had never voted specifically on an act to admit Ohio into the Union. In 1953 Congress retroactively admitted Ohio to the Union as of March 1803.

7. Lawton T. Hemans, *The Life and Times of Stevens Thomson Mason* (Lansing: Michigan Historical Commission, 1920), 53–54.

8. *Scioto Gazette*, August 17, 1831.

9. "Attorney General Opinion," *Message of the Governor of Ohio at the Second Session of the Thirty-third General Assembly* (Columbus, OH: James B. Gardiner, 1835), 39.

10. *Monroe Sentinel* (Michigan), reprinted in *Cleveland Herald*, July 23, 1835.

11. Hemans, *Life and Times*, 423–44.

Robert Lucas

1. Robert Lucas to William Kendall, in "Biography of Robert Lucas by a Citizen of Columbus," *Ohio Archaeological and Historical Publications* 17 (1908): 167–68.

2. In the first case, which involved New York and New Jersey, New York boycotted the proceedings. The second, between Massachusetts and Rhode Island, came before the court in 1834, and not until 1838—the year Lucas became governor—did it finally decide how to rule on it. *New Jersey v. New York*, 30 U.S. 5 Pet. 284 (1831); *Rhode Island v. Massachusetts*, 37 U.S. 12 Pet. 657 (1838).

3. *Ohio Statesman* (Columbus), November 22, 1839.

4. *Missouri Argus* (St. Louis), November 29, 1839.

5. Claude S. Larzelere, Harlow Lindley, and Bernard C. Steiner, "The Iowa-Missouri Dispute Boundary," *Mississippi Valley Historical Review* 3, no. 1 (June 1916): 80–81.

Daniel Webster

1. Wendell Phillips, *Speeches, Lectures, and Letters* (Boston: Lee and Shepard, 1894), 45.

2. *Maryland Gazette and Political Intelligencer* (Annapolis), May 23, 1822.

3. *Bangor Register* (Maine), April 6, 1826.

4. J. Chris Arndt, "Maine in the Northeastern Boundary Controversy: States' Rights in Antebellum New England," *New England Quarterly* 62, no. 2 (June 1989): 205–23; *Boston Courier*, January 16, 1832.

5. Maurice G. Baxter, *One and Inseparable: Daniel Webster and the Union* (Cambridge, MA: Harvard University Press, 1984), 41, 276–77, 285, 502; Irving H. Bartlett, *Daniel Webster* (New York: Norton, 1978), 200–207, 281–86.

6. Wilfred Ellsworth Binkley and Malcolm Charles Moos, *A Grammar of American Politics: The National Government* (New York: Knopf, 1949), 265.

7. Ephraim Douglass Adams, "Lord Ashburton and the Treaty of Washington," *American Historical Review* 17, no. 4 (July 1912): 779.

8. Arndt, "Maine," 219–220; George Ticknor Curtis, *Life of Daniel Webster*, 5th ed., vol. 1 (New York: D. Appleton, 1893), 278–83; Richard N. Current, "Webster's Propaganda and the Ashburton Treaty," *Mississippi Valley Historical Review* 34, no. 2 (September 1947): 189.

9. Current, "Webster's Propaganda," 189; Arndt, "Maine," 221; J. P. D. Dunbahin, "Red Lines of the Maps: The Impact of Cartographical Errors on the Border between the United States and British North America," *Imago Mundi: The International Journal for the History of Cartography* 50 (1998): 105–25; Lawrence Martin and Samuel Flagg Bemis, "Franklin's Red-Line Map Was a Mitchell," *New England Quarterly* 10, no. 1 (March 1937): 105–11.

10. Machias Seal Island, between the Gulf of Maine and the Bay of Fundy, remains under dispute to this day. See Paul Schmidt, "Machias Seal Island: A Geopolitical Anomaly" (master's thesis, University of Vermont, 1991), http://www.siue.edu/GEOGRAPHY/ONLINE/Schmidt.htm.

11. "An Account of the Post-Mortem Examination of the late Hon. Daniel Webster," *New York Journal of Medicine* (1853): 281.

12. Ralph Waldo Emerson, *The Works of Ralph Waldo Emerson*, vol. 2 (New York: Hearst's International Library, 1914), 557.

James K. Polk

1. Hans Sperber, "'Fifty-Four Forty or Fight': Facts and Fictions," *American Speech* 32, no. 1 (February 1957): 5–11; Edwin A. Miles, "'Fifty-Four Forty or Fight': An American Political Legend," *Mississippi Valley Historical Review* 44, no. 2 (September 1957): 291–309.

2. Translated in *The Liberator* (Boston), May 23, 1845.

3. Walter R. Borneman, *Polk: The Man Who Transformed the Presidency and America* (New York: Random House, 2008), 194–96.

4. R. L. Schuyler, "Polk and the Oregon Compromise," *Political Science Quarterly* 26, no. 3 (September 1911): 460–61.

Robert M. T. Hunter

1. Robert M. T. Hunter, *Speech on the Subject of the Retrocession of Alexandria to Virginia in the House of Representatives, May 8, 1846* (Alexandria: Printed at offices of *Alexandria Gazette*, 1846), 8, 11.

2. *South Port American* (Wisconsin), July 10, 1846.

3. *Raymond Gazette* (Mississippi), July 17, 1846.

4. *National Intelligencer* (Washington, DC), May 23, 1803.

5. The canal to which Hunter referred was the Alexandria Canal, which crossed the

Potomac from the terminus of the C&O Canal at Georgetown and continued along the Virginia side of the river to Alexandria.

6. Amos B. Casselman, "The Virginia Portion of the District of Columbia," *Records of the Columbia Historical Society*, vol. 12 (1909): 116–17.

7. Frederick Merk, "Dissent in the Mexican War," *Proceedings of the Massachusetts Historical Society*, 3rd series, vol. 81 (1969): 120–36.

8. *National Intelligencer*, January 1, 1838; January 14, 1846.

9. Mark David Richards, "The Debates over the Retrocession of the District of Columbia, 1801–2004," *Washington History* 16, no. 1 (Spring/Summer 2004): 54–82.

Sam Houston

1. James L. Haley, *Sam Houston* (Norman: University of Oklahoma Press, 2002), 7–26.

2. John P. Erwin, son-in-law of the secretary of state, was appointed postmaster for Nashville (Sam Houston's congressional district) over numerous nominees Houston had forwarded to President John Quincy Adams. Houston had some choice words regarding the fitness of the secretary of state's son-in-law, who took offense and enlisted a well-known duelist, John T. Smith, to deliver the note bearing his challenge. Smith, accompanied by General White, serving as his witness, approached Houston, but Houston refused to accept a note from one who was of lower station, as provided in the *code duello*. White took issue with Houston's interpretation of the *code duello*, thus insulting Houston's honor and resulting in White's accepting Houston's challenge to meet on the field of honor.

3. Alex W. Terrell, "Recollections of General Sam Houston," *Southwestern Historical Quarterly* 16, no. 2 (October, 1912): 113–36.

4. Haley, *Sam Houston*, 52–61.

5. M. K. Wisehart, *Sam Houston: American Giant* (Washington, DC: Luce Publishers, 1962), 56.

6. *Niles' Weekly Register* (Washington, DC), August 27, 1831, citing the *Nashville Banner* with a note stating "The editor of that paper says it is published as a 'matter of business.'"

7. *New York Herald*, December 7, 1836. The copy of the president's message obtained by the *New York Herald* differs, in the section quoted, from the final draft sent to Congress, which appears in the *Register of Debates*, appendix, 24th Cong., 2nd sess., 1.

8. William Carey Crane, *Life and Select Literary Remains of Sam Houston* (Philadelphia: Lippincott, 1884), 368–69.

9. *Congressional Globe*, appendix, 31st Cong., 1st sess., 102. Later, Abraham Lincoln, in his acceptance speech for the Illinois Republican Party's nomination for Senate in 1858, declared, "A house divided against itself cannot stand." Though stated without attribution, the words in his printed text were enclosed in quotation marks.

John A. Sutter

1. John A. Sutter Sr., "Reminiscences," manuscript (Bancroft Library, University of California–Berkeley), 23; Albert L. Hurtado, *John Sutter: A Life on the North American Frontier* (Norman: University of Oklahoma Press, 2006), 58.

2. Report of Thomas O. Larkin (April 12, 1844), *New York Herald*, June 22, 1844.

3. Hurtado, *John Sutter*, 158.

4. John A. Sutter Jr., *The Sutter Family and the Origins of the Gold Rush Sacramento*, ed. Allan R. Ottley (Norman: University of Oklahoma Press, 2002), 17.

5. Hurtado, *John Sutter*, 239–41.

6. *The Alta California* (San Francisco), August 1, 1850.

7. *Memorial of John A. Sutter to the Senate and House of Representatives of the United States, in Congress Assembled* (Washington, DC: Washington Sentinel, 1876).

James Gadsden

1. Richard Kluger, *Seizing Destiny: How America Grew From Sea to Shining Sea* (New York: Knopf, 2007), 127.

2. Allan Nevins, *Ordeal of the Union: A House Dividing, 1852–1857* (New York: Scribner, 1947), 490.

3. Ibid., 498.

4. Frank Cosentino, *Almonte: The Life of Juan Nepomuceno Almonte* (Ontario: General Store Publishing, 2000), 91.

Stephen A. Douglas

1. *Mississippian and State Gazette* (Jackson), January 20, 1854; *Daily Cleveland Herald*, January 25, 1854.

2. *Charleston Mercury* (South Carolina), November 29, 1859.

3. J. G. Holland, *The Life of Abraham Lincoln* (Springfield, IL: Gurdon Bill, 1866), 301–2.

John A. Quitman

1. *Memphis Daily Appeal*, August 9, 1855.

2. Robert E. May, *The Southern Dream of a Caribbean Empire, 1854–1861* (Baton Rouge: Louisiana State University Press, 1973).

3. *London Times*, September 24, 1849; *New York Herald*, May 10, 1849.

4. Tom Chaffin, *Fatal Glory: Narciso López and the First Clandestine U.S. War against Cuba* (Charlottesville: University Press of Virginia, 1996), 204–14.

5. Clark E. Carr, *Stephen A. Douglas: His Life, Public Services, Speeches, and Patriotism* (Chicago: A. C. McClurg, 1909), 12.

Clarina Nichols

1. *New York Herald*, July 20, 1859.

2. Clarina Nichols, "The Responsibilities of Woman," speech at the Woman's Right Convention, October 15, 1841, in *Woman's Rights Tracts*, no. 5 (Boston: R. F. Wallcut, 1854), 1.

3. Diane Eickhoff, *Revolutionary Heart: The Life of Clarina Nichols and the Pioneering Crusade for Women's Rights* (Kansas City: Quindaro Press, 2006), 30–34.

4. Nichols, "Responsibilities," 14–15.

5. Ibid., 15.

6. Ibid., 17–18.

Lyman Cutler's Neighbor's Pig

1. U.S. Department of State, *The Northwest Boundary: Discussion of the Water Boundary Question; Geographical Memoir of the Islands in Dispute; and History of the Military Occupation of San Juan Island* (Washington, DC: Government Printing Office, 1868), 183.

2. Scott Kaufman, *The Pig War: The United States, Britain, and the Balance of Power in the Pacific Northwest, 1846–72* (Lanham, MD: Lexington Books, 2004), 11–12.

3. Andrew Fish, "Last Phase of the Oregon Boundary Question: The Struggle for San Juan Island," *Quarterly of the Oregon Historical Society* 22, no. 3 (September 1921): 188–89.

4. Kaufman, *Pig War*, 41; L. U. Reavis, *The Life and Military Services of Gen. William Selby Harney* (St. Louis: Bryan, Brand, 1878), 51, 171–75; *New York Herald*, July 9, 1845.

5. Kaufman, *Pig War*, 43; Tom H. Inkster, "Storm over the San Juans," *Montana: The Magazine of Western History* 17, no. 1 (Winter 1967): 42–43.

6. Herbert Hunt and Floyd C. Kaylor, *Washington West of the Cascades*, vol. 1 (Chicago: Clarke, 1917), 199.

Robert W. Steele

1. "Constitution of the State of Jefferson," *Rocky Mountain News*, August 20, 1859. The boundaries stipulated in this constitution—lat 43° N, long 102° W, lat 37° N, and long 110° W—differ markedly from those that had been stipulated in H.R. 835. Further confusion exists due to an error of unknown origin in which different northern, western, and southern borders are cited in sources such as the *Columbia Encyclopedia*, 6th ed. (New York: Columbia University Press, 2004) and in the initial printings of, unfortunately, my previous book, *How the States Got Their Shapes*.

2. There was a different Robert W. Steele (1857–1910), who served as chief justice of the Colorado Supreme Court.

3. Stephen Harriman Long, *Account of an Expedition from Pittsburgh to the Rocky Mountains*, vol. 3 (London: Longman, Hurst, Rees, Orme, and Brown, 1825), 236.

4. Frederic L. Paxson, "The Territory of Colorado," *University of Colorado Studies*, vol. 4 (Boulder: University of Colorado, 1906–7).

5. *Rocky Mountain News*, September 19, 1860.

6. Ovando J. Hollister, *The Mines of Colorado* (Springfield, MA: Bowles, 1867), 93.

Francis H. Pierpont

1. Marian Mills Miller, ed., *Life and Works of Abraham Lincoln*, vol. 6 (New York: Current Literature, 1907), 206.

2. *National Intelligencer* (Washington, DC), October 30, 1829.

3. *The North American and Daily Advertiser* (Philadelphia), July 14, 1842; *Boston Daily Atlas*, June 26, 1845.

4. "Oration of Mr. Webster," *National Intelligencer*, July 8, 1851.

5. Remarks of Judge Alston G. Dayton, in *Statue of Governor Francis Harrison Pierpont: Proceedings in Statuary Hall* (Washington, DC: Government Printing Office, 1910), 47–48.

6. Vasan Kesavan and Michael Stokes Paulsen, "Is West Virginia Unconstitutional?" *California Law Review* 90, no. 2 (March 2002): 691–727.

7. James Morton Callahan, *Semi-Centennial History of West Virginia* (Charleston, WV: Semi-Centennial Commission of West Virginia, 1913), 146.

8. *North American and United States Gazette* (Philadelphia), June 19, 1863.

9. *Cleveland Herald*, May 13, 1863.

Francisco Perea and John S. Watts

1. W. H. H. Allison, "Colonel Francisco Perea," *Old Santa Fe: A Magazine of History, Archaeology, Genealogy and Biography* 1, no. 2 (October 1913): 217.

2. Deren Earl Kellogg, "Lincoln's New Mexico Patronage: Saving the Far Southwest for the Union," *New Mexico Historical Review* 76 (October 2000): 511–33.

3. Allison, "Colonel Francisco Perea," 218.

Sidney Edgerton and James Ashley

1. James M. Ashley to William H. Hunt, April 28, 1892, in J. M. Ashley, "The Naming of Montana," *Montana Magazine of History* 2, no. 3 (July 1952): 66; Sidney Edgerton to William H. Hunt, May 23, 1892, in Anne McDonnell, "Edgerton and Lincoln," *Montana Magazine of History* 1, no. 4 (October 1951): 44.

2. Martha Edgerton Plassmann, "Biographical Sketch of Hon. Sidney Edgerton," in *Contributions to the Historical Society of Montana*, vol. 3 (Helena, MT: State Publishing, 1900), 336–37.

3. Hubert Howe Bancroft, *The Works of Hubert Howe Bancroft*, vol. 31 (San Francisco: History Company, 1890), 643; James M. Hamilton, *From Wilderness to Statehood: A History of Montana, 1805–1900* (Portland, OR: Binfords & Mort, 1957), 274; Merle W. Wells, "How Idaho Became a Territory," in Richard W. Etulain and Bert W. Marley, eds., *The Idaho Heritage* (Boise: Idaho University Press, 1974), 32n, 44.

William H. Seward

1. Frederic Bancroft, *The Life of William H. Seward*, vol. 2 (New York: Harper, 1900), 135.

2. Ibid., 151, 225.

3. Frank A. Golder, "The Purchase of Alaska," *American Historical Review* 25, no. 3 (April 1920): 411–12.

4. *New York Herald*, March 31, 1867; *Albany Evening Journal*, April 1, 1867; *Columbus Ledger-Enquirer*, April 4, 1867.

5. *Milwaukee Daily Sentinel*, April 3, 1867; *Cincinnati Daily Gazette*, April 4, 1867.

6. George E. Baker, ed., *The Works of William H. Seward* (Boston: Houghton, Mifflin, 1884), 574; *Congressional Globe*, appendix, 40th Cong., 2nd sess., 402, 403, 491

Standing Bear v. Crook

1. *United States ex rel. Standing Bear v. Crook*, 25 F. Cas. 695 (1879).

2. Valerie Sherer Mathes and Richard Lowitt, *The Standing Bear Controversy: Prelude to Indian Reform* (Urbana: University of Illinois Press, 2003), 14; Stephen Dando-Collins, *Standing Bear Is a Person: The Story of a Native American's Quest for Justice* (Cambridge, MA: Da Capo Press, 2004), 37; James A. Lake Sr., "Standing Bear! Who?" *Nebraska Law Review* 60, no. 3 (1981): 469.

3. Testimony Relating to the Removal of the Ponca Indians, 46th Cong., 2nd sess., Senate Report no. 670, 51.

4. Mathes and Lowitt, *Standing Bear Controversy*, 25n, 50–52, 60.

5. Stanley Clark, "Ponca Publicity," *Mississippi Valley Historical Review* 29, no. 4 (March 1943): 507.

Lili'uokalani and Sanford Dole

1. Eugene Tyler Chamberlain, "The Hawaiian Situation," *North American Review* 157, no. 445 (December 1893): 731.

2. Caspar Whitney, *Hawaiian America: Something of Its History, Resources, and Prospects* (New York: Harper, 1899), 135.

3. William A. Russ Jr., "The Role of Sugar in Hawaiian Annexation," *Pacific Historical Review* 12, no. 4 (December 1943): 341; L. A. Beardslee, "Pilkias," *North American Review* 167, no. 503 (October 1898): 473.

4. Edmund Janes Carpenter, *America in Hawaii: A History of the United States Influence in the Hawaiian Islands* (Boston: Small, Maynard, 1899), 185–86.

5. *New York Times*, July 7, 1897.

6. Henry Miller Madden, "Letters of Sanford B. Dole and John W. Burgess," *Pacific Historical Review* 5, no. 1 (March 1936): 71–75.

7. *Los Angeles Times*, January 15, 1922.

Alfalfa Bill Murray, Edward P. McCabe, and Chief Green McCurtain

1. From the point of view of Congress and many American Indians, communal ownership of the land enabled those in leadership roles to enrich themselves while the majority of the tribe remained mired in poverty. See Angie Debo, *The Rise and Fall of the Choctaw Republic*, 2nd ed. (Norman: University of Oklahoma Press, 1961), 249, 254.

2. *Cherokee Advocate* (Tahlequah, OK), September 19, 1896.

3. *Idaho Daily Statesman* (Boise), August 8, 1911.

4. Keith L. Bryant Jr., *"Alfalfa Bill" Murray* (Norman: University of Oklahoma Press, 1968), 38.

5. Daniel F. Littlefield Jr. and Lonnie E. Underhill, "Black Dreams and 'Free' Homes: The Oklahoma Territory, 1891–1894," *Phylon* 34, no. 4 (December 1973): 352.

6. Jere W. Roberson, "Edward P. McCabe and the Langston Experiment," *Chronicles of Oklahoma* 51, no. 3 (Fall 1973): 350, 355.

7. Donald A. Grinde Jr. and Quintard Taylor, "Red vs. Black: Conflict and Accommo-

dation in the Post Civil War Indian Territory," *American Indian Quarterly* 8, no. 3 (Summer 1984): 211–29; Michael F. Doran, "Slaves of the Five Civilized Tribes," *Annals of the Association of American Geographers* 68, no. 3 (September 1978): 335–50.

8. *Fort Worth Star-Telegram*, December 28, 1910; *Pawtucket Times* (Rhode Island), December 28, 1910.

9. Associated Press report, *New York Times*, October 16, 1956.

Bernard J. Berry

1. *New York Times*, January 7, 1954.

Luis Ferré

1. Hearing before the House Committee on Resources (serial no. 105–16), 105th Cong., 1st sess., 85.

2. Luis Ferré, *Autobiografía de Luis A. Ferré* (San Juan: Grupo Editorial Norma, 1992), 20. At the time of his father's death in 1959, the company was valued at $50 million. See *New York Times*, November 14, 1959.

3. *New York Times*, March 29, 1946.

4. César J. Ayala and Rafael Bernabé, *Puerto Rico in the American Century* (Chapel Hill: University of North Carolina Press, 2007), 225–26.

5. *Chicago Tribune*, May 2, 1954.

6. Ayala and Bernabé, *Puerto Rico*, 226.

7. Kal Wagenheim with Olga Jimenez De Wagenheim, eds., *The Puerto Ricans: A Documentary History* (New York: Praeger, 1973), 288.

8. Ibid., 287–89.

David Shafer

1. *Chattanooga Times Free Press*, February 2, 7, 21, 28, 2008.

2. *Chattanooga Times Free Press*, March 5, 2008.

3. *Athens Banner-Herald*, February 21, 2008; *Atlanta Journal-Constitution*, March 27, 2008.

4. Gregory Spies, "The Mystery of the Camak Stone," *Professional Surveyor Magazine* (March 2004), http://www.profsurv.com/magazine/article.aspx?i=1215.

5. E. Merton Coulter, "The Georgia-Tennessee Boundary Line," *Georgia Historical Quarterly* 35 (December 1951): 269–306.

6. *Virginia v. Tennessee*, 148 U.S. 503 (1893); *Georgia v. South Carolina*, 497 U.S. 376 (1990).

Eleanor Holmes Norton

1. James D. Richardson, ed., *A Compilation of the Messages and Papers of the Presidents, 1789–1897*, vol. 2 (Washington, DC: Government Printing Office, 1896), 47.

2. "Dover Resolves," *New Hampshire Gazette*, January 14, 1774.

3. Joan Steinau Lester, *Fire in My Soul: Eleanor Holmes Norton* (New York: Atria Books, 2003), 54.

4. Johnny Barnes, "Towards Equal Footing: Responding to the Perceived Constitutional, Legal, and Practical Impediments to Statehood for the District of Columbia," *University of the District of Columbia Law Review* 13, no. 1 (Spring 2010): 59.

5. *Washington Post*, September 23, 1920; August 7, 1940; August 8, 1967; June 18, 1971; May 16, 1984; January 25, 1985; May 27, 1987.

6. *Washington Post*, November 19, 1991.

7. Orrin G. Hatch, "'No Right Is More Precious in a Free Country': Allowing Americans in the District of Columbia to Participate in National Self-Government," *Harvard Journal on Legislation* 45 (2008): 287–310.

Index

*Page numbers in **bold** indicate illustrations*

Photography Credits